HUMAN BEHAVIOR IN ORGANIZATIONS

Second Edition

Rodney C. Vandeveer
Purdue University

Michael L. Menefee
*University of North Carolina
at Pembroke*

Prentice Hall
Upper Saddle River, New Jersey
Columbus, Ohio

Library of Congress Cataloging-in-Publication Data

Vandeveer, Rodney C.
  Human behavior in organizations / Rodney C. Vandeveer, Michael L. Menefee.—2nd ed.
    p. cm.
  ISBN 978-0-13-503811-6
  1. Organizational behavior.   I. Menefee, Michael L.   II. Title.
  HD58.7.V363 2010
  302.3'5—dc22

                                                                    2008050597

Editor in Chief: Vernon Anthony
Acquisitions Editor: Gary Bauer
Editorial Assistant: Megan Heintz
Production Coordination: Elm Street Publishing Services
Project Manager: Christina Taylor
Senior Operations Supervisor: Pat Tonneman
Art Director: Diane L. Ernsberger
Cover Designer: Diane Lorenzo
Cover Image: Stockbyte
Manager, Image Resource Center, Rights and Permissions: Zina Arabia
Manager, Cover Visual Research and Permissions: Karen Sanatar
Image Permission Coordinator: Richard Rodrigues
Director of Marketing: David Gesell
Marketing Manager: Leigh Ann Sims
Marketing Assistant: Les Roberts

Photo Credits: Chapter 1: Getty Images–Digital Vision, Fountain Group; Chapter 2: Corbis/Bettmann; Chapter 3: AGE Fotostock America, Inc., Walter Bibikow; Chapter 4: Getty Images Inc.–Image Bank, Kevin Hatt; Chapter 5: Stockbyte; Chapter 6: Photolibrary.Com; Chapter 7: Stock Boston, Eric Neurath; Chapter 8: Getty Images, Inc.–Taxi, Darren Robb; Chapter 9: Getty Images, Inc.–Taxi, Ken Reid; Chapter 10: Getty Images Inc.–Stone Allstock, Ken Fisher; Chapter 11: Getty Images Inc.–Image Bank, Marc Romanelli; Chapter 12: Getty Images Inc.–Image Bank, Steve McAlister; Chapter 13: Getty Images Inc.–Image Bank, Butch Martin, Inc.; Chapter 14: Getty Images, Inc.–Photodisc, Ryan McVay; Chapter 15: Photolibrary.Com; Chapter 16: Photolibrary.Com; Chapter 17: Getty Images Inc.–Stone Allstock, Tim Flach; Chapter 18: Woodfin Camp & Associates, Michael Abramson; Chapter 19: AP Wide World Photos; Chapter 20: United Nations, Muldoon; Chapter 21: Getty Images, Inc.–Photodisc., Emanuele Taroni; Chapter 22: Getty Images Inc.–Hulton Archive Photos, Chris-Ware; Chapter 23: Photolibrary.Com.

This book was set in New Aster by Integra Software Services Pvt. Ltd. and was printed and bound by Edwards Brothers. The cover was printed by Lehigh-Phoenix Color/Hagerstown.

Pearson Education Ltd., London
Pearson Education Singapore Pte. Ltd.
Pearson Education Canada, Inc.
Pearson Education—Japan

Pearson Education Australia Pty. Limited
Pearson Education North Asia Ltd., Hong Kong
Pearson Educación de Mexico, S.A. de C.V.
Pearson Education Malaysia Pte. Ltd.

Prentice Hall
is an imprint of

www.pearsonhighered.com

10 9 8 7 6 5 4 3 2 1
ISBN-13: 978-0-13-503811-6
ISBN-10:   0-13-503811-1

This book is dedicated to the many who assisted in its development. They are

Mary Jo Vandeveer

Sandy Menefee

Vern Dahlstrom

*The many Purdue students in the
Human Behavior in Organizations classes*

And a special dedication to

Dr. Gavin Sinclair (1961–2000)

Coauthor and dear friend

Contents

Chapter 6

Chapter 7

Chapter 8

Chapter 9
Leadership   118

Chapter 10
Decision Making   140

Chapter 11
Communication   154

Chapter 12
Conflict   168

Chapter 17

Human Resources II: Company Policies   234

Chapter 18

Organizational Culture   248

Chapter 19

Motivation in Organizations   260

Chapter 20

Organizational Change   270

Chapter 21

Power and Politics   280

Self-Assessment Tests

The self-assessment tests and the explanations are from *Prentice Hall's Self-Assessment Library 3.4 Online Version,* by Stephen P. Robbins, 2009. This book contains material from this self-assessment library in Appendix 1 and in the following chapter self-assessments:

The idea for this book originated with Dr. Gavin Sinclair, the past course coordinator for the Human Behavior in Organizations course at Purdue University. Dr. Sinclair was a gifted writer who wanted to create a course where learning meant being actively involved. He wanted to write a book to which the students could relate and get involved, through cases and exercises. The result of his effort was this book, which was first used at Purdue in 1999. It was very positively received by both students and instructors. It helped turn the classroom into a dynamic interactive learning experience; enrollment in the class increased as word got out among the students about how interesting and useful the class had become. Since the first version of this book, thousands of students in the Human Behavior in Organizations course were asked to comment and make suggestions for improvement. Their continued input, suggestions, and comments were also incorporated into this edition.

TEXTBOOK FEATURES

This book features chapter opening cases; concise chapters; newspaper cartoons such as *Dilbert, Cathy,* and *Dagwood* to lighten the presentation; current movie and television references like *Gladiator, Castaway,* and *CSI*; exercises aimed at helping students learn more about themselves; concise chapter summaries; and cases to stimulate classroom discussion. Additional end-of-chapter case studies have been added for in-class and out-of-class assignments. The goal of this book is to provide students with the basics of Human Behavior in Organizations in a way that will help them envision how they will fit into organizations and be successful in their leadership roles. It is hoped that the knowledge, skills, and insights discovered in this book will serve students well over the course of their careers as well as in their personal lives.

TEXTBOOK ORGANIZATION

The book is divided into five parts. Each of these parts is designed to teach a different aspect of human behavior in organizations:

Part One presents the big picture. This introductory section is designed to acquaint students with the concept of organizational behavior and why it is important. Many students probably have not given much thought to organizations and how they operate. This part is also designed to illustrate that only through the use of a systematic study of individual and organizational behavior can we begin to accurately predict individual and organizational behavior. This is a critical skill for organizational leaders responsible for dealing with individuals at any level. We have found that the more students learn about organizations, particularly how the organization affects them and how they affect the organizations, the more interested students become in the topic of organizational behavior.

In **Part Two,** students are challenged to learn more about themselves through the use of self-assessments, case studies, and discussion points. Many students probably have not considered how their personality influences other people, or explored their own values and attitudes. The first chapter in this section encourages students to learn more about their own and their fellow students' personalities, abilities, and learning styles. Students are always interested in themselves and what new insights they may gain, which encourages them to undertake a systematic study of behavior. We also reinforce the idea that through a systematic study of behavior we can begin to anticipate behavior based on personality, ability, and learning styles, which will assist in the development of leadership skills.

The second chapter in this section addresses perception. We are all different and may not perceive things the same way. We begin to recognize that perception is reality to the perceiver, and it is on this level that the leader must learn to operate. The third chapter in this part challenges students to understand their own and others' values and attitudes. Understanding values and attitudes prepares learners to think about their goals and aims in life. We must take charge of our own destiny, for if we do not, someone else will. The final two chapters in this part cover what motivates people, and how to understand and cope with stress.

Part Three helps students come to terms with dealing with other people in and through teams. This is the leader's role. In Part 2, readers discover insights about themselves. Building on these insights in Part 3, students then move to exploring their own behavior patterns and how their behavior affects others. Among the most frequently asked questions employers pose to interviewees is, "Do you know how to work in teams?" or "Do you consider yourself a team player?" and "What experience do you have as a leader?" Once again, this part stresses the importance of conducting systematic studies of the behaviors of teams and the relationship between the leader and followers, resulting in effective performance. The topics covered in this part include teamwork, group behavior, leadership, decision making, communication, conflict, and negotiation. The people skills developed from reading this part can help students relate well and work well with other people both on the job and off the job.

Part Four is designed to help students understand organizations and behaviors that occur in organizations. Upon graduation from school or a course of study, students face an important organizational decision. That decision is whether to become "the little fish in the big pond" or "the big fish in the little pond." Will students work better in large organizations or smaller organizations? Once again, systematic study will provide insights into the advantages and disadvantages of each type of organization. Part Four covers a variety of topics, including organizational structure, the jobs people do, the employment process from job analysis to employee selection and retention, organizational culture, organizational motivation, organizational change, politics, and power. Much attention in this section is given to the "goodness of the fit" between the organization and individual.

Part Five explores effort, ethics, and success in the organization. Using the knowledge, skills, and discoveries learned from the previous chapters, students gain insight into what it takes to be successful in organizations and begin to think about the effort they give to their jobs as well as the ethics they and the organization have.

The appendices of this book provide classroom assignments and exercises building on the knowledge, experience, and lessons learned in the previous sections.

STUDENT SUMMARY PROJECTS

Appendix 1 contains **assignments that capture students' insights about their own behaviors, tendencies, and styles.** The collection of assessments affords students the opportunity to reflect on what was learned over the course of the instructional period. At the end of the course of instruction, the students prepare a paper reflecting on five thought-provoking questions that draw on the knowledge gained and their discoveries about themselves. Through this systematic study of self, much is gained and shared. The realization of personal growth and the understanding of self are very powerful.

Appendix 2 contains a **team assignment for students to reflect on their experience in a group/team project.** They are asked to share their discoveries of what occurred in the group development process and to talk about team roles, trust, communication, leadership, and all the other aspects studied over the course of instruction. At the end of the course of instruction, each team makes a presentation on an instructor-approved topic relating to an individual, team, or organizational behavior. This appendix also provides supplements to support the instructor and students in this assignment. The students are then challenged to analyze the process and write a paper on the experience, noting the lessons learned.

Prentice Hall's Self-Assessment Library 3.4 Online Version by **Stephen P. Robbins**—The online access card to the Self-Assessment Library 3.4 (SAL 3.4) is packaged with this textbook at no additional charge when the text is purchased new. SAL 3.4 is a unique learning tool that allows you to assess your knowledge, beliefs, feelings, and actions in regard to a wide range of personal skills, abilities, and interests. A scoring key is provided to allow for immediate individual analysis. This single volume of 68 research-based instruments is organized into three parts—What About Me?, Working with Others, and Life in Organizations—and offers you one source from which to learn more about yourself.

Companion Web site—The Web site is your 24/7 study tool at www.prenhall.com/vandeveer. This Web site greatly enhances the learning experience by letting students see sample test questions, view major essay questions over chapter content, find Web sites related to the chapter, and get a summary of the material in the chapter. The Web site is the perfect companion to the textbook.

INSTRUCTOR'S RESOURCES

Instructor's Manual—The instructor's manual has material to help prepare lectures, in-class exercises, quizzes, assessments, and case studies. This user-friendly manual helps instructors make this class a positive learning experience by involving the students in the learning process.

Test Bank—The test bank allows the instructor to create the right test for the class. Both true/false questions and multiple-choice questions are provided to test basic concepts of each chapter. Over 200 additional questions have been added to the test bank for this second edition, offering greater diversity in selection of test questions. The test bank complements all the material covered in the chapters.

Test Generator—The test generator allows the instructor to create custom tests for his or her classes. This is especially valuable when the instructor teaches multiple sections and/or coordinates classes with multiple instructors. Each class can have its own test, and each test reflects the instructor's view on what is important in each of the chapters.

PowerPoint Slides—The user-friendly PowerPoint presentations add a visual flair to any lecture or discussion. The PowerPoint presentation can be shown in class via computer, or the Power Points can be downloaded for overhead slides. These PowerPoints cover all the major material in the book.

ACKNOWLEDGMENTS

Even though Dr. Gavin Sinclair has passed away, his influence encourages us to continue writing this book and to make it as instructor- and student-friendly as possible while teaching the concepts of human behavior in organizations in a dynamic and interactive way.

Special thanks to the reviewers of this text: Randy Sleeth, Virginia Commonwealth University, Richmond, VA; Jim Hatchell, Purdue University, West Lafayette, IN; Joy Colwell, Purdue University-Calumet, Hammond, IN; G. A. Wynn, University of South Florida, Tampa, FL; and David Frantz, Purdue University, West Lafayette, IN.

RODNEY VANDEVEER is an associate professor in the School of Technology at Purdue University. Rodney has been teaching courses in organizational behavior and emerging world-class leadership strategies since 1994. Prior to his teaching career, Rodney spent many years in business and industry working as Director of Human Resources, Plant Manager, Director of Operations, and Manager of Labor Studies for such companies as the Allen Bradley Company, RCA, and the Rostone Corporation. Rodney has his B.S. from Purdue University and an M.S. in Management from Indiana Wesleyan University.

Rodney serves on the Executive Board of the Sagamore Council of the Boy Scouts of America where he is the recipient of the Silver Beaver award for distinguished service to youth. Rodney is a retired officer from the United States Army Reserve program. He remains active in various community programs and in consulting.

MICHAEL MENEFEE is the Thomas Family Distinguished Professor of Entrepreneurship in the Carolina Commerce and Technology Center at the University of North Carolina at Pembroke. He was a professor and former head of the Organizational Leadership and Supervision Department at Purdue University. Prior to coming to Purdue, he was a professor at Tennessee Technological University and the William Henry Belk Distinguished Professor of Business Administration with the University of North Carolina Pembroke. He received his B.S. in Management from Northern Illinois University and his M.S. and Ph.D. from the Krannert Graduate School of Management at Purdue University. He also has an ABSC from Moody Bible Institute. He has written more than 200 publications in the management field and served as president of the Southern Industrial Relations and Human Resource Association, the Southwest Case Research Association, and the Academy of Strategic and Organizational Leadership.

Dr. Menefee spent eight years in the construction and building materials business, five years in high-technology firms, and three years in the electronics industry. He has consulted for more than thirty years with many companies and institutions, including General Motors, Teledyne, Tenneco, Canadian American Lumber Limited, NASA, the Kettering Foundation, Coca-Cola, Hardees, Harrison Steel, Fairfield Manufacturing, Esterline, Cummins Engine, and Duriron. He has also consulted with local and state governments in the area of economic development.

PART

1

THE BIG PICTURE

Introduction

Understanding human behavior in organizations is a critical skill for leadership and success in organizations. We all work or are involved in organizations of some type, and we all need to interact with other people. This book provides a reflective insight into human behavior and divides the topic into five sections:

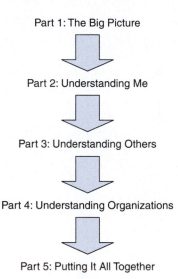

Part 1: The Big Picture

⬇

Part 2: Understanding Me

⬇

Part 3: Understanding Others

⬇

Part 4: Understanding Organizations

⬇

Part 5: Putting It All Together

In Part 1: The Big Picture, we will introduce the topic of **organizational behavior** and explain why this is an important and challenging field.

In Part 2: Understanding Me, we will discuss individual behavior and explore topics like personality, attitudes, motivation, and stress. Much of this section is based on applied psychology.

In Part 3: Understanding Others, we move into group behavior. We start with the idea that all people are different and then discuss how to motivate, lead, and communicate with others in a group setting.

In Part 4: Understanding Organizations, we expand beyond group behavior to organizations. We address issues like the structure of organizations, human resource policies, and

organizational culture. We also apply some individual concepts, like motivation, to the organization.

In Part 5: Putting It All Together, we assemble some take-home lessons from this book. We talk about what it takes to succeed in an organization and describe some typical career paths.

This book focuses on creating understanding of human behavior of self, in groups, and in organizations, as a leadership skill. An important accessory to this book are the online Self-Assessments. Throughout the book, we will be asking you to complete various self-assessment exercises. These exercises are designed to help you personally apply the principles in this book. Appendix 1 gives you an opportunity to capture and summarize your scores on these assessments. Individually, the assessments have marginal value. Collectively, however, your results on these tests construct a valuable profile that you can use to assess your strengths and weaknesses.

The Self-Assessment (SA) program is an integral part of your learning. As you scan the chapters, you will notice various SA inventories at the beginning of each chapter. This is a conscious and deliberate effort. Completing the SA accomplishes these important tasks:

- It will provide an introduction to the material in the chapter and help you personally apply the principles in this book.
- It provides a snapshot of various characteristics, attitudes, behaviors, or tendencies.
- It will create a historical profile or catalog for future reference.

Each time you complete an SA, turn to Appendix 1 of this book and use the duplicate recording form listed for the chapter. This appendix becomes the catalog that will reveal an ultimate course profile. As each SA is completed, record your score(s) both at the chapter location and at Appendix 1.

Mood, fatigue, and a host of other factors may influence and potentially distort your responses to SA questions. Make every effort to make unbiased choices as you navigate

The online Self-Assessment is an important part of this book, providing insights into self, propensity for teamwork, and fit for organizational structure.

the SA questions. The result will be a final profile that will be useful to you both now and in the future.

A final word about the SA program. The back jacket of the Access Card displays an index of the SA library. There are 67 assessment exercises. However, this book references about half of the assessment exercises. All of the assessments are useful, and you may wish to consult some not specifically listed in the text for further study. Please note that the individual assessment exercises are not necessarily sequential by chapter. For example, Chapter 2 directs you to exercises 1.A.2, 1.A.3, 1.A.4, and I.A.5 in that order. Chapter 3 then skips forward to exercise 2.C.4.

CHAPTER 1

What Is Organizational Behavior?

LEARNING OUTCOMES: WHAT IS ORGANIZATIONAL BEHAVIOR?

1. Define organizational behavior (OB).

2. Explain some of the differences in organizations.

3. Understand the need for systematic study of organizational behavior.

4. Describe an organization.

5. Recognize that OB depends on contingencies.

The Card Game

It was Friday night and the "boys" were getting together for their weekly round of poker games. The good friends had grown up together and graduated from the same high school. Bob, Joe, Ted, and Hal were all forty years old.

Bob is a mild-mannered accountant who works for a large manufacturing company. He graduated from a local college with a degree in accounting. Bob is married and has four children ranging in age from five to sixteen years. He has been with the same company for eighteen years.

Joe is a flamboyant mechanic at a local garage. He went to a local community college and finished with a degree in auto mechanics. Joe is on his fourth marriage and has three children by his first three wives. He has worked for eight garages over the last twenty years.

Ted is an extrovert and the purchasing agent for a supply company. Ted never went to college but learned on the job how to be a purchasing agent. He has been with three companies, and every change has come with advancement. Ted is divorced and has two children by his former wife. He likes people and loves making a deal.

Hal is a quiet librarian for a local college where he earned a degree in English. He has remained single and lives with his parents. Although he could earn more money working for another area school, Hal has not tried to change jobs and has been in the same job for the last eighteen years.

As usual, the conversation turns to their organizations. Bob says he is happy where he is in a stable environment with little change. Joe says Bob's job is too boring for him. "I like excitement and change," Joe says. "If my job gets too boring or I do not like it, I just leave." Hal chimes in that stability is a good thing, and job security is key in an organization. Ted comes back with this retort, "Job security is not that great. I move up, or I move on."

Which one of these men is right, or does the answer depend on the individual and organization?

Welcome to *Human Behavior in Organizations!* ∎

Almost every textbook covering the topics discussed in this book is called **Organizational Behavior.** The title of this book is *Human Behavior in Organizations* because this phrase is more descriptive. The overall objective of this book is to help you understand and predict human behavior in organizations and help you use this understanding to be more effective in organizations. This, in turn, will help you be more successful in life. The first chapter gives an introduction to the study of organizational behavior and what it means.

How can you understand an organization? How can you understand the people within an organization? There are many books on management theory and corporate policy, but some find the best description in the comic strip *Dilbert*.

Whenever I go into a company, I see literally hundreds of *Dilbert* comic strips taped to cubicles. Scott Adams, the creator of *Dilbert*, certainly hits a chord. Many people who have not worked in a big company do not understand *Dilbert*. That's because their experience with organizations does not fit the image of corporate America as portrayed in the comic strip.

Source: Dilbert, June 9, 1998. © Scott Adams/Distributed by United Feature Syndicate, Inc. Reprinted by permission.

Other people may relate with Dagwood Bumstead, with his carpool and his tyrannical boss, Mr. Dithers, in the comic strip *Blondie.*

Source: Blondie, December 9, 1997. Copyright © 1997. Reprinted with special permission of King Features Syndicate, Inc.

Still other people may relate to *Cathy,* as a professional woman trying to succeed in her organization.

Source: Cathy, October 26, 1998. © 1998 Cathy Guisewite. Reprinted with permission of Universal Press Syndicate, Inc. All rights reserved.

The study of organizational behavior, normally referred to as OB, is the study of how individuals and groups are influenced by others. Organizational behavior is an interesting topic because there are so many different types of **organizations** (just as there are many different comic strips portraying organizations), and human behavior varies greatly depending on your gender, background, and experiences. Even with all this diversity, some common principles can be pulled together to help us understand organizational behavior. These common principles are the subject of this book.

Let's look at one simple organizational behavior issue. When you meet somebody, what do you call him or her? Do you call your professors by

Organizations come in many shapes, sizes, and flavors.

their first names or do you call them Professor So-and-so? A class that calls the instructor by his or her first name suggests a certain degree of informality. It's the same way in an organization. The way people address one another is a common organizational behavior principle for understanding the dynamics of the organization.

I once worked in a fairly formal company. Most of the top Ph.D. researchers were addressed as "doctor," especially by outsiders. One day a person came to interview with the Chief Science Officer, whose name was Dr. Bobalosivich. When the interviewee met Dr. Bobalosivich, the interviewee said to him, "Your name is pretty hard to pronounce. Can I just call you Bob?" Needless to say, the interviewee's poor understanding of the principles of organizational behavior cost him any chance at getting the job.

More formally stated, **organizational behavior** is the study of human behavior in the workplace, the interaction between people and the organization with the intent to understand and predict human behavior. It is simply a study of the interpersonal skills needed to pursue a successful career in today's diverse world. In the case of the interview cited previously, an understanding of organizational behavior would have suggested to the person being interviewed that the company was a fairly formal organization. This would have been clear by watching the interaction between people in the company. Given this information, we could have predicted that the Chief Science Officer would have been offended when the interviewee wanted to call him "Bob."

> **Organizational behavior** is the study of human behavior in the workplace, the interaction between people and the organization with the intent to understand and predict human behavior.

SYSTEMATIC STUDY

Everyone develops an understanding of human behavior through common sense and personal experience. If you do something nice for a person, you generally expect that person to be appreciative. Once in a while, you will run into a rude person and you factor this exception into your understanding of human behavior. With some experience, you can start to predict when a person will be appreciative and when the person will not. In most cases, common sense and experience serve a person well.

Try taking this survey to test your common sense. Answer these questions as either true (T) or false (F).

1. _____ When employees are happy they are more productive.
2. _____ Friendly, trusting, and approachable bosses can motivate their workers.
3. _____ Leaders who exhibit a stable behavior, regardless of the situations they face, make the best leaders.
4. _____ Experiences have shown us that interviews where the interviewer leads with the statement "tell me about yourself" are very effective selection methods.
5. _____ A challenging job appeals to everyone.
6. _____ When people feel a little intimidated, they will work harder and do their best.
7. _____ Nonspecific goals allowing individuals to work at their own pace will motivate individuals to work harder.
8. _____ Money is a motivator for all employees.
9. _____ Most people are more concerned about their own salaries than they are about the salaries of others.
10. _____ Conflict has a negative effect on work group effectiveness.

When it comes to organizational behavior, many of the ideas we get from personal experience or common sense are wrong. The answer to each of the questions in the survey is *false*. For example, common sense may tell you a good way to motivate people is to pay them more money. Well, it might make good common sense, *but it's wrong*. Studies show that a person's salary needs to be fair, but you can't motivate people simply by paying them a higher base salary. You can, however, motivate workers by giving them bonuses as a form of recognition or motivate salespeople by paying them sales commissions to acknowledge the effort put forth on sales. How you pay a person more money can make a difference in his or her level of motivation.

What about giving people a nice certificate of appreciation and telling them what a good job they are doing? When this is done and one is sincere it has been shown to motivate people more than increasing their salary. Recognition is a powerful motivator to people, even though the total cost of a certificate and a "thank you" is practically nothing.

In the study of organizational behavior, we throw away a lot of common sense and intuition in favor of systematic study. With people as our key focus, how do we study them and the organization? Hindsight tells us the institution and common sense solutions do not work. What is the answer? It requires a scientific and systematic approach. **Systematic study** refers to well-constructed studies that examine certain aspects of human behavior. We move beyond the casual, everyday observation to a more scientific approach. If we want to know if a higher salary motivates people, then we look at studies where researchers have carefully measured the effects on motivation when people are given a raise. Even if these results go against our intuition, we are better off trusting the results of these systematic studies. Regardless of how adept you may be in solving problems and developing new ideas, very little can happen if you cannot communicate your ideas and encourage others to work with you. An understanding of human and organizational behavior and the development of strong interpersonal skills requires a systematic study to become effective.

People and organizations are complex. They cannot be explained using simple models or plain common sense. To understand the science of OB, a systematic study considers cause and effect. If people are paid a higher salary (the "cause"), what does this do to their productivity (the "effect")? In this example, salary is the independent variable, the variable that is being changed. Productivity is the dependent variable, the variable that changes as a result of the change in salary. Many other dependent variables can change as a result of a change in an independent variable. The four dependent variables studied the most in organizational behavior are productivity, absenteeism, job satisfaction, and turnover. Organizations are always looking for policies that will increase productivity, decrease absenteeism, increase job satisfaction, and decrease turnover.

Studying organizational behavior will help you learn about human behavior in organizations faster than simply relying on personal experience. Many managers in organizations have tried to motivate their employees by increasing their base salary, and eventually they learn this does not work. They could have saved a lot of time and effort by reading about the systematic studies that have examined this exact question. We want to save you time and effort by explaining the general rules of human behavior in organizations.

Systematic study means we rely on scientific studies, not intuition.

WHAT IS AN ORGANIZATION?

Organizations are not only companies. The principles in this course apply equally to companies, sororities, and bowling teams. Broadly speaking, **organizations** are simply groups with two or more people who share a certain set of goals and meet at regular times. Whether it's a multinational company or a sorority, all organizations have certain things in common. For example, they all have **group norms,** the notion of what constitutes proper behavior and what does not.

All organizations have procedures to make decisions: they vote, they reach a consensus, or the leader makes the decision. All organizations have a way to discipline members who do not perform up to expectations. In a company they may be fired; on a bowling team, they may have to pay for drinks for the rest of the team.

All organizations have to deal with a similar list of issues. How does the organization make decisions? How is the authority distributed? How are people in the organization compensated for their efforts? These are the questions we answer in this book, regardless of the type of organization. Many times we will use company examples, but the same principles apply to all types of organizations.

Perhaps the most important concept to remember as you study organizational behavior is that human behavior depends on **contingencies;** that is, it depends on the circumstances or the situation. In fact, the individual human behavior displayed at a given time is a function of the individual and the environment or situation. For example, a person may behave one way in church and another way at a party. Behavior can be predicted, but it depends on the situation. Is a person a good leader? It depends on the situation. What is the best way to motivate a person? It depends on the situation. How can you stop a destructive rumor? What is the best method to handle conflict? The answer to each of these questions depends on the people involved, the situation, and the environment.

An **organization** is a group with two or more people that share a common set of goals and meet at regular times.

Contingency refers to factors that vary based on the circumstances of specific situations.

CHALLENGES IN UNDERSTANDING ORGANIZATIONAL BEHAVIOR

Understanding human behavior in organizations has been getting more difficult in recent years. Forty to fifty years ago, most major corporations were dominated by middle-aged white men. It was a fairly homogeneous group of people with similar values, backgrounds, training, and behaviors. In recent years, companies have become multinational, with a much more diverse population that includes more women and minorities. Many young people are running some of the most influential companies in the world, such as Internet companies. Vast differences in hierarchies and layers of management, challenges brought on by "reengineering," downsizing, the globalization that results in outsourcing jobs, the use of teams, and mergers create additional areas to study in organizational behavior. Today, to understand organizational behavior we need to consider cultural differences, racial differences, age differences, and gender differences along with all the other organizational behavior issues like motivation, leadership, communication, stress, decision making, conflict, and power.

Career paths are also changing. In the past, people often started working for a company right after high school or college and stayed with that company for their whole careers. It is much different now. Many people will work for six or more companies in their careers, and each move will bring new challenges in understanding human behavior in that particular organization. Successful people today are taking charge of their own careers instead of depending on a company or organization for success. This book will help you prepare for the ever-changing and complex multinational and multicultural workforce.

SUMMARY

Organizational behavior is the study of human behavior in the workplace, the interaction between people and the organization with the intent to understand and predict human behavior. It is an applied field that studies what people do in organizations. The understanding of individual, group, and organizational behavior is critical to one's success as a leader or a follower, and it requires a systematic study to even begin to grasp all of the variables that affect behavior.

Three important points from this chapter will reverberate throughout this book:

- It is within organizations that the differences in behavior are observed. An organization is a group of two or more people that share a common goal and meet at regular times. There are many types of organizations, ranging from small groups to clubs to companies; however, the same principles apply to all organizations.
- Do not rely on your intuition. This leads to making assumptions and 97 percent of assumptions are flawed. When assumptions are flawed, ideas are wrong; therefore a systematic study is required. Systematic studies refer to well-constructed studies that examine the many aspects of human and organizational behavior.
- Organizational behavior focuses on improving productivity, employee performance, job satisfaction, decision making, conflict management, uses of power, leadership, change, and much more.
- With a systematic study, human behavior can be understood and predicted, but it often depends on the contingencies of the situation.

CASE STUDY

In 2003, John and Helen Carter were a couple in their early 30s who had been married for ten years. John was a math teacher at the local high school and Helen sold real estate. They had two children, John Jr. (Johnny), eight years old, and Amy, five years old. They lived in suburban Indianapolis. They had been going to the Sinners Community Church. They were fairly happy there until their friend and pastor resigned and left the community to be a pastor at a bigger church in Dallas. The church members invited several potential pastors to interview for the position of pastor. The members could not agree on a candidate and the church programs began to suffer without the usual leadership. The youth program was one area that suffered the most. Wednesday night activities were eliminated. Later, the Sunday night activities for youth ceased along with the youth basketball program on Saturdays. Promises were made by the deacons that the programs would return after a new pastor was chosen. After months of waiting, John and Helen were losing patience with the situation.

When the family was in their den on a cold Saturday night in December, the children decided to say something to the parents about the situation at church.

Johnny proclaimed: "I don't want to go to church tomorrow. It is so boring and there is nothing happening at the church anymore. Many of my friends don't come anymore."

Amy chimed in: "I don't like it either. None of my friends go here anymore and there is nothing to do. My teacher isn't very good either. We would be better off staying at home."

Helen said: "Johnny and Amy are right. Why don't we stay at home and have church here?"

John said, after careful thought: "Well, I guess you guys are right. It hasn't been the same after Pastor Thompson left for Dallas."

The family decided to stay at home and have church there. After several weeks, John and Helen ran into Bill and Sue Franklin at the building supply store. They had all been good friends at the Sinners Community Church and the Franklin's kids, Charlotte and Bob, were the same age as Johnny and Amy.

Bill said: "I haven't seen you guys in long while. How are things going?"

John replied: "Things are going okay. How about you?"

Bill continued: "We're fine. We haven't seen you at church lately. Are you going somewhere else?"

John replied: "No, we are just having church at home with the kids. To be honest, we just couldn't stand to go there anymore."

Bill agreed: "I know what you mean. Things just seem to be getting worse and worse with no new pastor in sight."

Sue chimed in: "Maybe we could meet with you guys. We sure do miss seeing you and we were planning on leaving the church anyway."

John agreed: "That's a great idea and we can go out for lunch afterward."

The Carters and the Franklins began meeting every Sunday at 10 A.M. for "home church" and Sunday school. After a while, the word spread to other members of Sinners Community Church about what the Carters and Franklins were doing. Although the church leadership was critical of what they were doing, many other families wanted to join them. When the number of people attending "home church" at the Carters grew to more than twenty, John and Bill thought about moving to a larger location. The group was enthusiastic about the move. Many people offered to give money weekly to rent a facility. A local school was found to be a perfect site and people agreed to pay the school weekly and clean up after they left.

Helen suggested that there be Sunday school classes for the children of different ages. Helen agreed to teach preschool kids and Sue agreed to teach elementary school kids. Bill agreed to teach adult Sunday school and John said he would take on the job of preaching the sermons for now. Betty, a friend now involved with the group, agreed to take the older elementary school kids after they started complaining about being with the younger kids. Fred saw a need for a teenage program and volunteered to run it.

Eventually Fred, Bill, and John got together and decided that this effort should be organized.

Fred stated: "We've got to get organized and find out who is doing what and when."

Bill agreed: "You are right! I've got my wife doing one thing, me another, and the kids doing something else. Don't get me wrong, we are busy, but we love it!"

John added in: "You guys are right. This is the way church used to be and it is good to have it back."

The group agreed to elect deacons, to assign people to teaching and other activities, to explore renting the school on a long-term basis, to seek a pastor, and to explore getting tax-exempt status as a church.

In 2005, the new Saints Community Church had a part-time pastor; a deal with the school to rent the building on Sundays and Wednesday nights; a Sunday school program with three children's classes, two teen classes, and three adult classes to accommodate the 150 regular attendees; and a board of deacons.

In 2007, the Saints Community Church had its own building, full-time pastor, 250 members, ten deacons, twelve Sunday school classes, a teen program, a youth basketball league, and a senior citizen group.

In class discussion:

- Discuss what has happened in this situation and why?
- Key: This shows how a family can become a group and a group can become an organization.
- As the group grows, notice the pressure to become more organized.

Out of class questions:

1. What has happened to this family?
2. How did this family become a group?
3. How did this group become an organization?
4. Was there a need to organize? Why?

1. From the definition of organizational behavior, what do we study?

2. What can we hope to gain from a systematic study of human behavior in the workplace?

3. If we conduct a systematic study of the various elements of behavior, what are the advantages of being able to predict behavior and how might these predictions improve your organization and your leadership?

4. The study of human and organizational behavior occurs within organizations. What is changing in the workplace and within organizations that necessitates a systemic study?

PART

2

UNDERSTANDING ME

Personality, Ability, and Learning

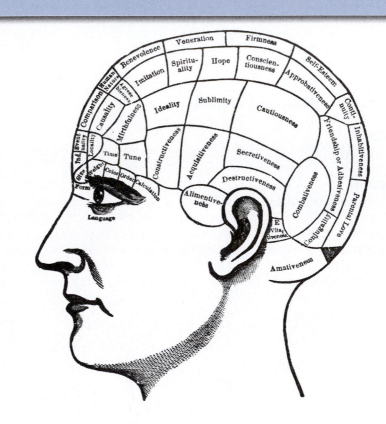

LEARNING OUTCOMES: PERSONALITY, ABILITY, AND LEARNING

1. Explain the factors that define a person's personality, ability, and learning style.

2. Explain the differences between Type A and Type B personalities.

3. Discover one's own personality type using the Jungian Type Indicator.

4. Outline the two types of ability.

5. Understand when learning has occurred.

6. Describe the various theories for learning.

7. Contrast the four learning styles.

8. Through self-assessment, gain a greater understanding of one's own personality and learning styles.

Name: _____

Section Number: _____

SELF-ASSESSMENT TESTS

Please complete the following exercises online, accessible with the Access Card packaged with this text, before reading this chapter.

EXERCISE I.A.2: WHAT'S MY JUNGIAN 16-TYPE PERSONALITY?   Result _____

The Jungian 16-Type Indicator (J-16) is a popular personality framework. It classifies people as extroverted or introverted (E or I), sensing or intuitive (S or N), thinking or feeling (T or F), and perceiving or judging (P or J). These classifications can then be combined into sixteen personality types. What value can the J-16 have for you? It can help you understand your personality, your strengths, and your weaknesses. It can help you in making successful career decisions when you try to find jobs that align well with your strengths and avoid those jobs that are a poor fit.

EXERCISE I.A.3: AM I A TYPE A?   Score _____

This instrument measures the degree to which you're competitive and rushed for time. The Type A personality describes someone who is aggressively involved in a chronic, incessant struggle to achieve more and more in less and less time. More specifically, people who are Type A are always moving, walking, and eating rapidly. They feel impatient with the pace of most events. They strive to do two or more things at once, they do not cope well with leisure time, and they are obsessed with numbers. They measure their success in terms of how many or how much of everything they acquire. People with Type B personalities are the exact opposites of those with Type A personalities.

EXERCISE I.A.4: HOW WELL DO I HANDLE AMBIGUITY?   Score _____

Having intolerance of ambiguity means that you tend to perceive situations as threatening rather than promising. You prefer more structured situations. In contrast, people who score high on tolerance respond better to change and tend to be more creative. A high tolerance for ambiguity makes you more likely to be able to function in a work world where there is less certainty about expectations, performance standards, and career progress.

EXERCISE I.A.5: HOW CREATIVE AM I?   Score _____

Creativity is the ability to combine ideas in a unique way or to make unusual associations between ideas. A creative person develops novel approaches to doing his or her work or unique solutions to problems. For managers, creativity is useful in decision making. It helps them to see options that others might not. All jobs, of course, don't require high creativity.

You should also record your scores on these exercises in Appendix 1.

NOTES

The Seminars

Rob and Jill are attending their first company full-day management development seminar. After attending the morning sessions on new quality assurance measures and the afternoon seminar on diversity training, they get together with some coworkers the next morning at the break to discuss what had happened. Jill is an extrovert with a degree in social sciences, and Rob is an introvert with a mechanical engineering degree.

Jill tells the group that the morning session was totally boring and the afternoon session was really good. Rob pipes in that he does not agree. He really liked the number crunching and getting into the methodology of quality measurement, but he was not a big fan of the touchy-feely stuff discussed in the afternoon session. Jill counters that the diversity seminar hit home on certain personal issues she has encountered and that the morning session went right by her.

These two people went to the same seminars, heard the same speakers, and received the same material. How could their reactions to the training be so different?

Welcome to Personality, Ability, and Learning! ∎

Three factors that define a person are personality, ability, and learning style. We will discuss these three factors in this chapter. The self-assessment tests are a critical part of this chapter to help you understand yourself better.

PERSONALITY

Who do you think has the best personality of the characters in *CSI*, the popular CBS television series on crime scene investigations? Is it Grissom, Katherine, Greg, Sarah, or Nick? Or maybe you would choose Warren or Brass?

All five characters have different personalities. Greg, the laboratory technician, is extroverted with a youthful, yet realistic, enthusiasm. Katherine Willows, the senior female CSI, is loyal and determined. Grissom has a wise and cautious demeanor. Sarah is kind but tough when she needs to be. Nick is aggressive and brash, and he sometimes does things that seem more emotional than logical.

If you have watched episodes of the original *CSI* series, you could probably predict how these five characters might act in a situation. If these characters had to get to the other side of a rock wall, Nick would probably try to blast his way through, Greg would find a way to fly around, Sarah would find a door, Katherine would try many different options, and Grissom would use logic and intuition and show up on the other side. Their behavior is predictable based on their personalities.

All of these characters tend to be likeable. It's tough to say which one has the best personality. It doesn't really matter. The more important question is this: *How can we understand their personalities so we can interpret and predict their behavior?* The same is true in real life. Instead of deciding whether you like a person's personality or not, it is better to accept the

One's **personality** is the individual, distinctive qualities responsible for one's identity. One's personality is the sum total of ways an individual reacts to and interacts with others. Accept that everyone has a unique personality.

other person's personality as a given and figure out how that personality drives his or her behavior. With this understanding, you can relate better to this person. A person's personality is a combination of heredity, environment, and the situation. Therefore, one's personality is the sum total of ways an individual reacts and interacts with others.

It is, therefore, essential to understand your own personality and know how your personality "fits" with others. Anyone who has worked in a job involving interacting with other people knows that certain personality stereotypes stand out. This personality trait is an advantage in some circumstances but a disadvantage in others. If an extroverted person needs to meet with some people that he or she has never met before, being extroverted can be an advantage. An extroverted person is usually less nervous about meeting people for the first time. Being extroverted can be a disadvantage during the meeting, however, if the extroverted person talks all the time and never listens to what the other people have to say. An extroverted person needs to be extra cautious about monopolizing conversations. Understanding your personality type helps you know where you can take advantage of your personality traits and where you need to be cautious.

One simple example of different personality types is **Type A** and **Type B** personalities. Type A people are the ones who are always going, always trying to get five things done at one time. People with strong Type A personalities are obsessed with numbers and measure their success in terms of how much of everything they acquire.[1]

People with Type B personalities are more laid back. Interestingly enough, in North America 50 percent of the people are Type A and 50 percent are Type B. It is not better to be one type or the other, but you can predict certain behavior with Type A personalities (e.g., they can't sit still) and other types of behavior with Type B personalities (e.g., you can't get them going). You are not going to motivate Type A personalities by offering them a relaxing vacation on the beach, but they might be excited if you offer them a whitewater rafting trip. Someone with a Type B personality would probably take the beach vacation. Are you a Type A or Type B? You can take a test on the self-assessment CD to find out.

According to the self-assessment test, I am a Type _____.

Probably the best-known personality test is the **Myers-Briggs Type Indicator (MBTI)**.[2] This instrument has been around for more than 60 years, yet it remains very influential in helping to sort out the differences in personality types. This tool classifies people into different personality types based on four different characteristics. There is not a "right" way to score on these four dimensions. You are what you are. Once you know what you are, however, you can see how this personality type can be an advantage or disadvantage in different situations and try to adjust your behavior accordingly. Many of today's *Fortune* 500 companies use the test in some form or another as a key component of an executive training program.[3] Please note, the Myers-Briggs is not an indicator of success and does not measure intelligence or skills. It does help leaders discover their own personal styles and how they are perceived by their peers and subordinates. It reflects a natural preference in behavior.

The first characteristic measured by the MBTI is whether a person is **introverted (I)** or **extroverted (E).** The letter after the word is a way to keep track of different personality characteristics. Some people like to be by themselves (I), other people get energy from being with others (E). People who are extroverted tend to focus on the outer world of people and external events. They direct their energy and attention outward and receive energy from external events, experiences, and interactions. People who are introverted tend to focus on their own innerworld of ideas and experiences. They direct their energy and attention inward and receive energy from their internal thoughts, feelings, and reflections. It is not better to be an **I** or an **E**; these personalities are just different. It doesn't mean a person is loud or shy but rather how people absorb and process information.

The second personality characteristic is whether a person is **sensing (S)** or **intuitive (N).** An S trusts things he or she can see, hear, and touch. People who prefer sensing like to take in information through their eyes, ears, and other senses to find out what is actually happening. They are observant of what is going on around them and are especially good at recognizing the practical realities of a situation. An **N** uses intuition and draws conclusions from things that cannot be sensed. People who prefer intuition like to take information by seeing the big picture, focusing on the relationship and the connections between the facts. They want to grasp pattern and are especially good at seeing new possibilities and different ways of doing things. Katherine is probably an S because she is realistic about things. Grissom is probably an N because he is always relying on logic and intuition.

The third personality characteristic is whether a person is **thinking (T)** or **feeling (F).** A T is logical. People who prefer to use thinking in decision making tend to look at the logical consequences of a choice or action. They try to mentally remove themselves from a situation to examine it objectively and analyze cause and effect. Their goal is an objective standard of truth and the application of principles. Their strengths include figuring out what is wrong with something so they can apply their problem-solving abilities. An **F** is more emotional. People who prefer to use feeling in decision making tend to consider what is important to them and to other people. They mentally place themselves in a situation and identify with the people involved so that they can make decisions based on person-centered values. Their goal is harmony and recognition of individuals, and their strengths include understanding, appreciating, and supporting others. Grissom is probably a T; Nick is definitely an F. Engineers tend to be Ts; artists tend to be Fs.

The fourth personality characteristic is whether a person is **perceiving (P)** or **judging (J).** Ps usually try to understand a situation carefully before taking action. People who prefer to use their perceiving process in the outer world tend to live in a flexible, spontaneous way, seeking to experience and understand life, rather than control it. Plans and decisions feel confining to them; they prefer to stay open to experience and last-minute options. They enjoy and trust their resourcefulness and ability to adapt to the demands of a situation. Js are more likely to quickly decide what needs to be done and then just do it. People who prefer to use their judging process in the outer world tend to live in a planned, orderly way, and they want to regulate and control life. They make decisions, come to closure, and move on. Their lifestyles are structured and organized, and they like to have things settled. Sticking to a plan and schedule is very important to them, and they enjoy their ability to get things done. Katherine is probably a P because she would always be sure to carefully understand a situation before doing anything. Greg and Nick are probably Js because they would quickly judge a situation and then take action.

Your results on the MBTI will be four letters based on how you are classified on these four characteristics. For example, if you are an ENTJ, this means you are extroverted (E), intuitive (N), thinking (T), and judging (J). Since there are four characteristics with two possible letters for each, there are sixteen different personality types as measured by the MBTI. To give you a feel for the different types of personalities, Table 2–1

The result of an **MBTI** test is a four-letter description of your personality.

Table 2–1 MBTI Personality Types

Definitions of some of the unusual terms:
Questor: someone who searches for something.
Conservator: someone who protects something or someone.
Trustee: someone who takes care of things.

INTP	INFP	ESFJ	ESTJ
Architect	Questor	Seller	Administrator
ENTP	**ENFP**	**ISFJ**	**ISTJ**
Inventor	Journalist	Conservator	Trustee
INTJ	**INFJ**	**ESFP**	**ESTP**
Scientist	Author	Entertainer	Promoter
ENTJ	**ENFJ**	**ISFP**	**ISTP**
Field Marshall	Teacher	Artist	Craftsperson

Source: MBTI Personality Types adapted from *Please Understand Me*, David Kiersey and Marilyn Bates, p. 70. Used by permission of PNB Co., P.O. Box 2748, Del Mar, CA 92014.

presents the sixteen possibilities with a one-word description for each. The information for this table was adapted from the book *Please Understand Me* by David Keirsey and Marilyn Bates. This book has a wealth of information on interpreting MBTI results, and if you are interested in learning more about MBTI, this is a great book to read.

The self-assessment CD has a simplified version of the MBTI. You can get the four-letter descriptor of your personality from the self-assessment CD.

According to the test, I am a _____ _____ _____ _____.

As noted, personality differences can be expected in the workplace; however, if you are Southwest Airlines, the last thing you need is a dysfunctional team at 30,000 feet in the air. To make sure that doesn't happen, Southwest Airlines decided to give the Myers-Briggs Type Indicator assessment to determine the psychological preferences of the aircraft team and other employees.[4] The MBTI tool was used to aid team building, conflict resolution, and leadership programs. Southwest uses the assessment as a diagnostic tool to help employees identify how obstacles, stress, and potential conflict may arise. It is used to help team members recognize and celebrate their differences. The teams then use this knowledge to achieve better results. Elizabeth Bryant, director of Southwest's University of the People, noted that Southwest found the assessment can provide a foundation for building trust in developing teams. The assessments helped the team members understand the reasoning behind their coworkers' behavior, which, in turn, helped build trust and empathy within the departments. "In these classes, we saw a lot of 'aha' moments," says Bryant. "Behaviors that might have once caused misunderstanding and frustration now are viewed through a different filter."[5]

There are other ways to classify personalities in addition to the MBTI. All of these tests end up measuring essentially the same thing, however, so if you are familiar with MBTI, you are pretty well covered.

Once you understand your personality, how does that help you interact with others? We've already talked about how understanding your personality can help you adjust your own behavior in different situations. Understanding personality types should also help you appreciate how other people are different. We know that some people are more extroverted and some people are more introverted. It's not good or bad; that's just the way it is.

You have probably heard a person say, "That person is too pushy" or "That person just sits in the corner and never says anything." It is better to accept these different personality types and try to work within these boundaries. If a person is introverted, you may need to give that person more time to warm up to you. If a person is extroverted, try not to be turned off if he or she comes on too strong. In a work environment, having different personalities around can be a big advantage. Extroverts tend to work in the sales jobs, and introverts tend to handle the analyst jobs.

Now that we have discussed a few of the many personality profile assessments, we need to consider how personality profile assessments are being used in the workplace. Human resource professionals use personality profiles to analyze their organizations' overall leadership and staffing strengths and to find a variety of candidates who possess the diverse personalities and styles that their organizations need.[6] Expanding the use of personality assessments offers professionals new uses for a number of tools. Personality assessments are used in recruiting, hiring more diverse employees who fit in, and helping new hires become acclimated to an organization more quickly. They are also used to help supervisors and managers coach their subordinates and to design needed leadership development programs. A word of caution is also needed at this point. Do not use personality assessments as a means to "weed out" applicants but rather use them as a tool to address and improve the overall organization.

Here is the bottom line on personality:

- Leader, know thyself. Understand your own personality and use this information to adjust your behavior.
- Instead of making value judgments about other people's personalities, accept these differences and use this information to understand and predict behavior.
- Personality assessments may be used to analyze an organization's overall leadership and staffing strengths and weaknesses.

ABILITY

How did you choose your major and, ultimately, your future profession? Hopefully you chose something that you find interesting and that fits your abilities. In the movie *Happy Gilmore*, Happy (Adam Sandler) wanted to be a hockey player. Unfortunately, Happy couldn't skate or handle the puck very well. These are not good characteristics for a hockey player! He tried out for the hockey team year after year, but he never made it. Hockey was not his calling.

One day Happy picked up a golf club and found that he could hit the ball more than 400 yards (that's a very good characteristic for a golfer). In the movie, Happy becomes a professional golfer and everything turns out okay. Some people think they don't have the ability to succeed, but maybe they are just playing the wrong game.

Ability is the *capacity* to do something. Happy Gilmore had the capacity to hit the golf ball a long way for many years before he actually used this skill. Some people have the ability to make straight As, but they may never achieve those grades.

Ability can be broken down into **intellectual ability** and **physical ability**. Intellectual ability is the capacity to do mental activities. For example, an SAT test tries to measure a person's ability to do the intellectual tasks required to succeed in college. An IQ test measures general intelligence. There has been a good amount of research over the past ten years evaluating intellectual abilities. Some researchers believe intelligence is better understood by dividing it into four parts: cognitive, social,

Ability is the *capacity* to do something. That doesn't mean you actually do it.

emotional, and cultural.[7] Cognitive intelligence entails knowing and perceiving. As society became more complex, intellectual competences became more sophisticated. Social intelligence can be defined as the intelligence that lies behind group interactions and behaviors. Emotional intelligence is the capacity to recognize our feelings and those of others, to motivate ourselves, and to manage our own emotions and those in our relationships.[8]

Physical ability includes such traits as how fast one can run, how much weight one can lift, and how high one can jump. Some people might think physical ability is only important for jobs that involve manual labor, but this is not true. Physical ability also includes things like dexterity, which is a trait that surgeons need, or stamina, which helps international salespeople maintain exhausting travel schedules.

All people have different sets of abilities, and all jobs require different sets of abilities. If you can match your particular set of abilities with the right job, you will probably be more successful in life. This is known as the **job-ability fit,** the fit between a person's abilities and the requirements of a job.

The **job-ability fit** is the fit between a person's abilities and the requirements of a job.

A good way to find a person's best job-ability fit is through the *Strong Interest Inventory*. This test is available from any career counseling office. This test measures one's abilities and compares these abilities with a set of abilities of people who are successful in different professions. The outcome of the test is used to match the test taker to compatable professions.

Gavin Sinclair said that, "when I hit my midlife crisis, I took the *Strong Interest Inventory* to help evaluate new career options." The test said the best profession for Gavin would be a college professor, which came as a complete surprise to him. However, becoming a professor turned out to be a good fit with his abilities (even his student evaluations supported this finding). These job-ability fit tests don't always give the right answers, but they can challenge you to consider some new options that you might not have considered before.

LEARNING

Learning is any relatively permanent change in behavior that occurs as a result of experience.

Learning is how we go beyond our basic personalities and abilities. We learn to modify our behaviors in different situations and we learn new skills. Any relatively permanent change in behavior that occurs as a result of experience is defined as learning. There are three basic theories of learning: classical conditioning, operant conditioning, and social learning. After a review of these theories, there is a self-assessment test that can offer a better understanding of your learning style.

Classical Conditioning

Classical conditioning (Pavlov) is passive.

The theory of **classical conditioning** came from a series of famous experiments conducted by Ivan Pavlov.[9] Pavlov rang a bell and then immediately presented a dog with a piece of meat. The dog would salivate at the sight of the meat. He repeated this process many times, each time ringing the bell just before he presented the meat to the dog. After a while, the dog would salivate simply at the sound of the bell. The dog associated the sound of the ringing bell with the meat. This is an example of classical conditioning. It is a passive learning process where a person responds to a certain stimulus, even though normally there would be no response to that stimulus. It is unlikely that a dog would salivate at the sound of a bell if the dog hasn't been preconditioned to associate food with a bell ringing.

Adriamycin is a common chemotherapy drug. It has a distinctive red color, which is noticeable when it hangs in an IV bag. Chemotherapy patients often become sick to their stomachs and throw up after getting Adriamycin. One of the major cancer centers in Boston redecorated their lobby with a red color that is very close to the color of Adriamycin. Many cancer patients walked into the newly redecorated lobby, saw the red color, and threw up (which quickly resulted in the next redecoration project). They had associated the red color with throwing up. It was a totally reflexive response; probably some of the patients didn't even know why they suddenly felt nauseous.

Operant Conditioning

The theory of **operant conditioning** came from the work of B. F. Skinner.[10] He found that people are more likely to repeat a certain behavior if they are rewarded for that behavior. For example, if you study hard for a test and get rewarded with an "A," you will be more likely to study hard for the next test. If you study hard and get a bad grade, you may decide that studying hard doesn't really help.

Operant conditioning is common in organizations. If you do a good job planning an event, you may be recognized for your important contribution. On the other hand, if you do a lot of work and no one seems to notice, you may decide not to work so hard on planning the next event.

One of the most important lessons to learn in an organization is to reward people for good performance because they will be more likely to repeat the good performance in the future.

Operant conditioning (Skinner) is active.

Social Learning

Social learning is simply learning through experience.[11] Earlier in this book we suggested that one already knows a lot about human behavior based on one's common sense and experience. This is the same as saying that knowing a lot about human behavior is a result of social learning. The more accurately one perceives situations and identifies patterns of behavior, the higher one's level of social learning.

Social learning is learning through experience.

Learning Styles

Everyone has a different learning style. Table 2–2 is one way to look at a person's learning style.

Table 2–2   Learning Styles

Bodily-Kinesthetic	These people are **active learners.** They like to experience things themselves and explain what they have learned to others.
Visual-Spatial	These people **remember what they see.** These types of learners tend to forget spoken words and ideas.
Verbal-Linguistic	These people **remember much of what they hear and more of what they hear and then say out loud.** They benefit from class discussions.
Logical-Mathematical	These people like to **reflect on concepts.**

The following self-assessment test will help you understand your learning style.

Your Learning Style

Rate each of these statements on the following scale:

(1) Rarely   (2) Sometimes   (3) Usually   (4) Always

1. _____ I enjoy physical activities.
2. _____ I am uncomfortable sitting still.
3. _____ I prefer to learn through doing.
4. _____ When sitting, I move my legs or hands.
5. _____ I enjoy working with my hands.
6. _____ I like to pace when I'm thinking or studying.
7. _____ I use maps easily.
8. _____ I draw pictures/diagrams when explaining ideas.
9. _____ I can assemble items easily from diagrams.
10. _____ I enjoy drawing or photography.
11. _____ I do not like to read long paragraphs.
12. _____ I prefer a drawn map over written directions.
13. _____ I enjoy telling stories.
14. _____ I like to write.
15. _____ I like to read.
16. _____ I express myself clearly.
17. _____ I am good at negotiating.
18. _____ I like to discuss topics that interest me.
19. _____ I like math at school.
20. _____ I like science.
21. _____ I solve problems well.
22. _____ I question how things work.
23. _____ I enjoy planning or designing something new.
24. _____ I am able to fix things.

SCORING		
Bodily-Kinesthetic	(total for questions 1–6)	_____
Visual-Spatial	(total for questions 7–12)	_____
Verbal-Linguistic	(total for questions 13–18)	_____
Logical-Mathematical	(total for questions 19–24)	_____

**Please record your scores on the *Pathways to Learning* test
in Appendix 1.**

The category with the highest score on the self-assessment test is your preferred learning style. Here are some strategies to take advantage of each particular learning style (from *Keys to Success: How to Achieve Your Goals*, Carter, Bishop, Kravits, and Butcher, Prentice Hall, 1999).[12] If you scored a relatively high score in two or more categories, you should read the tips for all of those sections.

BODILY-KINESTHETIC

- Study in a group in which members take turns explaining topics to each other and then discussing them.
- Think of practical uses of the course material.
- Pace and recite while you learn.
- Act out material or design games.
- Use flash cards with other people.
- Teach the material to someone else.

VISUAL-SPATIAL

- Add diagrams to your notes whenever possible. Dates can be drawn on a time line, math functions can be graphed, and percentages can be drawn on a pie chart.
- Organize your notes so that you can clearly see main points and supporting facts and how things are connected.
- Connect related facts in your notes by drawing arrows.
- Color-code your notes using different colored highlighters so that everything relating to a particular topic is in the same color.

VERBAL-LINGUISTIC

- Talk about what you learn. Work in study groups so that you have an opportunity to explain and discuss what you are learning.
- Read the textbook and highlight no more than ten percent.
- Rewrite your notes.
- Outline chapters.
- Recite information or write scripts and debates.

LOGICAL-MATHEMATICAL

- Study in a quiet setting.
- When you are reading, stop periodically to think about what you have read.
- Don't just memorize material; think about why it is important and what it relates to, considering the causes and effects involved.
- Write short summaries of what the material means to you.

Source: "Strategies to Take Advantage of Each Learning Style," from Carol Carter, Joyce Bishop, and Sarah Lyman Kravits, *Keys to Success: How to Achieve Your Goals, 2nd Ed.* Published by Allyn and Bacon, Boston, MA. Copyright © 1998 by Pearson Education. Adapted by permission of the publisher.

The leader of a group needs to understand that people in the group may have different learning styles. If you want to help them learn, you should present information in a way that will appeal to all the different learning styles discussed in this section.

SUMMARY

Three key factors that define a person are personality, ability, and learning style.

An individual's personality is the way we characterize that person. Some have a pleasant personality while others may be abrasive. Some may be loud while others may be quiet. We often use a series of assessments to assist in the classification of one's personality. With the *MBTI* we have:

- Extroverts (outgoing) and introverts (reserved)
- Sensing or intuitive
- Thinking or feeling
- Perceiving or judging

Another classification of personality is Type A (always on the go) and Type B (laid back) personalities that describe how people act.

Ability is defined in two ways—physical ability and intellectual ability. Physical ability includes ability to perform certain physical activities, including lifting, running, dexterity, and stamina. Intellectual ability means ability to perform mental activities such as critical thinking and math.

Learning can occur in several ways. Classical conditioning makes learning passive. Operant conditioning makes learning active. Social learning means learning through experience. Learning style describes the way we learn:

- Bodily-kinesthetic learning happens through experience (by doing).
- Visual-spatial learning happens when people remember what they have seen.
- Verbal-linguistic learning happens when people remember what they hear and say.
- Logical-mathematical learning occurs when people reflect on concepts.

CASE STUDY

The Jasper Company had been trying to create an advertising campaign to market their new mop. This mop is a technological breakthrough with the ability to resist stains, odor, and bacteria. The mop can be submerged in a pail of water and all the grime will come off. Grime in the pail will not adhere to the mop no matter how dirty the water gets. Bob Smith, the president of Jasper Company, told the heads of the operations, marketing, design, and engineering departments that he wanted the best person from each department to work on a marketing committee for the new mop. Bob felt if all the departments worked on the project then all the departments would feel a sense of ownership and involvement. Operations sent Bill Jones, an up-and-coming manager, who is outgoing, logical, decisive, and intuitive. Bill is a no nonsense and get-the-job done type of individual. Marketing sent their star employee, Mike Melvin. Mike is a popular, hands-on, passionate, flashy, and quick acting individual. He is often referred to as a mover and a shaker. The design department sent Helen Pitts to the committee. Helen is a shy, skeptical, caring, and cautious person. She is very creative and highly professional. The engineering department sent Sandy Brown. Sandy is an intuitive, needs-to-see for herself, logical thinking, and careful individual. She is a first-rate engineer and always strives to do things right.

When time came for their first meeting, the conference room was set and Bob knew that his hand-picked team would come up with some great ideas. Bill opened the 9 A.M. meeting.

Bill said, "Let's get on with this meeting. I don't want it to take all day."

Mike chimed in, "Bill is right and I have just the plan we should follow right here."

Bill retorted, "What do you mean you have a plan? We haven't done anything yet."

Sandy jumped in, "I think we ought to sell the mop on its technical merits as the best cleaning device ever. I have the test data right here."

"Who needs test data?" Mike replied. "What we need is sizzle and test results are not sizzle. I want to show you all how to sell something. I want to put the mop in the hand of a young attractive model in an evening dress who is mopping the floor."

Helen finally jumps in, "Your idea is crass, degrading to women, and unrealistic. We need to take our time and be creative on this promotion. I have lay-out designs that we can use. People will love to see the features of the mop in these multi-colored drawings."

Mike fires back, "You know what you can do with those drawings and your bad attitude. Nobody wants to see your drawings. That is just one dumb idea."

Bill, trying to restore order, said "I am taking charge of this meeting. So, everybody sit down and shut up. I want this wrapped up and on Mr. Smith's desk by end of business today. We need to stay on task."

Mike shouts back, "Just who put you in charge? Why should any of us listen to you? You think that you are better than the rest of us."

Bill replies, "I am certainly better than a hot head like you and someone needs to take charge."

Helen said, "I still think we should take our time on this and do it right. I think we should see everyone's ideas and try to work together."

After going at it all day, the group accomplished nothing. The ideas that had been presented were lost because they had forgotten to have anyone take notes.

After going back and forth all day on how the mop should be sold to the public, the members left the meeting fed up with each other with no real solution in sight. News of this got back to Bob Smith and he called a meeting of his department heads.

Bob started the meeting by commenting, "I thought I told you people to send me your best employees. What I ended up with was a bunch of losers who produced absolutely nothing in a day's time. Where was all this brilliance you have been promoting within your staffs?"

There was a good minute of silence until Ralph, the operation department head, spoke.

Ralph said, "Bill is the best person I have and if things broke down, it wasn't his fault. He must have been working with the wrong people."

Sally, the head of the design department, responded, "I can assure all of you that Helen is my best employee and it wasn't her fault that things did not get done."

Mark, the head of engineering, chimed in, "It couldn't be Sandy fault. She is a top-flight engineering and I will stand behind her 100%."

Chuck, the head of marketing, responded, "Mike is the best sales and marketing man in the business. He knows his stuff and couldn't be the problem."

Bob closed the meeting and sent the heads back to their departments. He could not believe what the department heads had said. He just knew that someone must be at fault for the failure of the meeting. He was both disappointed by the failure of the meeting and baffled by his employees' behavior.

In class discussion:

1. Due to the lack of a leader in the marketing meeting and the different personalities involved how might this have been handled better?

2. How should the meeting have been run to get the most out of the people involved?

DISCUSSION QUESTIONS

1. Explain the theory of operant conditioning, classical conditioning, and social learning, and provide an example to illustrate this method of learning.

2. All people have a different set of abilities. Discuss the importance for understanding individual differences in abilities.

3. Explain the differences between a Type A personality and a Type B personality. Which type is better? Explain why.

4. What type of personality would you want your boss to have? Explain.

5. Are the two concepts of ability (intellectual and physical) mutually exclusive (have no relationship to each other) or are they complementary (related to each other)?

CHAPTER 3

Perception

LEARNING OUTCOMES: PERCEPTION

1. Recognize the three factors influencing perception.

2. List the shortcuts used to the advantage, or detriment, of understanding others.

3. Explain the fundamental attribution theory.

4. Through self-assessment, gain insight on how one's own perception influences understanding of people and situations.

Name: _____

Section Number: _____

SELF-ASSESSMENT TEST

Please complete the following exercise online, accessible with the Access Card packaged with this text, before reading this chapter.

EXERCISE 38: HOW WELL DO I
MANAGE IMPRESSIONS?   Score _____

Score _____   Score _____   Score _____   Score _____

   This instrument assesses one's management of image. As the analysis notes, most of us are concerned with the image that others have of us, their perception. Impression management is a process by which people attempt to control the impressions others form of them. The instrument itself assesses five impression management strategies from self-promotion to ingratiation to exemplification to intimidation to supplication. It is important for people to know their style and how that style might fit into an organizational culture.

   You should also record your score on this exercise in Appendix 1.

NOTES

The Big Game

Fred and Jerry were members of a very good high school basketball team. The team was playing for the sectional championship after finishing the regular season with a 14-6 record and easily winning the first round of sectional play by beating a team with a 3-18 record. The 40-point win in that game did much to build the team's confidence, maybe too much.

The championship game was not going well for the boys' team as they trailed by a score of 34-28 at the half. The second half did not go any better and although they were the favored team, they lost by a score of 70-54. After the game, the local television station's sports anchor, Tex Routman, interviewed Fred and Jerry to ask what had happened. Fred told Tex that the officiating was bad all night, the other team fouled too much, the gym was too hot, coaching decisions were poor, and fan support for their team was lousy.

Jerry indicated in his interview with Tex that he had had an off night, the team was overconfident, and they were simply outplayed by the other team. Tex left shaking his head not only about the loss but also about the conflicting stories the two athletes told.

Jerry and Fred had played for the same team in the same game under the same circumstances. How could their stories be so different? Welcome to Perception! ■

How do you look at the world? A big part of understanding and predicting behavior is understanding how a person perceives a situation. A person's behavior is based on his or her perception of reality, not reality itself.

Have you seen the movie *A Beautiful Mind?* In this movie, John Nash (played by Russell Crowe) lives his life like everything is real, but three of the characters he responds to are make-believe. Once he starts to figure things out, Nash's behavior has to change. *A Beautiful Mind* illustrates the most important lesson about **perception:** *People's behavior is based on how they perceive reality, not reality itself.* Nash thought his best friend, his friend's niece, and an undercover agent were all real, so he acted that way. Once he perceived these people were just figments of his imagination, his behavior had to change accordingly. *Finding Forrester, The Sixth Sense,* and *The Matrix* are three additional film examples that dramatize how perception is reality.

Here is a real situation where a perception completely distorted reality. On board a Northwest Airlines flight in March 2001, two passengers seated next to one another, a man and a woman, were talking on their cell phones prior to take-off. An announcement was made to turn off all cell phones and electric devices in preparation for departure. The man complied, but the woman continued to talk. After a few moments, the man said to the woman, in a conversational tone, "Stop talking on your cell phone, doing so could bring the aircraft down." Another passenger heard only the phrase "could bring the aircraft down." This passenger immediately left her seat and notified a flight attendant that the man who had spoken to the woman about the phone had actually threatened to bring the aircraft down. The flight attendant told the captain who then returned to the gate area and notified the authorities. The man was arrested and

People's behavior is based on how they perceive reality, not reality itself.

Perception is a process by which individuals organize and interpret their sensory impressions to give meaning to their environment.

removed from the airplane. Later in the day the situation was cleared up and the man was allowed to continue his travels.

As this illustrates, perceptions vary from person to person. Different people perceive different things about the same situation. But more than that, we assign meaning to what we perceive. And the meanings might change for a certain person. One might change one's perspective or simply adjust things to mean something else. As a result, sometimes we are confused by the way people act, and it is often because we don't understand how other people perceive the world. We tend to think everyone perceives the world the same way we do, but that assumption often leads to misunderstanding. To understand a person's behavior, we must first understand how that person perceives a situation. Only then can we understand and predict that person's behavior.

THREE FACTORS THAT INFLUENCE PERCEPTION

Perception is influenced by three factors:
- Perceiver
- Target
- Situation

Perception is influenced by three factors: the perceiver, the target, and the situation. I often ask students to tell me what they perceive about me: How old am I? Am I married? What are my political beliefs? What are my religious beliefs? Was I in a fraternity in college?

In this case, the students are the **perceivers.** They are the ones trying to answer the questions about me, the **target.** They are sorting out these perceptions in the context of observing me in class, the **situation.** Their perceptions of me might be different if they knew me from another situation.

Perception is simply the way people interpret the world around them. In my perception game, different people perceive, or interpret, me differently. I do not wear a wedding ring. As a result, some people automatically interpret this to mean I am not married. When these people interpret the world, they make a conclusion about the marital status of people based on the societal norm that a married person wears a ring. In my case, this doesn't work. I am married, but I don't wear a ring. Sometimes clues can be misleading.

Projection is attributing a person's own characteristics to another person.

Selective perception is when people selectively interpret what they see based on their interest background, experience, and attitudes.

Stereotyping is attributing a specific trait to a person based on the characteristics of the group to which a person belongs.

Much of the way my students perceive me is based more about themselves, the perceivers. If a student is in a fraternity and generally has a good opinion about me and the way I act, he is more likely to guess that I was in a fraternity. This tendency is called **projection.** Other people with very strong religious beliefs may pay special attention to whether I had given any hints about my religious faith. This is called **selective perception,** where people selectively interpret things about the target based on the perceiver's interests or background. Some students may guess I have liberal political beliefs because I am a professor, or they may guess I have conservative beliefs because I am from Indiana. In both cases, the students are **stereotyping,** judging me based on my being a part of a certain group. As you can tell, projection, selective perception, and stereotyping can all lead to errors in perception, so a person needs to be careful.

Halo effect is when a general impression is made about an individual because of a single positive characteristic.

A **contrast effect** occurs when an impression is made based on a comparison with others, ranking the individual higher or lower on the same characteristics.

Other examples of how students perceive me can come at course review time. Most of my students like the fact that I *try* to be funny. They may give me a high teaching rating simply because I am entertaining. This would be an example of the **halo effect,** where a person is perceived in a certain way because of a single characteristic. My students think I am a good teacher because of a single characteristic: I try to be funny. I may also get good teaching ratings because of the **contrast effect,** meaning I might be bad but *contrasted* with other professors, I am perceived to be pretty good. A professor who has a trait that students dislike (like giving hard tests) may be rated low on all traits. This is called the **horn effect.**

So far we've talked about how the characteristics and beliefs of the perceivers can affect perception. There are also some special characteristics of the target that can make a big difference in perception. If I were especially young or old, that might have made students more curious about my age. I had one professor who was 87 years old and still going strong, so everyone knew about him because he was so unique. Since I am considered middle aged, nobody pays much attention to how old I am. The more unique an attribute of a target, the more likely it will be noticed.

Finally, the third element of perception is the situation. If a student meets me outside of class, he or she may form different perceptions of me. To use an extreme example, I have a college friend who became manager of a Hooters restaurant. I had not seen him for many years, and he happened to be coming to town for the grand opening of the new Hooters. He asked me to stop by and see him, which I did. The first person I saw when arriving at Hooters was one of my students. She made sure to tell everyone in the class where I was that Friday night. The same weekend I also gave a speech at a local church, and the mother of one of my students was there and told her son that she had met me. He also told many of the students where I was that Sunday. My students' perception of me probably varied based on which situation they heard about.

To summarize, perception is formed by the perceiver, the target, and the situation. When trying to understand people's behavior, try to see the world as they see it. When perceivers look at a target, are they influenced by projection, selective perception, or stereotyping? Does the target have any special features? What is the situation in which this is taking place? Remember that expectations can distort our perceptions. We tend to see what we expect to see.

ATTRIBUTION THEORY

Some people believe they control their own destiny. Others believe that circumstances control them. This is called locus of control. The people that believe they control their destiny are said to have an **internal locus of control.** People who believe that circumstances control them are said to have an **external locus of control.** Did you see Mel Gibson in the film *Conspiracy Theory?* He definitely had an external locus of control. He always believed someone or something was controlling his life.

Based on the self-assessment test at the beginning of this chapter, do you have an internal locus of control or an external locus of control? If you have an external locus of control, you need to be especially careful about blaming external factors for your problems.

Perception leads quite naturally to judgment. After you perceive something, you then try to make a judgment on how this fits with everything else you know. If you heard that your professor was at Hooters, you might make a judgment. If you see a person without a wedding ring, you make a judgment (which may be that the person is single or perhaps not).

One way to make a judgment about people's behavior is based on **attribution theory.**[13] Attribution theory suggests that a person tries to understand whether another person's behavior is caused by internal or external factors. For example, I may have a student who comes late to class every day. Based on attribution theory, I might want to determine if this behavior is internally or externally caused. So after class I ask the student, "Why are you always late to class?" If the student answers, "My

Horn effect is when a general impression is made about an individual based on a single negative characteristic.

Internal locus of control: people who believe they control their own destiny.

External locus of control: people who believe that external factors control them.

Attribution theory: trying to decide if another person's behavior is internally or externally controlled.

class before this is at the airport, and it takes an extra ten minutes to get to your class," I will think his behavior is externally caused. He is late because of external circumstances beyond his control. If instead the student says, "I have a hard time waking up for this 1:30 P.M. class," I will probably conclude that his behavior is internally caused, meaning it is something that he could control.

How People Apply Attribution Theory

What if I am not convinced that it really takes an extra ten minutes to walk to my class? What if there are four students who have the same class at the airport before my class, and all four are always ten minutes late? This behavior shows **consensus,** meaning everyone who faces a similar situation exhibits the same behavior. In this case, I am more likely to believe that an external factor caused these students to be late.

People also look for **consistency** in a person's actions to determine if that person's behavior is driven by internal or external factors. If my tardy student is ten minutes late only part of the time, there must be more to the story. Maybe the professor of the prior class lets them out early sometimes, and on those days the student makes it to class on time, so the student's tardiness on some days is still externally caused.

Finally, people look at **distinctiveness** to determine if a person's behavior is the result of internal or external factors. If my late student has a class immediately after mine in the same building and is always on time for that class, his tardy behavior in my class shows distinctiveness, meaning his behavior is different in different situations. Distinctiveness usually means the person's behavior is more likely to be the result of some external factor rather than something under the person's control.

Attribution theory, or deciding if a person's behavior is caused by external or internal factors, leads to some interesting biases. Have you ever known someone who has every excuse in the book for not getting something done? This person blames every bad outcome on external factors. Yet when something good happens, he or she is quick to take credit. This is called **self-serving bias,** meaning the person thinks that anything good is the result of internal factors under the person's control, and any bad things are the result of external factors that cannot be controlled.

On the flip side, have you ever known a professor who simply doesn't like a certain student? If the student says she had to miss an exam because her car broke down, the professor thinks she still could have found a way to get to class. As a result of the absence the professor believes the student cannot possibly get a good grade on the exam. If the student gets a good score on an exam, the professor thinks the student must have been cheating. The professor is exhibiting **fundamental attribution error.** The professor attributes the negative behavior as internally caused with this student, and successes (the good grade) are perceived to be the result of external factors, the cheating.

A PERSONAL EXAMPLE

A good student of perception can make some pretty amazing predictions of behavior. One night I went to a bar with a friend from work. He was thirty-something, a manager in HR (human resources, or personnel, as they used to be called), and single. He was a keen student of the bar scene. He would spend many hours every week hanging out at the bar "studying" this topic. I, on the other hand, got married when I was twenty and am far less knowledgeable about the bar scene.

Consensus: everyone that faces a similar situation exhibits the same behavior.

Consistency: showing the same behavior in the same situation all of the time.

Distinctiveness: showing different behavior in different situations.

Self-serving bias: a person thinks that anything good is the result of internal factors and anything bad is the result of external factors.

Fundamental attribution error: a person attributes a behavior to internal factors when it was actually an external factor outside of the person's control.

After sitting in the bar for about fifteen minutes, my friend turned to me and said, "See that guy with the red sweater? He's going to go over to the woman with the blue shirt who is sitting at the bar."

I looked over the situation and said, "No way. He is way on the other side of the room. He doesn't even see her." Two minutes later, the guy with the red sweater went over to the woman with the blue shirt at the bar.

"Now they're going to go over to the table by the window," my friend predicted.

"How can you know that?" I asked, not learning my lesson the first time. "There is plenty of room at the bar, and there are five other tables that are closer." The couple went over to the table by the window.

"Next she is going to put her hand on his shoulder," my friend said. Being burned twice, I shut up. She put her hand on his shoulder. Before I take this story too far, the point is that if a person has experience perceiving a certain situation, he or she can make some pretty good predictions about what will happen. This not only applies in bars. It happens at basketball games, in class, at church, at parties, and in the workplace.

The most important thing to remember from this chapter is that people's behaviors are based on how they perceive reality, not reality itself. If you do not understand how a person is acting, it may be because that person perceives the situation differently than you.

Perception is influenced by three factors:

- the perceiver
- the target
- the situation

Some common mistakes that distort a person's perception are

- Projection—attributing a person's own characteristics to another person
- Selective perception—interpreting things based on the perceiver's interests and background
- Stereotyping—judging persons because they are part of a group
- Halo effect—a person is well perceived based on one or two positive characteristics
- Contrast effect—a person is regarded positively or negatively based on a comparison to others
- Horn effect—a person is poorly perceived based on one or two negative characteristics

Attribution theory is trying to understand if a person's behavior is under his or her control, which is called an *internal locus of control*, or whether the behavior is driven by outside factors, which is called an *external locus of control*. People look for consensus, consistency, and distinctiveness to try to make this determination.

If a person thinks that good things are always due to internal causes but bad things are due to external causes, that person has a *self-serving bias* (unless by some miracle that is always the case). If a person always attributes another person's behavior to internal causes when in fact there are external causes, the person judging the other person is making a *fundamental attribution error*.

CASE STUDY

The Situation

The Allen Company had just recruited and hired four people to be production supervisors from various universities. Ron and Bill were each told to take two of the new employees for assignment in their departments. The men have seen these new employees previously for only thirty minutes during their company interviews. Ron and Bill now have to decide which two employees would work best in their respective departments and give their recommendation to human resources for placement. Ron, thinking it would be nice to work directly with Bill on this issue, called for a meeting. The meeting was set for Wednesday afternoon at 2:30 and the human resources department needed the final recommendations by Friday at noon. The new people were going to report to human resources on Monday morning.

The Decision Makers

Ron, a white male, grew up in an affluent neighborhood in the western Chicago suburbs. He attended private schools including the finest prep school in the area. After prep school, he was accepted at an Ivy League college. He was a member of a top fraternity on campus and was jokingly referred to as "the big man on campus." He graduated near the top of his business school class. After college, he married a woman from a prominent East Coast family who was a member of a campus sorority. They have one infant child. This is his first job since graduating from college and he is viewed by the company as someone on the fast track. His job as production supervisor can be viewed as a temporary assignment on his way to the top.

Bill, an African-American male, grew up in a tough Chicago neighborhood and enjoyed playing sports. Bill's parents were divorced when he was young and he had to work his way through school. He attended night classes at the local junior college, while working a day job. He did well and earned a scholarship to the state university in the area. The scholarship helped, but he still needed to work part-time while attending classes. He worked hard and finished near the top of his class. He has been with the company for five years and is

also considered a candidate for advancement based on his work ethic and drive. He and his wife have been married for five years and have two children. Bill is viewed by the company as a solid performer and someone who can get things done in production.

The New Employees

Fred, a white male, graduated from an Ivy League college and was a fraternity member. He is single, but does have a girlfriend from college who was a member of a sorority. He is a business school graduate with a degree in management. This would be his first job as his parents paid his way through college and he spent his summers traveling and attending private camps.

Lauren, an African-American female, grew up in the inner city and came from a broken home. In high school, she was motivated to achieve success to get out of her neighborhood and have a better life. Her older brother was murdered in a drive-by gang shooting and many of her classmates were involved in gangs. Drugs and alcohol were common in her neighborhood and school. She was able to get a scholarship at a state university and took full advantage of it. She graduated at the top of her class in systems management and was determined to have a better life for herself.

Sarah, a white female, is from the western Chicago suburbs. She grew up in the same vicinity as Ron and attended the same prep school he had. She went to a prestigious private university in the Midwest. She was considered to be personable and was popular on her campus. Although her grades were mediocre due to pursuing social activities on campus, she made a good impression on people and graduated with a degree in communications. This was going to be her first real job as she did not work during high school or college.

Chuck, a white male, grew up on a farm. He spent his entire life on the family farm. He worked hard to do farm work and attend high school. He was a star athlete in high school, earning varsity letters in football, basketball, and baseball. He was very popular and had been elected class president, captain of the football team, and homecoming king. He received a full scholarship to the state university to play football. Although he was good, he was not recruited to play professional football after college. He graduated with a solid B average in technology. Deciding he wanted to try something new, he applied for the production supervisor position and accepted the offer to join the Allen Company.

The Meeting

Bill and Ron met to go over the ground rules for the interviews and final selections. They agreed that each candidate would receive a conference call from Bill and Ron on Thursday and that they would make their final decisions that afternoon and pass the results on to human resources.

The Interviews

Fred was the first person called. During the course of the interview, Ron discovered that he and Fred had belonged to the same fraternity as well as having the same major. Ron seemed to dominate the interview. The second interview was with Lauren. During the interview, Bill realized they were from the same neighborhood. Bill took the lead in this interview. Sarah was the next person interviewed. Sarah spent most of her time talking about sorority life and growing up in the suburbs. Chuck was the last person interviewed. He talked to Bill and Ron about working hard on the farm and playing sports.

The Outcome

Bill and Ron met after a short break to finalize their decisions. Bill had two clear favorites he wanted for his department and Ron had two people he wanted. Ron spoke up and said that he really liked Fred and Sarah. Bill did not put up a fight and stated that he really wanted Chuck and Lauren to work with him.

Questions

1. Why did Ron pick Fred and Sarah?
2. Why did Bill pick Chuck and Lauren?
3. Were their decisions predictable and why?

1. Discuss the three factors that influence perception.

2. Explain the difference between the halo effect and the horn effect in perception.

3. Explain the self-serving bias as part of attribution theory.

4. What has influenced your perception of reality?

5. What is the problem of stereotyping?

CHAPTER 4

Values and Attitudes

LEARNING OUTCOMES: VALUES AND ATTITUDES

1. Recognize the need for studying values.

2. Describe the differences in values between generations and cultures.

3. Explain the differences between values and attitudes.

4. Explain cognitive dissonance.

5. Recognize the three components of attitudes.

6. Through self-assessment, gain a greater understanding of one's own values.

Name: _____

Section Number: _____

SELF-ASSESSMENT TEST

Please complete the following exercise online, accessible with the Access Card packaged with this text, before reading this chapter.

EXERCISE I.B.1:   WHAT DO I VALUE?

Record your top four terminal values:

1. _____
2. _____
3. _____
4. _____

Record your top four instrumental values:

1. _____
2. _____
3. _____
4. _____

Values are basic convictions of what is right, good, or desirable. Your values reflect what you think is important. There are, of course, no right or wrong values. This self-assessment merely gives you some directive insights into your value structure.

You should also record your score on this exercise in Appendix 1.

Notes

The Bad Company

After working for Boso Industries for more than ten years each, Helen and Marge get notice that their vacation time will be reduced, their salary frozen for the next three years, their benefits cut, and their sick days eliminated. Helen and Marge had already been unhappy with their jobs. Their workloads had increased as the company cut back on staff, and their boss was constantly pressuring them to work harder.

Helen reflected on the fact that the company had always provided them employment even in difficult economic times. She said she could live with a little dissatisfaction and accept the new round of cuts.

Marge, on the other hand, stated that the conditions in the organization were lousy. She said the job was already bad with increasing workloads and poor supervision. The current cuts were unacceptable.

Later that week, Jane, the supervisor, came to Helen for her reaction. Helen informed Jane of her intent to stay on the job and thanked Jane for keeping her. Marge found Jane and told her she did not find the new cuts acceptable and she resigned and left the company.

Why had these two workers responded differently in this situation? Welcome to Values and Attitudes! ■

A person's attitude can be a major factor in determining his or her success in life. In this chapter, we will define values and attitudes, and then you can take a survey to understand whether or not you have a "good" attitude.

Do you think abortion is right or wrong? What about capital punishment? Gay rights? Your basic notions of what is right and what is wrong are called **values.** Your values help you answer these questions about abortion, capital punishment, and gay rights, which are three controversial issues. Different people have different opinions about what is right and what is wrong on many issues.

Values are the basic notions about what is right and wrong.

WHAT DETERMINES YOUR VALUES?

Surprisingly, a significant part of your values is determined by genetics. Studies on identical twins offer proof of this.[14] Identical twins who are separated at birth end up having values similar to each other, even if they grew up in totally different environments. Because a large portion of your values is determined by genetic factors, values tend to be fairly stable over time. Your basic notion of what is right and what is wrong probably will not change much over your lifetime.

There is an old adage that states you are what you are because of where you were when, and that applies here. There are other factors that also impact one's value system. Environmental factors like parents, friends, and teachers help shape one's ideas of right and wrong. Religious beliefs can be an important factor for many. Activities and associations early in life such as 4-H Club, Boy Scouts and Girl Scouts, Big Brothers and Big Sisters, and a whole host of other organizations may impact values later in life. Whatever the source, everyone ends up with a certain moral code of what is right and what is wrong, and these values strongly influence behavior.

In the 2008 presidential election, the values of the different political candidates became an issue. Some people believed the Reverend Jeremiah Wright had an impact in helping to form presidential candidate Barack Obama's values. Billy Graham, the well-known minister, has one set of values. Larry Flynt, the publisher of *Hustler* magazine, has a different set of values. Billy Graham and Larry Flynt will react differently to a situation because of their different values. **If you want to understand a person's behavior, you must understand his or her values.** One way to understand this is to look at terminal and instrumental values. **Terminal** values are the end states that you hope to achieve. **Instrumental** values are the means of achieving these terminal values. For example, I have a terminal value to have a comfortable life. My strong work ethic is the instrumental value that will help me achieve a comfortable life.

> **Based on the self-assessment test at the beginning of the chapter, does your list of terminal and instrumental values capture what you really think is important? Do you reflect these values to other people?**

VALUE DIFFERENCES BETWEEN GENERATIONS

Certain generations tend to have some common values that came from growing up in the same environment.[15] People who grew up during the Great Depression, known as the Builders, developed strong values built around family and religion, believed in hard work, bringing excellent strengths to a team, and were loyal workers. People growing up following World War II, the Boomers, were influenced by family and education, the Vietnam War and the Cold War, challenged leadership, and had an attitude that anything can be accomplished. They were considered the "me" generation, who placed a heavy emphasis on the acquisition of wealth and focused on their own personal goals. Those who came of age in the late 1960s to the mid 1980s, the Busters and Generation X, are more likely to be influenced by the media, value diversity, began thinking globally, have a concern for the natural environment, and believe in strong relationships. People growing up today, the Bridgers or Generation Y, are influenced by friends, media, and sport stars; are confident, ambitious, and community-oriented. They know technology and have a greater entrepreneurial spirit.[16] A lack of understanding of these value differences between generations can cause problems with communication, use of technology, working relationships, teams, and acceptance of diversity. It's always interesting when the first question a new young employee asks a long-time manager is, "How much vacation do I get my first year?" This is not a bad question, but different generations tend to have different values so it may be interpreted the wrong way. The young employee values flexibility, while the long-time manager values loyalty to the employer.

Whenever interacting with a person of a different generation, you might want to keep some of these generalizations in mind. These are only generalizations, however, so *actual results may vary!*

VALUE DIFFERENCES BETWEEN REGIONS AND CULTURES

Television, movies, music, the Internet, and easier access to travel have been shrinking the geographical differences in values between people. There are still substantial differences in regional values. However, within the United States, people in the Midwest and South tend to have more conservative values than people on the East Coast or West Coast. Rural values tend to be more conservative than urban values.

Value differences are even greater between countries. Arab countries have different values than Western countries. Third World countries have different values than more developed nations. Much of the value differences between countries and cultures is based on socioeconomic conditions or religious beliefs. Keep these generalizations in mind when dealing with people from different geographical regions or cultures. The differences in values may or may not hold true. The cultural differences are probably more likely to be true than the geographical differences. If you plan to interact with people from a different culture for a prolonged period of time, take the time to learn about that other culture.

WHAT'S THE DIFFERENCE BETWEEN VALUES AND ATTITUDES?

In the movie *Titanic,* Rose (Kate Winslet) is engaged to marry Cal (Billy Zane). It seems to be a good arrangement, and Rose's mother is especially happy because it will maintain their social position. Rose and Cal are both members of high society, and they would seem to share many of the same values. Then Jack (Leonardo DiCaprio), a poor boy who had barely scraped up enough money for accommodations in a lower-class berth, comes along. Rose's initial attitude toward Jack is negative. Jack is clearly below her status in life. Rose was raised with values to associate only with people of high social status. Over time, however, Rose's feelings and **attitude** toward Jack change.

Attitudes are more complicated than values. People's attitudes come partly from the way they think as a result of their values (the **cognitive component** of an attitude), but attitudes also depend on how you feel about something (the **affective component** of an attitude) and what you are prepared to do about how you feel (the **behavioral component** of an attitude). If I ask you for your attitude about a certain television show, your answer will depend on whether you think the show is consistent with your values, how you feel about the show, and whether you like the show enough to make a special effort to watch it each week. Your attitude can change over time. Maybe one day you decide you are tired of watching that show. Attitudes about something can change quickly, while values tend to be fairly stable over time.

In the case of Rose, her attraction to Jack does not necessarily mean her values changed. Maybe her attitude toward Jack changed because the affective and behavioral components of her attitude overwhelmed the cognitive component. Attitudes can change much faster than values. Rose's attitude toward Jack went from negative to positive in a fairly short time.

It is also possible that Jack may have pushed Rose to think about her real values. Some values that may have been hidden, like respect for all people regardless of their status in life, may have become more important to Rose than the values of being "proper" or respecting her mother's wishes. A conflict between two values is called **cognitive dissonance.**

Attitudes have three components:

- Cognitive
- Affective
- Behavioral

Cognitive dissonance is a conflict between two values or between values and behavior.

Throughout the movie, Rose felt conflict between her values as her relationship with Jack developed. The conflict between two values put Rose in a state of cognitive dissonance, and she was forced to rethink her values to eliminate this conflict.

Cognitive dissonance can also occur when people are asked to choose between their values and a behavior. For example, in an episode of the television drama *ER*, a Catholic doctor is told to perform an abortion. This dilemma puts her in a state of cognitive dissonance. In most cases, the value wins out. You can't repeatedly get people to do something against their basic values. Eventually the cognitive dissonance becomes too great and the person does something to eliminate the conflict.

ATTITUDES IN AN ORGANIZATION

A person's attitude toward his or her job is an important consideration in an organization. As mentioned in Chapter 1, job satisfaction (along with productivity, absenteeism, and turnover) is one of the four key variables in the study of organizational behavior.

Job satisfaction is not simply job happiness. Job satisfaction is a person's attitude that includes, among other things, a feeling of fair play. Promotions, pay, opportunity, and the work environment are all factors that influence a person's job satisfaction.

What if a person is not satisfied with a job? He or she has four options, depending on if the person wants to do something active or passive, constructive or destructive. If a person wants to do something active and constructive, he or she can voice his or her concerns, hoping that the organization will respond and do something to improve the person's job satisfaction. If the organization is not responsive to the employee's frustration, this is the point the employee may turn to a union as a means to get his or her voice heard. A passive and constructive option is to simply stay loyal to the organization, accept being dissatisfied, but continue to do the job. According to the 2007 Walker Loyalty Report, employee loyalty has leveled off for the first time in a decade, with 34 percent of the workers being truly loyal—meaning they like the company they work for and plan to stay at least two years.[17] Experts say a happy and loyal employee is the best kind. A loyal employee is more likely to be a positive worker who shares his or her positive attitude with others. A passive and destructive option is to neglect the job and do the least possible because you are unhappy. Finally, an active but destructive option is to exit, or leave, the organization. That is not to say

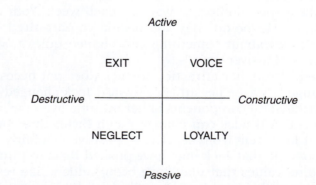

Figure 4–1 Responses to job dissatisfaction.

Source: Responses to Job Dissatisfaction. Reprinted with permission from *Journal of Applied Social Psychology*, 1985, Vol. 15, No. 1, pp. 88–103. © V. H. Winston & Son, Inc., 360 South Ocean Boulevard, Palm Beach, FL 33480. All rights reserved.

that leaving the organization is a bad thing to do; it is just destructive from the organization's point of view if the employee who leaves has performed well for the organization.

Other factors to consider are organizational commitment and job involvement. Organizational commitment is the extent to which people believe in the organization and see themselves as part of it.[18] The greater this belief, the harder a person is willing to work to help the organization achieve its goals. Job involvement is the extent to which people believe their jobs are important and see themselves as part of the work. The belief is that people will work harder if they think their jobs are important and worth doing.[19] These responses to job dissatisfaction are summarized in Figure 4–1.

Values are the basic notion of what is right and what is wrong, and values are fairly constant over time. Attitudes are an evaluation one makes about something. Attitudes have three components:

- A cognitive component, which is based on one's values
- An affective component, which is how one feels about something
- A behavioral component, which is how one acts about something

Cognitive dissonance is a conflict between two values or between values and behavior. To understand people's behavior, you need to understand their values and attitudes.

People who are truly successful in life (however you choose to define *successful*) seem to have one thing in common: a positive mental attitude. Whenever I was hiring a person, I would always look for someone with a "can-do" attitude. A positive attitude can overcome many shortcomings in ability or experience. Too often people become discouraged by the difficult situations that they confront in life.

Charles Swindoll, minister, author, and motivational speaker, has a good quote relating to life's difficulties and attitudes:[20]

> *The longer I live, the more I realize the impact of attitude on life. Attitude, to me, is more important than the facts. It is more important than the past, than education, than money, than circumstances, than failures, than successes, than what other people think or say or do. It is more important than appearance, giftedness, or skill. It will make or break a company . . . a church . . . a home.*
>
> *The remarkable thing is we have a choice every day regarding the attitude we will embrace for that day. We cannot change the inevitable. The only thing we can do is play on the one string we have, and that is our attitude. I am convinced that life is ten percent what happens to me and ninety percent how I react to it. And so it is with you . . . we are in charge of our Attitudes.*

Bad things may happen, but that doesn't mean that one should become negative. Maintaining a good attitude in times of difficulty will result in more success in whatever one chooses to do. How is your attitude? Try taking the following test.

ATTITUDE ADJUSTMENT SCALE

Please think of your current job or a job that you had in the past, and then rate your attitude about that job. Read these statements and choose a score of 1 to for 10 each. A "10" means your attitude could not be better in this area. A "1" means that your attitude could not be worse in this area. Be honest.

	SCORE
1. If I were to guess, I feel my boss would currently rate my attitude as a	_____
2. Given the same opportunity, my coworkers or peers would rate my attitude as a	_____
3. Realistically, I would rate my current attitude as a	_____
4. In dealing with others, I believe my effectiveness would rate a	_____
5. My current creativity level is a	_____
6. If there were a meter that could gauge my sense of humor, I believe it would read close to a	_____
7. My disposition, the patience and sensitivity I show to others, deserves a rating of	_____
8. When it comes to not allowing little things to bother me, I deserve a	_____
9. Based on the number of compliments I have received lately, I deserve a	_____
10. I would rate my enthusiasm toward my job and life during the past few weeks as a	_____
TOTAL SCORE	_____

Attitude Adjustment Scale adapted from Crisp: *Attitude, 3rd Edition* by Elwood N. Chapman. © 1995. Reprinted with permission of Aptius Education, www.aptius.com.

Score

A score of 90 or over is a signal that your attitude is "in tune" and no adjustments seem necessary; a score between 70 and 90 indicates that minor adjustments may help; a rating between 50 and 70 suggests a major adjustment is needed; if you rated yourself below 50, a complete overhaul may be required.

CASE STUDY

The Coworkers

Dejuan Brown grew up in a small town in west Texas. His father, Darius, worked in the oil fields and had enjoyed steady employment with the same company since he graduated from college. Darius was a strict parent, a reliable employee, a model citizen, a good husband, and a pillar of the local Baptist church. He believed in getting a good education, honoring the Lord, and always doing right by others. There was no liquor of any kind in his house and smoking was absolutely prohibited, even among guests of the home. Pastor Dewayne Allman from the Faith Baptist Church described Darius as one of the best men he had ever met and his family as models of the faith. Dejuan's mother, Lashea, was a stay at home wife and mother. She taught the children values and set the example for them. She was very soft spoken and even tempered. The children knew that if they were disobedient they would have to answer to Darius who was a lot stricter than Lashea and tended to use his belt to settle discipline problems.

Dejuan and his sister, Helen, were taught to not use drugs, alcohol, or tobacco. They also were taken to church every Sunday morning, Sunday night, and Wednesday night. The children grew up to be very respectful of others, especially people like teachers, neighbors, and fellow church members. When Dejuan graduated from the local Christian high school, he was near the top of his class. He had done very well and was offered a scholarship at a Christian college in Texas. After four years, Dejuan earned a degree in management and sought employment in Texas, but not in his home town. After interviewing with several firms, Dejuan decided to go to work at Redtech. Redtech was a fast-growing manufacturing company that made custom rubber and plastic products for various industrial manufacturers. Redtech sought to hire the best and the brightest people for long-term employment. Dejuan liked the idea of long-term employment because he had seen the job stability that his father had enjoyed with the oil company where he worked. Dejuan had impressed Redtech management with his down-home style and honest way of doing things.

Bill Williams grew up in a poor section of downtown Houston. His father was never married to his mother and left just after Bill was born. Bill's mother, Mary Lou, was never around much for Bill and his two sisters and two brothers. She was always working and trying to make money to pay the bills. When she was at home, she spent time with different men, drinking alcohol, or using drugs. Bill and his brothers and sisters saw a lot of men come and go from their home. None of them ever married Mary Lou and the men were not interested in the children. The children had to fend for themselves. Ray, Bill's older brother, became involved in a gang and started selling drugs. Bill was determined to stay away from gangs after Ray was killed in a gang-related shooting. Tim, his younger brother, got involved with a gang and ended up in juvenile detention for carjacking. Bill's two older sisters were able to finish high school and find jobs in the community. By this time, Bill wanted to get out of the neighborhood by any means possible. Bill began hustling pool, playing cards, and shooting dice for money. Many times the games were fixed and Bill was able to make money easily. He always claimed to be great at taking advantage of the suckers. Bill had developed a street mentality that stated the end always justifies the means. Bill was able to finish high school by way of some academic dishonesty that was never proven by the school administration, which tended to look the other way. Bill decided his lifestyle of hustling was only good for so long, and he decided to enroll in a public college in Houston that reserved a certain number of places for students from low-income families in the community.

Bill decided to hustle his way through college by paying off other students to write his papers and sometimes take his tests, especially those given online. Bill had developed some bad habits over the years and was a heavy drinker and smoker as well as recreational drug user. After five years of taking classes and using opportunity money given to him by the school and money he got from hustling, he got his degree in general studies. Knowing that he had to get clean from drugs to pass the drug tests for potential employers, Bill stopped using drugs but he became more dependent on alcohol. Redtech, seeking to hire local employees, hired Bill after he successfully passed his drug test.

The Job

After serving their mandatory 120 day probationary period with Redtech, Dejuan and Bill were assigned to the same department as supervisors on different shifts. Redtech stressed teamwork and the concept of one big happy family. Dejuan was determined to play by his set of rules. Everybody on Dejuan's shift was expected to be at work on time and work a full shift. Dejuan's knew the rules and he enforced them. He was fair but firm in his treatment of the employees. He quickly developed a reputation of being honest and hard working if not hard nosed. Bill was more of a free spirit. He usually came in a little late and did not mind if his employees did the same. He was always "cutting a little slack" for people on the job by not strictly enforcing the rules or quality standards. His employees were known to use alcohol at work. Bill claimed that it helped settle their nerves and that it was okay for them to drink just as long as they did not get drunk. Bill was known to have a bottle of whisky in his desk for medicinal purposes.

The Situation

The people who worked on Dejuan's shift began to complain about how strict he was and how they had to go back and re-do parts made on Bill's shift. They wanted to know why the people Bill supervised could come in late and get special privileges. The work done on Dejuan's shift always met or exceeded specifications.

Bill's employees began working partial shifts, drinking more on the job, and goofing off. Bill's shift was falling further and further behind in both quantity of work and quality of work as the workers became less serious about their jobs.

Questions

1. What caused Dejuan and Bill to behave in different ways even though they work at the same job for the same company?
2. What part do values and attitudes have in determining work behavior?
3. How can this situation be fixed by the management of Redtech?

1. Explain the differences between values and attitudes.

2. Provide an example of the differences in values between generations and share how this knowledge would benefit you.

3. Explain how understanding a person's values can provide a level of understanding in that person's behavior.

4. In understanding attitudes, what are the components and which is the hardest to change and why?

5. Can you change your attitude?

6. How difficult is it to change one's values? Explain your answer.

> **Ability** *is what you're capable of doing.*
>
> **Motivation** *determines when you do it.*
>
> **Attitude** *determines how well you do it.*
>
> —*Lou Holtz*[21]

> *The greatest discovery of my generation is that one can change his or her life by changing his or her attitude.*
>
> —*William James*[22]

Motivation

LEARNING OUTCOMES: MOTIVATION

1. Describe the five levels of Maslow's needs hierarchy.

2. Outline the three areas of Alderfer's ERG model.

3. Differentiate between Hertzberg's hygiene factors and motivators.

4. Contrast McGregor's Theory X and Theory Y.

5. Describe the impact of three points of the McClelland needs theory.

6. Explain the goal-setting theory for motivation.

7. Illustrate the equity theory for motivation.

8. Illustrate the reinforcement theory in practice.

9. Explain the relationship between the three contingencies of Vroom's expectancy theory.

10. Through self-assessment, gain a greater understanding of one's own motivational needs.

Name: _____

Section Number: _____

SELF-ASSESSMENT TESTS

Please complete the following exercises online, accessible with the Access Card packaged with this text, before reading this chapter.

EXERCISE I.C.1: WHAT MOTIVATES ME?

Growth Needs Score   _____
Relatedness Needs Score   _____
Existence Needs Score   _____

This instrument taps into the three needs of growth, relatedness, and existence. It is based on the ERG Theory. If you consider all four items within a need category to be extremely important, you would obtain the maximum total of 20 points. College students typically rate growth needs highest. However, you may currently have little income and consider existence needs to be most important. Note that a low score may imply that a need is unimportant to you or that it is substantially satisfied. The implication is that everyone has these needs, so a low score is usually taken to mean that this need is substantially satisfied.

EXERCISE I.C.4: WHAT'S MY VIEW ON THE
                NATURE OF PEOPLE?   Score _____

This instrument was designed to tap into your view of human nature. It is based on Douglas McGregor's Theory X and Theory Y. McGregor proposed that individuals tend to view others in either negative or positive terms. The negative stereotype, which he called *Theory X*, sees human beings as primarily lazy and disinterested in working. In contrast, *Theory Y* views them as responsible and hard working under the right conditions. Your score can give you insights into your inherent view of people. However, you are not locked into a particular management or leadership style based on your view of human nature. Your views reflect a tendency, not a mandate.

You should also record your scores on these exercises in Appendix 1.

NOTES

The Burger Den

The Burger Den is a local fast-food restaurant that caters to high school students. Several high school students worked there after school and on the weekends. It was a fun place to work, and Rodney and Mary Jo, the owners, were graduates of the local high school. Three of their best employees were Cindy, Susan, and Chuck. All these employees were high school seniors. All were well respected on the job, at the high school, and in the community.

All of them worked in the kitchen area in food preparation. Chuck had the drive and the desire to be a manager. His goal was to be in charge of the weekend crew. Cindy was a popular girl who wanted to interact with customers. Susan wanted to be recognized by Rodney and Mary Jo for her work with the Burger Den.

After giving it much thought, Rodney and Mary Jo decided to make Chuck the weekend manager, to make Cindy the cashier, and to make Susan the employee of the month with a plaque with her name on it to be displayed in the restaurant. All three employees were very happy with the outcome. Later, Rodney noted that both productivity and morale increased.

Why did Rodney and Mary Jo make the decisions they did? Welcome to Motivation! ■

What gets you going? What makes you work hard toward a goal? In the Iron Man Triathlon competition, the participants swim 2.4 miles, cycle 112 miles, and then run 26 miles. What motivates these determined people? In this chapter we will look at some of the models of motivation and what drives people to do what they do.

In the movie *Rudy*, starring Sean Astin, we find a young man, Rudy, who has been told all his life that he is not good enough, not smart enough, and not big enough to play football. However, Rudy has a passion to play football for Notre Dame University. He is motivated to live his dream and he goes out for the team as a walk-on player. He serves as little more than a human tackling dummy against the starting players. In one sequence of events we find Rudy really emotionally down when he meets the groundskeeper in the concourse of the stadium. The groundskeeper reminds Rudy that his drive to excel has to come from within himself, and he can't give up now. Bloodied but unbeaten, Rudy goes on and earns the respect of his coach and the other Notre Dame football players, who finally give him one shot at his dream. *Rudy* is based on a true story and is an unforgettable testament to the power of dreams and one's own motivation to triumph.

What is motivation? From early research by Abraham Maslow to the more recent research on Victor Vroom's Expectancy Theory, we discover people have needs and wants. **Motivation** is the willingness of a person to exert effort to satisfy needs and wants. Many triathletes are motivated to finish an Iron Man competition. It's a badge of honor. They are willing to invest many hours in training to accomplish this goal. Other people want or need a lot of money, and they are willing to work very hard to achieve this. The goals may be different, but motivation starts with a desire to satisfy needs and wants.

Motivation is the willingness of a person to exert effort to satisfy needs and wants.

The ideas and thoughts of motivation have certainly taken on new meanings in recent years. Research continues to try to determine what works and what does not work when it comes to motivating people. We see some individuals performing at a much higher level than ever thought possible. Yet other individuals have all the intellectual and physical capabilities, but they just don't seem to be able to make "it" come together. Why? Where does motivation come from? Can anyone really be motivated? If so, how is it done? These questions and many more will be explored in this chapter.

> What are your **needs** and **wants?** Money? A family? A car? A desire to help other people? These needs and wants are the basis for what will motivate you in life. Please answer the other questions in the Chapter 5 section of Appendix 1 before moving on.

This chapter discusses nine theories that provide different ways to look at motivation. These nine theories make up the majority of the motivational theories needed when working with others and in trying to understand what alternatives can be used to motivate others. Since there are so many theories of motivation, it is easy to get them confused. Just remember that these are all different ways of describing how people are motivated, and different theories apply better to different situations.

MASLOW'S HIERARCHY OF HUMAN NEEDS

Abraham Maslow was a clinical psychologist and a pioneer in the development of **needs theories.** Little existed in the way of empirical, scientific studies of motivation until Maslow's research. He based his theory on twenty-five years of experience in treating individuals with varying degrees of psychological health.[23]

Based on his experience, Maslow contended that every person has needs that follow a certain order, or hierarchy, of priority. Maslow's theory points to five different levels of needs, illustrated by Figure 5–1.

Lower-Order Needs

1. **Physical needs,** such as food, air, water, clothing, and sex. These are the most basic needs of a person.
2. **Safety and security needs,** whereby a person seeks protection or some kind of assurance that one isn't going to lose everything he or she worked so hard and so long to achieve.

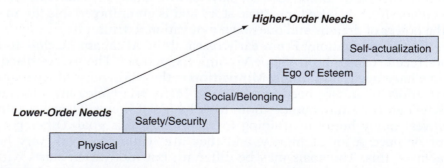

Figure 5–1 Maslow's hierarchy of needs.

Higher-Order Needs

1. **Social or belonging needs,** which state that everyone wants respect and trust of others. We need friends and friendship, acceptance, a sense of belonging to a social system, and the feeling of being liked and loved.

2. **Ego or self-esteem needs,** which include the needs of individuals to strive for independence, power, status, prestige, recognition, position, pride in self and work, self-esteem, meaningful work, and authority.

3. **Self-actualization,** which is the level where people are pleased with themselves and their accomplishments. The Army used a slogan in recruiting new soldiers that captures this idea, "Be all that you can be in the U.S. Army."

These five levels of needs are divided into lower- and higher-order needs. The first two, physical and safety needs, are classified as **lower-order needs** because they are satisfied externally (i.e., they are *extrinsic* needs). The last three, the social, self-esteem, and self-actualization, are termed **higher-order needs** because these needs are met from internal satisfaction (i.e., they are *intrinsic* needs). Maslow's theory notes the lower-order needs must be satisfied before addressing the higher-order needs.

Lower-order needs are satisfied externally.

Higher-order needs are satisfied internally.

The 2000 movie *Castaway* staring Tom Hanks as Chuck Noland, a FedEx systems engineer, illustrates this theory very well. Chuck was at the ego and esteem level of the hierachy, with a lot of status, recognition, and power in his job. His life is abruptly changed when a harrowing plane crash leaves him isolated on a remote South Pacific island. Noland immediately reverts to level one in the hierarchy where he is totally consumed with staying alive. He figures out how to collect drinking water, gather fish, and perform other tasks to meet his physical needs. Soon he moves to level two of the hierarchy when he discovers a cave that provides some shelter and protection from the elements and he then figures out how to make fire, which adds to his comfort. He then gets to level three, social needs, when he invents "Wilson" from a volleyball. Wilson becomes a "friend," with whom he shares his thoughts and feelings. This third level need was so strong that as he was escaping the island, he strapped Wilson to the raft so they could escape together. Later as Wilson became dislodged from the raft, Noland began swimming to recover Wilson because of the strong social need, almost drowning in the attempt.

Maslow's needs theory is widely recognized and appears to be logical. However, research indicates that needs are not met in a linear fashion. When it comes to motivation, we find that people are a little more complex than this theory takes into consideration. People do not move neatly up the Maslow hierarchy. So where do we go from here? To answer this question we need to look at several other theories.

ALDERFER'S ERG MODEL

Clayton Alderfer's research takes Maslow's five-step approach and develops a three-part model labeled Existence, Relatedness, and Growth (ERG) to explain motivation.[24] Unlike Maslow, Alderfer said that more than one need might be operative at the same time. The ERG model (see Figure 5–2) also suggests that if the gratification of a higher-level need is stifled, the desire to satisfy a lower-level need increases. The ERG model is supported by contemporary research studies and is reflective of the individual having needs working in all three areas at the same time.

The **existence needs** in Alderfer's model encompass the physical and safety/security needs discussed in Maslow's theory. The **relatedness needs** include the social needs, social esteem needs, and interpersonal

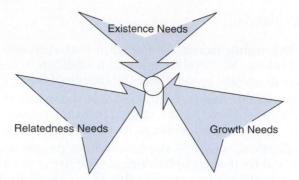

Figure 5–2 The ERG Model: The circle represents the individual. These needs are acting on the individual. Multiple needs may be operative at the same time.

safety needs. The **growth needs** encompass both the internal self-esteem needs and the self-actualization needs discussed in Maslow's needs theory.

Based on the self-assessment test at the beginning of this chapter, which of these needs had the highest score and is most important to you? Which of these needs had the lowest score? Is that because this need is unimportant to you, or have you substantially satisfied this need?

More than one of these needs can be operative at the same time. Let's look at an example. We constantly read about disasters such as floods, tornadoes, hurricanes, and earthquakes where homes and property have been destroyed. We could all certainly agree that the families and individuals affected by these natural disasters have existence needs. At the same time they still have a need to feel that they are appreciated and connected to others. Satisfying the relatedness needs may help in the emotional and psychological recovery from these disasters. This may be through family, church, community, or even the Red Cross or Salvation Army. Either way, the existence needs and relatedness needs are certainly present, and both needs are influencing individual behaviors at the same time.

HERZBERG'S MOTIVATION–HYGIENE THEORY

One of the more widely known and influential views of motivation is that of Herzberg. Herzberg was among the first industrial psychologists to consider and write explicitly about the notion of human growth needs. He interviewed 200 engineers and accountants from different companies and asked them to describe incidents at work that made them feel "exceptionally good" or "exceptionally bad" about their jobs. From these interviews, Herzberg concluded that satisfaction (feeling good) and dissatisfaction (feeling bad) are independent concepts, not opposites on a single continuum as traditional views had held.[25]

Herzberg's theory argues that jobs must feature a number of characteristics to permit them to arouse and then satisfy growth needs. His **motivation–hygiene theory** suggests several work-related factors will lead to dissatisfaction rather than satisfaction. In his theory, he contends that satisfaction is on two different scales.[26] First, on the motivation scale, there is **satisfaction** or **no satisfaction;** on the hygiene scale is **dissatisfaction** or **no dissatisfaction.**

Herzberg reasoned that these motivator factors had the potential to motivate workers to higher levels of performance because they provided opportunities for personal satisfaction. The absence of these motivator factors would leave them feeling somewhat neutral toward their jobs.

Motivation–hygiene theory contends there are two different sets of job factors. One set satisfies (**motivators**); one set prevents dissatisfaction (**hygiene** factors).

Although they could not induce workers to higher levels of performance, hygiene factors could create great dissatisfaction if they were not met. Hygiene factors could make a worker dissatisfied, but they could not create more than a neutral feeling toward the job even if they were ideally met. For example, workers expect to have good working conditions in which to perform their work. If the working conditions are considered bad, then according to Herzberg, workers will become dissatisfied. If the working conditions are good and meet the workers' expectations, then there is no dissatisfaction. As this example illustrates, an organization must maintain good hygiene factors to remain healthy.

Let's look at another example. Suppose you receive a very good salary increase today. How do you feel? Well, according to Herzberg, you are not dissatisfied. However, if one year or even two years go by without another increase, what happens? You will start to become dissatisfied. Thus, an organization must maintain this hygiene factor (pay) to prevent dissatisfaction and thus remain in good health.

In a similar manner, let's look at the motivators. Motivators satisfy intrinsic needs and, over time, maintain a level of importance. As an example, the letter of recognition or the award you received a year or so ago still provides a sense of accomplishment and pride as it did when you received it. In many cases, the recipient puts his or her certificate or trophy in a prominent place for others to view. Five, ten, or even twenty years later, it still provides a sense of accomplishment and recognition. It continues to motivate. In this example, we see recognition is a motivator. In fact, recognition is perceived to be one of the strongest motivators.

Herzberg's argument is unique because it suggests that the factors that motivate employees are quite different from those that lead to dissatisfaction. Figure 5–3 shows the relationships of satisfiers and dissatisfiers

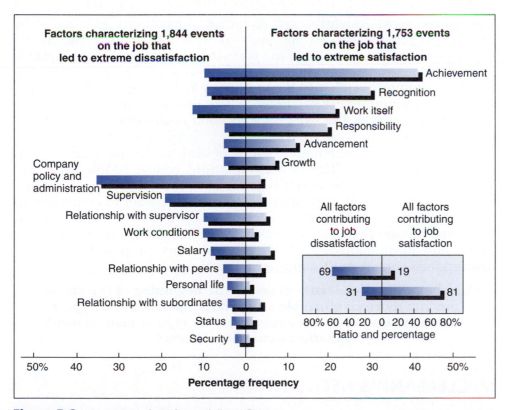

Figure 5–3 Comparison of satisfiers and dissatisfiers.

Table 5–1 The Presence or Absence of Certain Factors

What If	Are present on the job . . .	Are not present on the job . . .
Satisfiers-Motivators	Then there will be job satisfaction.	Then there will be NO job satisfaction.
Dissatisfiers-Hygiene Factors	Then there will be NO job dissatisfaction.	Then there will be job dissatisfaction.

present on the job. When satisfiers are present in the workplace, there will be job satisfaction. In other words, when satisfiers are present, the worker will be motivated to perform at a higher level of performance. When hygiene factors are met (present) on the job, there will be no job dissatisfaction. However, when hygiene factors are not met on the job, there will be job dissatisfaction and the degree of dissatisfaction is based on how well the hygiene factors are met (Table 5–1).

In comparison to Maslow, we can see that some factors are met internally while others are external to the individual. The satisfiers are on the higher-order needs or satisfied internally. The hygiene factors are external or lower-order need factors. Even though the research data that support this theory are mixed, the motivation–hygiene theory has had a substantial influence on the thinking of managers and researchers. It is probably safe to say that the theory is one of the most widely known theories of motivation in managerial circles.

McGREGOR'S THEORY X AND THEORY Y

One of the most insightful and enduring observations ever made by behavioral science concerning work is that of Douglas McGregor. McGregor was acutely aware of the pervasiveness of a set of assumptions held by managers concerning human beings at work. He referred to this set of assumptions as **Theory X** and **Theory Y**.[27] Managers who hold the Theory X assumptions are pessimistic about workers' capabilities.[28] They believe that people dislike work, seek to avoid responsibility, are not ambitious, and must be supervised closely.

Theory Y is an alternative, more optimistic set of assumptions. Managers that hold to Theory Y assumptions believe people do accept responsibility, can exercise self-control, have the capacity to innovate, consider work to be as natural as rest or play, and want to contribute to the organizational goals if given the opportunity. McGregor argues that these assumptions accurately describe human nature in far more situations than most managers believe. He therefore proposed that these assumptions should guide managerial practice.

Based on the self-assessment test at the beginning of the chapter, are you more comfortable as a Type X manager or a Type Y manager? Based on this tendency, what type of management situation would fit you best?

McCLELLAND'S NEEDS THEORY

David McClelland was a researcher interested in determining why some people succeed as managers and others do not. His research suggests there are three different needs that motivate people toward their success in work and their relationships. These are a need for achievement, a need for power, and a need for affiliation.[29]

The Need for Achievement

Some people are high in their need for **achievement.** This is a drive to excel, to achieve in relation to a goal or standard, and to succeed. In the movie *Pretty Woman*, starring Richard Gere and Julia Roberts, Gere's character is a workaholic and he is obsessed with his work and the need to achieve. He is constantly working when he is away from the office, and he is often preoccupied by the thought of getting back there. Those high in achievement tend to set moderately difficult goals that offer a challenge to themselves. High achievers also want specific feedback on their performance. They need to know how well they are doing toward the completion of the task and want constant feedback. Those high in their need for achievement tend to think about their work while away from their job and they may find it difficult to separate themselves from their work until a specific task is completed. Because of this, high-need achievers tend to assume personal responsibility for getting things done. My uncle has a high need for achievement. When I was visiting him in his home, I could not help noticing the walls of his den were filled with plaques and certificates of accomplishment. I asked him which of these was the most important to him. His response: "The next one."

> The need for **achievement** is the drive to accomplish challenging goals.

The Need for Power

The need for **power** reflects an individual's desire to influence others' behavior toward the accomplishment of goals and objectives. People with a high need for power like to work and are concerned with control, discipline, and self-respect. There are positive and negative sides to this need. The negative aspect occurs when the relationship is characterized by competition where one wins and one must lose. In a work setting, the strong need for power may prove detrimental to the organizational goals. The leader with a positive orientation to power would focus on accomplishing the group goals and helping employees obtain the feeling of empowerment.

> The need for **power** is the desire to control others, to influence others' behavior according to your wishes.

The Need for Affiliation

The need for **affiliation** can take us back to the third step in Maslow's theory, which indicates that we have a need to belong, a need to be part of a social group. Recent research also confirms that we desire and need this affiliation; however, the need is at different levels. Those with a high need for affiliation prefer to spend more time maintaining social relationships and joining groups. They want to feel they belong. Individuals with high affiliation needs may not be the most effective managers or leaders because they have a hard time making difficult decisions without worrying about the impact their actions may have on their social relationships. Some say that individuals high in their need for affiliation have a tendency to think with their heart and not with their mind.[30]

> The need for **affiliation** is the desire for close relationships with others.

Interestingly, the research in McClelland's needs theory has shown that the need for affiliation and power tends to be closely related to a manager's ability to accomplish a task in the most friendly, yet timely, manner. However, the individual who has a high need for power and a low need for affiliation may make the most powerful and best manager.[31] In fact, it is argued that a high power motive may be a requirement for managerial effectiveness.[32] It has been suggested that a high power need may occur simply as a function of one's position in a hierarchical organization. This suggestion proposed that the higher the level an individual rises in the organization, the greater is the individual's position power and power motive. As a result, powerful positions would be the stimulus to a high power motive.

GOAL-SETTING THEORY

The premise underlying **goal-setting theory** is that behavior is regulated by values, intentions, and goals. A **goal** is what a person tries to attain, accomplish, or achieve. Goal setting is recognized widely by managers as a means to improve and sustain the employees' performance. Based on research of the goal-setting theory, several interesting and critical findings have emerged:[33]

- An individual provided with specific hard goals performs better than a person given easy, nonspecific goals. To just say "do your best" does not work any better than setting no goals. Goal specificity seems to act as an internal stimulus.

- Goals must be understood and accepted by the individual for the goals to become motivating factors. Providing a means for employee involvement in the goal-setting process provides ownership of the goals. When employees have ownership of their goals, they will try harder to achieve them. Although participative goals may have no superiority over assigned goals when accepted by the employee, participation does increase the probability that employees will agree to and act on more difficult goals.

- Feedback is critical. People tend to do better when they get feedback on how well they are progressing toward their goals. This feedback acts to guide behavior.

The goal-setting theory builds on the individual's need for a sense of achievement and growth.

EQUITY THEORY OF MOTIVATION

The **equity theory** provides a simple framework for understanding how people decide whether or not they are being treated fairly in their relationships. Given the importance of role relationships within organizations, it is essential to have a framework whereby these relationships can be evaluated.

Let's look at an example. Jane Reynolds works for a large bank and has the title of Account Manager. She has been with the bank for seven years. She recently found out that her salary is $6,000 per year less than another woman, Mary Seneck. Mary also has the title of Account Manager and has only been with the bank for four years. Jane believes they perform nearly identical duties and are both above average performers for the bank. How do you think Jane feels? She is probably upset, but why? Jane believes they both do the same amount of work; she believes she is an above-average performer; she knows she has been with the bank longer, yet she makes $6,000 per year less than Mary does. What do you think her reaction might be in response to this perceived disparity?

What Jane has done is evaluate the inputs (performance, tenure, above-average work) and outcomes (wages), and she has determined there is an imbalance in pay. This example demonstrates the equity theory of motivation. It occurs all the time. The equity theory proposes that people are motivated to maintain fair and equitable relationships between themselves and others. Jane evaluated various inputs such as seniority (of which she has more), job titles, the belief that she and Mary do nearly identical tasks, and the feeling that they are both above-average performers. She then compares this with the output—the difference in salary—to determine there is an equity issue. It is the perception of equity that counts. Mary, for example, may feel that she contributes far more than Jane and views the salary difference as fair. Figure 5–4 illustrates the need for balance between the inputs and the outputs to achieve equity.

Some managers are accused of showing *favoritism*. This is another example of the equity theory. People will consider many factors to evaluate equity, but the primary variables appear to be gender, length of service, position held in the organization, and the amount of education. In this comparison, if it is determined by the outputs to be unfair and not equitable, the motivation for one to contribute either positively or negatively is affected.[34]

Equity comparisons lead people to behave in a way that restores equity. Research has shown that some of these actions include:

- Changing the inputs to try to find equity.
- Changing the outcomes.
- Changing the person of comparison.
- Looking at another measurement.
- Changing one's self-perception toward the situation.
- Asking to move to a different job to establish a different reference point.
- Simply choosing to leave.

In our example, Jane might choose to change the inputs by reducing her performance. She has restored equity by adjusting her effort to a level that she feels is consistent with the output (i.e., pay level) she receives when compared to Mary. Alternatively, Jane might choose to change the measurement she considers in her comparison. Perhaps Mary has more education or experience in other organizations. When Jane takes this into consideration she may feel that the additional education is worth the $6,000 pay differential. She has thus restored equity in her mind.

Professional athletes face similar dilemmas. Should a rookie's compensation be as high as the experienced players on the team? Can this problem be addressed by having pay scales based on tenure and past performance? Also consider the dilemma of senior corporate management when they must recruit a replacement for a middle or senior manager. It is not uncommon that a company finds it needs to "up the ante" significantly to induce a person to join the company. This is at the expense of pay equity, and although companies try, pay secrecy or confidentiality just does not exist. Recently in some fields, it is really a job seeker's market. As a result, you may be offered a higher starting salary than the salary of a person who has been with the organization for several years. Is it fair? It really depends from whose viewpoint you are looking, doesn't it?

In any case, the bottom line on equity theory is this: People are highly motivated to seek equity and to adjust for any inequities they may believe exist in their work.

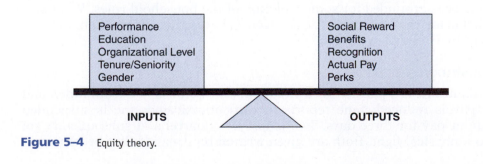

Figure 5–4   Equity theory.

REINFORCEMENT THEORY

Some authors argue that the reinforcement theory is not a motivation theory but, more correctly, a methodology to alter behavior. Others point out that if an individual is aware that a particular performance may elicit a reward or perhaps alter an unpopular situation, then the individual will be motivated to adjust his or her behavior. In fact, the individual may intensify his or her effort. For this reason, we view the application of reinforcement as an effective theory of motivation.

Reinforcement may come in various packages, depending on how we want to shape a response. The packages are conventionally seen as positive reinforcement, negative reinforcement, punishment, and extinction.[35]

Positive Reinforcement

Positive reinforcement means providing a positive response when a person demonstrates the desired behavior.

We generally strive to influence others in a favorable or positive way. Consider the following illustrations. It is common in many retail businesses to select an employee of the month. The thought is that by having such a program, employees will be motivated to seek recognition. In some cases the reward may be "sweetened" with money, a personal parking space, or valued merchandise awards. Conventional wisdom says everyone has a chance to win. However, in reality, winning may be within reach of only a few. Consider what it says about the employees who are not chosen. Are they losers? Special care must be taken to include everyone if the program truly is to be an effective motivator for the entire organization.

A local grocery chain has a system of recognition that seems to work well. A hotline has been established for customers to register their likes and dislikes. When a customer comments favorably about an employee, that employee is recognized by the senior leadership with a letter and a metal gold star. It is not insignificant that the head of the meat department wears a plastic placard on his uniform prominently displaying his multiple gold stars. The program works.

Everyone likes personal service at a restaurant. Here is a way for you, the reader, to test the reinforcement theory. The next time you eat at a restaurant, estimate your tip for the server BEFORE you place your order. Tell the waiter that you believe the service will be outstanding and simultaneously personally present the tip. This backward act is reinforcement. Can you visualize your potential service for that meal? While this simple experiment may not elicit five star service every time, when it works, it really works.

Negative Reinforcement

Negative reinforcement means rewarding by taking away uncomfortable consequences.

Negative reinforcement is rewarding people by taking away uncomfortable consequences or something unpleasant. The negative situation is removed; thus negative reinforcement is a reward, not a punishment. Consider the baseball coach whose practice is to order the entire team to run laps for every error committed in a ball game. Will the players make an extra effort to be errorless if doing so eliminates laps? Perhaps a teenager is grounded for some violation of the household rules. What sort of behavior may we expect if the teen believes that proper conduct will result in extended privileges?

Punishment

Punishment is the application of an undesirable consequence for an undesired behavior.

Punishment is a penalty for a violation. Sam returns late from lunch and his pay is reduced. Jane reports to work intoxicated; she is suspended without pay for three days. Two employees quarrel and subsequently get into a physical fight. Both are given written reprimands that become part of their personnel files. Suspension, demotion, termination, and reprimand are all examples of punishment.

Extinction

Visualize a classroom where a particular student invariably seeks to be called on or alternatively speaks out with an opinion on every issue. At the outset, most instructors politely respond to the student until it becomes a disruption. At some point the instructor will ignore the student, thus removing any form of reinforcement for the disruptive action.

Extinction is the reduction in frequency of undesired behavior by removing the reward for such behavior.

THE EXPECTANCY THEORY

In 1964, the book *Work and Motivation* by Victor Vroom discussed the **expectancy theory** of work motivation. Vroom's theory seeks to predict or explain the task-related effort expended by a person. According to the expectancy theory (see Figure 5–5), motivation results from deliberate choices to engage in activities to achieve worthwhile outcomes.[36] The expectancy theory views motivation as the result of three different expectancies. The first is the belief that one's effort will affect performance, or the effort-to-performance expectancy. The second is the belief that one's performance will be rewarded, or the performance-to-reward expectancy. And third, the reward or outcome will satisfy an individual need, called the reward-to-need satisfaction expectancy. Let's look at this model in a little more detail.

Expectancy theory says that motivation results from deliberate choices to engage in activities to achieve worthwhile outcomes.

Step 1: Effort-to-Performance Expectancy

Effort-to-performance expectancy is a person's perception of the probability that effort will lead to successful performance, the performance needed to obtain the reward. If we believe our efforts will yield high enough performance to receive a desired reward, then this expectancy can be very high. If we believe our performance will be the same regardless of how much effort we put forth, then the expectancy would be low. As an example, the production line to build cars at an automobile plant is controlled by the speed of the line and not the operator. The operator's effort to increase the number of cars produced would prove fruitless, and his effort-to-performance expectancy would be low. However, if you are building a piece of equipment on your own, you have the necessary parts and support to meet a higher production schedule, and you control the flow of production, then you could have a high effort-to-performance expectancy. In organizations where management sets standards or goals so high that they are out of workers' reach, the expectancy is that increased effort will not lead to sufficient performance to reach the level desired and expectancy will be low.

Step 2: Performance-to-Reward Expectancy

Performance-to-reward expectancy is a person's perception of the probability that performance will lead to a certain reward or other desirable outcome. This part of the theory suggests that if one's performance meets

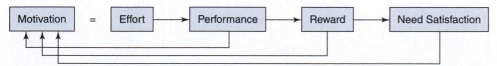

Figure 5–5 The expectancy theory.

a desirable organizational goal, then one should expect a reward for exceeding performance expectations.

Step 3: Reward-to-Need Satisfaction Expectancy

An outcome or reward is anything that might potentially result from performance. For the reward to act as a motivational factor, the reward has to meet a felt need. If the reward does not meet a need, then the reward may become a demotivator.

For example, suppose your boss tells you that if you continue to work hard and generate high results, you will be promoted into management. Suppose you don't really want to go into management. You know that management personnel have to work extra hours without extra pay, have meetings on weekends, and have to travel and be away from home for long periods of time. You are at a point in your life that you really don't find this sort of reward attractive. It just doesn't meet your needs. What might happen to your performance? It may actually drop. When trying to motivate others, one should make sure the reward meets employees' needs.

The expectancy model does seem to be applicable in the work environment; however the manager must know the desired reward of his or her employees. Several studies have supported various parts of the theory. Research has also confirmed expectancy theory claims that people will not engage in motivated behavior unless they:

- believe their efforts will lead to performance.
- believe their performance will lead to the desired rewards.
- value the expected rewards, which satisfy some need or strong desire.

So what can we take away from this discussion on motivation? How might one be able to use this in the workplace? For example, if you still think money is the number one motivator, according to Herzberg you're wrong. Money is important, but if someone doesn't like his or her job or the way he or she is treated, he or she won't be satisfied regardless of the amount of money paid. While money is important to employees, what tends to motivate them to perform at high levels is the thoughtful, personal recognition that signifies true appreciation for a job well done.[37] Here are some basic guidelines:

- Design rewards based on the individual's personal preferences. To understand what is important to each employee it is essential to get to know and talk to each employee.
- Reward for achievement. The goal setting theory is at work here. Rewards should be based on what is actually done. Rewards should be given as soon as possible after the desired behavior.
- Find people doing things right. Give praise when earned.

Source: Dilbert, June 25, 1997.© Scott Adams/Distributed by United Feature Syndicate, Inc. Reprinted by permission.

- Provide recognition when deserved. Recognition must be genuine and meaningful. Personally thank employees for doing a good job.

- Recognition and awards of appreciation address the intrinsic needs. A pat on the back, a sincere handshake, and public recognition in front of peers work.

- Involve your people in the decisions that affect them. People have a need to be involved, which helps them to feel engaged in the business.

- Listen to your people. Listening creates trust and respect in your people. Listening allows people to vent their frustrations and it communicates that you care.

- Give your people a chance to grow personally and professionally. Help them learn new skills. This creates a partnership and commitment to the organization and leadership.

- Be visible. Get to know your people by their first names. First-name recognition communicates a level of comfort and appreciation for employees and fosters an environment of trust.

- Celebrate successes. For example, in a company with 380 employees, after one million hours passed without lost time from an accident, there was a celebration with a dinner served by the president and managers. The employees then set a goal for three million hours without an accident, and after reaching that goal, they celebrated with jackets and another dinner.

- Build your organization around teams. Take time for team- and morale-building meetings and activities.

Motivation is the willingness of a person to exert effort to satisfy wants and needs. As noted in the needs theories of motivation, motivation is intrinsic and is a driving force.

- According to **Maslow's needs hierarchy,** human needs fall into five groups: physiological, safety, social and belonging, esteem and ego, and self-actualization. When a need at one level is essentially satisfied and is no longer a driving force, that need loses its strength and the next level need is activated.

- **Alderfer's ERG model** takes Maslow's five levels of needs and compresses them into three interactive needs. This more contemporary model shows multiple needs being active at the same time, and this model is supported by research. This theory demonstrates that the individual worker is complex and has multiple needs all interacting at the same time. That makes the manager's task much more challenging.

- **Herzberg's motivation–hygiene theory** divides job factors into satisfiers and dissatisfiers. The satisfiers are the motivators, and the dissatisfiers are the maintenance or hygiene factors. Problems arise in business and industry today when management attempts to motivate through the use of the hygiene factors. Management will try to motivate with policies, procedures, and pay increases; as noted by Herzberg's model, this only prevents dissatisfaction and only for a short period of time. It does not motivate.

- **McGregor's Theory X and Theory Y** approach motivation from the manager's perspective. The manager with the Theory X perspective believes people are inherently lazy and will try to avoid work, therefore requiring an assertive and directive form of management. The manager with the Theory Y perspective believes people enjoy work as much as play and will seek responsibility. Those with the Theory Y perspective will use a more participative and self-controlled style of management for motivation.

- **McClelland's needs theory** explains that certain needs people strive to satisfy are acquired from the culture. His research centers on three needs of particular significance in understanding managers and workers: the need of achievement, need for power, and need for affiliation. The need for power is the primary motivator of successful managers.

- The **goal-setting theory** is an important part of all major theories of motivation. Goals that are more specific and difficult but achievable will result in higher performance than easy goals. When workers participate in setting goals, the goals are accepted by the workers and, with some sort of feedback provision and rewards, they are more effective in motivating the worker.

- The **equity theory** explains how people are motivated by fairness. A person will make a determination of equity by evaluating all of the inputs and outputs of a situation. If the person perceives the situation to be unfair, he or she may use a variety of ways to find equity in the situation.

- According to the **reinforcement theory,** the consequences of an action (rewards and punishments) determine a person's motivation for engaging in certain behaviors. People learn to repeat behaviors that bring them pleasurable outcomes and learn to avoid behaviors that lead to uncomfortable outcomes.

- The **expectancy theory** is based on the idea that motivation results from deliberate choices to engage in certain activities to achieve worthwhile outcomes. The expectancy theory model is based on effort-to-performance expectancies, performance-to-reward expectancies, and reward-to-need satisfaction expectancies.

Find something you really love that gets you going, so that every day you want to make yourself better. Once you find that, it's easy to stay motivated.

—Kerri Strug, Olympic gold medalist in gymnastics[38]

John Mayweather was the owner and president of JMC, Inc., an electronics repair business. He had six employees who did the repair work on everything from copiers to computers. Four of the employees were new, younger workers and two were experienced veterans. John highly valued his two veterans, Rodney and Vern. Both previously had jobs with major companies that had closed their operations in the area. Both men wanted to stay in the area and work on electronics. When John advertised in the local newspaper, the two men applied for the job and John was so impressed he decided to hire them both. As the business grew, John added younger employees from the local technical college. These people had associate of science degrees in electronics but little business experience. Jim, Marty, Mary Jo, and Sandy were all good employees, but John thought they were looking around for something better. Many of their classmates had been hired by big electronics chain stores. These big stores paid more, had better benefits, and offered a company car to employees. The current employees liked working for John, who has a friendly demeanor and offers a family-type atmosphere in his company, but some wondered about their future with a small company. Rodney and Vern are paid $20 per hour and the rest of the repair people are paid $15 per hour. All have basic medical insurance with hospital, doctor, and prescription coverage; a matching 401(k) retirement plan; and a reimbursement plan for business-related mileage for using their own cars at 44 cents a mile.

One night after work the younger employees decided to go out for dinner at Frank's Bar and Grill. After being there for about fifteen minutes, they were joined by Steve and Tom, their classmates from the technical college. Marty asked Steve what he was doing. Steve informed them that he is working for MegaMart, a large chain retail electronics store, in repairs. Mary Jo asks how that is going and Steve tells them he is making $18 per hour with a full benefit program that includes all kinds of insurance like hospitals, doctors, dentists, prescriptions, and eye care as well as a paid retirement plan and company car for work. Steve also says that senior repair staff like Ted, a technician with five more years of experience than Steve, can make up to $25 per hour. Tom said he was working for his family and was making $12 per hour with just basic medical benefits including prescription, doctor, and hospital. Before the topic of life at JMC, Inc., came up the conversation moved to sports and the local social scene. The old friends enjoyed their evening together.

Steve and Marty had a friendly rivalry in high school and college in everything from prettiest girlfriend to fastest car. Jim and Tom were close friends in high school and at the technical college. Mary Jo and Sandy really were not involved with the guys and seemed to pal around with each other.

The next day at work, Marty seemed to be distracted. He was not quite his usual happy self. His condition worsened as he thought about how much better Steve was doing with his job. Jim was having a good day and he picked up the slack from Marty. Jim was convinced he had a good job and worried about his friend Tom who was not doing all that well in the family business. Mary Jo and Sandy looked at each other and thought that their jobs were good.

Finally, Rodney approached Marty and asked him what was wrong. Steve told Rodney and Vern that he had run into Steve and that Steve is making $3 dollars an hour more and had better benefits and a company car. He went on to say that senior people like Ted, who is a friend of Rodney's and Vern's, is making $25 per hour. Rodney's response was that $25 is serious money. Vern was less impressed with the MegaMart operation and said that big stores can be hard work environments. Rodney's response was that at that wage he could live with some pain. Steve, Rodney, and Vern all went back and refocused on finishing the day's work.

Marty decided to go to MegaMart and apply for a job. He was warmly greeted and offered a job at $18 per hour plus all the benefits. Marty accepted the job and gave his one week notice at JMC, Inc. After finding out from Vern that Marty was leaving, Rodney went over to MegaMart and met with the manager. He was offered $25 per hour plus the benefits and accepted their offer. He told John that he also was leaving in one week.

John felt compelled to have a meeting with the rest of the employees. He started the meeting by telling them that Rodney and Marty were leaving and that he hoped the rest of them would stay at JMC, Inc.

Vern spoke first and said, "I like working at JMC and I don't have a reason to leave."

Jim also stated, "I am good with staying here."

Sandy and Mary Jo looking at each other echoed, "We are staying with you, John."

John was relieved about the others staying, but could not figure out what had happened to Rodney and Marty. They were great employees and all of sudden they are gone. John decided to ask Rodney about what had happened. Rodney informed him that the younger employees had run into a friend of theirs who worked for MegaMart and found out how well he was doing there. Marty went over there and got a better job. Rodney went on to say that his friend, Ted, worked there and was making more money than he was.

Rodney concluded the conversation with, "Face it, John, you are no MegaMart and never will be."

To which John responded, "No, Rodney, I am no MegaMart and never want to be one."

John was now planning his next trip to the technical college and putting together a newspaper advertisement to look for two new employees. He was curious why some of his people had decided to leave and others had decided to stay given the same set of circumstances.

Questions

1. How would Equity Theory account for the behavior of the employees?

2. How would Expectancy Theory account for the behavior of the employees?

3. What job factors are important to employees?

DISCUSSION QUESTIONS

1. Explain the motivational need approaches of Maslow, Alderfer, and Herzberg.

2. Describe the relationship of the three expectancies in Vroom's expectancy theory.

3. What are the manager's responsibilities in the employee/employer motivational relationship?

4. List three conditions needed to make the goal-setting model effective.

5. Share an experience illustrating the equity theory of motivation.

CHAPTER 6

Stress

LEARNING OUTCOMES: STRESS

1. Define stress.

2. Explain the relationship of the two determinants of stress.

3. Recognize conditions of positive stress and negative stress.

4. Describe the ways a person reacts to stress.

5. Outline three ways stress affects an individual.

6. Discuss stress management techniques.

7. Through self-assessment, gain a greater understanding of one's own level of stress.

Name: _____

Section Number: _____

SELF-ASSESSMENT TEST

Please complete the following exercise online, accessible with the Access Card packaged with this text, before reading this chapter.

EXERCISE III.C.2:   HOW STRESSFUL IS
                     MY LIFE?   Score _____

    Stress and change go hand and hand. Stress is part of our daily lives and will probably always be. It is up to us to try and learn how to manage stress. This instrument measures the impact of life changes on people and how stress is created. Several of the questions relating to retirement may not appear applicable; however, the rest of the questions offer insights and can easily apply.

EXERCISE III.C.3:   AM I BURNED OUT?   Score _____

    Burnout is exhibiting chronic and long-term stress. This instrument was designed to provide you with insights into whether you're suffering from burnout.

You should also record your score on this exercise in Appendix 1.

NOTES

Pick Up the Pace

Harry was a no-nonsense kind of person. He was always ready for the challenge of his job of production supervisor in a plastic products company. He bragged that he could out-work, outthink, and outwit anyone. His work was always well done. He was the golden boy of management. He was well respected and well rewarded by management.

His department and his workers were considered the best in the company. He trained his people to be the best and expected them to perform. His department was always chosen for the more challenging jobs that needed to be done quickly. They never let the customer down.

As the business grew, more and more jobs were sent to Harry's department. At first, they met the challenge of custom order plastics. As more orders came in and the time frames to finish the orders shortened, the quality of work diminished. There were now errors and missed deadlines that had not happened before. Harry noticed the workers who normally came to work on time were showing up late or not at all. Several shouting matches between employees had occurred in a department known for people who got along. Harry was experiencing headaches and he was not able to sleep well at night.

After six months of trying to cope with the situation, Harry quit his job and went to work for a competitor. Many of his best employees followed him to a more peaceful work environment.

What happened to Harry and his employees?

Welcome to Stress! ■

It is 4:30 P.M. on a Monday. Rumors have been flying there is going to be a cutback in the hourly and professional ranks soon. You know the number of incoming orders have not been enough to support the organization's staffing. A new product line that shows promise could offset some of the expenses but is still six months away from being in place. Just minutes ago, you received a call from your boss demanding your presence at a meeting in his office the next morning. He ended his conversation with "Be there!" How do you feel? Pretty stressed, right?

Work stress is a primary cause of both physical and mental illness in our society. The cost to businesses and society is significant. What is stress? **Stress** is the way we react, physically and emotionally, to change.[39] Stress is a general term we apply to the pressures we feel in our lives and it is the wear and tear our bodies experience as we adjust to our continually changing environment. When we as individuals are faced with work or personal demands, uncertainty in the outcome of a situation, or a decision that carries a level of importance, we feel stress.[40]

Stress is an unavoidable fact of life. American business owners say they are more stressed out now than ever before.[41] A certain level of stress may actually improve performance and decision making. When stress becomes too great, however, it is termed to be dysfunctional, and performance and decision making may deteriorate.

Stress is the way we react physically and emotionally to demands where the outcome is uncertain and important.

We need to understand stress and learn to master it. If we do not, then stress may affect us behaviorally, psychologically, and/or physically. In this chapter, we want to answer four questions:

- What are the positive and negative aspects of stress?
- How does a person react to stress?
- What are the effects of stress?
- What are some stress management techniques?

WHAT ARE THE POSITIVE AND NEGATIVE ASPECTS OF STRESS?

Positive Stress

As we can see in Figure 6–1, stress can be positive. Stress helps us concentrate. For example, you may have a big exam coming up. If the outcome is uncertain and the test is important to you, you will experience stress. Because of this stress you will undoubtedly study harder and longer and learn more from the extra effort. Without the stress, the extra effort may not be forthcoming. Think for a moment about an Olympic runner competing in the 100-meter run. With the uncertainty of the outcome and the importance of this recognition, a runner will practice for years for a 10-second event. Without that stress, the level of effort and performance never would have happened.

When we experience positive stress, we tend to feel:[42]

- Better focused
- Energized
- Motivated
- Aware of options
- Challenged rather than intimidated

Positive stress can help us concentrate and focus. When positive stress enhances our individual or group performance, it is termed **functional stress.** Our physical stress response helps us to meet challenging situations. It is an automatic and essential fact of life.

Negative Stress

Stress may also become a negative force in our lives. In today's world, many situations appear to be overbearing and just too much, which can cause performance to deteriorate. High stress may be dysfunctional.

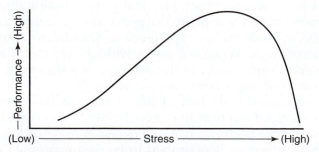

Figure 6–1 The relationship between stress and job performance.

Source: The Relationship Between Stress and Job Performance, from *Managing Stress* by K. C. Brewer, American Media Publishing, March 1995. Reprinted by permission of the National Seminars Group, a Division of Rockhurst University Continuing Education Center, Inc.

When stress is too high, turnover of employees will increase. Stress may become a constant, ongoing cycle. There is no relief or relaxation for the individual, and when this occurs, negative stress may bring on physical, behavioral, and/or psychological problems. With negative stress one tends to feel:[43]

- Tense
- Anxious
- Angry or depressed
- Withdrawing from or lashing out at others
- Frustrated

When negative stress begins to affect individual or organizational performance, it is considered to be **dysfunctional stress.** The good news is we can learn to manage the stress in our lives and assist those around us who need help in coping with stress.

HOW DOES A PERSON REACT TO STRESS?

Stress is often the result of change, and we are all affected by change. Since the world is constantly changing, we all have stress. It is best to find ways to manage stress or even use it as a positive force. Let us look at this in a little more detail, beginning with individual stress.

Whether the cause of our stress is physical or mental, we can respond in three basic ways:[44]

- **Avoid.** We can attempt to ignore a stressful situation and hope that whatever is causing stress will go away. A common avoidance technique is reliance on alcohol or drugs. This behavior soon becomes destructive to the individual and the situation. Pretending the stress does not exist will not resolve the issue for you.
- **Resist.** We can fight the stress. If the stress is coming from our boss, coworkers, or spouse, we can view stress as an assault by an external source and fight it. This is really a defensive response and often makes the stress worse.
- **Confront/Adapt.** We can work to identify the real cause of our stress and eliminate it. If this is not possible, then we figure out how to adapt so it won't destroy our lives.

Some individuals seem to thrive on stressful situations, while others are overwhelmed by stress. Research has identified at least five variables that help to explain why some people thrive on stress while others do not: perception, locus of control, job experience, social support, and type of personality.

Perception

An individual's perception of a situation will influence the level of stress. To the individual, his or her perception of reality *is* reality. Perception then will moderate the relationship between a potentially stressful condition and an individual's reaction to it.[45] Stress lies in an individual's interpretation of the factors in a given situation, thus increasing or decreasing individual stress.

Locus of Control

Locus of control is a personality attribute. People with a high **external** locus of control believe their lives are controlled by outside forces.

Those with a high **internal** locus of control believe they control their own destiny.[46] When externals and internals confront a similarly stressful situation, the internals are more likely to believe they can have a significant effect on the outcome. Therefore, they act to take control of the event. The externals are likely to blame others and their environment and become defensive. Because they are more likely to feel victimized in stressful situations, externals are more likely to experience stress.

Job Experience

The greater the job experience, the more comfortable the employee becomes with the environment of the work situation and with fellow employees. With this gain in job experience, stress is reduced or disappears. From an organizational behavior viewpoint, this interaction between level of experience and job stress makes perfect sense. People who remain with an organization longer are those with more stress-resistant traits; otherwise they would have left due to the stress.[47] Also, people eventually develop coping mechanisms to deal with stress. The longer a person is with an organization, the more likely he or she is to become fully acclimated to the environment. Longer tenure generally reduces a person's stress level.

Social Support

Research suggests that with a stronger relationship with fellow workers and managers and the support from one's family, one is better able to handle stress.[48] Social support systems moderate the negative effects of stress, even high levels of stress. Involvement with family, friends, associates, and the community can provide the support one needs to make job stressors and the stressors of life more tolerable.

Type of Personality

A person with a Type A personality is characterized by feeling a chronic sense of time urgency and by an excessive competitive drive. The Type A person is trying to get more done in less time. In the past, researchers believed people with Type A personalities were more likely to experience stress on and off the job than workers with Type B personalities. Those with Type A personalities were believed to be at a higher risk for stroke or heart disease.[49]

A closer analysis of the evidence, however, has produced new conclusions. It has been found that only the hostility and anger associated with Type A behavior are actually related to heart disease. Just because a person is a workaholic, rushes around a lot, and is impatient or competitive does not mean that he or she is feeling the negative effects of stress. In fact, it is the quickness to anger, the persistently hostile outlook, and the cynical mistrust of others that are harmful, and not all people with Type A personalities possess these negative traits.

WHAT ARE THE EFFECTS OF STRESS?

The effects of stress can be viewed in three different ways: physiologically, psychologically, and behaviorally.[50] We want to examine these effects in more detail to better identify when stress starts to become dysfunctional.

Physiological Stress

No matter how hard we try, we cannot keep stress locked inside or ignore it. Doctors estimate that 75 percent of all medical complaints are stress related.[51] The most common complaints include:

Insomnia/sleep disorders	Muscle aches
Sexual dysfunction	High blood pressure
Indigestion/vomiting	Heart attack/stroke
Ulcers/diarrhea	Chronic illness (flu, colds, etc.)
Headaches	Hives

All of these may be related to the negative stress that we experience every day. The opportunity for stress today seems to be unrelenting and more intense than ever before. In our study of the organization and the individual, we must learn how to control the stressors in our environment and modify our behavior in responding to them.

Psychological Stress

Job dissatisfaction is the simplest and most obvious psychological effect of stress. Recent statistics show that 75 percent of workers indicate they feel stress on the job. Stress-related illnesses and decreased productivity cost American businesses more than $150 billion each year. Psychological stress can be caused by feeling a lack of control due to:

- Undefined job responsibilities
- Not having adequate resources to complete a job
- Lack of recognition
- Lack of feedback due to no method for performance evaluation
- Employees taken for granted
- Boredom due to one's skills not being utilized
- Lack of priorities

Tension, anxiety, fear, irritability, poor work performance, and procrastination are some additional symptoms of psychological stress. The evidence suggests that jobs providing a low level of variety, significance, autonomy, feedback, and identity to employees create stress and reduce satisfaction and involvement in the job.

Behavioral Stress

Behaviorally related stress in the workplace may cause changes in productivity, absenteeism, and turnover. Individual reaction to behavioral stress may result in changes in eating habits, increased smoking or consumption of alcohol, hurried speech, nervousness, and sleep disorders.

What are some actions businesses might undertake to reduce or prevent workplace stress? Here are some suggestions:

- Make sure the orientation training for new hires is complete and then follow up with a second orientation training session to review questions that may arise within the first two weeks of a new job.
- Provide adequate training. Never put an employee into a performance situation without adequate training in the new task.

- Make sure all management knows how to properly communicate and coach employees.
- Provide immediate feedback on decisions.
- Communicate often. Address any workplace rumors by being proactive with plans and decisions.

WHAT ARE SOME STRESS MANAGEMENT TECHNIQUES?

Based on the self-assessment test at the beginning of this chapter, are you suffering from burnout? There are several ways to manage the stress of yourself and your employees.

Establish Personal Priorities

Establishing personal priorities will relieve stress by establishing an objective means for evaluating time demands and give a basis for saying "no" to demands that conflict with priorities.

Physical Exercise

Physical exercise such as aerobics, walking, jogging, swimming, and riding a bicycle has long been recommended by physicians as a way to deal with excessive stress levels. This departure from the work environment provides a mental and physical diversion from work pressures and becomes a means to "let off steam."

Time Management

Find a time management system that is convenient to use. A good time management system allows you to keep track of appointments and to organize important aspects of your life. Say "no" to projects that don't fit into your time schedule, don't fit your values or goals, or compromise your mental and physical health. Delegate those tasks to others that they are capable of doing. As a youth group leader I discovered delegating responsibility to the parents of the youth got them involved and committed to the program, provided the necessary support for new activities, and allowed me to accomplish more with the program. It also allowed me extra time to do things and to get to places. Examples of events that belong on your calendar include deadlines, work projects, telephone calls, long-range planning, meetings, and exercise.

Relaxation

Relaxation stimulates the body's parasympathetic nervous system, which controls stress responses like respiration, heart rate, and digestion. When we relax these areas, we feel calmer and more in control. Relaxation methods should be practiced once or twice daily for 5 to 15 minutes. A quiet, comfortable place and comfortable clothes are essential.[52] The basic components of most relaxation programs are

- **Concentration-Focusing.** The purpose is to concentrate totally on relaxation. Some methods to accomplish this are music and a repeating tone or beat.
- **Deep Breathing.** The purpose is to counteract and reduce the flow of adrenaline and cortisone in the body. This should feel natural, not forced.

- **Progressive Muscle Relaxation.** By tensing and then relaxing certain muscles, you become more aware of the tension in your body and can consciously reduce it.
- **Gentle Muscle Stretching.** Feeling limber and relaxed helps you cope with stress more effectively. Methods such as yoga, tai chi, and other programs help achieve this.
- **Visualization/Imagery.** By visualizing a peaceful setting and picturing yourself in it, you can reduce or eliminate much of the mental tension that comes with stress.
- **Music Therapy.** Popular choices of music are natural sounds and "New Age" music.
- **Social Support.** Develop a circle of friends with whom you feel comfortable sharing your problems and concerns. Just having someone listen to you often opens up new avenues for solutions.
- **Get adequate rest.** Recent research studies have shown that getting too little sleep, five hours or less a night, is detrimental to one's mental and physical health. Studies show that not getting enough sleep or getting poor quality sleep on a regular basis increases the risk of having high blood pressure, heart disease, and other medical conditions. Not getting enough sleep can be dangerous—for example, you are more likely to be in a car accident if you drive when you are drowsy. Research further notes the average individual requires between seven to eight hours of sleep per night to perform at peak levels.[53]
- **Pets.** Studies have shown having a pet may help some reduce stress. The comfort and companionship pets provide their owners can help reduce stress, keep them healthier, and even increase self-esteem. One of the most surprising ways that pets relieve stress occurs when you simply pet your pet. It's been shown that petting an animal reduces the heart rate, blood pressure, and arteriosclerotic process. "Pet therapy" is widely used in nursing homes, prisons, hospitals, and schools to reduce loneliness, anger, depression, and stress.[54]

SUMMARY

Stress is the way we react, physically and emotionally, to change. Stress may be a positive or negative force. Stress may be mild or severe. The level of uncertainty and the degree of importance will determine the amount of stress one feels. The greater the level of importance and the higher the level of uncertainty, the higher the level of stress. The duration and severity of stress is dependent on how powerful the causes are and how long the causes continue.

People react to stress in three basic ways. They may elect to avoid stress and hope whatever is causing it goes away. They may resist stress by becoming defensive. Or they may choose to confront and/or adapt to the stress. If the cause is something one cannot change, one may choose to adapt to the change as a means to resist the stress. Or one may confront the stress, address the real cause, and find a resolution.

Positive stress is termed *functional stress* and incites improved performance. Negative stress is termed *dysfunctional* and impedes individual or group performance. Negative stress, left unchecked, may show itself physiologically, psychologically, and/or behaviorally. Job-related stress impacts employee satisfaction and performance and tends to decrease job satisfaction.

Several proven stress management techniques can be beneficial to the organization and the employee. Those suggested in the text are to:

- Establish personal priorities
- Do physical exercise
- Use time management
- Relax any way that works

Stress management needs to be part of an overall wellness program. The results have proven to add to the health and welfare of the employees and to contribute to the company's health, and its bottom line.

CASE STUDY

Bill Patterson grew up in a family of four in suburban Chicago. Growing up, Bill enjoyed a good home life with little concerns about money, marital problems, sibling rivalry, health issues, or neighborhood problems. Bill's father was a surgeon at the local hospital and earned an extremely good income. He gave his family everything they needed or wanted. Bill's parents had been happily married for twenty-five years. Bill's mom was a stay-at-home mother who took charge of helping the children. Bill's older sister, Carla, had been a cheerleader, member of the National Honor Society, and homecoming queen in high school. Bill had lettered in football and track and had been a member of the National Honor Society. He had his own car and life in high school was great.

He went to the state university and majored in business. He had a nice scholarship that paid for his tuition and his family paid for his housing and other expenses. He was popular on campus and enjoyed a good life. He was able to go on trips over Spring break and in the summer to Florida, Mexico, and the Caribbean. He graduated near the top of his class even though he openly admitted to not doing as well as he could have because of an active social life. That social life had included a good deal of time in his senior year with Susan, an art major from Wisconsin, and Sharon, an economics major from Iowa. Bill had been successful in keeping the two of them apart and they apparently did not know about each other. Bill would tell Susan he had a meeting and would go see Sharon. Bill told Sharon he was studying on the nights he was with Susan. By this time, Susan and Sharon were both thinking that Bill was seriously interested in them and they both started to talk about marriage with Bill. Bill liked them both but the "m" word was hard to handle. He was sure that either Susan and/or Sharon would have moved on by now, making his choice easy, but they had not.

In his last semester, Bill had interviewed for jobs with a large retailer in Chicago, a large trucking firm in Iowa, and a large cheese manufacturer in Wisconsin. Bill entered interviewing knowing that he would probably only get one offer and he would take it. He had great interviews with all three companies. He was invited to visit and tour all three companies. He had enjoyed the trips and could see himself working for any of the companies. To his surprise, he got offers from all three companies. The large retailer gave him a chance to go home to Chicago and earn $40,000 per year with full benefits. The trucking firm gave him the chance to be close to Sharon's home and make $45,000 plus benefits. The cheese manufacturer had offered him $48,000 plus benefits and it was only 25 miles from Susan's family. He had told each company that he was really interested in working for them, but he needed more time. They each agreed to give him two weeks before they moved on to other candidates for employment.

Bill had not been good about keeping his offers quiet as he had told his parents, Susan, and Sharon about his offers. His parents were excited that Bill was coming home to Chicago. The family could be back together again as Bill's sister Carla, a journalism graduate, had taken a job in the suburbs with a local newspaper. Bill's father told him that it was good that he had the opportunity to come home. He also said that he would introduce Bill to his banker and work on finding him a house in the area. His mother also informed Bill that Sandra, his high school girlfriend, had returned home and was asking about him. Bill got to thinking about all the good times he and Sandra had shared in high school and thought maybe getting together with her again might not be a bad idea. They had drifted apart when they decided to go to different colleges. Needless to say, Bill had forgotten to tell his parents about Susan and Sharon.

Bill complicated matters further by going on weekend trips home with both Sharon and Susan to meet their parents. Both sets of parents were impressed with Bill and had been led to believe by their daughters that Bill was "Mr. Right." Both sets of parents had called Bill to congratulate him on getting a job in their area. Both expressed delight that after the marriage their daughter and new husband would be living so close to them.

Bill was really impressed with himself initially. He thought that this is just like being on *The Apprentice* and *The Bachelor* at the same time. He had the jobs and he had the girls. After thoughts of Don Trump saying, "you're

hired" and of him passing out red roses had passed, it dawned on him that he was in a real mess. He thought about how he would tell the girls, their parents, his parents, and the companies. The more he thought about it, the more tense and anxious he became. He started to have headaches and muscle aches. He started to ignore cell phone calls from the girls and his parents. He was having difficulty sleeping and had indigestion.

Every day, he woke up thinking, which girl do I want and which job do I want? One day, the cheese manufacturer job offer was on top and the next day, the choice would be going home to the retailer. The trucking company presented a good compromise. The girls were even more difficult to sort out. He thought about high school and wanted Sandra. Then, he would think about college and become torn between Sharon and Susan. Then, what was he going to do about his family?

With every passing day, Bill became more stressed. He had lost weight, did not feel good, could not sleep, and was irritable with friends. He also had final exams coming up and needed to do well on them. With three days left before a decision had to be made, he went to the student hospital and asked to see a doctor. The doctor told him that what he was going through was acute stress and that stress had caused his problems. The doctor told Bill that the only cure for this problem was to make final decisions about the job and girls and to let everyone involved know his decision. He was also told to expect some repercussions from his decisions. After this had passed, he was told to get on with his studies and graduate.

Bill decided to go home, take the retail job, and start seeing Sandra. The companies understood Bill's decision and wished him well. Sharon and Susan were less enthusiastic about his decision and let him know about it. Two unpleasant calls from Wisconsin and Iowa ensued. Bill was able to pass his final exams and graduate. After a short time, Bill's stress diminished and his physical problems disappeared.

Questions

1. What were Bill's problems?
2. How had Bill helped create his own problems?
3. Can stress cause physical problems?
4. Was the doctor's advice right for Bill?
5. What additional advice might you suggest to prevent this sort of stress?

DISCUSSION QUESTIONS

1. Identify and discuss the stressors in your life, their sources, and ways to address your stress.

2. Explain how stress may be positive. Provide some examples.

3. Explain the differences in the personality attributes of internal and external locus of control.

PART

3

UNDERSTANDING OTHERS

Turning People into Team Players

LEARNING OUTCOMES: TURNING PEOPLE INTO TEAM PLAYERS

1. Explain the popularity of teams in the workplace.

2. Identify the different team player roles.

3. Illustrate the difference between role expectation and role perception.

4. Describe social loafing.

5. Contrast the cultural differences between groups of people.

6. Explain synergy in teamwork.

7. Through self-assessment, gain a greater understanding of one's own orientation to being a team player.

Name: _____

Section Number: _____

SELF-ASSESSMENT TEST

Please complete the following exercise online, accessible with the Access Card packaged with this text, before reading this chapter.

EXERCISE II.B.6:   HOW GOOD AM I AT BUILDING
                      AND LEADING A TEAM?   Score _____

The authors of this instrument propose that it assesses team development behaviors in five areas: diagnosing team development, managing the forming stage, managing the conforming stage, managing the storming stage, and managing the performing stage. Based on a norm group of 500 business students, your score will help you determine which quintile you fit.

You should also record your score on this exercise in Appendix 1.

NOTES

The Team

Joe, the vice president of operations at an auto parts plant, tells Frank he must convert the department he manages into a team.

"Our whole company is going with this new team approach," Joe tells Frank, "and that includes your people."

Up until now, Frank's workers have worked well independently, but stayed in two different groups. The younger workers tended to work well together and were always trying new things and pushing the envelope. Many of them played softball together and were involved in many activities together outside of work. Their view of the older workers was that they were just putting in time and hanging around until retirement.

The older workers also tended to get along well together and stuck to traditional methods and ways of doing things. They often called the younger workers "troublemakers" and "rebels." They saw the younger workers as bucking the system and creating problems. The older workers went bowling together and saw each other after work to play poker and drink beer.

Joe is aware of Frank's situation but does not want to get involved. He tells Frank this is a departmental issue and Frank will have to deal with it.

What does Frank do to create a team?

Welcome to Turning People into Team Players! ■

"Teamwork is the essence of life. If there is one thing on which I'm an authority, it's how to blend the talents and strengths of individuals into a force that becomes greater than the sum of its parts."

—Pat Riley, NBA coach[55]

Part 2 of this text provided the tools to conduct a complete analysis of yourself: your personality, abilities, way of perceiving, values and attitudes, sources of motivation, and strategies for dealing with stress. There were two reasons for focusing so much attention on trying to help you understand yourself. First, if you understand yourself, it helps you set your future direction in life and helps you identify your strengths and weaknesses. Second, it helps you realize that **all people are different and that's okay.** Not only is it okay, but also, as we will see, it is essential.

Usually people are too judgmental about other people. "That guy is too pushy," or "my roommate always wants to stay in her room and never wants to party." It may seem obvious, but just because a person is different doesn't mean something is wrong with him or her. Take the Jungian 16-Type Personality test, for example. Some people score as introverts, some people score as extroverts. Is one type better than another? In general, no. Some tasks or jobs are better for introverts, and some are better for extroverts, but you cannot say that one type is universally better than the other. If you feel a person is too introverted for your tastes, it is better to accept that fact and act accordingly. As we saw in the section on "Understanding Me," most personal traits are either genetic or strongly ingrained in a person. It is unlikely that you could change a person much anyway.

All people are different and that's okay. For teams, **diversity** can be an advantage.

This is not to say that there is no absolute right or wrong. Some behavior is wrong, and one should take a stand against truly bad behavior. In 90 percent of cases, however, people make judgments about other people that are not based on an issue of right or wrong, but simply on an issue about people being different.

The fact that people are different is a huge advantage when working as a team.[56] Having a diverse collection of people on a team makes things more difficult in the beginning. People are naturally less comfortable with people who are different from themselves. As a project progresses, however, the different perspectives of a diverse team can become a huge advantage.

When most of us were growing up, we didn't learn much in school about teamwork. In most cases, if you worked together with a classmate, it was called *cheating*, not teamwork. Lately, there has been a big push to incorporate team projects into school courses. Why is that?

WHY TEAMS?

With so much technical information to learn in college, it is sometimes difficult to justify spending time studying teamwork. In the past, people made the same argument about communication skills. Over the past ten or twenty years, however, people have really started to appreciate the need for good communication skills. Teamwork skills are in a similar category as communication skills. Teamwork is something people need to master to be successful in their future lives, no matter what they end up doing. In fact it is said, "If it is not being done by teams, it is probably not being done."[57]

There are three key reasons for learning about teamwork. The first is that team skills are needed and valued by employers. About 80 percent of U.S. organizations use teams to accomplish tasks.[58] As technology advances, people's skills are becoming more and more specialized. Teamwork skills are needed to get a group of specialists together and accomplish a task. When multiple skills are needed to complete a task, teams have an advantage over individuals.

A second reason to learn about teamwork is to develop interpersonal skills, which are highly relevant to teamwork activities. One of the major reasons that first-time managers fail is poor interpersonal skills. While technical skills may get a person through the early part of his or her career, when the person moves up into management positions, technical skills become less important and the interpersonal and teamwork skills become essential. Even if a person is not destined to become a manager, learning about teamwork can help teach how to participate effectively in a team. Teams are appropriate where knowledge, varied experience, multiple skills, abilities, and judgment are needed.

The final and most compelling reason for learning about teamwork is to capitalize on complementary skills leading to improvements in productivity and performance. Teams certainly provide an advantage when the decision or task will benefit from multiple skills, varied judgments, or a variety of experiences. There is probably no better example of teamwork than the Fantastic Four. For those of you who missed Saturday morning cartoons or Marvel comic books, the Fantastic Four is a group of four superheroes: Mr. Fantastic, The Invisible Woman, The Thing, and The Human Torch. Even though individual superheroes are more popular (underscoring another cultural bias against teams), the Fantastic Four could stack up against Superman any day.

WHAT TEAMWORK SKILLS DO WE NEED TO LEARN?

The Fantastic Four have to combine their individual skills and abilities to solve problems. For example, say the Fantastic Four were pursuing a bad person, but a bridge over a river up ahead was washed out. The Thing, even though he has incredible strength, would be powerless to cross the raging water. Mr. Fantastic, however, is able to convert his body into a highly elastic state. He could stretch across the river to form a temporary bridge, and The Thing could travel across safely on Mr. Fantastic's back. Thanks to teamwork, The Thing's incredible strength could then be used to help accomplish the task.

Not many people will turn out like Superman—fully equipped with all the tools necessary to confront any problem. Remember, even Superman needed some help when it came to kryptonite. Most people end up developing special skills that need to be combined with other people's skills to accomplish a task, just like the Fantastic Four. If people do not learn teamwork, they will not understand how to access the unique skills and abilities of others, and they will be severely limited in what they can accomplish. This is the first and most important teamwork skill people need to learn: **You can accomplish more if you take advantage of the unique skills and abilities of others.** Many people are certain that they need to do everything themselves. This attitude carries on when they go into industry, causing a lack of efficiency that eventually hurts them and the company.

Even after people realize that other people have skills that could help them, many aspects associated with teamwork must be developed. In this realm, managing and leading teams is a must. The second biggest hurdle to promoting teamwork is getting people to recognize that **all people are unique and perceive the world differently.** For example, say an engineer needs to give a presentation to a group of investors, and the engineer is told to work with a coworker who majored in communications to put the presentation together. The engineer might be frustrated with the approach taken by the communications person. "Why spend half an hour explaining that concept when a mathematical equation would give the precise information in less than one minute?" the engineer might ask. Because the audience might not understand a mathematical presentation. Unless people learn that other people think differently than they do and perceive the world in a different way, they will not develop the tools they need to work effectively in teams, especially in teams that include both technical and nontechnical members.

As people work in teams, they will take on different roles toward the accomplishment of the goals. A **role** is a set of expected behavior patterns attributed to a team member in a given position. As people take on the different roles within particular situations, they have a **role perception** of what is required for their roles. One's perception of what his or her role involves determines one's behavior in response to that role. As an example, if one is selected to be the team leader, the leader will have a role perception of what he or she is supposed to do as the leader. In a like manner, others also have expectations of each role. In the above example the rest of the team members will have certain **role expectations** of the individual who has the role of team leader. Most people believe they understand the roles of team leader and follower; however, without communicating the expectations and perceptions, it will often result in disappointment with the performance. Unfortunately, these roles on teams have been assigned positive and negative connotations. When the role perception of the leader and the role expectation of the other team members are not congruent,

> Through **teamwork,** more can be accomplished by using the skills and abilities of several individuals.

> **Role** is a set of expected behavior patterns attributed to a team member in a given position.

> **Role perception** is how the individual believes he or she is to act in a given team role.

> **Role expectation** is how others on the team believe or expect other members to behave.

Table 7–1 Team Roles

Leader	Directs and facilitates action
Creator	Initiates creative ideas
Promoter	Champions ideas after they're initiated
Assessor	Offers insightful analysis of options
Organizer	Provides structure
Producer	Provides direction and follow-through
Controller	Examines details and enforces rules
Maintainer	Fights external battles
Adviser	Encourages the search for more information
Linker	Coordinates and integrates

Source: Team Roles based on *Team Management: Pratical New Approaches* by C. Margerison and D. McCann, Gloucestershire, UK: Management Books 2000 Ltd., 1996. Reprinted by permission.

Role conflict may occur when the role perception and the role expectations are not congruent.

there is the potential for **role conflict.** A more complete list of team roles is provided in Table 7–1. This table lists the many critical roles in teams.

A review of these team roles emphasizes why it is so fortunate that people are different. If you have a controller personality, aren't you glad there are other people around who can act as a creator? If you are a linker, aren't you glad other people are natural producers? If you learn nothing else from this chapter, you should learn that people are different and that's not only okay, but it is also a great advantage.

Another way to look at team roles is to recognize that all successful teams include three necessary skills:

- Technical expertise
- Problem solving/decision-making skills
- Interpersonal skills/communication

Combining workers into teams does not always work. In a few instances some assigned members may turn out to be noncontributors. In many situations, this noncontribution manifests itself as **social loafing**—that is, coasting on the team effort. The leader of an especially talented team must be alert to any member who may be likely to coast.

Social loafing is the tendency for individuals to put forth just enough effort to get by when working with teams.

It may also happen that what seems to be a good team fit fails because a team member is disruptive and seeks personal attention that detracts from the team effort. A case in point is the signing of Dennis Rodman in 1999 to play for the Los Angeles Lakers NBA basketball team. Rodman is a great basketball player but, for various reasons, was disruptive to the team effort.

Based on the self-assessment test at the beginning of this chapter, are you good at building and leading teams? Are you a team player?

Some people have a natural inclination toward working with others. Other people need to learn teamwork. It is a skill just like any other skill. If you are not naturally a team player, you need to learn team skills to be effective in an organization.

WHAT ABOUT GENDER DIFFERENCES?

For a given job, the differences between men and women are not that great.

So far we have emphasized how people are different. Just to confuse you, now we are going to talk about how men and women are the same. We could go on for hundreds of pages talking about all the studies on the differences between men and women. Instead, we will give you a break and make the following statement: For a given job, there is not much difference between men and women. In fact, there are more differences within each gender than there are between the genders.[59]

For a given job is a key part of that statement. Most people attracted to a certain job are interested in that job because of their personalities, their abilities, their motivation, and so forth. Once people have chosen jobs based on these individual factors (which are different for all people), they are likely to find themselves surrounded by people who are much the same as they are, whether they are men or women. Creative people tend to end up in jobs that reward creativity. Whether the creative person is a man or a woman is less important than the fact that the person is creative.

In the movie *GI Jane*, the base leader started out treating Lieutenant O'Neil (played by Demi Moore) differently. She was given a separate bunk, separate bathroom, and different standards for the Navy SEAL training. She objected to this because she was attracted to being a Navy SEAL for all the reasons that men were attracted to being SEALS: She was aggressive and wanted to blow up stuff. She did not see her gender as an important difference compared to the commonalities she had with the other SEAL trainees. The differences between Lt. O'Neil and the rest of the SEAL trainees were not nearly as big—even though there was a gender difference—as the difference between the SEAL trainees and me (I might be male, but I am still a wimp). Gender is usually not the big factor in a given job. The big factor is the personal attributes that led a person to that profession.

When comparing different jobs, there are big differences, but they are usually based on perception, not gender. The perspective of managers is different than that of assembly-line workers. Male and female managers surely have more in common than male managers and male assembly-line workers on most work-based attitudes and actions. Admittedly this is a simplification, but you should look for the differences in people based on individual characteristics rather than the differences in people based on gender. As a team leader, understanding these individual characteristics will enhance one's ability to build the team on the individual strengths and form more effective teams.

The bigger problem with gender differences usually comes from people's attitudes. Since everyone has not read this book (yet), some people believe there are fundamental differences between men and women who are doing the same job. People who hold this belief base their behavior on this perception, and this is often the source of many of the gender problems seen in workplace teams today.

WHAT ABOUT CULTURAL DIFFERENCES?

There can be strong cultural differences among people. Some cultures emphasize certain characteristics. In some cultures, for example, the barter system is the accepted way to purchase almost everything. In other cultures, you are expected to use currency to buy things. Environmental differences between cultures can create, on average, fundamental differences between groups of people. The key phrase in this statement is *on average*. There is a fine line between stereotyping and recognizing cultural differences.

Stereotyping is attributing a specific trait to a person based on the characteristics of the group to which that person belongs. For example, many people in Third World countries think that all Americans are rich. On average, it is true that Americans are richer than people in Third World countries. What is true on average, however, is not necessarily true

Stereotyping is attributing a specific trait to a person based on the characteristics of the group to which a person belongs.

when looking at an individual. Is a specific American person richer than a specific person from a Third World country? It is impossible to know without having information about the two people.

This is the danger in discussing cultural differences. It is true that there may be some differences, on average, when comparing one group with another group. You should not take these differences and assume they apply to everyone. These cultural differences are a starting point that should not be accepted until confirmed by the individual person's behavior.

A good movie that illustrates cultural differences is *Rising Sun*. In this movie, the character played by Sean Connery, who is an expert on Japanese culture, acts as a mentor to the character played by Wesley Snipes. Connery and Snipes are two police detectives trying to solve a crime committed at the headquarters of a Japanese company. Throughout the movie, Connery shows how certain aspects of Japanese culture influenced the Japanese characters to act differently than if they had been brought up in American culture. While this general framework was helpful, the Japanese characters still exhibited substantial individual behaviors that were sometimes inconsistent with cultural stereotypes.

When you interact with another culture, you must be conscious of all the possible differences. For example, nonverbal communication and gestures are very different between cultures. Using the American gesture for *okay* in Brazil is definitely not okay. In Brazil, the *okay* gesture is equivalent to the American *one-finger salute*.

Business practices also vary widely between cultures. In some cultures, it is customary to start a negotiation with a ridiculous starting offer. In still other cultures, doing this suggests that you are not serious. In other cultures, any negotiation is seen as distasteful and you are expected to simply present your final offer.

Different cultures have different concepts of time. In some cultures, a morning meeting could mean the meeting starts at 6 A.M., while in other cultures it means an 11 A.M. start. Getting back to someone quickly could mean within the same day, or it could mean a response three months later.

The workday is also structured differently in different cultures. Some cultures run on an 8-to-5 schedule with a short break for lunch. In other cultures, a long lunch break is the norm, and people come back to work until 7 or 8 P.M.

Cultural differences exist, and they are often very strong. You need to be aware of these cultural differences and factor in this information without stereotyping people.

Synergy

Building a force that is greater than the sum of its parts is the hallmark of a team. A common misconception is that being part of a group is equivalent to being part of a team. This is just not the case. A movie comparison provides an illustration. In the movie *A Simple Plan* two brothers and a friend stumble onto a small crashed airplane that contains $4 million. These three men form what they believe to be a team whose goal is to ultimately split the $4 million. While each person is different, together they do not merge into a single force. Each develops his own agenda, and the result is failure. On the other hand, consider the three NASA astronauts featured in the movie *Apollo 13*. Each has a function: commander, pilot, and navigator. When the flight was placed in jeopardy, the three worked in concert to rescue the mission. Their effort was not without conflict, but their teamwork brought the spacecraft and the astronauts home safely.

A football team is not successful without both an offense and a defense. A baseball team combines the efforts of pitchers, hitters, and fielders to achieve success. The Boston Pops Orchestra integrates brass, percussion, and strings to demonstrate their excellence. What makes all these teams successful? The combining of elements that results in something greater than the individual parts is called **synergy.** This is discussed in greater detail in the next chapter. Positive synergy occurs at the point where complementary functions are fashioned together into a cohesive unit. For example, a baseball team made up of only pitchers will likely see little or no success even if the pitchers are all great pitchers. There must be complementing skills for a team to achieve success. This is what true teams are about. Whether in problem solving, decision making, working on a task, or developing a new product, when individuals work as a team the alternatives to the problem are greater, the decision is better, the productivity is improved, a better product is developed, people's affiliation needs are met, and synergy develops.

Synergy is building a force that is greater than the sum of its parts.

CHARACTERISTICS OF GOOD TEAM BUILDING

Good team building does not just happen. It requires hard work and an attitude of willingness to work together. The following points will help highlight some of the more critical characteristics for good team building.

- High level of interdependence among team members. The North American culture stresses being independent and interdependent. Members of successful teams rely on each other for success. One must put self second to the goals of the team.

- Development of mutual trust and respect. Trust is the foundation for effective leadership and teamwork.

- Team leaders must possess good people skills. As noted above, strong interpersonal skills are required for effective team leadership. Effective communication skills, time management, and an understanding of motivation techniques are all required.

- Team roles are defined and understood. Roles will change based on the tasks and goals of the group but success is dependent on each member understanding how he or she can contribute to the overall success and then just do what needs to be done.

- The team must have clear goals and objectives. If you want everyone to strive for the same goal, each and every team member must understand, accept, and share the goals of the team. Team decisions are made based on the attainment of the goals and objectives.

- The team must have the capacity to create new and innovative ideas. Due to peer pressure and the drive to attain goals, teams need to be aware of groupthink and group shift. Having the capacity to be creative and accept change is important for team success and survival.

Today, about 80 percent of businesses and organizations use some form of teams. Working in teams can lead people to be more productive. The team skills needed for increased productivity are

■ Technical expertise
■ Problem solving/decision making
■ Interpersonal skills/communication

People in the team can, and will, assume various roles such as creator, promoter, assessor, organizer, producer, controller, maintainer, adviser, and linker during the teaming process.

Members of the team will have role expectations of each team member, and each member will have a role perception of what they are to do and how they are to act.

Social loafing or coasting occurs when a team member puts forth just enough effort to get by when working with others and "rides" on the success of the other team members.

Two areas of concern in team building are gender differences (differences between men and women) and cultural differences (differences between people of different cultures). The cultural differences tend to be more significant than gender differences.

Synergy is when the team is able to accomplish more working together than working individually.

CASE STUDY

It was a typical semester at State University. The courses were underway and the instructors were getting used to their students and vice versa. The history department had hired Dr. Menefee, a new professor right out of graduate school. Believing that he could make Introduction to World History interesting for his class of non-history majors, he devised a plan to put people into teams and let the teams work on various projects. The teams were going to complete papers on various history topics from research done outside of the classroom. The team's responsibility was to create in-depth papers on topics from the lectures. The four five-person teams were chosen by counting off numbers 1 to 4 in class. Dr. Menefee told the students their entire grade for the semester would be based on six team papers and all the members of the team would receive the same grade.

The student reaction was very positive at first. There would be no quizzes, no tests, and attendance did not matter. All the students taking this course were non-history majors trying to fulfill a general education requirement in liberal arts and sciences. The mentality of getting the credit and moving on was prevalent. The class was composed entirely of sophomores and freshmen. The GPAs for the class ranged from 1.55 (on probation) to 3.88 (on the dean's list).

The first team had Sarah, Bob, Fred, Obi, and Lauren. Sarah was a sophomore with a GPA of 3.88 and was determined to make high grades to get into law school. She was a take-charge person and wanted things done right every time. Bob was a freshman partier who had amassed a 2.01 GPA and felt pretty good about not being on probation. Fred was a freshman working a nearly full time job to pay for college. He was doing fairly well with a 2.79 GPA. Obi was a freshman from Japan. He was very smart, but had language problems, and these difficulties resulted in him earning a GPA of 1.95. Lauren was a sophomore who had just pledged a sorority. She had a GPA of 2.33.

The second team had Bill, Mike, Tim, Sue, and Ashley. Bill was a sophomore, had a 3.75 GPA, and was president of the sophomore class. Mike was a sophomore with a 3.55 GPA and he was assistant editor of the student newspaper. He had the reputation for putting the paper together and getting it out on time. Tim was a freshman with a 3.50 GPA and the ability to work with people and get things done. Sue was a freshman with a 3.22 GPA and the ability to encourage others. Ashley was a sophomore with a 3.45 GPA and she grew up in a strict home and had learned to obey the rules.

The third team was composed of Nick, Tony, Gail, Wendy, and Gwynn. Nick was a sophomore business major with a 2.25 GPA and the philosophy of do what you have to do to get through liberal arts and science courses. Tony was a freshman jock with a GPA of 2.11. Tony just wanted to stay eligible for football and he had aspirations of going pro. Gail, a sophomore, had a GPA of 2.45 and just wanted to get through this course with a C. Wendy had a GPA of 2.18 and had no interest in history. Gwynn, a freshman, with a GPA of 2.08, wanted to stay off of probation.

The fourth team was composed of Roger, Linda, Meagan, Lindsey, and Paul. Roger, a freshman, was the worst student in the class with a 1.55 GPA. He hated college, but came only because his parents pushed him into it. Linda, a freshman with a 1.99 GPA, enjoyed the party scene and could not care less about world history. Meagan, a sophomore, had a 2.01 GPA and was more interested in finding a husband than getting a degree. Lindsey, a sophomore with a 2.19 GPA, was just trying to get a passing grade to finish off her last liberal arts and science course. Paul had a GPA of 2.25 and felt he could take a D in this course and still stay in good academic standing.

In the middle of the semester, Dr. Menefee noticed some interesting trends with the teams. Team Two was clearly dominating the class. Their three assignments were in on time, typed perfectly, and superior in content. The team had gotten scores of 98, 99, and 100 on the three papers. Team One had gotten scores of 82, 83, and 81 on their three papers. The papers contained minor word processing errors and one was one day late. Team Three had earned scores of 72, 74, and 75 on their three papers. Their work was sometimes late with word processing and content errors. The Fourth Team was definitely struggling with scores of 60, 64, and 59 on the three papers. Their work was full of word processing errors, poor content, and all the papers were delivered after the due date.

Dr. Menefee decided to discuss their work with each team individually. Team Two was the first to see Dr. Menefee. He explained he was pleased with their work and asked them how they had done it. Bill explained he took the lead on the papers, Mike organized the work, Sue encouraged the team to stay on task and look for the best information, and Ashley was the closer, making sure it was proofread for content and word processing and making sure the finished copy was handed in on time. All the students said the team worked well together.

Dr. Menefee met with Team One and told them their work was good. Only Sarah, Fred, and Obi showed up for the meeting. Sarah shared that Bob was under the weather and Lauren was at a sorority meeting. He asked them how the team was working. Sarah was starting to answer the question when Fred had to leave to go to work. Sarah complained that she had to do all the work herself because Fred was always working, Lauren was caught up in her sorority, and Bob never shows up. Obi said he tries to help, but his English is not so good. Sarah said "I try hard to do A work, but I cannot do it all myself even with the help I get from Obi and sometimes Fred. Bob and Lauren contribute nothing to this team."

Dr. Menefee met with Team Three and told them that their work was just average. The team reacted positively to that comment. Nick said the team worked well together and produced a paper that satisfied them. They indicated they were pleased with the C grade.

Dr. Menefee met with Team Four and told them that their work was below average. Paul spoke on behalf of the team and stated that they were not history majors and the assignments were too tough. Roger chimed in with, "you really need to cut us some slack here Doc." After the meeting, Dr. Menefee was convinced that none of them was trying very hard.

Questions

1. Describe what happened with each team and why it happened.
2. Was there any social loafing in the teams?
3. Why was Team Two doing better than the other teams?
4. Is giving the same grade to everyone on the team a good idea?

DISCUSSION QUESTIONS

1. Discuss why teams may have an advantage over individuals in decision making and job performance.
2. Which team role champions ideas after they're initiated?
3. Discuss ways to address team members who are social loafers.
4. Discuss some of the cultural differences between individuals on teams.

CHAPTER 8

Group Behavior

LEARNING OUTCOMES: GROUP BEHAVIOR

1. Describe the types of groups.
2. Outline the reasons people join groups.
3. Describe the five states of group development.
4. Explain the punctuated equilibrium model.
5. Discuss the three types of teams.
6. Review the issues critical to team organization and success.
7. Explain groupthink, groupshift, and escalation of commitment.

The Group

Ned and Todd were discussing the new maintenance contract. "I really hate doing business with Crandall Services because they make you wait so long before they do anything," Ned said.

Todd added, "They are not at all friendly, and many times I have had to have them come back and fix jobs they messed up."

"I am definitely not voting for Crandall this time around," said Ned.

"Me either," chimed in Todd.

At the department meeting, Bob, the division head, said, "Let's go with Crandall again because they always give us super service."

Ann replied, "Right you are Bob."

Larry said, "You sure know how to pick a winner in Crandall."

Jane chimed in, "I am all for that."

Bob looked at Todd and Ned and asked, "What about you fellows? Are you in or not?"

Ned and Todd responded, "We are in."

What happened here with Ned and Todd?

Welcome to Group Behavior! ■

Group behavior. Group dynamics. Teams. For business and industry to be successful in today's competitive marketplace, we find a vast majority of businesses going to the team concept with the goal of using everyone's capabilities and knowledge. For this effort to be successful, those involved in teams must understand group behavior and the dynamics of a group.

This chapter explores the types of groups, the reason people join groups, the behavior within groups from the time they come together to the time they separate, and many other critical points of group behavior. We then discuss how a group becomes a team. The chapter is divided into the following sections:

- Types of Groups
- Why Do People Join Groups?
- Group Development
- The Punctuated Equilibrium Model
- Types of Teams
- Team Issues
- Virtual Teams
- A Word of Caution

TYPES OF GROUPS

Let's begin with developing an understanding of what a group is. Social scientists have formally defined a **group** as a collection of two or more interacting individuals with a stable pattern of relationships who share common goals and who perceive themselves as being a group. With this definition, we begin by exploring the two basic types of groups, **formal** and **informal.**[60]

A **group** is a collection of two or more interacting individuals with a stable pattern of relationships who share common goals.

Formal Groups

There are two types of groups, **formal** and **informal.**

The formal group is defined by the organizational structure. Within a company you may have the human resource group, the accounting group, the engineering group, and so on. Each group is identified through an organizational chart. The reporting relationships are formal.

Formal groups may be subdivided into command groups and task groups.

Formal groups are defined by the organizational structure.

- The organizational chart defines **command groups.** As an example, the vice presidents report to the president of the organization. The manufacturing supervisors report to the operations manager. In both examples, the reporting relationship of each group is defined by the organizational structure.

- A **task group** is just that. It is a group formed to complete a task. For example, you may have a group project in a class to make a presentation. Your group would be a task group, because the group is formed to complete the task of making a presentation.

Informal Groups

Informal groups are groups that formed to respond to common interests or social interaction.

Informal groups are simply groups sharing relationships or alliances that are not formally structured or determined by the organizational chart. We will explore two different types of informal groups: interest groups and friendship groups.

- In **interest groups,** we find people working together for a common interest and not because of any organizational chart. A group coming together to support a political candidate, a model train club, and Students Against Drunk Drivers (SADD) are all examples of interest groups. Each group shares a common interest.

- In **friendship groups,** the focus is on people bonding together and sharing common characteristics. This really goes back to motivation theory, where we find that people have a need for affiliation, to feel loved, and to have a sense of belonging.

WHY DO PEOPLE JOIN GROUPS?

Research has identified several reasons people join groups. The primary reasons are

- **Security.** There is strength in numbers. This is why we see coalitions, people who come together to support a cause. By belonging to a group, individuals can feel stronger and know they are not alone. Groups allow individuals to reduce their stress and insecurity by sharing with others.

- **Status.** There is often status associated with joining a group. Inclusion in a certain group is deemed important by others because it provides a sense of identity, recognition, and status. In the college setting, we see men and women joining fraternities, sororities, clubs, and organizations. Why is that? It's fun, it satisfies part of our social needs, and it also gives identity and status.

- **Self-esteem.** As noted earlier, groups can fulfill our social needs. Interaction with others helps us feel needed and appreciated.

- **Power.** This is closely related to the security reason for joining groups. What we often cannot do alone, we can do through the group working together. A sense of synergy adds power to our performance; again, there is strength in numbers.

- **Goal Achievement.** At times a task requires more than one person to accomplish it. By sharing the load, the tasks are broken down into manageable sizes, making the goal easier to attain.
- **Organizational Culture.** Many organizations are team based. Various organizations have found teams to be the preferred mode of operation and have evolved into a team organizational culture. Hewlett-Packard and Johnsonville Sausage are two examples of organizations that embrace this new environment. To be successful within this type of organization, workers are required to become part of a task or command group and must learn how to work in the team environment.

GROUP DEVELOPMENT

When a group comes together, it often goes through a five-stage process of group development,[61] though it doesn't always follow the linear path shown in Figure 8–1. Some groups will go through the stages in a different order or skip some stages, but this is a good general model to describe a group's development. The five stages of the Tuckman Model are forming, storming, norming, performing, and adjourning.

1. **Forming.** The first stage in group development is the realization that by coming together, workers may be better able to meet their individual and collective needs. This often leads people to discover a common goal and develop relationships that will help them better reach their goal. After this initial discovery, the group is formed. In the **forming** stage, group members get to know each other and begin to develop ground rules.

   Forming is characterized by caution, confusion, and uncertainty.

2. **Storming.** Once the group is formed, its members move into the **storming** stage. This stage is characterized by members showing

   Storming is characterized by tension, hostility, and intragroup conflict.

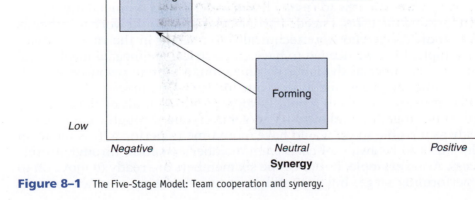

Figure 8–1   The Five-Stage Model: Team cooperation and synergy.

resistance, and perhaps some hostility, to the control of other group members. Group members are struggling to find out how they fit into this new entity. They are trying to find acceptance and explore the need for trust in others. The identification of each person's role starts to take place as members of the group begin to have understanding of and support for one another.

Norming is characterized by establishing group norms and close relationships.

3. **Norming.** From this point the group moves into the **norming** stage. In the norming stage, the group members are learning how to work together. Norms are acceptable standards of behavior shared by the group members. Most norms are informal and are determined by the situation. A group's success and even survival depends on norms, for they allow some predictability of others. Norms increase the group members' satisfaction and help the group develop an identity. Leadership and team member roles are understood, new and the group begins moving toward the transformation to a team.

    It is important to realize the group may revert back to the storming stage for a number of reasons. For example, a member such as a *Seldom seen Steve* does not show up for meetings, or a *Do it all Dottie* tries to do all the work because she doesn't trust the rest of the team, or *Always right Arnie* will not accept or recognize others' ideas or contributions because he believes he has all the answers. Storming sometimes occurs when a new member is added to the group. New norms will develop and old norms are relearned.

Performing is characterized by focusing on the accomplishment of the task.

4. **Performing.** After norming, the group goes to the **performing** stage. In this stage of group development, group members work together to get their job done.

Adjourning is characterized by wrapping up activities and getting closure.

5. **Adjourning.** Once the job or task is completed the group has served its purpose. If the group is a temporary group, it moves into the final stage, **adjourning,** which is when the members of the group wrap up their activities.

In the movie *Seabiscuit*, the group forms behind Charles Howard and then it storms. During the storming stage the jockey, owner, and trainer disagree on the method to train and care for the racehorse, Seabiscuit. The disagreement became so strong that the jockey threatened to leave; however, the group began to norm and finally perform by winning the challenge race and beating the champion racehorse, War Admiral.

A Personal Example

While working at RCA making color televisions, I was asked to put a group together to explore ways we could increase line production without adding any capital expenditures. As the project leader, my task was to bring together the various people I felt were necessary to research our assignment and to make recommendations to our management team. We were given three months to research and make the recommendations.

In forming the team, I needed people who I felt could work together as well as individuals who were technically competent in the various areas. For example, I felt we needed to have an electrical engineer, a mechanical engineer, a member of the labor organization, a human resource specialist, a facilities engineer, and at least one industrial engineer.

Recognizing the group would have to go through all of these stages, I had to put together a plan to try to get everyone through each stage as quickly as possible so we would have more time to perform. It is the team leader's task to be aware of each team member's position throughout this process. As an example, if four of the six members are ready to move on to the performing stage, but you still have two members who are not yet through the storming stage, this will definitely hinder the group's effectiveness and efficiency in trying to complete the tasks. As the group leader, one has to know this process and work to get those two group members through the storming and norming stages. By doing this, it allows them to become part of the team quicker and to become more productive.

One of the very first things I did as the formal leader of the group was to take the group out for dinner just to get everyone to know each other on a personal basis. This helped to eliminate several of the defensive barriers early in the process and allowed us to move on to the norming stage fairly quickly.

In the norming stage, we discussed group member roles, assignments, partnerships, meeting times, communication issues, and other critical aspects for successful completion of the project. Once everyone was through this stage, we were ready to start work. One might ask, "How long does all of this take?" and the answer can certainly vary. It depends on the project, the level of interaction between the members before the assignment, the length given for completion of the project, the frequency the team meets, the synergy developed, and a whole host of other variables.

Once the group was through the norming stage and moved into the performing stage, the effectiveness and efficiency of the group certainly increased. The group actually became a **team.** In this example, a team is defined as a group whose members have complementary skills and are committed to a common purpose or set of performance goals for which they hold themselves mutually accountable.

Teams are organized around work processes rather than functions. Out of this level of cooperation the team will experience **synergy.** The difference between a work group and a work team is the ability to create positive synergy. Synergy is defined as working together in a manner where the total output is greater than the sum of the individual parts. In our example, the work team generated positive synergy through combined effort with the results of the performance being greater than what was possible through any individual effort.

As a result of our team coming together at RCA, we were able to develop a plan and make recommendations that resulted in increasing the production of the number of televisions. The recommendations allowed production to increase from 640 sets per line per day to 968 sets per line per day. We were able to do so without any capital equipment expenditures.

A **team** is a group whose members have complementary skills and are committed to a common purpose or set of performance goals for which they hold themselves mutually accountable.

Synergy is building a force that is greater than the sum of its parts.

The Five Dysfunctions of a Team

Not all groups make the transition to teams. As you have probably experienced by now, it is hard to grow into a group and hard work is required by all group members to make the transition. Patrick Lencioni, in his book, *The Five Dysfunctions of a Team*, outlines five dysfunctions a group will need to overcome to get through the storming stage.[62] They are

■ **Dysfunction** #1. The absence of trust is number one. This essentially stems from the team's unwillingness to be vulnerable within the group. Team members who are not genuinely open with one another about their mistakes and weaknesses make it impossible to build a foundation of trust.[63] Trust lies at the heart of leadership and it also lies at the heart of teams and teamwork. Without trust, teamwork is impossible. Trust is the confidence among team members that their peers' intentions are good and there is no reason to be protective or careful around the group. In essence, teammates must get comfortable being vulnerable with one another. The leader needs to build synergy through the building of relationships that are built on trust.

- **Dysfunction #2.** Fear of conflict. The failure to build trust is damaging because it sets a tone for conflict. Teams that lack trust are incapable of engaging in unfiltered and passionate debate of ideas. Instead, they resort to veiled discussions and guarded comments.

- **Dysfunction #3.** The lack of healthy conflict is a problem because it ensures the third dysfunction of a team: lack of commitment. Without having aired their opinions in the course of passionate and open debate, team members rarely, if ever, buy into and commit to decisions, though they may feign agreement during meetings.

- **Dysfunction #4.** The avoidance of accountability is the fourth dysfunction. Because of this lack of real commitment, team members develop an avoidance of accountability. Without committing to a clear plan of action, even the most focused and driven people often hesitate to call their peers on actions and behaviors that seem counterproductive to the good of the team.

- **Dysfunction #5.** The failure to hold one another accountable creates an environment where inattention to results can thrive. This can occur when team members put their individual needs (such as ego, career development, or recognition) or even the needs of their divisions above the collective goals of the team.

Another way to understand this model is to take the opposite approach—a positive one—and imagine how members of truly cohesive teams behave:

1. They trust one another.
2. They engage in unfiltered conflict around ideas.
3. They commit to decisions and plans of action.
4. They hold one another accountable for delivering results according to plans.
5. They focus on the achievement of collective results.

Once again there are some actions the leader can take to improve the group's transition. For example:

- Provide some sort of mediation resources when conflict becomes difficult for the group to manage.
- Review the mission statement, purpose, and expectations of the group to redefine the organization's action plan.
- Conduct a group decision-making activity.
- Discuss and review the member roles.
- Develop a "rebuilding" team activity.
- Remind everyone that the storming stage is a natural part of the formulation of a group.

THE PUNCTUATED EQUILIBRIUM MODEL

Another model for group development is the punctuated equilibrium model (Figure 8–2). This model focuses on the timing and performance of groups.

According to this model, the first meeting sets the group's direction. Certain behavioral patterns and assumptions emerge in this meeting through the stages of forming, storming, and norming. These patterns of behavior may appear as early as the first few seconds of the group's life and once set, the direction becomes almost indelible. It is unlikely to be reexamined throughout the first half of the group's life. During this period, the

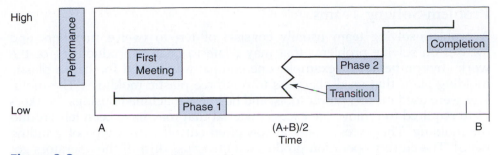

Figure 8–2 The punctuated equilibrium model.

Source: The Punctuated-Equilibrium Model, from "Time and Transition in Work Team: Toward a New Model of Group Development" by C. K. G. Gersick, *Academy of Management Journal*, 31(1), 1988, pp. 9–41. Copyright 1988 by Academy of Management. Reproduced with permission of the Academy of Management in the format Textbook via Copyright Clearance Center.

group tends to stand still or become locked into a fixed course of action. Even if it gains new insights that challenge initial patterns and assumptions, the group is incapable of acting on these new insights in this first phase.

At some point the group goes through a transition. This brings the team to Phase 2 of the project where the team is more productive. This phase is characterized by a final burst of activity to complete the team's work, moving it to the performing stage in group development.

One of the most interesting discoveries made in these studies was that each group experiences its transition at the same point in its calendar—precisely halfway between its first meeting and its official deadline—despite the fact that some groups spent as little as an hour on their project while others spent six months or longer. It's at the midpoint that the groups universally experience a **midlife crisis.** This midpoint functions like an alarm clock, creating a sense of awareness and urgency that time is limited and the group needs to "get in gear."

This model can be used to describe some of the experiences with student teams and term projects. At the first meeting, introductions occur, a timetable is established, and work assignments often are made. The group members evaluate each other and form opinions; however, these most often are not shared. From this point the group may agree to meet on a regular basis to carry out its activities; however, not much happens until about half of the allotted time has passed. At this point there is a renewed sense of urgency, discussion becomes more open, and the group moves aggressively to make the necessary changes. If the right changes are made, the next phase of time finds the group developing a first-rate project. The group's last meeting, which will probably occur just before the project is due, lasts longer than the others and is much more productive than previous meetings. In this meeting, all final issues are discussed and details resolved. When the project is complete, the group moves to the adjourning stage of group development.

In summary, the punctuated equilibrium model certainly possesses a challenge to look for ways to improve group performance earlier in the cycle. The long periods of inertia interspersed with a brief renewed sense of urgency by the members' awareness of time and deadlines invite teams to explore new alternatives to improve performance sooner in the timeline of the project.

TYPES OF TEAMS

Let us take what we know so far about the group process and see how this applies to specific types of teams. The three different types of teams are problem-solving teams, cross-functional work teams, and self-managed work teams (sometimes referred to as self-directed work teams).

There are three types of teams:
- Problem-solving
- Cross-functional
- Self-managed

Problem-Solving Teams

A problem-solving team usually consists of ten to twelve members and focuses on solving problems that may relate to quality, productivity, or the work environment. For example, one company I worked for had a plastic molding plant that used fiberglass to reinforce plastic moldings. The moldings were used in cars, power tools, and business machine housings. Workers were required to remove the excess material that may have been left around the molding. This excess material was often cut off with a type of grinding wheel. The cutting operation produced a fiberglass dust. If the operators got the dust on their arms, they would itch from the fiberglass particles. A "Dust Team" was formed to help address the dust problem. They were a very popular team, and they made a big difference in the working environment.

Cross-Functional Work Teams

A cross-functional team brings together workers from different areas, functions, and even levels of the organization to focus on a task. The example given earlier in this chapter of the team coming together to look at ways to increase the line production for the manufacture of televisions is a good example of a cross-functional work team.

Self-Managed Work Teams

The self-managed work team, also known as a *self-directed work team*, usually is made up of ten to fifteen workers who take over management of the process. The team may also take over many of the responsibilities of their former supervisors and managers.[64] In the book *The Flight of the Buffalo*, author Ralph Stayer tells of employee teams at Johnsonville Sausage taking over the reigns of management. Employee teams did the hiring, firing, budgeting, scheduling, and other tasks normally done by supervisors. This raises the question, "What happens to the supervisors?" For one thing, not as many are needed, which lowers costs. Supervisors become trainers, teachers, coaches, and mentors to the teams. As business continues to reduce costs through greater employee involvement in decision making, empowerment of employees through self-directed work teams may very well be the trend of the future.

While the concept of self-managed work teams is admirable, research has produced some surprising findings.[65] While employee job satisfaction seems to be higher in the self-managed work team, employees also seem to have higher absenteeism and turnover rates than the traditional organizational structure.

TEAM ISSUES

Listed here are eleven issues that are integral to team organization and success.

Size	Leadership
Team Skills	Reward Systems
Authority	Group Decision Making
Geography	Team Meetings
Goals	Trust
Timing	

Size

The size of a team will affect the team's overall behavior. Problem-solving teams seem to generate more and better solutions with ten to twelve members. The diversity, varied experiences, multiple skills, and judgment of the larger number prove to be an advantage. However, smaller teams tend to be more effective and efficient in completing a task. Teams of five to seven members seem to provide the best elements of both small and large groups.[66] A team that is too large invites **social loafing** by members within the group.[67] Social loafing is the tendency for individuals to put forth just enough effort to get by when working with others. They don't carry their fair share of the workload, and others in the group must make up the difference.

Team Skills

Any team that is formed should have three functions represented with at least one member representing each function: technical expertise, problem solving, and communicating.[68]

Authority

Whenever the leadership sees the need to create teams, there must be a conscious effort to staff the team with the expertise and authority to achieve the team's goals and objectives. Without the proper authority, the team will become frustrated and ineffective.

Geography

The advent of technology in the form of electronic communication expands the team opportunity to the worldwide arena. It is feasible and encouraged to link widely diverse elements of global organizations through teams. Ford Motor Company first developed the forerunners for the Contour and Mystique passenger cars in Europe. The electronic link was a cost-effective methodology to transfer information from Europe to the United States.

Goals

One of the major reasons teams experience diminished success is due to vague and unclear direction. Even the best people in an organization will function ineffectively without clear goals.

Timing

Teams function most effectively and efficiently with a clear agenda that assigns responsibility with an equally clear time line. Teams take time to develop and emerge as one productive unit. To reduce the time needed to make the transition to a team, many organizations will provide team assignments through training or exercises to enhance team members' dependency on one another.

Leadership

Teams are not unlike any other successful organization with regard to leadership. However, many leaders are not equipped to handle the change to teams. New skills such as patience, communications, working through committees, giving up authority, and learning to deal with others outside their normal realm of influence suddenly become critical. Committees that go nowhere can often trace their ineffectiveness to a lack of team leadership. While the leadership function may not be assigned to any one individual in a team situation, strong and competent leadership is necessary for a team to succeed. Some teams may allow leadership to emerge as needed, others may assign a leader based on the situation or task, or management may assign others to fulfill the leadership function. Leaders of teams often find themselves in the role of team facilitator.

Reward Systems

Typical reward systems in many organizations provide recognition and reinforcement for the leader or the leadership element. In a team setting, rewards should be shared with the entire team. In fact, make an effort to celebrate with team recognition and rewards. A plaque with the team members' names along with individual plaques recognizing each team member reinforces the team's cohesiveness.

Group Decision Making

Teamwork implies group decision making, a process that is risky and challenges accountability. However, numerous studies support the advantages of group decision making as normally being superior to individual decision making, especially when the decision is enhanced by the application of diverse skills, judgment, and experience.[69] With group decision making, more information and knowledge through the shared experiences and education is available. More diverse views are shared increasing the quality of the decision making. Decision making through consensus increases the legitimacy of the decision; however, group decision making is more time consuming and there is increased pressure on the minority to conform.

Team Meetings

Due to the nature of multiple members, team meetings are often necessary to ensure adequate communication and allocation of resources that are being used. Meetings need to have a purpose and focus. To make team meetings more effective there are several things the team leadership can do. For example, prepare a meeting agenda and distribute the agenda in advance. Through the availability of e-mail, this can be done electronically with assignments for reports sent to all the team members prior to the meeting. Establish specific time parameters and keep the discussion focused. As the leader, encourage and support participation of all the members. Have someone keep the minutes of the meeting and make them available for review by the rest of the team members immediately after meeting

Trust

Of all the issues that influence success and team efficiency, trust is the most significant.[70] Without team trust, the quality of the teamwork will suffer. Some organizations have gone to elaborate means to create a sense of trust among the team players. A popular trust-building demonstration is a game staged between two potential team players using a ladder as a prop. One participant is asked to climb the ladder three or four rungs to a small platform. The team partner stands at ground level behind the person on the ladder, out of eyesight. The team member on the platform is then blindfolded. The team member on the ground asks the elevated partner to fall backward, assuring that he or she will protect the other from any injury that could result from the fall. In virtually every case apprehension is visibly evident, especially among strangers. People do not want to risk their personal safety unless trust has been developed.

The trust equation suggests that we should be willing to share dependency, but that willingness does not come without a price. Team members will generally trust other team members who they do not personally know if those team members are part of a larger common bond.

Teams that develop and maintain high levels of trust have several expectations from their team members. As demonstrated in the ladder exercise, a significant expectation is the feeling of **dependency,** given a particular situation. I have confidence that you, my team member, will react in a way I can **predict.** Further, if you tell me something, I can believe you because team members deal with one another **ethically** and with **integrity.** The team becomes a family within a family.

The ladder exercise also demonstrates a need for **competence** if the exercise is to be successful. If the person on the ladder feels the team member who is selected to be the safety net is either too small or too weak to accomplish the task, it doesn't matter how ethical or loyal that person may be. Trust will not be developed. Likewise, if we create a team where one or more of the team members do not have the experience, education, or abilities to participate, trust will be diminished. For example, the plant nurse may be a poor team member if the task is to discover innovative ways to revise circuit boards.

VIRTUAL TEAMS

Virtual teams are emerging with the advent of new technology in communication and teleconferencing capabilities. By virtual, it is meant that electronics are used to enable the flow of information.[71] A virtual team is a group of people using technology to communicate and function as a team while working from different locations. This means the team members may be in the same building or located any place in the world. As such the virtual teams' meetings are in a virtual office; however, occasional face-to-face meetings are encouraged to avoid a feeling of isolation. Virtual teams can be incredibly successful; however, virtual teams need to develop trust and a sense of identity among the team members.

A **virtual team** is a group of people using technology to communicate and function as a team while working from different locations.

A WORD OF CAUTION

Organizations are forming teams at an ever-increasing rate. The evidence suggests cost advantages to using teams. Workers also find that many social and job satisfaction needs are met in teams. However, we need to understand several disadvantages as we discuss teams. Three of these disadvantages are **groupthink, groupshift,** and **escalation of commitment.**

Groupthink

Groupthink is a type of thinking in which team members share such strong motivation to achieve consensus that they lose the ability to evaluate alternative points of views critically. With groupthink:

- Group members rationalize any resistance to the assumptions they have made.
- Group members apply direct pressure on those who express doubts about any of the group's shared views or they question the validity of arguments that support the alternative favored by the majority.

Groupthink occurs when group conformity overrides reality.

- Group members who have doubts or hold differing points of views seek to avoid deviating from what appears to be group consensus by keeping silent about misgivings and even minimizing to themselves the importance of their doubts.
- There appears to be an illusion of unanimity. If someone doesn't speak, it is assumed that he or she is in full accord. Abstention becomes viewed as agreement with the group's decision.

How can a group prevent groupthink? Here are several suggestions to minimize this problem:

- Groups that are highly cohesive and have more discussion seem to have less groupthink. Promote open discussion.
- Groups with impartial leaders who encourage member input generate more discussion with alternative solutions.
- Leaders should avoid expressing a preferred solution early in the group's discussion because this tends to limit critical analysis.
- The group should not be insulated, or the group will generate and evaluate fewer alternatives.
- Use **brainstorming.** Get team members to generate all kinds of ideas (even crazy ones) without stopping to censor or evaluate any of the ideas. After the list of ideas has been generated, the team goes back to evaluate each idea.

Groupshift

Groupshift occurs because of a lack of individual responsibility, which causes the group shifts to become more conservative or more risky.

Working in groups can take away individual responsibility. As a result, sometimes groups may act more extreme than individuals, either more risky or more conservative.[72] This often happens when a core of the group takes an extreme position toward greater conservatism or greater risk and the rest of the group goes along with it.

Escalation of Commitment

Escalation of commitment is staying with a course of action beyond where it is reasonable.

Escalation of commitment is a tendency to stay committed to a chosen course of action even though feedback indicates otherwise.[73] In spite of negative feedback or information that does not support your decision to continue, one is compelled to give it another try. As an example, what if you buy a used car for $3,500? You know the car needs new brakes and will require another $200 to fix. You invest the $200 and fix the brakes. You then notice the car needs a new set of tires costing another $300. Of course you need the latest in CD players, so you decide to spend another $500 for the sound system. All of a sudden, you have $4,500 invested in the car. When driving the car you notice it seems to be pulling to the left. You have this checked out and you are told the steering mechanism is shot and you need new shocks. You find out this is going to cost another $1,000. The escalation of commitment principle indicates there is a very strong tendency to go ahead and invest another $1,000 to "save" the $4,500 you already have invested. The commitment escalates with each new expenditure.

Good decision makers will recognize when escalation of commitment is occurring and know when to call it quits. In doing so, they recognize that they need to make the best decision for the current situation regardless of the costs that may have been incurred in the past.

SUMMARY

Groups can be classified as formal groups and informal groups. Formal groups are defined by the organizational structure and can be either command groups based on the organizational chart or task groups formed to complete a project.

The reasons people join groups are for security, status, power, goal achievement, and organizational culture.

The process of group development is based on five stages:

- Forming is realizing that people will be working together in a group.
- Storming is the conflict that occurs in building a group.
- Norming is setting acceptable standards of behavior.
- Performing is doing the task.
- Adjourning is ending the group.

A time base model of group development is the punctuated equilibrium model, which is based on improving performance over time from the first meeting to the transition period to the completion.

There are three types of teams:

- Problem-solving teams that focus on solving problems.
- Cross-functional teams that include workers from different areas that focus on a task.
- Self-managed teams that manage a process.

Eleven issues are important to team organization and success: size, team skills, authority, geography, goals, timing, leadership, reward systems, group decision making, team meetings, and trust.

A virtual team is a group of people using technology to communicate and function as a team while working from different locations.

Three problems with using teams are groupthink (desire to get a consensus), groupshift (lack of individual responsibility), and escalation of commitment (staying with a bad plan).

CASE STUDY

The community was becoming aware that it had a problem with gangs in the neighborhoods. There had been a carjacking by a teen with a gun. Graffiti had started to appear on people's houses and garages. The markings were distinctive and were associated with two gangs. The two gangs were the Bad Boys and the Losers. The Bad Boys were associated with blacks and whites who had lived in the community for some time. The Bad Boys were more of a nuisance or a right of passage gang until their neighborhood had an influx of Hispanics. The Hispanics, wanting to establish themselves, had formed the Losers. The Bad Boys, feeling the pressure of a new gang, refused to back down. You could sense the friction in the community as each gang tried to recruit new members and establish their turf. What had been an occasional school fight had escalated to drive-by shootings aimed at rival gang members. Although no one had been hurt so far in these drive-by shootings, the violence was starting to spread to ordinary citizens. People were being robbed, harassed, and threatened by gangs. Property had been vandalized and some cars had been stolen.

After many letters to both City Hall and the newspaper, the city officials agreed to have a meeting on gang activity with the public invited. The meeting was set for 2 P.M. on a Wednesday, in April, in City Hall chambers. As the officials sat down for the meeting, they noticed there were only a few people present and most of them were senior citizens. The senior citizens expressed concerns over graffiti on their houses, purse snatchings, and break-ins. The officials decided that it was a problem for senior citizens and promised more patrols in the neighborhoods where they lived. The next day the newspaper reported the gang problem was minimal and senior citizens would be protected.

The newspaper and the city government immediately were criticized by the citizens for not addressing the whole problem of gangs and minimizing gang activity. The city officials fired back that they had held a meeting on gang activity and only a few people came. The citizens fired back that not many people could attend a meeting held at 2 P.M. on a Wednesday. One man wrote that he had to work for a living not like the lazy bunch of do-nothing politicians at City Hall. While the war of words continued between the public and the city, gang activity increased and a woman was shot in a drive-by shooting on her own porch.

This act brought more pressure on people to get together and deal with the issue of gang violence. The city officials agreed to hold a night meeting on Wednesday night. The churches protested that move as it interfered with mid-week services. The meeting was moved to Tuesday and the group met at City Hall. It became apparent that City Hall was going to be too small for the crowd that came. The meeting was then moved to a school auditorium. After two hours of hearing from a variety of people, it was decided that something needed to be done about gang violence. A second meeting was set for the next Tuesday night to continue the discussion.

The next meeting generated much hot discussion between the various parties. Some people argued that the gang members were just misguided children that needed love and affection. Others claimed that the gang members were nothing more than hoodlums and that vigilante groups should be formed to hunt them down. Many references were made to the *Death Wish* movies in which the hero takes back the streets by killing off gang members. Many people indicated they had guns and were not afraid to use them. Others were advocating more peaceful approaches to deal with the gangs. Others were afraid of being caught in the crossfire of the rival gangs and the vigilantes. After two hours of arguing and debate, a third meeting was set to go over how things should be done.

The third meeting brought back many people determined to find out how to address the gang problem. It was decided by the group that one person should speak at a time. The police reminded people not to take the law into their own hands. The public agreed to do that unless they were personally attacked and had to defend themselves. The group agreed to search for solutions that made their community a better place to live by removing the gangs or at least minimizing their impact on the community. This two-hour session clearly established the ground rules for future meetings and helped to solidify the group.

A fourth session was held that aimed at coming up with a plan to minimize gang influence and violence. The police said they could use any help from the community they could get. The citizens suggested neighborhood watch groups that would report suspicious activity to the police. The police agreed to check out any reports from these neighborhood watch teams. School officials agreed to watch activities in and around the schools and the police volunteered their help in monitoring schools, especially the junior high and high schools. Parents said they would talk to their children about gangs and monitor them for any gang-type activity. Homeowners agreed to paint over graffiti and help their older and poorer neighbors keep graffiti off their property. Everyone agreed to try all these suggestions and see how things went.

After two months, the crime and the graffiti were clearly down. The police were using tips to pursue gang members and put them in detention. The schools were suspending students for gang and violent activity. Parents were watching the activities of their children more closely. Churches and youth organizations began to work more with youth and to provide more after-school opportunities. The city recreation department started forming teams in various sports that students could participate in after school and during the summer. The neighborhood watch groups were working to reduce crime in the neighborhoods and graffiti. The situation was clearly improving and the members of the group felt future meetings would not be necessary unless things changed. All of the members of the group agreed to keep doing what they had promised. The group disbanded with the knowledge they had made a positive difference.

Questions

1. When did forming occur for this group?
2. What do you suppose storming looked like for this group?
3. What was accomplished in the norming stage?
4. What happened in the performing stage?
5. Why did the group decide to adjourn?

DISCUSSION QUESTIONS

1. Analyze the key issues at each stage of the group development process.

2. Apply Tuckman's five-stage theory of group development to a group to which you belong. Discuss ways you can recognize these stages of group development.

3. Discuss various ways to recognize groupthink.

4. Discuss ways to overcome the problem of groupthink.

CHAPTER 9

Leadership

LEARNING OUTCOMES: LEADERSHIP

1. Discuss the trait theories of leadership.

2. Explain the behavioral theories for understanding leadership.

3. Describe Fiedler's contingency model for leading.

4. Outline the Hersey and Blanchard Situational Leadership® theory.

5. Describe the characteristics of the charismatic leader.

6. Contrast the differences between transactional and transformational leaders.

7. Through self-assessment, gain a greater understanding of one's own leadership style.

Name: _____

Section Number: _____

SELF-ASSESSMENT TEST

Please complete the following exercise online, accessible with the Access Card packaged with this text, before reading this chapter.

EXERCISE II.B.1:   **WHAT'S MY**
LEADERSHIP STYLE?   **People Score** _____

  Task Score _____

This leadership instrument taps the degree to which you are task or people oriented. Task orientation is concerned with getting the job done, while people orientation focuses on group interactions and the needs of individual members. The best leaders balance their task–people orientation to various situations. A high score on both would indicate this balance.

If you are too task oriented, you tend to be autocratic. You get the job done, but at a high emotional cost. If you are too people oriented, your leadership may be overly laissez-faire. The best leaders are those that can balance their task–people orientation.

EXERCISE II.B.4:   **DO OTHERS SEE ME**
AS TRUSTWORTHY?   **Score** _____

Effective leaders have built a trusting relationship between themselves and those they see to lead. This instrument provides you with insights into how trustworthy others are likely to perceive you. The higher the score, the more you are perceived as a person who can be trusted. If you want to build trust with others, look at the behaviors this instrument taps, then think about what you can do to improve your score on each.

You should also record your score on this exercise in Appendix 1.

NOTES

The Leaders

Van works as head of the parts department of Acme Company. His job is to make sure that all the production lines have all the parts they need and to maintain the parts inventory. Van has twelve employees working for him. The employees are basically unskilled, and many have been assigned here because they do not fit in anywhere else. The educational level of this department is the lowest in the company.

Tom, who was in the same high school class as his friend Van, is head of the research and development department. He also has twelve employees. Five of his employees have Ph.D.s, five have master's degrees, and two have bachelor's degrees, including the laboratory technician and the secretary. This is by far the best educated department in the company.

Van and Tom were having lunch when the topic of leadership came up.

Van was quick to say, "You really need to ride herd, let them know who is boss, and tell them what to do to get the work done."

Tom disagreed, "You have to give them the opportunity to succeed, create a friendly and supportive environment, and make sure you are there for them when they need you."

Van said, "What are you talking about? I have to supervise these people constantly to keep them from fouling up."

Tom responded, "I check on them occasionally, but I trust them to get the jobs done."

Van replied, "If I acted like you, I would be looking for a new job!"

Tom replied, "If I acted like you, I wouldn't have any staff!"

Who is right in how to lead people?

Welcome to Leadership! ■

"The problem with most leaders today is they don't stand for anything. Leadership implies movement toward something and convictions provide that direction. If you don't stand for something, you'll fall for anything."

—Don Shula, former NFL coach[74]

It really doesn't matter how smart you may be in spotting problems or how brilliant you are with generating great ideas on what needs to be done to move your organization forward: very little will happen if you can't get those who you work with to accept what you have in mind. It requires leadership.

The concept of leadership and the application and demonstration of leadership in an organization is central to the health and prosperity of that organization. In a survey of more than 750 readers of *Chief Executive* magazine, the Center for Creative Leadership found that CEOs believe good leadership is critical to a company's success.[75] Nearly 79 percent of the respondents ranked leadership as one of the five most critical factors in achieving a competitive advantage. In this same survey nine out of ten of the CEOs surveyed saw the development of leaders to be an important personal responsibility. Another survey by Robert Half International found 53 percent of managers questioned considered leadership and motivational skills the most important talent a manager should have. Sixty-six percent said they possessed "limited motivational skills but only 12 percent thought they excelled.[76] People management skills and other "soft" skills, many of which we cover in this text, are indeed hard skills to learn.

Leadership is the art and science of getting the job done through the willing efforts of others. With this definition, the essence of leadership is to influence other people's behavior toward certain goals or objectives. Leaders articulate and define what has previously remained implicit or unsaid. They invent images, metaphors, and models that provide focus for movement and change. They preach the vision. They lead by example. **Leadership is active.** It is present or it is absent. To say that a person is a poor leader or that an organization lacks leadership simply means that there is a leadership void.

Are leaders managers, or conversely, are managers leaders? In either case the answer may be yes or no. We all strive to be that person who is both a successful leader and a successful manager. Generally, we would like to work for or report to someone who is both. Leadership is an ability, the art of being able to influence, while management is a process. Oprah Winfrey's audience watches her program because of a respect for Oprah. She is clearly considered an influential person and probably is seen as a leader. The producer and director of the television program are responsible for the planning, organizing, directing, and controlling of the production assets that make the show successful. They are the skillful managers. Influencing the actors and cast members to extend themselves in their performance to make it believable is leadership.

We will consider and investigate the following leadership theories:

- Trait theory
- Behavioral theory
- The contingency approach
- Some contemporary approaches to leadership

TRAIT THEORY

The **trait theory** of leadership focuses on an individual's personal attributes, which suggest a particular leadership style. Some may say that certain individuals are *born leaders*. Why is a particular student elected class president? What are the characteristics of the football and basketball team captains that distinguish them from their teammates? What criteria do students use to select a team leader for a class project? When you reflect on these examples, you may respond that the people chosen just seemed to be the right person for the job. They demonstrated traits or characteristics that fit the image of what a leader should be.

Table 9–1 includes a short list of typical leadership traits and individual examples. This list, while not all-inclusive, illustrates the trait concept.

BEHAVIORAL THEORY

Trait theory is descriptive; however, taken alone, it fails to consider how leaders interact with their followers. If we were to subscribe to trait theory, then we would simply review a cast of 50 and single out those men and women who appear to be born with desirable leadership traits.

The transition from what leaders *seem to be* to what leaders *do* opened the door to the study of the behavioral approach. The behavioral approach lends credibility to the belief that leadership may be learned. Rudy Giuliani,

Leadership is the ability to influence others.

Trait theory focuses on an individual's personal attributes.

Behavioral theory focuses on what leaders do.

Table 9–1 Typical Leadership Traits

Leadership Trait	Individual Example
Ambition and energy	FDNY
	Martin Luther King, Jr.
Desire to lead	Barack Obama
	John McCain
Honesty and integrity	Mother Teresa
	Rudy Giuliani
Self-confidence	Bill O'Reilly (Fox News)
	Rosa Parks
Intelligence	Albert Einstein
	Warren Buffett
Job-relevant knowledge	Steve Jobs
	Oprah Winfrey

mayor of New York during the September 11 terrorist attack, says, "Leadership does not simply happen. It can be taught, learned, developed."[77]

Studies conducted at the Ohio State University (OSU)[78] and at the University of Michigan (UM)[79] are frequently cited as landmark studies that introduced behavioral leadership thinking. These two studies introduced the concept of task and relationship. This concept endures today. A third behavioral model that we will discuss is the **Management Grid.**

*The OSU and UM studies introduced the concept of **task** and **relationship.***

The Ohio State University Study

The researchers identified two leader behavior characteristics:

- **Initiating Structure.** The leader has a clear orientation toward mission or task accomplishment.
- **Consideration.** We might commonly call these leaders *people persons*. The leaders that display this behavior are friendly, open, and concerned about the well-being of their followers.

Consider the following examples from two motion pictures. In the movie *Saving Private Ryan*, General George C. Marshall, the supreme military head of all U.S. forces in World War II, demonstrates a compassion for Private Ryan and his family over the recent loss of his three brothers in combat. That movie scene illustrates a compassionate Marshall demonstrating **consideration.** In another movie example, Colonel Jessup, the fiery Marine Corps commander in *A Few Good Men*, appears to be the opposite of General Marshall. Personal considerations do not influence Colonel Jessup's decisions; his focus is mission accomplishment. Colonel Jessup, while fictional, presents an example of a leader exhibiting **initiating structure** behavior.

University of Michigan Study

This research is similar to the Ohio State University study identifying these behavioral characteristics:

- **Production oriented.** Get the job done.
- **Employee oriented.** While it may be important to accomplish the task, those that displayed this behavior were found to place a high priority on the needs of their followers.

The Managerial Grid

The final behavioral theory model discussed is the Managerial Grid, which was created by Blake and Mouton. The authors, through the use of surveys and inventories, charted various leader behaviors. If a company, business, or organization were to subscribe to the use of this tool, the results could reveal leadership deficiencies that need attention. Recall that the behavioral approach suggests that leaders may be molded, developed, or perhaps even homegrown, an attitude that leadership is a learning experience.

The grid is not an abstract idea or concept that is rarely discussed outside the hallowed halls of academia. United Airlines provides a case in point. Some time ago, the decision makers at United created a leadership education program that focused on the team activity in a typical airliner cockpit. While it is properly recognized that the captain is in charge and is ultimately responsible, United was seeking to improve the team relationships in a functioning work environment.

One of the instruments used in United's program is the **Managerial Grid** (Figure 9–1). The Grid becomes a useful tool as crew members address issues of experience, conflict, and team building in the cockpit.

In a broader sense suppose a supervisor completed a survey and scored 9,1 (Authority-obedience) on the grid. The grid finding suggests the supervisor could benefit from education to improve her people skills. Because the evaluation points to a less-than-desirable score in the interpersonal skills area, perhaps the supervisor would reevaluate her ability to communicate with those under her leadership. Perhaps training in

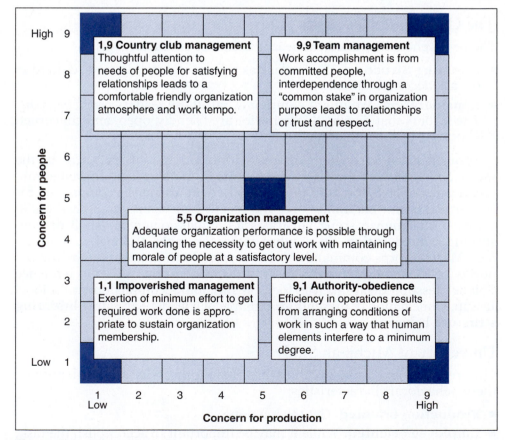

Figure 9–1 The managerial grid.

Source: The Managerial Grid. Reprinted by permission of *Harvard Business Review.* An exhibit from "Breakthrough in Organizational Development" by R. R. Blak, J. S. Mouton, L. B. Bares, and L. E. Greiner, November/December 1964. Copyright © 1964 by the President and Fellows of Harvard College. All rights reserved.

delegation, motivation, and managing conflict would provide a greater balance between the directive behavior and the supportive behavior.

CONTINGENCY THEORY

As leadership theory continued to mature, it became clear that a significant leadership dimension was being ignored. That dimension is the **situation.** Linking the situation with the leader's behavior and with the follower's attitude creates the **contingency theory.** We offer two applications of the contingency theory. They are the contingency model and the situation leadership theory.

The Contingency Model

Fred Fiedler, in his book, *A Theory of Leadership Effectiveness*, studied the interaction of leader style (behavior) and the leader-follower situation. Fiedler postulates the following from his study.

- A leader's style is either task oriented or relationship oriented.
- A leader's style or behavior is fixed and there is relatively little change in the leader's style over time.
- The situation is not fixed and may be altered to fit a particular leader style.
- Since style is relatively fixed and since Fiedler believes the situation may be altered, he argues that careful consideration must be given to the leadership situation when selecting and matching the leaders to tasks.

Fiedler explains the interaction of these postulates with the creation of the contingency model. The model has three elements, each of which is related to the leader-follower situation.

Part 1 is **position power,** the degree to which a leader's position enables the leader to ensure compliance. For example, there is no question as to the authority of a head football coach. While he may delegate play calling, he may also step in at any point and change the activity. Most coaches routinely take charge late in a close game, and no one argues. They exhibit strong or high position power. On the other hand, consider an ad hoc committee of students representing the fourth floor of a dorm. By a majority vote, the group chooses committee member Jack to act as chairperson. If committee members subsequently choose to be inattentive and late to meetings or fail to accomplish a particular task, Jack has little authority to issue sanctions. Jack has weak or low position power.

Part 2 is **task structure,** the degree of clarity for goal accomplishment. There is no question that the goal of the football team is to win the game. This is a case of high task structure. The dorm committee's goal, however, is not always clear. Vagueness may exist, a situation of low task structure.

Part 3 is **leader-member relations.** What is the nature of the relationship between the leader and the members? Michael Jordan said publicly and privately he would only play for Coach Phil Jackson and the Chicago Bulls. This is a demonstration of good leader-member relations. Conversely, Dan Reeves in the early 1990s was the head coach of the Denver Broncos, ironically his opponent in the 1999 Super Bowl when he was head coach of the Atlanta Falcons. The media reported that the Denver Broncos were never Super Bowl winners under Reeves's leadership. The media further reported that the relationship between Reeves and John Elway, the Broncos' quarterback, was anything but cordial, a classic example of poor leader-member relations.

Fiedler proposes that organizational situations can be measured. Is the leader's position power strong or weak? Is the group task structure high or low? Are leader-member relations good or poor? Fiedler charts these relationships as shown in Table 9–2.

The **contingency model** links the situation with the concept of task and relationship.

There are three elements of the leader-follower contingency model:
- Position power
- Task structure
- Leader-member relations

Table 9-2 Situation Leader Match

SITUATION/ OCTANTS	I	II	III	IV	V	VI	VII	VIII
LEADER-MEMBER RELATIONS	GOOD	GOOD	GOOD	GOOD	POOR	POOR	POOR	POOR
TASK STRUCTURE	HIGH	HIGH	LOW	LOW	HIGH	HIGH	LOW	LOW
POSITION POWER	STRONG	WEAK	STRONG	WEAK	STRONG	WEAK	STRONG	WEAK
Therefore, the actual situation is	FAVOR-ABLE	FAVOR-ABLE	FAVOR-ABLE	MODER-ATE	MODER-ATE	MODER-ATE	UNFAVOR-ABLE	UNFAVOR-ABLE
The recomended style is	TASK	TASK	TASK	RELA-TIONS	RELA-TIONS	RELA-TIONS	TASK	TASK

KEY

MODERATE = Moderately Favorable

TASK = Task-Oriented

RELATIONS = Relationship-Oriented

Situation Leader Match adapted from *A Theory of Leadership Effectiveness* by Fred E. Fiedler, McGraw-Hill, 1967, p. 34. Used by permission of Fred E. Fiedler.

In the first three octants, leader-member relations are good while task structure and position power vary. In these cases, the leadership situation is favorable and a task-oriented leader should be successful. In octant II, the well-liked team member, who has no real position of appointed authority, can orient on the task without much argument from the team members. Perhaps this is why a well-liked team member can pick up the slack in the absence of the appointed leader. Try to visualize a scenario to fit the other seven situations (octants).

Recall that Fiedler suggested that knowing a leader's style becomes the critical path. He further proposed that a leader's style is relatively fixed. So just how do we discover the style? Fiedler created a short survey that measures leadership style. Follow the instructions on the following sample survey and measure your style before proceeding.

Fiedler proposes that a leader's style is fixed.

Least Preferred Coworker (LPC) Survey

*The **LPC Survey** measures a leader's style.*

Think of the one person with whom you can work *least well*. He or she may be someone you work with now, or he or she may be someone that you worked with in the past. He or she does not have to be the person you like least well, but should be the person with whom you had the most difficulty in getting a job done. This person may be a former supervisor, peer, or subordinate.

Rate this person as he or she appears to you on a scale from 1 to 8 for the sixteen attributes listed in Table 9–3 and then sum the scores. Be alert; the scale changes periodically. The result is your LPC or Least Preferred Coworker score.

Fiedler tells us that those who score low view their least preferred coworker unfavorably. This leader will likely have a task-oriented style, while those who score high see their least preferred coworker in a more favorable way and are likely to be relationship oriented. A single survey or inventory without other supporting evidence is, of course, weak at best.

Table 9–3 Least Preferred Coworker Survey

Pleasant	8	7	6	5	4	3	2	1	Unpleasant
Friendly	8	7	6	5	4	3	2	1	Unfriendly
Rejecting	1	2	3	4	5	6	7	8	Accepting
Helpful	8	7	6	5	4	3	2	1	Frustrating
Unenthusiastic	1	2	3	4	5	6	7	8	Enthusiastic
Tense	1	2	3	4	5	6	7	8	Relaxed
Distant	1	2	3	4	5	6	7	8	Close
Cold	1	2	3	4	5	6	7	8	Warm
Cooperative	8	7	6	5	4	3	2	1	Uncooperative
Supportive	8	7	6	5	4	3	2	1	Hostile
Boring	1	2	3	4	5	6	7	8	Interesting
Quarrelsome	1	2	3	4	5	6	7	8	Harmonious
Self-Assured	8	7	6	5	4	3	2	1	Hesitant
Efficient	8	7	6	5	4	3	2	1	Inefficient
Gloomy	1	2	3	4	5	6	7	8	Cheerful
Open	8	7	6	5	4	3	2	1	Guarded

Source: Least Preferred Coworker Survey, adapted from *A Theory of Leadership Effectiveness* by Fred E. Fiedler, McGraw Hill, 1967, p. 268–269. Used by permission of Fred E. Fiedler.

Sum your responses and record the score _____.

However, scores less than 40 tend to be low LPC, while scores over 60 represent a tendency to high LPC.

The next step is to match the leader to a particular situation. Favorable and unfavorable situations are suited to task-oriented leaders while moderately favorable situations are suited to relationship-oriented leaders. Since leader style, according to Fiedler, is fixed, we merely alter the situation to suit the leader's style. If a task-oriented leader faces a situation counter to his style, then Fiedler tells us to change the situation. Options include:

- Replace the task-oriented leader with a relationship-oriented leader.
- Make an adjustment to either the leader's task structure or position power, or alternatively, adjust both.

The essence of Fiedler's work is that we can alter the situation to fit the leader. This is necessary since a leader's style is relatively fixed.

Situational Leadership® Model*

Ken Blanchard and Paul Hersey view the contingency theory differently than Fiedler. Their concept, **the Situational Leadership® theory,** focuses on the follower. The follower's ability and his willingness to accomplish a task are the central leadership issues that guide the behavior of a leader. Hersey and Blanchard believe that a leader can and will adjust his or her behavior and style as follower ability and willingness changes. They identify the following four flexible leadership styles.

The **Situational Leadership®** **model** proposes that a leader's style is flexible and may be adjusted to fit the situation.

1. **Directive/Telling, Style 1 (S1).** The leader is specific as to the actions to be taken to accomplish particular tasks. Some consider this authoritarian leadership, the sort of thing we visualize that goes on in a military entry level training unit. This is high task and low relationship.

*Situational Leadership® is the registered trademark of the Center for Leadership Studies, Inc. www. situational.com

2. **Coaching/Selling (S2).** The leader continues to be task specific. However, the leader role becomes one of encouragement for the follower. An example is an employer's actions toward a new employee his first day on the job. This demonstrates high task and high relationship. This style approximates the 9,9 leader from the Blake and Mouton managerial grid.

3. **Participating/Supporting (S3).** The leader and the subordinate share in the decision making. The leader seeks the follower's input and expertise; it is no longer necessary to be specific with task identity. A laboratory director's relationship with his lead research chemist is an illustration. Here we have high relationship and low task.

4. **Delegating (S4).** There is little leader involvement; the follower manages independently. A salesperson who is not located at the home office functions with little contact from his or her supervisor. He or she is experiencing low relationship and low task.

Hersey and Blanchard next characterize followers in terms of their ability and readiness to accomplish a task. The model application varies in three ways. First is the amount of directive behavior employed by the leader ranging from high to low. Second is the amount of supportive behavior used by the leader. Third is the amount of follower involvement in the decision making. Here are the four follower readiness situations.

1. **Readiness 1 (R1).** The follower lacks task competency and personal confidence. The follower is both unable and unwilling to participate in the decision-making process.

2. **Readiness 2 (R2).** The follower is willing but lacks the competency to accomplish the goal without help or guidance from the leader. The follower is willing but unable to work unsupervised.

3. **Readiness 3 (R3).** The follower has the competence to manage the task; however, the follower either does not understand what is to be accomplished or perhaps lacks the motivation. He or she is able but unwilling.

4. **Readiness 4 (R4).** The follower is able and willing. He or she possesses both the skill and the motivation for task accomplishment. The follower is able to manage himself or herself well, building credibility through his or her impact and positive results. In essence the follower becomes his or her own leader.

Figure 9–2 charts the leader-follower transition. Hersey and Blanchard believe that a follower at R1 needs a leader who demonstrates a style common to S1, a directive leader supervising a follower who is unable and unwilling. This circumstance occurs frequently for the new hire. The new employee is not aware of policies, norms, or other conventions that are the accepted practice for the organization. The unknown can create anxiety and uncertainty as new skills are introduced. Most leader behavior in such a situation would include clear specific guidelines and direction found in a directive leader style. We can make the case that over time the follower will learn and progress in his or her understanding of organizational norms that will improve the follower's willingness to accept new tasks. Hersey and Blanchard see this as normal growth.

A creative person who works well in the absence of close supervision will rapidly progress to an S4/R4 relationship. There may be other followers who are perfectly content to report for work each day looking to their leader, boss, or supervisor to create the day's activity complete with education and examples if necessary. The leaders and followers in the high-turnover fast-food business may spend the majority of their time at

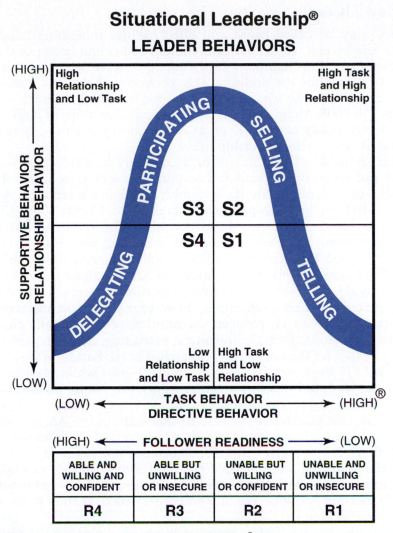

Situational Leadership®
LEADER BEHAVIORS

(HIGH)	High Relationship and Low Task		High Task and High Relationship

SUPPORTIVE BEHAVIOR
RELATIONSHIP BEHAVIOR

PARTICIPATING

SELLING

S3 | **S2**

S4 | **S1**

DELEGATING

TELLING

Low Relationship and Low Task | High Task and Low Relationship

(LOW)

(LOW) ◄———— TASK BEHAVIOR ————► (HIGH)®
DIRECTIVE BEHAVIOR

(HIGH) ◄———— FOLLOWER READINESS ————► (LOW)

ABLE AND WILLING AND CONFIDENT	ABLE BUT UNWILLING OR INSECURE	UNABLE BUT WILLING OR CONFIDENT	UNABLE AND UNWILLING OR INSECURE
R4	**R3**	**R2**	**R1**

Figure 9–2 Hersey and Blanchard's Situational Leadership® model.

Source: From "Hersey and Blanchard's Situation Leadership Model," *Management of Organizational Behavior,* 6th ed., by P. Hersey and K. Blanchard.

S1/R1, whereas the head chef at a five-star restaurant would likely be at an S4/R4 relationship with his or her supervisor.

The concept of task and relationship is retained in the Hersey/Blanchard model. Their model differs from Fiedler in that Hersey/Blanchard believe it is normal behavior for leaders to adjust their style when the situation changes.

CONTEMPORARY APPROACHES

Four recent theories have some basis in what we know of the current leadership environment.

- Attribution theory
- Charismatic and visionary leadership
- Transformational versus transactional leadership
- Emotional intelligence

Attribution Theory

This theory may be called cause and effect. When something happens, pleasant or unpleasant, the leader or dominant individual becomes the focus. Ben Bernanke, the chairman of the Federal Reserve, was often given a great deal of blame for the declining U.S. economy of the first decade of 2000. However, Bernanke was not criticized for lowering the interest rate several times in 2008. Many attribute the economic downturn of 2007–2009 to his monetary policy actions. Even as the economy declines, Bernanke continues to survive in his leadership role.

When a sports team fails to win or a company falls into despair, the players are not generally replaced and corporate America does not rebuild new factories or replace employees. Invariably the leader is replaced. A lack or apparent lack of leadership is not tolerated. In March 2006, Calvin Sampson was hired as the new head coach for the Indiana University basketball program. Sampson replaced Mike Davis, who took over for Hall of Fame coach Bob Knight in 2000. Coach Sampson, while the head coach at Oklahoma University, was under NCAA sanctions for violations that were caused by excessive phone calls to recruits. As a result, Oklahoma University placed itself on a self-imposed two-year probation and reduced scholarships from 13 to 11, reduced the number of phone calls coaches could make to recruits, limited off-campus recruiting, and cut paid visits down from 12 to 9 for the last season. On arrival at IU, Sampson was found to have made 577 impermissible calls from 2000–2004 while at Oklahoma University and was punished by the NCAA, restricting future phone calls to recruits. Sampson had the opportunity to start with a clean slate at IU; however, within the first year he was back in trouble with the NCAA. At Indiana University, he was participating in three-way conversations in violation of NCAA sanctions. Sampson forfeited a $500,000 pay increase and one scholarship for the following season.[80] In 2007, Sampson's contract was bought out by the university and he was released. As a result, the Indiana basketball team and leadership continue to suffer and are trying to rebuild to the high status they once achieved.

The reverse is also true. Exxon Mobil posted record sales of $404.5 billion and earnings of $40.5 billion in 2007. Much of the success was attributed to Rex Tillerson who became president of the company in 2001 and CEO in 2006. Rising oil prices have fueled the rise of Exxon Mobil and have put oil businesses in the international spotlight. Tillerson has become not only a successful corporate leader, but also an expert in the field of world energy, having published several articles on the subject.[81]

Charismatic and Visionary Leadership

It is not unusual to look at charismatic and visionary leadership separately. However, they complement one another when viewed together. The following list identifies the principle characteristics of this type of leadership.

- The leader demonstrates **self-confidence.**
- The leader has a **vision.**
- The leader clearly **articulates the vision.**
- The leader has **strong convictions about the vision.**
- The leader's **behavior is out of the ordinary.**
- The leader is **perceived as a change agent.**
- The leader is **sensitive to the organizational environment.**

Vision is the core of leadership. The leader's job is to create the vision for the organization in a way that will engage both the imagination and the energies of its people.[82] The vision must reflect the organizational values and the leader must communicate in a way that will allow the organization to understand, embrace, and support the vision. The vision moves the people and the people are the organization.

Let's go back to the 2008 Democratic Presidential nomination campaign for an excellent illustration of these characteristics at work. Senator Hillary Clinton is a successful leader, a U.S. Senator, and a former First Lady. She is the wife of a popular former president, Bill Clinton, and has significant super-delegate support. How can Hillary lose? The challenger, the new senator in Washington, D.C., Barak Obama from Illinois, is not given much of a chance early in the campaign. During the campaign, Senator Clinton generally tends to the business of the government and her relationship with Bill Clinton. Barak Obama travels the country, frequently by bus, holding town meetings and speaking directly to potential voters. He works hard at convincing anyone who will listen that he has a vision different from both presidents Bush and Bill Clinton, who together have held the White House for the last 20 years. He bashes high gas prices, foreign policy, housing foreclosures, bad economic conditions, and deficit spending. He argues the need for better education and he pledges change when elected. Barak Obama's charisma and vision set him apart from Senator Clinton.

Transformational versus Transactional Leadership

Transformational leadership is an extension of **transactional leadership.** In some respects transactional leadership provides a foundation on which transformational leadership builds. Bernard M. Bass's research identifies the following key leader characteristics:[83]

TRANSACTIONAL LEADERSHIP

- **Provides contingent rewards.** Reward effort and provide recognition for achieving goals through bonuses, pay raises, and awards.
- **Management by exception** (active). Watch for and seek out deviations from norms and take corrective action where deficiencies exist. Evaluate production rejection rates, check for waste, and monitor customer feedback.
- **Management by exception** (passive). Changes are made when standards are not met. Missed production goals and sales shortfalls are examples.

TRANSFORMATIONAL LEADERSHIP

- **Charisma and inspiration.** The leader creates and communicates a vision for the organization.
- **Intellectual stimulation.** The leader promotes intelligence and careful problem solving.
- **Individualized consideration.** The leader gives personal attention to his followers and treats each employee individually.

To illustrate the concept, consider the story of a successful retail business that creates its own technology. Our example focuses on the organizational function that creates the technology, the research and development (R&D) group. In the normal course of R&D business, the director (leader) administers contingent rewards by implementing pay increases and recognition for good work. He is also careful to review reports of work in progress, checking for errors, waste, and completeness. By accomplishing these tasks, he is fulfilling his transactional role as a leader.

In addition to these activities, this particular leader, with the support of senior management, directs that every Wednesday afternoon is "free" time for all his employees. He is not suggesting this is time for golf or personal time; instead the time is set aside for the R&D staff to work on anything they choose. They are free to use the R&D resources, tools, and publications; it is a time to be creative. This is a particularly important and busy time for the leader, so he ensures that his calendar is always free of distractions. He spends Wednesday afternoons passing through the various labs encouraging work, cheerleading, and showing genuine excitement at new developments. What a great business opportunity. Sure it is expensive; however, one new product like a Prozac or Viagra can turn the fortunes of a company. This transformational activity is acted out daily in small privately owned companies where the owner (leader) visits each company department every day, coaching and inspiring his team.

Emotional Intelligence

Great leaders move us! They ignite our passion and inspire the best in us. Have you ever known a leader who just seems to know what to do at the right moment? He or she seems to know how to work the organization to revive its workforce, creating a renewed sense of pride and commitment. New research suggests that the most effective executives use a collection of distinct leadership styles, use these styles at just the right time, and have high levels of emotional intelligence.[84] In other words, emotional intelligence, or EI, is a great predictor of successful leadership. **Emotional intelligence** refers to the leader's ability to recognize one's own feelings and those of others for self-motivation and for managing emotions in themselves and in relationships with others. As a result, leaders providing the best results do not rely on only one leadership style but can incorporate many styles seamlessly and in different measures. The keystone of emotional intelligence is an awareness of one's own feelings as they occur. This enhanced self-awareness is the first step in EI development. This research found four fundamental capabilities composed of specific sets of competencies.[85]

Self-Awareness (Personal Competence)
- Self-awareness is the ability to monitor and control one's own feelings as well as to identify and understand the feelings of others.[86]
- Emotional self-awareness: the ability to read and understand your emotions and to recognize their impact on work performance and relationships. For example, when leaders high in EI become angry, they will use their anger to energize themselves into taking appropriate action.
- Accurate self-assessment: a realistic evaluation of your strengths and limitations
- Self-confidence: a strong and positive sense of self-worth

Self-Regulation (Personal Competence)
- Self-regulation is the ability to monitor and control one's own feelings and emotions in order to avoid reacting inappropriately.[87]
- Emotional self-control: the ability to keep disruptive emotions and impulses under control
- Transparency: a consistent display of honesty and integrity; trustworthiness
- Adaptability: flexibility in adapting to changing situations or overcoming obstacles
- Achievement orientation: the drive to improve performance and to meet an internal standard of excellence
- Initiative: a readiness to act and seize opportunities
- Optimism: seeing the upside in events

Social Awareness (Social Competence)

- Social awareness is the ability to engage in appropriate behavior and actions given the emotional content of the situation.[88]
- Empathy: skill at sensing other people's emotions, understanding their perspective, and taking an active interest in their concerns
- Organizational awareness: the ability to read the currents of organizational life, build decision networks, and navigate politics
- Service orientation: the ability to recognize and meet the follower, client, or customer needs

Relationship Management (Social Competence)

- Inspirational and visionary leadership: guiding and motivating with a compelling vision
- Influence: Wielding a range of tactics for persuasion
- Developing others: the propensity to bolster the abilities of others through feedback and guidance
- Change catalyst: proficiency in initiating new ideas, managing, and leading people in a new direction
- Conflict management: the ability to resolve disagreement and orchestrate resolutions
- Building bonds: proficiency at cultivating and maintaining a web of relationships
- Teamwork and collaboration: competence at promoting cooperation and building teams.

Interestingly, no leader, no matter how outstanding, has strengths across the board in every one of these many EI competencies. Highly effective leaders typically exhibit a critical mass of strength in a half dozen or so EI competencies.[89] In fact, when high performers were compared with average performers in senior management positions, nearly 90 percent of the difference in their effectiveness was attributable to emotional intelligence factors rather than basic intelligence. IQ is certainly required for leaders to lead; EI is required for leaders to lead successfully.[90] The good news in all of this is that we can learn the skills necessary for high EI.

PRACTICAL APPLICATION

Trait theory, behavioral theory, contingency theory. What is to be learned from all of this discussion on leadership? Consider the following:

- We lead people.
- Leadership is situational.
- Should we ignore leaders and focus on the followers?
- Has our sense of leadership changed over time?

We lead people and people are different from reports and machines. State-of-the-art information systems and the finest tools, equipment, or machines are useless without competent people. People are an organization's most expensive asset in terms of aggregate acquisition and maintenance. People are also the most expensive cost when education, turnover, and absenteeism are considered. Therefore, it is imperative that leaders visit as many employees personally as is possible each day. Leaders who accept this responsibility coach, motivate, and encourage their followers to make something positive happen. We cannot win without people!

Leadership is situational. A military decision maker appears to be task oriented in crucial situations. It is difficult to involve the entire command when success hangs in the balance.

Mergers and acquisitions are common occurrences in the marketplace today. The demand for leaders is ever present. When EMC, a Massachusetts-based information infrastructure provider, began its transformation, the plan called for renovating its entire product set, acquiring more than 35 companies, and building out centers of technology excellence across the globe. EMC faces the knowledge management challenge in preparing young managers and up-and-coming executives to replace retiring top-level baby boomers. What gave EMC the edge, the company argues, is its focus on distinct leadership training and development.[91]

In a privately owned company, the owner tends to be task oriented early in the business and organizational development. However, as the unit matures, and the size of the organization expands, the leader must take less of a hands-on approach.

Sports coaches, especially football coaches, walk both sides of the street. Normally, the head coach permits his position coaches to make calls, plays, and adjustments as they see fit. When the game is on the line and time is scarce, the head coach often shortens the range of influence of the assistant coaches. A university faculty administrator may be the opposite extreme of the military decision maker. Task accomplishment, while important, is often secondary to maintaining compatible relationships with faculty members.

Where should the leadership focus be? Perhaps we should de-emphasize the behavior of the leader and emphasize the behavior of followers as a judge of a leader's success. Is the team successful? Are the people creative? Are the workers thinkers or do they simply react? For some, this may seem to be a throwback to the attribution theory. Maybe, but there are some who could not care less whether the leader is task oriented or relationship oriented. Their bottom line is measured in success.

Now is a good time for you to review your responses to the self-assessment test at the beginning of the chapter. Where do you score? Do you find yourself leaning to task or relationship? Perhaps you have a balance between the two. If so, go with it. If not, educate yourself, critique your performance, and seek that elusive balance.

Finally, what has happened to leadership over time? We have been experiencing an evolution of leader behavior. In the early twentieth century, we were influenced by people like Henry Ford. He was a tough taskmaster who likely was not influenced by work councils or anything that would suggest that he was not in total control. The post–World War II generation, often referred to as *baby boomers,* found themselves in the midst of a leader transition. Theory X was challenged by Theory Y. Team synergy replaced unilateral decision making. Finally, the concept of transformational leadership as an extension of a leader's transactional role makes perfect sense in the world as we know it today.

Harvey Mackay[92] wrote that former President Dwight D. Eisenhower would demonstrate leadership with a piece of string on a table. When he pushed the string, it always crumpled; however, when he pulled the string, it always followed in a straight line. What is the lesson demonstrated here?

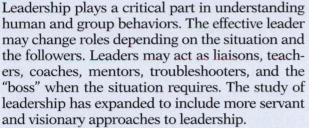

Leadership plays a critical part in understanding human and group behaviors. The effective leader may change roles depending on the situation and the followers. Leaders may act as liaisons, teachers, coaches, mentors, troubleshooters, and the "boss" when the situation requires. The study of leadership has expanded to include more servant and visionary approaches to leadership.

Leadership can be further explained by exploring four different approaches. These four approaches are trait theory, behavioral theory, contingency theory, and contemporary theories.

Trait theory is based on an individual's personal attributes as a leader and implies the leader is born with these traits.

Behavioral theory is based on the relationship between getting the job done (task) and concern for the employees (consideration). The behavioral theory notes one can be trained in leadership skills and these skills can be learned.

The contingency theory of leadership from Fiedler is based on the leader's power position, task structure, and leader-member relations. Blanchard and Hersey state that the contingency theory of leadership is based on the leader's task behavior (getting the job done), the leader's supportive behavior (taking care of the workers), and follower readiness (measure of ability and willingness to work).

Contemporary approaches include:

- attribution theory (cause and effect)
- charismatic and visionary leadership (self-confidence, vision, ability to articulate the vision, behavior out of the ordinary, reputation as a change agent, sensitivity to the organizational environment)
- transactional leadership (change things)
- transformational leadership (change people)

People should seek to understand their own leadership styles, the workers, the work to be done, and the situation. Self-assessment can provide greater understanding of leadership style.

Leader's Exercise

The following discussion is one person's experience with successful leaders. Leader success was measured by the overall success of the organization in terms of growth, goal achievement, and profitability. Some of the leader characteristics presented may seem to be bold and harsh. The real-world work experience can be that way. Not all successful leaders demonstrate all the behaviors. However, several of the **eight attributes** were observed in more than one leader. Please read the following and then complete the exercise that follows.

What Characteristics Do Successful Leaders Share?

1. **They are unconventional.** They are never intimidated, and they never permit themselves to be at the mercy of staff people, rules, policies, or regulations when it comes to making business decisions. The establishment of formal rules, boundaries, limitations, and fences, while necessary in most environments, is only important on their terms. Such mundane matters must never get in the way of running a business.

2. **They are and will always be visionaries.** This is a truly remarkable characteristic. There are few real visionaries. A visionary is someone who can see an opportunity, figure out how to make it work (often without staff support and agreement), and finally, communicate the vision. The communication or explanation of the vision may be skeletal; however, there will be enough detail that the support troops can figure out how to make it work. Business "experts" said the founder of Federal Express was crazy when he had the vision for an overnight delivery business. He even got a D on an assignment that described the idea. He stuck with his vision and made it a reality. It is now so successful that businesses worldwide cannot operate without FedEx.

3. **They see themselves as invincible and tell you so.** Martha Stewart is an American business magnate, author, editor, and homemaking advocate. She is also a former stockbroker and fashion model. Over the last two decades, Stewart has held a prominent position in the American publishing industry; she is the author of several books and hundreds of articles on the domestic arts, editor of a national housekeeping magazine, host of two

popular daytime television programs, and commercial spokeswoman for Kmart. In 2001 she was named the third most powerful woman in America by *Ladies Home Journal*. She had become an American icon in the business world. Then, according to the U.S. Securities and Exchange Commission in a federal indictment, Stewart avoided a loss of $45,673 by selling all 3,928 shares of her ImClone stock in late 2001. The day following her sale, the stock value fell 16%.[93] After a highly publicized, five-week jury trial that was the most closely watched of a wave of corporate fraud trials, Stewart was found guilty in March 2004 of conspiracy, obstruction of an agency proceeding, and making false statements to federal investigators, and she was sentenced in July 2004 to serve a five-month term in a federal correctional facility and a two-year period of supervised release. Following her release from prison in March 2005, Stewart launched a highly publicized comeback, and was once again involved in *Martha Stewart Living* magazine.[94] She is back on top once again.

4. **They appear to be ruthless.** To challenge them straight up is courting disaster. Their eyes are daggers, and their tongue is a saber. However, it takes unusual diplomacy, psychology, and timing to bargain or reason with them. Trust me, I know from experience.

5. **They avoid conflict.** They do not object to a good fight; however, they allow underlings to do the disagreeing and fight it out in the arena. All the while they are intently listening and watching. They never become *decisively engaged*. In other words, leaders never lose the ability to influence the action. There is always a Plan B. Usually the debate is about one of the leader's visions or ideas. Successful leaders hire and gather around them people who are brighter than they are. This generally creates debate that allows the leader to consider and capitalize on another's ideas, where appropriate.

6. **They practice absolute control.** The "wheel" communication technique describes the leader's mode of operation. That is, the leader is at the center of the decision-making process. All decisions are cleared with the boss before implementation. This type of leader wants to always feel the pulse of the organization. I recall when the CEO of a company demanded to be the final approval authority for every new corporate headquarter's hire even though the company was approaching $1 billion in revenue. We are talking about every hire, including support staff.

7. **They have no fear.** Defeat a competitor, drive him from the business, and capture his market share. I do not believe they would routinely stand up in the face of machine gun fire or openly challenge the law. However, each would certainly move to the brink without reservation.

8. **They take maximum risk.** Two men in the late 1980s believed they saw a great retail opportunity in a business that was failing badly. These two men mortgaged their homes and pledged all their assets to the bank to generate the required working capital to buy the business and begin operations under new ownership. Few supported their vision. At the time interest rates were near all-time highs and the U.S. economy was struggling. These men faced a potential financial disaster. However, in three short years, the partners had retired all debt and began a period of extraordinary business growth. They were considered foolish at the outset; however, later their business was hailed as a model for others.

The Dynamic Products Company was a successful manufacturing company that specialized in high-technology products for industrial and commercial purposes. The manufacturing part of the business depended on research and development to give them new products. The research and development group consisted of ten research scientists with Ph.D's from major universities and their manager, Dr. Bob Williams. Dr. Bob as he was known throughout the company was a brilliant researcher and led the way to many patents for the company. He always insisted on being on a first name basis with his scientists and supported their research activities in any way he could. It was not uncommon for the scientists to go to Bob when they needed help with their projects. Bob had earned their respect over the years and new scientists were somewhat in awe of him.

When asked about his management style, he would comment, "What management style? I am just one of the boys in lab." He let people have total control of their projects. He would get them any equipment, assistance, or space they needed. All of the scientists had keys to the laboratory facilities and could work pretty much when they wanted. Bob showed a high level of trust in his scientists and they appreciated him for that. Bob, despite having apparent lack of management style, always got great results from his team. They would often finish projects ahead of schedule and under budget. Fred, one of the scientists, was known for working in the middle of night and at other odd times. One time, he walked off the golf course on the fourteenth hole on a Saturday and went to the lab to work on his project. He once left a party at his own home to go to the lab to work on his project. His wife and friends became used to his behavior and it was referred to as a Fred Moment. Even though Fred may be an extreme example of a scientist not working on a schedule, others also found it easier to work late at night or early in the morning. Mike was an example of the morning person. Mike was at the lab at 6 A.M. most days and would leave around 3 P.M. or when he got tired. Brian was the night person and preferred to work from 3 P.M. to midnight. As it happened, there seemed to be people coming and going all the time in the lab. The rest of the plant used a traditional 8 A.M. to 4:30 P.M. schedule, with a half an hour off for lunch. The plant guards were used to the scientists and let them in whenever they came.

The president of the company, Roger Jones, viewed the results of the laboratory as a great success story despite the scientists' unusual way of doing business. He was quoted as saying that the laboratory is one of the true success stories of the company, with the number of new products they have created, the number of patents they have received, the help they have been to customers, and the cost efficiency of their operation. Roger was a big fan and ardent supporter of Dr. Bob and the scientists in the lab.

In 2008, Roger had reached retirement age and decided to step down as president and spend more time with his family. The board of directors reluctantly accepted his resignation and commended him on the outstanding job he had done as president. The company had been very successful under Roger's leadership. Some board members thought that Roger had been too much of a nice guy as president and now it was time to bring in someone who could exert more authority over the workers, especially the odd-balls in the laboratory. Thinking that the company needed a more forceful president, they hired John Green. John had been a colonel in the army prior to being president of a relatively small technology plastics manufacturer. He was a no-nonsense type of boss who believed firmly in strict enforcement of all rules and regulations.

Once hired as president, he had a meeting with all the managers, including Dr. Bob. He quickly informed them that he felt the old way of doing things had to change and the company needed to be more efficient. He insisted that all employees work between the hours of 8:00 A.M. and 4:30 P.M. He told the production people there would be no overtime unless he approved it. He informed Dr. Bob the new lab hours were from 8:00 A.M. to 4:30 P.M. Dr. Bob tried to explain to John that his scientists were salaried employees and not hourly employees. John told him that he did not care what they were. They would be there during regular hours or else.... John went on to say if Dr. Bob could not get the job done, he would hire someone else to run the lab.

At first Dr. Bob ignored John demands and continued to run the lab as it had always been run. The guards had always let the scientists come and work whenever they wanted and continued to do so until John ordered the guards to not let anyone in during non-business hours. The scientists went to Dr. Bob for help. Dr. Bob went to John and tried to explain the situation but John would have none of it. The meeting ended with John telling Dr. Bob to enforce the rules or resign.

Deciding that working for John was not an option, Dr. Bob began talking to other companies about employment. With his reputation, it was easy for him to find a job as laboratory manager with Advanced Products Group, a growing company. When Dr. Bob left, things got worse for the scientists as Tom Young, an underling of John's at his old company and in the army, was brought in to clean up the perceived problems in the laboratory. Tom had worked as a production manager and had been a drill sergeant in the army. He had picked up some college credits in the army, but did not have a degree. Tom was completely loyal to John and would do anything he said.

John introduced Tom to the scientists in a closed meeting. Tom informed the scientists there was one way to do things in the lab and that it was his way. From that point on, every employee was expected at work during business hours and each scientist would give him a report every week on what he or she was doing. The reports were due by 9 A.M. every Friday. Tom also informed them he would direct all activities and assignment of personnel. If the scientists wanted anything, they had to request it in writing to Tom. Tom also made his presence felt in the laboratory by stopping work and making the scientists answer questions about what they were doing. It rapidly became apparent to the scientists that Tom had no idea how to run a laboratory and Tom did not trust them.

Dr. Bob realized his new company needed skilled scientists to expand their operations. Dr. Bob went to Dale Davis, his boss, about the possibility of hiring his old staff. Dale said, "I will personally welcome anyone you bring in and will pay them more than they are making now." Dr. Bob called Joe, his senior scientist at Dynamic Products Company, and asked him how it was going. Joe told him the place is a mess and said, "I am trying to find a new job." Dr. Bob offered Joe a job while they were on the phone and told Joe to bring any of his colleagues with him to Advanced Product Group. Joe accepted the job and started calling the other scientists. One by one, all the scientists called Dr. Bob looking for a job. Dr. Bob gladly hired all of them, including Fred. The next day the scientists told Tom that they all were quitting. Tom told them they could not do that. One of the scientists clicked on a CD player and Tom was treated to the classic verse of "Take This Job and Shove It" by Johnny Paycheck. The scientists happily departed Dynamic Products Company for Advanced Products Group and the opportunity to work with Dr. Bob once again.

Questions

1. Describe Dr. Bob's leadership style in terms of the Managerial Grid.
2. Why did Dr. Bob's leadership style work?
3. Describe the leadership style of John Green and Tom Young.
4. Why did John and Tom's leadership style not work with the scientists?

DISCUSSION QUESTIONS

1. The foregoing is intended to be a thought starter. In some cases there may be significant disagreement with whether these are positive characteristics. Prepare a written report that responds to the following questions.

   a. Have you observed any of these characteristics in leaders that you consider successful?

   b. Discuss the appropriateness of each listed behavior.

   c. Would you try to emulate any of these characteristics? If not, why not?

2. When we observe a success in our work life or our social life, we can identify the responsible person. Review the theories and make a selection of the leadership theory that makes the most sense to you. Discuss your selected choice with particular attention as to why that choice makes more sense than other alternatives.

3. What would be some of the consequences to an organization if the vast majority of the managers were 5,5 leaders under the Managerial Grid (Figure 9–1)?

CHAPTER 10

Decision Making

LEARNING OUTCOMES: DECISION MAKING

1. Explain the satisficing model for decision making.

2. Describe the workings of the implicit favorite model for decision making.

3. Outline the maximizing or rational decision-making model.

4. Discuss the various group decision-making techniques.

Name: _____

Section Number: _____

SELF-ASSESSMENT TESTS

Please complete the following exercise online, accessible with the Access Card packaged with this text, before reading this chapter.

EXERCISE I.D.1:   **AM I A PROCRASTINATOR?**   Score _____

Procrastination is a tendency to postpone, delay, or avoid performing tasks or making decisions. While this could be a positive thing if it allows one to gather more information before making a decision, chronic procrastination causes lost opportunities. If procrastination consistently hinders individuals from taking action, making decisions, or changing things in their lives, it could be a problem. However, really low scores on the procrastination scale could indicate that one often acts prematurely and could later regret his or her actions.

You should also record your scores on this exercise in Appendix 1.

NOTES

The Decision

The purchasing department is looking for a new secretary. The minimum requirements are a high school diploma, word processing at 45 words per minute, and two years of experience as a secretary.

Bob and Tom are the purchasing agents for the company and have to make the final decision. The human resources department has the responsibility to screen the applicants and only send those qualified to Bob and Tom.

Bob and Tom agreed to interview applicants on Wednesday morning. When Tom gets in, he gets an urgent phone call from the shop manager who needs more parts by the end of the week. The order must be placed before 11 A.M. today. Bob has a message on his answering machine from a supplier stating that he needs to call him back now.

The three candidates scheduled are Betty, Jean, and Mary. Betty is a high school graduate who can word process at a rate of 45 words per minute and has two years experience as a secretary. Jean has an associate's degree from the area community college, can word process at 80 words per minute, and has six years experience as a secretary. Mary has a bachelor's degree from a regional university, can word process at the rate of 95 words per minute, and has ten years experience as a secretary with five of those in a purchasing department.

Feeling the pressure, Bob and Tom want to get this decision made quickly so they can take care of their other issues. Betty walks in and does fairly well on the interview.

Tom says, "She meets all the qualifications. I say we take her and send the others home."

Bob responds, "Sounds good to me."

Tom calls the human resources department and tells the staff person there to give the job to Betty and cancel the other two interviews.

Did Bob and Tom make the right choice?

Welcome to Decision Making! ■

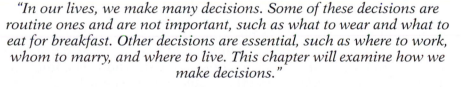

"In our lives, we make many decisions. Some of these decisions are routine ones and are not important, such as what to wear and what to eat for breakfast. Other decisions are essential, such as where to work, whom to marry, and where to live. This chapter will examine how we make decisions."

The job of a manager, above all, is to make decisions. At any moment on any given day, most managers are engaged in some aspect of decision making that impacts their organizations and the operations of the business.[95] Under ideal situations, managers and people like us have one decision to make at any given time, have perfect knowledge of that situation, have a perfect vision of the future, have one right way to go, choose the right way, and implement the decision flawlessly. Unfortunately, we do not live in a perfect world and do not always make the best decisions. In analyzing the decision-making process, one needs to look at the things in our world and the managers' world that are not perfect. Decision making would best be described as an exercise in evaluating trade-offs. We will look at three popular techniques to solve problems and make decisions: the satisficing model, the implicit favorite model, and the maximizing model (also known as the rational decision-making model). At the end of the chapter we will discuss group decision techniques.

THE SATISFICING MODEL

The satisficing model[96] begins by reducing the problem to a level where it can be easily understood. The satisficing model is a play on two words outlining the uniqueness of this model. After the basic criteria, or needs, have been determined, this decision-making model suggests the alternative chosen is the first alternative that is *satisfactory and sufficient enough* to meet the criteria of the decision. The advantage is that it is a quick way to make a decision that will meet our needs; however, for the sake of a quick decision, we may sacrifice making the best decision. This method does not explore all possibilities, but only takes the first one that is acceptable. As an example, let's say you are really hungry and only have $10 for dinner. You really like Chinese food, but the first restaurant you come to that has a dinner for less than $10 is an Italian restaurant. You eat the Italian meal even though you could have had a Chinese dinner for the same price. The result is that you did get a dinner for $10, but it was not the best dinner you could have gotten for $10. In this example, in order to satisfy your hunger, you sacrificed your preference for Chinese food. To further illustrate, let me share another situation where I used this decision-making model. I had a piece of equipment go down due to an electric motor burning out. I needed to get this piece of equipment back into production. Once I determined the minimum specifications, mounting hole, and size of motor, I began making calls to see who might have one. When I found a motor that met my minimum requirements, I purchased it. The motor was actually of a higher output than the one being replaced but the mounting patter worked and the voltage needs were met. I could have spent more time trying to find the exact power size and maybe even gone online to try to get one at a much lower price; however, time was important. I satisfied my need by sacrificing the best value. A person using the satisficing model will solve the problem but will not always come up with the best solution.

THE IMPLICIT FAVORITE MODEL

The implicit favorite model[97] implies that the decision maker has already determined the requirement for a solution and has determined a course of action; however, he or she wants to confirm the decision. The implicit favorite model starts by identifying the problem and establishing a favorite choice for the solution. Other alternatives will be generated and compared to the favorite. The favorite choice of the decision maker is confirmed and the implicit favorite will be chosen. In business, a job opening may need to be filled and the decision maker may have an implicit favorite candidate for a job. The decision maker will determine the criteria for the job reflective of the candidate's qualifications. Other candidates will then be judged against that criteria, but the favored candidate will normally be selected. In our restaurant example, the implicit choice would be the Chinese restaurant. Other restaurants would be considered, but you are going to the Chinese restaurant.

THE MAXIMIZING OR RATIONAL DECISION-MAKING MODEL

The maximizing or rational decision-making model differs from the satisficing and the implicit favorite model in that it seeks to find the best possible solution to a problem or, in other words, seeks the best decision. This method was detailed in Kepner and Tregoe's *The Rational Manager*.[98] This model is intended to allow the decision maker to find several possible solutions and to pick the best choice based on the needs and wants of the situation. In the rational decision-making model, the decision maker goes through the following stages:

1. Identify the need for a decision and prioritize the problems.
2. Identify the decision criteria—determine the Musts and Wants.
3. Allocate weights to the want criteria.
4. Develop the alternatives.
5. Evaluate the alternatives.
6. Select the best alternative.

The key to making a decision is to understand the problem.

Let's examine this in more detail and try to illustrate how this works through a model for decision making.

Identify the Need for a Decision and Prioritize the Problems

The first thing you should do is prioritize your problems. Assuming you have done so, what happens next? To understand the problem within this area you need to **identify the need for a decision.** Why is this problem an important one to solve? How does it affect your business?

The next step in the Rational Decision-Making Model is to **identify the decision criteria.** What things are necessary in order to have a positive outcome? To make the best decision you need to identify what must be done and the things you want to do.

Identify the Decision Criteria: Determine the Musts and the Wants

Before coming to a final decision, the decision maker needs to consider what must happen with the decision as well as what he or she wants out of the decision. Determining the musts and wants of your situation will help you to clearly see what is most important when choosing an alternative. A **must** is an absolute parameter to the decision. If a must is violated, that alternative is not considered. If a man is in the market for a new house and must spend less than $250,000, a house that costs $450,000 will not be considered. In fact, a house that costs $251,000 would not be considered.

To make the best decision, you need to identify the things that **must** be done and the things you **want** to do.

Allocate Weights to the Want Criteria

A want is something that is desired but not necessary. A person may want a white house, but may purchase a brown one if it meets his or her musts and some other wants. A want will not rule out an alternative, but it may make that alternative less attractive to the decision maker; thus allocating weights to the want decision criteria helps prioritize the wants. I normally use a scale of 1–10 with 10 being the best or highest rating. The stronger the want, the higher the number value given. When selecting a house due to job relocation, since there are three children in our family, we determine the number of bedrooms must be four but we would like to have five so there is room for guests. On bathrooms, we must have one in the master bedroom and one for the rest of the house; however we want three baths if possible. When we weighted the wants, the desire for the extra bath was given a higher value than the fifth bedroom. The bathroom received a want value of 9 and the fifth bedroom received a want value of 6.

Develop the Alternatives

A decision maker will usually generate alternatives or choices for action. The alternatives will be aimed at solving the problem or producing the best choice. The choices can be generated in a logical manner or by brainstorming. Using a logical approach will generate fewer alternatives, but they will be more thought out. Using brainstorming will generate more alternatives, but they will lack detail and may be more difficult to figure out.[99]

Picking the best choice starts by comparing every alternative to the musts. If an alternative violates a must, it will no longer be considered. After the musts are considered, the remaining alternatives are compared to the wants to determine which choice is the best decision.

Evaluate the Alternatives

Once the alternatives have been developed, **evaluate the alternatives** using the decision criteria. Which alternative best matches your wants and needs? Do some satisfy none of your needs and only your wants? Does one satisfy both? Carefully consider the positives and negatives of each alternative. These consequences could help you determine which alternative will satisfy the criteria and have a positive consequence once implemented.

Select the Best Alternative

After you have carefully evaluated the alternatives, **select the best alternative.** The following example illustrates how one works through this process.

The XYZ Company wants to buy a new printing machine for its production line. The company cannot pay more than $150,000 for the machine and wants a capacity of 75,000 units per day and a machine that can be set up in four weeks or less. The following machines are available:

Machine	Cost	Capacity per Day	Setup Time in Weeks
Print Magic	$165,000	87,500	6
Sharp Image	$150,000	72,500	5
Readi-Print	$100,000	84,500	3
Print and Go	$300,000	100,500	7
Print Pro	$125,000	93,000	2

Using the must system, the Print Magic and the Print and Go would not be considered because they exceed the company's budget and thus violate a must. The other three machines will continue to be evaluated.

The company wants a machine that can be set up in less than four weeks and has a daily capacity of at least 75,000 units. Looking at the remaining machines, the Sharp Image does not provide the needed capacity and it takes more than four weeks to set up. That leaves only two machines that satisfy both the company's needs and its wants, Print Pro and Readi-Print. If cost is of a greater concern, the Readi-Print becomes the best choice. If increased capacity and less setup time are the greater concerns, the Print Pro becomes the best choice.

The consequences of the decision also must be considered. If this choice is made, what will happen? In the purchase of a new machine, such factors as downtime, availability of parts and service, and training people to use the machine must be considered. This type of analysis is played out in a what-if scenario. Assume the decision has been made and ask, "What happens now? If the machine breaks down, how fast can it be fixed and at what cost? How long will it take the workers to learn how to operate the machine?" The purpose of this analysis is to anticipate the impact the decision will have.

After the decision is made, now what?

To help you understand this technique, let's look at this in more detail using a decision-making model. Keep in mind this works when purchasing a car, choosing a college, selecting a house, or finding a job. Many of you may be graduating soon and will be looking for a job. Some of you may be considering an internship for summer work. This model will help you make the decision.

Problem: Decide on a job offer

Criteria—Musts		Job Offer 1	Job Offer 2	Job Offer 3
Utilize my degree	XXX	Yes	Yes	Yes
Salary of $48,000	XXX	Yes	Yes	Yes
Medical insurance	XXX	Yes	Yes	Yes
Educational program	XXX	No	Yes	Yes
Criteria—Wants	**Weight**			
Southwest location	5	Yes-5	No-0	Yes-5
Small company—under 400 employees	7	Yes-7	Yes-7	No-0
Stock option program	6	Yes-6	Yes-6	Yes-6
Good team culture	9	Yes-9	Yes-9	Yes-9
Opportunity for advancement	10	Yes-10	Yes-10	Yes-10
Want $52,000+	8	Yes-8	Yes-8	No-0
Total	45	45	40	30

With this model job offer number 1 appears to be good but it violates one of the musts because it has no education program. The next best option that meets all of the musts and offers most of the wants is job offer number 2. This process takes a lot of the emotion out of the decision-making process and provides a much more objective approach.

As a side note, wouldn't it be interesting to use this model in selecting a spouse? What would the musts and wants look like? As intriguing as it might be, I must advise against using it for selecting a spouse.

Determining a Course of Action

After recognizing a problem at hand, **the decision maker must also consider several different possible courses of action.** These five different courses of action have different levels of urgency depending on the situation.

1. **Corrective action.** The obvious answer is to solve the problem by eliminating the cause of the problem. This is commonly called **corrective action.** If an engine is running rough because a spark plug fails to fire properly, the bad spark plug is removed and a new spark plug is installed. In evaluative decision making, a person chooses the

Five basic types of action can be taken in decision making and problem solving.

perceived best job out of the offers made. These actions are aimed at solving the problem or settling the issue.

2. **Interim action.** Sometimes, the decisions made are not simple. What if the decision maker does not have all the facts necessary to make a good decision and needs additional time before taking action? A manager may know what the problem is but has not yet determined the cause, or a job seeker may need additional time to make the last plant trip before choosing a job. In both of these cases the decision makers need more time. The additional time can be obtained by adopting an **interim action** strategy. The interim action strategy allows the decision maker to postpone the decision until a later date. This action only delays the decision-making process and is not the final decision. This strategy can be seen when a company places a person in an interim position until a permanent person is found for the job or when an employee asks the boss for more time before making a decision. This can also be seen by a job seeker asking a potential employer for more time before making an employment decision.

3. **Preventative action.** If a company knows from experience that a certain machine will break down on the production line, it will not purchase that machine. If you know that a certain company has laid people off with every downturn in the economy, you might not want to go to work for that company if job security is a priority. Some companies elect to replace all the light bulbs after a set number of hours, thus preventing the need to respond to burned-out bulbs. **Preventative action** is aimed at never letting the cause of the problem come into play.

4. **Contingency action.** Sometimes we anticipate a problem is going to happen, and we prepare to take care of it. If we know that a computer is going to crash sometime, we back up the system with data storage or a backup computer system. Parents will provide a babysitter with the necessary information for action in the event a problem should arise while they are gone. This is called the **contingency action** approach. The contingency action approach gives the decision maker a backup plan before things go wrong.

5. **Adaptive action.** Sometimes problems happen, and we have to live with them. When companies and people learn to live with their problems and make the best of the situation, that response is called **adaptive action.**

Who Makes the Decision?

Tannenbaum and Schmidt[100] summarize seven different possibilities:

Other issues to consider are quality, time, commitment, and control.

- The manager makes the decision and announces it.
- The manager sells the decision.
- The manager presents the ideas and invites questions.
- The manager presents tentative decisions subject to change.
- The manager presents the problem, gets suggestions, and makes the -decision.
- The manager defines the limits and asks the group to make the decision.
- The manager permits the subordinates to function within limits defined by the superior.

The decision-making process moves from being boss-centered at the top of the list to being subordinate-centered at the bottom of the list.

The quality of the decision usually increases with the input from employees or others. Additional people add perspective and knowledge that one lone decision maker may not have. The exception to this thinking is when the decision maker is the expert. Following a professional guide through a jungle would be preferable to having a group of tourists deciding on their own which way to go.

The time is increased by using additional people in the decision-making process. A lone decision maker can usually sort out the facts, generate alternatives, and make a decision faster than any group. If time is critical, the expert decision maker should make the call. If time is not critical, group decision making may be used to generate the best decision.

When commitment of the people involved is critical to the implementation of the decision, it is recommended that the people get involved in the decision-making process and perhaps even make the decision. A decision made by the group will tend to become the property of the group and the group members will be more committed to its successful implementation.

When the decision maker feels that he or she must maintain control of the process, the decision maker needs to make the decision. If the decision maker knows the best decision, then he or she needs to make that decision. If the decision maker needs the approval of the group or does not know the correct decision, he or she may want to go to a group decision-making process where the group makes the decision or the group provides significant input into the decision.

Any decision is always influenced by the decision maker's perception of reality. A younger manager may make a decision based on limited experience, while an older manager would make his or her decision based on years of experience. The younger manager may be more innovative but not see some long-standing issues. The older manager may be aware of long-standing issues but not be very innovative. Males and females may see a problem differently. The same may be said for people of different backgrounds, races, cultures, and religions.

GROUP DECISION TECHNIQUES

Several group decision-making techniques are available for those who want to work with others. The simplest of these is the **interacting technique.** With the interacting technique, a group of people simply engages in a face-to-face discussion to make a decision. If you and your friends were trying to decide what to do on a Saturday night, the interacting technique of discussion may center on activities such as seeing the latest movie, going bowling, restaurant hopping, going to a party, and eating pizza. The goal of this technique is to allow everyone to have a say before deciding what the best option for the group is.

Another group decision-making technique is **brainstorming.** In brainstorming, people are encouraged to be creative and come up with every possible solution they can think up. This freewheeling exchange can really generate many ideas, but the quality of some ideas may be lacking. The classic example is the brainstormers in a Burger King commercial who are told there are no bad ideas. They come up with the sushi sandwich. The real problem with this method is that it takes considerable time to sort through all of the ideas presented in order to make the right decision.

The **nominal group technique**[101] is a more sophisticated technique in group decision making than the two previously mentioned techniques of interacting and brainstorming. With the nominal group technique, members of the group are presented with the problem and asked to write down their ideas. After a period of time for individual deliberation, each member of the group is asked to present his or her idea to the group. These ideas are recorded and then the group discusses the ideas. The ideas are then ranked by members of the group and the final decision is made by choosing the idea with the highest ranking. With this technique, all the members of your group who want to go out on Saturday would present their one best idea to the group for consideration. The bowling, pizza eating, partying, and other ideas are discussed and ranked, with the highest ranking item being the chosen activity of the night. Nominal group technique has been criticized for limiting a person's ideas.

In the **Delphi technique,** people are not present in the same room. The problem is identified and people are asked to generate a solution. Each person is given an anonymous questionnaire that helps provide a solution to the problem. The responses are collected in a central location and distributed to the group. Each member is then asked to provide new solutions based on the information he or she have received from the central location. The process continues until the group reaches a consensus, in which all members agree to one solution. The major problem with the Delphi technique is that it can take a long time.

The latest technique geared to the computer age is **electronic meetings.**[102] People on networked computers can interact with one another to produce the best solution to a problem. The interaction can be anonymous with the results being posted as to which solution is chosen. This technique offers the advantages of being fast, anonymous, and honest. Electronic decision meetings are likely to become a more common option for group decision making.

SUMMARY

Two key factors should be considered when making decisions:

- Who is going to make the decision?
- What is the quality of the decision?

The satisficing decision-making model allows the problem to be solved with the first solution that meets the established criteria. It may not be the best solution. One may satisfy the need for a decision while also sacrificing other elements for the speed of a decision. If time is a top priority, this model works well.

The implicit favorite decision-making model provides the decision maker with a means to evaluate other solutions against a perceived best decision. Once all other solutions are found to be less favorable than the implicit favorite, the implicit favorite solution is selected.

The maximizing or rational decision-making model provides a model to assist in decision making. The steps are to:

- Prioritize the problems.
- Identify the decision criteria.
- Allocate weights to criteria.
- Develop the alternatives.
- Evaluate the alternatives.
- Select the best alternative.

You may select a course of action from five alternatives:

- Corrective action means finding a fix for the problem once it has occurred.
- Interim action allows the decision maker to postpone the decision.
- Preventive action is aimed at never letting the cause of the problem happen.
- Contingency action provides a backup plan in the event a problem occurs.
- In adaptive action, the decision is made to adapt to the situation rather than spend the time or money to fix or eliminate the problem.

If you know what action to take, you can save time and maintain control by making the decision yourself. When you are unsure about a decision or you need the commitment of other people, you should consider one of the group decision-making techniques. This will give you the benefit of other people's knowledge and experience as well as getting their commitment for the final decision.

The decision-making process moves from the decision being made by the boss at the top, to managers, teams, or individuals. The greater the need for involvement of others, the longer the decision-making process will take.

Group decision techniques may range from a face-to-face discussion (interacting technique) to a creative and open brainstorming session to generate ideas for possible solutions. The nominal group technique provides a more structured format involving multiple individuals. Through the use of an anonymous questionnaire, the Delphi technique provides a means to get individuals involved from different offices or locations. Using the electronic meeting as a decision-making tool is geared to those using computers and will become more common in the future.

CASE STUDY

Tom Allen, Rick Smith, and Tory Payne were all CPAs from the same university. They had gone to school together and had been friends their whole lives. One of the dreams they had was starting their own accounting firm in their hometown of Elm City. Tom had gone to work for a large CPA firm in Charlotte, NC. He had been there six years and did not like working in a big city. Rick had taken a job with the Internal Revenue Service. He was becoming tired of his job of auditing tax returns looking for mistakes. Tory had gone into the Army and served in the Quartermasters Corps. She liked the Army, but wanted to get involved in a private CPA practice.

Elm City High School was having the tenth reunion of their class at the Elm City Country Club. Tom was the first to arrive with his wife, Helen. They had been married for six years and had two sons, ages four and two. Helen was from a small town and had enjoyed being in Elm City with Tom and his parents. Rick was the next to arrive with his wife, Dolly. They had one child, a girl age three. Tory was the last to arrive with her husband. They had met in the Army and had no children.

As the evening progressed, the three ended up making the rounds of their classmates before settling into a group of six with their spouses. Tom commented on how much he enjoyed being back in Elm City after living in Charlotte. He went on to say he hated the traffic, congestion, and crime. Rick said that his job was boring and that he was looking for something else. Tory said that she was looking for civilian work now that her Army career was over. After discussing the matter, the three thought it might be a good idea for them to explore starting a CPA firm in Elm City.

They found the town was in need of a CPA firm since Mr. Roberts retired and closed his business. The other firm in town, Grady and Sons, CPAs, was very high priced and seemed to care about only rich clients and large businesses. This left the market open for a firm that could help individuals as well as small businesses. Currently, these clients were paying the high fees of the Grady firm or taking their business out of town.

The three agreed the first thing they needed to do was to find office space to rent. Each agreed to engage in a search for an office. They agreed the rent should not exceed $1500 per month and the office should have a reception area, private office space for each of them, and a storage area to keep records.

Tom started his search by checking the *Elm City Times*, the local newspaper, for listings of rental property. He then called all four real estate offices in town and got their listings. He also called all the office buildings in town to see what they had available. He then eliminated all properties over $1500 per month in rent. After that, he eliminated all properties that did not give him the space to have areas for reception, three offices, and storage. There were ten properties on his list and he went out to see all of them with Helen. He checked for location, appearance, and suitability. He and Helen concluded that five

of the properties were not in good locations for customers to find and park. Three of the office sites were very old and in need of repair. Two properties were in good locations, had a good appearance, adequate free parking, and were somewhat suited to the firm's needs. After talking to the two owners, the owner of the property on Main Street was willing to make changes to the office to better suit their needs at no additional cost. The owner of the property on Maple Street said their firm would be responsible for any changes and would have to pay for them. Tom was convinced the Main Street property was the best choice.

Rick started his search by calling Chuck, an old friend in the real estate business. Chuck told him that he had four properties for rent that may fit his needs, but he wanted Rick to see the one he owned first on Center Street. Chuck showed his property to Rick and assured Rick he would take care of anything that Rick wanted if he would rent there. Rick liked Chuck and wanted to rent from him. Chuck showed the other three properties to Rick, but Rick still wanted to rent the one that Chuck owned, even though two of the properties had a better location and parking and the third one had more space for the same rent. Rick had made his choice to go with Chuck's property.

Tory and her husband wrote down the criteria of $1500 per month rent and space for three offices, a reception area, and a storage area. They grabbed the newspaper and called the people with properties available and arranged to see the first property that day. Once there, they realized that the owner wanted more money than they wanted to pay. They left and called the owner of the next place on the list. They entered the property and felt that it was just too small for their offices. They called the owner of the next place on the list and arranged to see it the next day. The property on Division Street rented for $1500 per month and had five areas suitable for three offices, a reception area, and a storage room. Tory had found their new office.

Tom, Rick, and Tory were excited that they had found the right office for their firm. When they got together, Tory announced, "I have our office. It is on Division Street and meets every one of our criteria." Rick stated that he had his favorite and it was on Center Street. Tom claimed to have found the best spot for an office on Main Street. The three were perplexed on how they could arrive at three different decisions based on working with the same criteria.

The three are now faced with the problem of making a decision that best serves their needs and wants. They scheduled a meeting for the next day with the decision on what office space to rent hanging in the balance, as well as the future of the proposed firm. Their families were excited about moving to Elm City and hoped the they all could work something out to make the firm a reality.

Questions

1. What decision model did Tom use and why?
2. What decision model did Rick use and why?
3. What decision model did Tory use and why?
4. Which model generates the best decision and why?

DISCUSSION QUESTIONS

1. When is it advantageous to let the group get involved in the decision-making process?
2. When is it advantageous for the leader to make the decision?
3. Using the rational decision-making model, work though a decision illustrating all of the points for successful use of this model.

CHAPTER 11

Communication

LEARNING OUTCOMES: COMMUNICATION

1. Describe the communication process.

2. List typical barriers to effective communication.

3. Contrast the differences between the grapevine and rumors.

4. Discuss other considerations for effective communication.

5. Through self-assessment, gain a greater understanding of one's own communication skills toward listening and giving feedback.

Name: _____

Section Number: _____

SELF-ASSESSMENT TESTS

Please complete the following exercises online, accessible with the Access Card packaged with this text, before reading this chapter.

EXERCISE II.A.1:   WHAT'S MY FACE-TO-FACE
                   COMMUNICATION STYLE?   Score _____

Dominant _____   **Dramatic** _____
Contentious _____   **Animated** _____
Impression _____   **Relaxed** _____
Attentive _____   **Open** _____
Friendly _____

The higher your score for any dimension, the more that dimension characterizes your communication style. When you review your results, consider to what degree your scores aid or hinder your communication effectiveness. High scores for being attentive and open would almost always be positive qualities. A high score for being contentious, on the other hand, could be a negative in many situations.

Effective communicators have developed good listening skills. This instrument is designed to provide you with some insights into your listening skills.

You should also record your score on these exercises in Appendix 1.

NOTES

The Picnic

Jones Company was having its annual summer picnic and softball game. As usual, the food and beverages, including kegs of beer, were abundant. Hank, a design assistant, was enjoying himself by having some food and a few beers before the start of the softball game. Everyone was having fun and enjoying the festivities.

When the softball teams were chosen, Hank was playing second base on one team, and his boss, Marvin, was playing right field for the other team. In the sixth inning, Marvin hit a line drive to right field and decided to turn it into a double. The throw to Hank at second base was low and Marvin slid into Hank. Hank was somewhat dazed by the collision and the beers he had consumed.

After Hank got to his feet, Marvin told Hank he needed a report on the Smith job as soon as possible. This was the first and only time the Smith job was mentioned to Hank.

Two weeks later, an irate Marvin charged into Hank's cubicle and demanded the Smith report.

Marvin said, "Where is that Smith report? Haven't you been working on that for two weeks?"

Hank responded, "What Smith report? I don't know anything about it."

Marvin replied, "The one I asked you to get me at the softball game, you idiot!"

Hank replied, "I don't remember anything about it!"

Marvin replied, "Don't mouth off at me! Get it done now, period!"

Marvin left the area mad at Hank for being so stupid, and Hank started working on the Smith job still feeling mad at Marvin.

What happened here?

Welcome to Communication! ■

In a survey of 480 companies and public organizations by the National Association of Colleges and Employers, the ability to communicate ranked first among personal qualities of college graduates sought by employers[103] In another survey of 1,400 leaders, managers, and executives attending training with the Ken Blanchard Companies, 43 percent identified communication skills as the most critical skill set to possess, while 41 percent said that inappropriate use of communication or listening is the number one mistake leaders make. Eighty-two percent cited failing to provide appropriate feedback, praise, or redirection as a personal shortcoming, and another 81 percent weren't satisfied with their ability to listen or involve others.[104] The biggest source of interpersonal problems is poor communication.[105] Good communication is essential to be successful in life. With the above statistics it is amazing we are as successful as we are.

Did you ever have trouble getting someone to understand you? Did you ever have trouble understanding someone else? Do you ever have trouble listening to others, especially with a stereo or television on? These problems are associated with communication and can be corrected by becoming better communicators and listeners. In the business world, poor communication is the number one reason for interpersonal conflict in all levels of the organization. To lead effectively a person must be clear and confident in what he or she has to say and then must follow up.

The key to the communication process is to create understanding.

THE COMMUNICATION PROCESS

This chapter can be outlined by the basic communication process model in Figure 11–1.

What Causes Communication to Happen?

It can be difficult to understand someone even when that person speaks the same language as you do. The process of communication can be more difficult than it appears. The first step in the process is a stimulus or an idea that gets people to want to communicate with other people. That stimulus may be dramatic like a fire. It becomes imperative that we warn other people of the danger that the fire poses. It can be something as simple and nonthreatening as seeing a friend and wanting to tell him or her about something that happened today. Whatever the **source,** the stimulus or idea makes us want to communicate with others.

Constructing the Message

After experiencing the stimulus, our mind must construct the message. This process is called **encoding.** Encoding is the process of putting our thoughts into words, phrases, and sentences that another person can understand. The key to making this process work is to make sure that the person getting the message can understand it. Seek first to be understood. Many people try to use jargon and confusing words in an attempt to sound impressive. They may sound impressive, but they run the very real risk of being misunderstood.

Choosing the Channel

The old adage, "It's not what you say but how you say it," applies here. After the message is encoded, the sender has to pick the right medium of communication, or **channel.** Some communications lend themselves to the spoken word. If you saw fire coming out of your neighbor's house, you would probably run over to the house and shout "Fire!" at the people who live there. This would not be a good situation to use a written communication because something needs to be communicated now. Waiting for a written message would be too late to do any good.

If the message is simple or urgent, consider a verbal message. Verbal messages are usually communicated face-to-face or by telephone. The verbal message gives you the chance not only to deliver it quickly, but also the chance to get the reaction of the other person. An example of this would be if you asked someone to close the door and he proceeded to open a window. It would be obvious that there was some problem with that communication.

If you need to communicate how to do a relatively complex job to someone, a verbal message may not be adequate. Some of the instructions

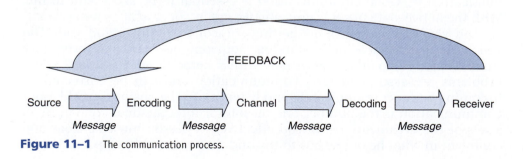

Figure 11–1 The communication process.

may be forgotten, and some steps may be confused with others. This would probably lead to failure in finishing the job correctly. In cases like this, it would be wise to put the instructions in writing so that the person can refer to them as he or she is doing the job. This will increase the chances that the job will be done right. As a rule, if the message is complex, multifaceted, or legally binding, put it in writing.

Written messages have been enhanced by technology. In addition to the traditional written document, there are also faxes and e-mails. Putting it in writing gives the person something to refer to and helps reduce misunderstandings between people about the message.

Understanding the Message

After the message is sent, it must be translated by the person who gets the message. The person who gets the message is called the receiver. The process of translating the message is called **decoding.** Thus, the receiver tries to understand the message by properly decoding it.

Unfortunately, the decoding process is not without problems. These problems are commonly referred to as **barriers** to communication because they prevent good communication from occurring.

Some typical barriers to communication include:

Barriers hinder good communication and can occur anywhere along the communication process.

1. **Unfamiliar language.** As you might expect, people with different native languages may have difficulty communicating with each other, but people can also be confused by jargon. What might be familiar to people living in one area of the country might be totally foreign to people living in another region. An example of this would be a Southerner asking for a poke at a store in the Midwest. Many people may not realize that the person is asking for a paper bag.

   Another example of unfamiliar language is professionals who routinely use jargon associated with their jobs. People working in that field would understand what they are saying, but when they use jargon outside of their professional group, people may not understand them at all. An example of this would be the term *cogs*. To an engineer, it would mean part of a gear; to a politician, it would mean a council of governments; and to an accountant, it would mean cost of goods sold. The solution to the barrier of unfamiliar language is to use common language that the receiver can understand.

2. **Improper timing.** Sometimes the receiver is just not ready to receive the communication. The receiver may be engaged in another activity, not in the right frame of mind, or not tuned into the conversation. If you are on the phone and someone in the room asks you a question, it is hard to concentrate on both conversations at the same time. Anger is also a problem because some people cannot focus on anything other than the object of their anger. Trying to get them to consider anything else is a futile endeavor. The solution to the barrier of improper timing is to choose the appropriate time when the receiver is ready to hear what you have to say.

3. **Noise and distractions in the environment.** A person can be subjected to noise such as machines, radios, telephones, people talking, and other environmental sounds. Distractions most often occur when a person tries to listen while doing some other activity. This situation is often made worse by the fact that the other activity may be providing information to the person who is involved in the conversation. An example of this is when a person is reading a report and trying to listen to another person. Another example is when a person is talking on the telephone while trying to carry on a conversation with a person in the office. It is easy to see that the conversation can become contaminated

by the other information source. This can lead to confusion and mistakes. The solution to this barrier is to eliminate the noise and the distractions. Eliminate noise by finding a quiet place, at least a quieter place than the current environment. Eliminate distractions. Try to focus on only one thing at a time.

4. **Attitude,** especially a bad one. A bad attitude toward the sender of a message can distort the message. An example is your feelings about a person who may have lied to you in the past. When that person starts speaking to you, you may have already made your mind up that the person is lying again even if that person is telling you the truth. Another example is when someone you dislike starts talking. It is easy to find yourself discounting what the person is saying because you do not like him or her. The solution is to hear what the person has to say before coming to a conclusion. Another example would be if the sender is telling you something that makes you feel defensive.

5. **Differences between people.** Differences can include gender, race, creed, age, education, intelligence, experiences, and other personal factors. An example may be someone with a Ph.D. trying to speak with someone who did not finish high school. Another example could be an 80-year-old person talking to a teenager about what is good music. The chances are fairly good that neither one is familiar with the other's music. The solution is for people to find a common frame of reference and try to see the situation from the other's point of view. Even with that said, communication can still be challenging because of the inherent differences between people.

6. **Relationship between the sender and the receiver.** This occurs when one person has a higher position or more status than the other person does. Examples are a boss talking to a subordinate or a parent talking to a child. The subordinate and the child may be inhibited in what they can say to the other person. The solution is for the higher-status person to try to put the other person at ease and speak at his or her level.

7. **Filtering.** In some cases, the sender may only give enough information to get a favorable response from the receiver. For example, my daughter might tell me she is going out with Christina and Joanna, and I would say, "okay." She may have left out that Tom, George, and Jason were also going, knowing if she had added that information I would have said "no."

8. **Selective perception.** The receiver may only hear selective parts of the message from the sender that are of particular interest to the receiver. You might tell your boss about plans for a new computer system, and the boss doesn't pay attention until cost numbers are mentioned.

Action or Response

If all goes well, the **receiver** will get the message. If the message requires a response, the receiver will need to consider how to respond to the message. If the message was not understood, the receiver should ask that the message be repeated or explained.

Looking for the Response-Feedback

Once the message has been decoded by the receiver, the sender may be looking for a response from the receiver, or **feedback.** If the communication was a command or a request, the sender will be monitoring to see if the receiver takes the appropriate action. If the appropriate action is not taken, the sender will probably want to send the message again perhaps by way of a different medium, such as putting it in writing if the first message is oral. If the message requires a response, the sender will be looking for the receiver to reply. If there is no reply or the response is inappropriate, the sender may have to send the message again in its original form or adapt the message in terms of content or medium.

One excellent way to give feedback is to paraphrase the message back to the sender, or repeat the message to the sender in your own words. If you have not understood the message as the sender intended, the paraphrasing technique can identify the problem.

Based on the self-assessment test at the beginning of this chapter, how good are your listening skills? This is a weak area for many people. How good are you at giving feedback? Good listening and feedback skills can eliminate many communication problems.

Communication within Organizations

People in organizations are expected to have good communication in the workplace. Researchers have linked effective communication strategies to productivity gains, efficiency improvements, cost reductions, improved morale, and decreased turnover.[106] Several forms of communication happen in the workplace, including **lateral** (peer), **upward** (superior), **downward** (subordinates), and **outside** (customers, suppliers, and others in the organization). (See Figure 11–2.) In lateral communication, people talk to their peers within their departments and those outside their departments at the same level in the organization. Although much of the lateral communication is work-related and used for solving problems or handling conflicts, some may be social in nature. This social communication is valuable in building good working relationships with people leading to increased cohesiveness and improved workplace satisfaction. In upward communication, the person talks to those above him or her in rank in the organization. Much of this communication is getting orders and information from superiors and passing along status reports and information to superiors. This feedback and valuable information allows for better decision making and provides opportunities for greater employee engagement.

In downward communication, the person is passing along orders and information to those at lower levels of the organization and getting information and status reports from them. When communicating with those outside the organization, the person is responsible for representing the organization and providing a positive view of the company. It is essential

Communication occurs in four different directions:
- Upward
- Downward
- Laterally
- Outside

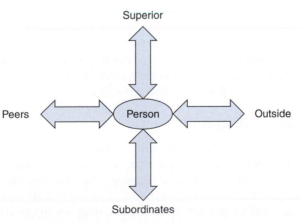

Figure 11–2 Organizational communication model.

that the organization have good relations with customers and suppliers to ensure future sales and continuing sources of material for operations. Good communication with government, citizens in the community, and others also are included in outside communication.

OTHER CONSIDERATIONS IN COMMUNICATIONS

The Grapevine and Rumors

The **grapevine** is the informal communication network within an organization.

Why do we participate in the grapevine or rumor mill? The truth is it is fun. It also fulfills an important gap in the information being received. Gossip in the grapevine in the form of rumors is everywhere in the organization. Most organizations have a well-developed **grapevine.** The grapevine is an informal part of communications within organizations. The grapevine passes along stories that get started and passed around by employees. Stories from the grapevine range in reliability from absolute truths to far-fetched, unbelievable tales. This may surprise you, but studies have shown that about 75 percent of the stories from the grapevine are accurate.[107]

Rumors are unsubstantiated stories that appear to be important, cause anxiety, and are ambiguous.

Rumors are a special part of the grapevine. Rumors usually refer to unsubstantiated stories that have three characteristics:

- The information appears to be important.
- The information creates anxiety.
- There is ambiguity.

The most effective way for dealing with rumors is by telling the truth. True stories in the rumor mill should be supported and lies should be discredited. Stories with half-truths should be explained to eliminate any wrong belief on the part of employees.

The classic example of a rumor mill is the story about one company that had lost two small orders due to being at full capacity in the production area. Despite operating at full capacity, the rumor mill quickly spread the story about the two orders being lost. The story later was revised to two large orders lost and then grew to the loss of two large customers. The story finally ended up with company on the verge of going out of business. When managers heard this rumor, they released the real truth about the situation and the rumor mill was temporary silenced.

Voice Tones

Sometimes the way we say things is more important than what we say. A voice tone can reflect how we really feel about what is being said. Have you ever noticed how a sharp, raised voice can mean anger? We want to be sure that our voice tones truly reflect what we are trying to communicate. When we have just exchanged harsh words with someone, how do we start our conversation with someone else? Is there a carry-over effect? Make sure that your voice tone is truly directed at the person to whom you are speaking.

Body Language and Gestures

Body language also influences the way people understand our message. Openness can be seen in a relaxed style with arms at one's side or arms open. A closed style indicating the person may be uncomfortable in the situation can be seen in arms held close to the body and standing a greater distance from the other person. Consider using an open style to promote friendliness and understanding in your conversations.

People often express themselves with their hands. Thus, people are really communicating their feelings by the use of their hands. Have you ever noticed the friendly gestures that drivers use on the road when someone cuts them off? Make sure your gestures support your verbal communications.

PRACTICAL APPLICATION

The American Management Association has suggested ten ways to make the communication process work better for people. These **Ten Commandments of Good Communication** are

1. **Seek to clarify your ideas before communicating.** Make sure you know what you are trying to say.

2. **Examine the true purpose of each communication.** How many times have we all said something that we wish we had not said? Thinking about the purpose of the communication will help prevent this from happening so much.

3. **Consider the total physical and human setting whenever you communicate.** For example, having a business conversation in a nonbusiness setting may not be taken seriously or remembered by the receivers.

4. **Consult with others, where appropriate, in planning communications.** It might be a good idea to ask another person if he or she understands the message before giving it to others.

5. **Be mindful of the overtones as well as the basic content of your message.** People can read things into our message by the voice tone and gestures that are used in the delivery process.

6. **Take the opportunity, when it arises, to convey something of help or value to the receiver.** One way to build good communications is by helping other people. If you have helped them in the past, they will probably listen favorably to you in the future.

7. **Follow up your communication.** It is a good idea to make sure that the receiver has gotten the message. You might follow up on the original message with another message, perhaps using a different medium.

8. **Communicate for tomorrow as well as today.** Remember that the way you communicate with someone today sets the tone for that relationship in the future.

9. **Be sure your actions support your communications.** People speak louder with their actions than they do with their words. A boss who is always late for work will have difficulty trying to tell people to be on time.

10. **Seek not only to be understood but also to understand—be a good listener.** People must take the time to listen to what others have to say if they want people to take time to listen to them.

Source: Ten Commandments of Good Communication from *Management Review,* American Management Association, October 1955. Copyright 1955 by the American Management Association. Reproduced with permission of the American Management Association in the format Textbook via Copyright Clearance Center.

CURRENT NEEDS AND COMMUNICATION

Communication is an easy process to explain and a hard process to use. Effective leaders/managers clearly communicate mutually set expectations, making sure everyone has clear objectives and performance measures.

Effective leaders/managers provide continuous feedback, give stretch goals to achieve, and ensure the achievements are recognized. There are miscommunications every day in life at work, in school, at home, or just being with friends. Communication problems have been linked to people quitting their jobs, being fired, getting divorces, leaving organizations such as churches and clubs, and having disputes with neighbors, friends, family, and others. The ten commandments of good communication can help people overcome these problems. Communicating to be understood and being a good listener are crucial. Another important aspect of communication is to think about what you are saying before you say it. As one may well put it, put your brain in gear before you put your mouth in gear, and remember today's communications set the tone for tomorrow's relationships.

SUMMARY

The communication process consists of (1) the source who encodes (constructs) the message, chooses the medium (channel), and sends the message, and (2) the receiver who decodes (understands) the message, takes appropriate action, and provides feedback to the source.

Barriers interfere with or hinder the communication process at any one of the different steps. Some of these typical barriers are unfamiliar language, improper timing, noise and distractions in the environment, attitude, differences between people, relationships between the sender and the receiver, filtering of the communication, and selective perception where the receiver hears selectively those parts that fit his or her understanding.

Informal communication in organizations includes rumors carried by the grapevine. Informal communication will often be believed over the formal communication. In fact, research has shown about 75 percent of the information shared through the grapevine is accurate. Rumors, on the other hand, refer to substantiated stories. The fact that the grapevine and rumors are often rampant is due to the perception that communication being shared formally by the organization does not provide the important information. In addition, the information shared by leaders may create anxiety or ambiguity that gives rise to rumors.

Communication can be altered by voice tones, body language, and gestures. People will believe what they see through the body language and gestures over what they hear. The ultimate goal of communication is to have understanding on the part of the receiver.

Sherrill's Gas Station and Convenience Store, which sits at the intersection of US Highway 31 and Indiana Highway 28, has a sign that reads "EAT HERE and GET GAS." Remember, communication is what the receiver understands and not always what the sender says.

CASE STUDY

Ajax Plastics Company was at full production and the orders for new injection molding products were increasing. Bill Bright, the president, was working with the bank to bring in money for an expansion of the business, including two new production lines and 20 new jobs. In the meantime, none of the orders they were getting could be filled on the timetables given them by the customers. Bill decided to have a meeting with his three production managers to discuss the issue.

Bill and the three managers met and developed a plan to deal with the situation. They decided they would make every effort to keep all of their customers. The larger customers that accounted for 80 percent of the company's revenue would be given priority. The other existing customers would receive next priority in getting their orders out on time. New customers, especially those with small orders, would be given last priority and told that their orders would be finished within four to five weeks. This strategy would keep all the big customers happy and would also meet the needs of most other customers.

Barnick Company was a local company that sold molded plastic products. Barnick had used an out-of-town plastic molder for all their work. A large order came from one of Barnick's customers and the out-of-town supplier could not handle the entire order. So, Barnick placed a call to Ajax for a small order and was told that the order would take four to five weeks to complete. The customer needed the products in three weeks. Barnick decided to go elsewhere for the products. Barnick understood Ajax's situation and agreed to talk to them in the future if a need arose.

Canbay Company was a plastic toy manufacturer. Their latest creation, Mr. Rubber Monkey, had created a sensation in the toy world. They needed someone to make extra toys to supplement their production. They contacted Ajax and were told that it would take four to five weeks to start production on the toys, even if Ajax could be given the mold from Canbay. As the two companies were discussing production plans, the demand for the toy dropped sharply and Canbay realized that they could now produce the number of toys needed. Canbay informed Ajax that their services were no longer needed. Both companies agreed to remain in contact and perhaps to work together in the future.

Bill ended the weekly meeting with the production managers by telling them how great things were going and how all the customers were happy except two potential customers that he thought he could get back to in the future when the production facility expanded. On the way out of the office, Bill commented to one of the production managers that he hated losing the Barnick and Canbay jobs. Alice, the office secretary, heard that comment and it stuck with her.

That Friday night, employees of Ajax were sitting in their favorite tavern, Al's Place. They were having a few beers and watching the baseball game on a large screen television. A few employees from Barnick and Canbay also happened to be in the bar. As the conversation turned to work, the Ajax employees told the others where they worked. The Canbay employees said that was too bad as Ajax had just lost a deal with Canbay for the production of a hot toy item. The Barnick people chimed in that Ajax had just lost a deal with them for plastic products. One Barnick employee said things must be getting rough for you guys at Ajax after losing these deals. The Ajax employees began to wonder about their company and their jobs.

Monday morning in the break room, Alice was having her morning coffee. She overheard some production workers talking about what they had heard in the bar on Friday night. Nick said it sounds like we are in big trouble if those guys were right about us losing the Barnick and Canbay jobs. Alice piped in that she had heard from Bill himself that he hated losing those jobs. The more the group thought about it, the more serious the situation was becoming. Nick went out and told workers about hearing it straight from Alice that the company was in serious trouble as a result of losing two large jobs. Joe passed along the information that Ajax had lost two huge orders and they were in trouble. Bob picked up this knowledge and informed people on his production line

that the company was in big trouble and some workers were going to be laid off. Fred, hearing what Bob had said, passed along to more workers the company was going under and they were all going to lose their jobs.

By late afternoon, workers were pushing the production managers for information about the company shutdown and the layoffs. The three production managers met and discussed the news they just heard from the workers. They concluded that the workers had it wrong and they needed to talk to Bill now. In their meeting with Bill, they told him about the stories of losing huge orders, the plant closing, and everyone losing their jobs. Bill told the production managers that all the stories were ridiculous.

Bill decided to call a factory meeting and address all the employees. The meeting was set that night in the high school auditorium. As Bill approached the podium, there were several anxious listeners in the audience. Bill told them that they had lost the Barnick and Canbay jobs because the Barnick timetable could not be met and the demand for the Canbay product had fallen. He went on to tell them that these were two very small jobs that would not impact the company at all. In fact, he told them about how they were arranging jobs to cover increasing demand for their products while keeping their customers happy. He went on to assure them their jobs were safe and plans were under way to add two new production lines and twenty new jobs.

The workers were relieved to find out the truth about the situation, but wondered why Bill had not told them more about company plans sooner. Bill, the managers, and workers left the meeting wondering how a wild inaccurate story about the company closing and everyone losing their jobs ever got started and spread around the company.

Questions

1. How did the rumor get started?
2. Was there any basis to the rumor?
3. What happened to the rumor as it spread throughout the company?
4. Did Bill handle this situation in the right way?
5. What could the company have done to prevent this rumor from happening?

DISCUSSION QUESTIONS

1. Discuss the barriers to communication that exist between the instructor and the students in the classroom.
2. Share some examples of communication through the grapevine and then discuss how the communication process may be improved to minimize the impact of the grapevine.
3. Demonstrate communication through the use of body language.
4. Share ideas for effective listening.

DID YOU KNOW . . .

People remember:

10 percent of what they read,

20 percent of what they hear,

30 percent of what they see,

50 percent of what they see and hear,

80 percent of what they say, and

90 percent of what they say and do.

If you tell 100 people something without repetition:

After 24 hours, 25 percent have forgotten it.

After 48 hours, 50 percent have forgotten it.

After 72 hours, 75 percent have forgotten it.

After one week, 96 percent have forgotten it.[108]

CHAPTER 12

Conflict

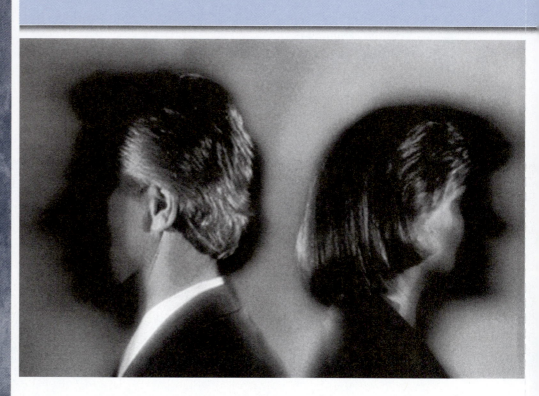

LEARNING OUTCOMES: CONFLICT

1. Define conflict.

2. Contrast the three views of conflict.

3. Describe the five conflict-handling strategies.

4. Discuss the use of a third party to resolve conflict.

5. Differentiate between conciliation, fact finding, fact finding with recommendations, mediation, and arbitration for seeking conflict resolution.

6. Through self-assessment, gain a greater understanding of one's own preferred conflict-handling style.

Name: _____

Section Number: _____

SELF-ASSESSMENT TEST

Please complete the following exercise online, accessible with the Access Card packaged with this text, before reading this chapter.

EXERCISE II.C.5: WHAT'S MY PREFERRED CONFLICT-HANDLING STYLE? Your Highest Score _____

Competing _____

Collaborating _____

Avoiding _____

Accommodating _____

Compromising _____

Research has identified five conflict-handling styles:

- **Competing.** A desire to satisfy one's interests, regardless of the impact on the other party to the conflict.
- **Collaborating.** Where the parties to a conflict each desire to satisfy fully the concerns of all parties.
- **Avoiding.** The desire to withdraw from or suppress the conflict.
- **Accommodating.** Willingness of one party in a conflict to place the opponent's interest above his or her own.
- **Compromising.** Where each party to a conflict is willing to give up something.

Ideally, we should adjust our conflict-handling style to the situation. For instance, avoidance works well when a conflict is trivial, when emotions are running high and time is needed to cool them down, or when the potential disruption from a more assertive action outweighs the benefits of a resolution. In contrast, competing works well when you need a quick resolution of important issues, where unpopular actions must be taken, or when commitment by others to your solution is not critical. However, the evidence indicates that we all have a preferred style for handling conflicts. In tough situations, this is the style on which we tend to rely. Your score on this instrument provides you with insight into this preferred style. Use this information to work against your natural tendencies when the situation requires a different style.

You should also record your score on this exercise in Appendix 1.

NOTES

The Conflict

The old church needed a new roof and the church board had the responsibility to decide how to fix it. Some of the board members wanted to buy an asphalt shingle roof with a thirty-year warranty, and some of the board members preferred a new type of metal roof, also with a thirty-year warranty. The issue created a great amount of anger on the board. Every time the issue of the roof was brought up, people would get mad and leave.

The chair of the board decided to put the roof issue on the agenda as the last item for all board meetings. This was done so the board could get other business finished. This continued for several weeks until the roof issue was not on the agenda and was not discussed at all. People preferred avoiding the roof issue rather than discussing it. A decision was never reached.

One night a severe thunderstorm struck the community and blew portions of the old roof off the church. This caused extensive water damage to the building and contents.

Did the church do the right thing by not making a decision? Welcome to Conflict! ■

Conflict is something we all face when working with others. Conflict is not always bad. Conflict can sometimes lead to more creativity and better ideas. It is important to deal with conflict in a constructive way.

The very nature of business activities and the individual interactions breed conflict. **Conflict** can be defined as a process where one party perceives that another party has negatively affected (or is about to negatively affect) something of concern to the first party. If no one is aware of a conflict, then it is generally agreed that no conflict exists. In many instances an employee will avoid actual or perceived conflict until the situation seems to be unmanageable.

As we can see, in our personal world and the business world, to succeed a leader must be competent in handling conflict. We can find ourselves in conflict with others over a variety of issues. It may be something as simple as what to have for dinner. You may prefer chicken, and the other person may want pizza. Deciding to have chicken tonight and pizza tomorrow night demonstrates your ability to resolve the conflict. Unfortunately, not all conflicts are this easy to solve. This chapter will look at conflict from several different angles.

> **Conflict** is a process where one party perceives that another party has negatively affected or is about to negatively affect something that the first party cares about.

DIFFERING VIEWS OF CONFLICT

Different people view conflicts differently. Some people, known as *traditionalists*, believe that conflicts should be avoided. This **traditional view** is probably unrealistic because life presents people with many conflicts. The second view of conflicts, known as the **human relations view,** is that conflicts are a natural part of life and that people need to learn how to resolve them. Most people believe this to be the case. When faced with life's conflicts, people need to learn how to handle them in the best way. A new way to view conflict is the **interactionist view.** With the interactionist view,

> Is conflict good or bad?
>
> Three views:
> - Traditional
> - Human relations
> - Interactionist

conflict is seen as a positive force that is needed for groups to perform effectively. Conflict keeps groups changing and innovative.

Some conflict is beneficial, and this type of conflict should be encouraged as a way to promote progress. If the conflict outcome supports the goals of the organization or improves performance, the conflict is viewed as being **functional.** When two managers are in conflict about the best way to improve productivity, and the conflict pushes them to come up with an idea that increases productivity by 10 percent, the conflict can be classified as functional.

If the conflict outcome does not support the goals of the organization or hinders performance, the conflict is viewed as being **dysfunctional.** When two managers disagree on which plan to use to increase quality and the dispute leads to a decrease in quality when one manager refuses to use the plan chosen, the conflict can be classified as dysfunctional.

Conflict management is achieving the desired conflict level.

INFORMATIONAL-BASED CONFLICTS

In some conflicts, resolution is easy and benefits both sides.

Some conflicts can be resolved when information is shared between the parties. This occurs because parties involved in a conflict situation seldom have perfect or complete information. When information is shared, the parties can easily make the right choice that will be agreeable to all concerned. The way to resolve informational-based conflicts is to share information, values, and points of view. For example, you and your friend are going to take a trip from your town to another city 300 miles away. You want to take the interstate because you want the trip to be as fast as possible, but your friend wants to take the highway because it is more scenic. Your friend knows that the interstate is being repaired in several areas and there will be lengthy delays. During the discussion on which way is the best, your friend tells you about the problem with the interstate and points out the fact that the highway will be faster than the interstate. Sharing this information has now made the choice of the highway the obvious one. You and your friend will be traveling down both the fastest and the most scenic route.

Strategies for Handling Conflict

Some situations are much more complex and require much more effort to resolve than just sharing information. These situations are known as *win-lose situations* because one side's win is typically the other side's loss. For example, you and a friend are trying to decide where to invest $1,000 that is currently earning 2 percent interest in a savings account at the local bank. Your friend wants to put the money into high-tech (risky) stocks that could earn 15 percent. You want to put the money in blue chip (conservative) stocks that could earn 8 percent. The problem is that if you invest all the money in risky stocks, there is no money left to put into conservative stocks and vice versa. The goal is to resolve this conflict without ruining the friendship.

In deciding how to handle a conflict, two key variables come into play. One is called **assertiveness.** Assertiveness is a measure of how much you want to have your way. If you feel strongly about something, you are going to be more apt to be assertive to get it. The other variable is **cooperativeness.** Cooperativeness is the measure of how much you want another person to get what he or she wants. If you want to establish a good relationship with other people and/or the decision is not important to you, you will be inclined to cooperate with those persons to help them get what they want.

Depending on the levels of assertiveness and cooperativeness, there are five general strategies for handling conflict: avoiding, accommodating, competing, compromising, and collaborating (see Figure 12–1):

- **Avoiding Strategy.** You and your friend may decide not to make a decision at all by leaving the money in the bank. In this case, the conflict is avoided when both parties decide to leave the money in the bank, but it is not the best use of the money because either choice would have been better than leaving the money where it is. In an organization sense, two managers may not like each other, and they do not have to deal with each other on the job. A possible solution to their conflict is to simply avoid each other and concentrate on doing their respective jobs. Avoiding is low in both cooperation and assertiveness.

- **Accommodating Strategy.** Under the accommodating strategy, you would want to give your friend what he or she wants to make your friend happy and preserve your friendship. In our example, all of the money would be invested in the high-tech stocks as requested by your friend. An accommodating strategy is low in assertiveness because you are not trying to have your own way, but it is high in cooperation because you are meeting the other person's demands. In other words, you choose to lose so that your friend can win. In an organization sense, a manager may want to accommodate another manager on a current conflict that may not be all that important in order to have the other manager accommodate him or her in a later conflict that may be important. The manager may accommodate another manager on the schedule of a rush job when the shop schedule is open and may want the other manager to accommodate him or her on delaying a job when the shop schedule is full. Accommodating can be a good way to build relationships and trade for favors in the future.

- **Competing Strategy.** Under the competing strategy, the main goal is to have your own way or win the conflict. In our example, you would vigorously pursue the conservative stock strategy even if it costs you your friendship. Competing is common in everyday life as people, schools, and companies try to beat their opponents. Competing, as you might have guessed, is high in assertiveness and low in cooperation. The outcome of

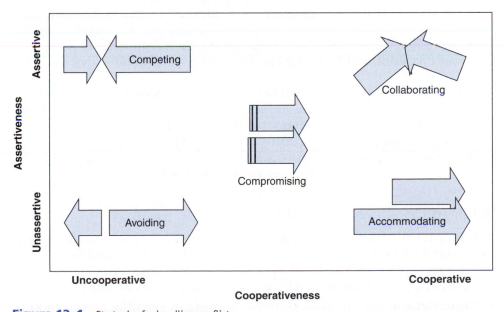

Figure 12–1 Strategies for handling conflict.

Source: Strategies for Handling Conflict from "Conflict and Negotiation in Organizations," by K. Thomas, in *Handbook of Industrial and Organizational Psychology*, 2nd ed., Vol. 3, M. D. Dunette and L. M. Hough (eds.), Palo Alto, CA: Consulting Psychologists Press, 1992, p. 668. Reprinted by permission of M. D. Dunette and L. M. Hough.

this strategy is that one party will win and the other party will lose. When trying to deal with another company in the marketplace, competing with them for customers is perfectly acceptable. The problem with competing occurs within the organization. People who should be working together for the good of the company often find themselves competing with one another. Competing within an organization probably is not a preferred strategy.

■ **Compromising Strategy.** Under the compromising strategy, the parties will try to work out the situation so nobody gets all that he or she wants, but everyone gets something. In our example, you and your friend may decide to invest $500 in risky stocks and $500 in conservative stocks. Neither gets all that you wanted, but both of you get something. Compromising involves both assertiveness and cooperation. Compromising is a popular way to resolve conflicts because neither side experiences a total loss and both sides experience some sense of winning. Compromise seems to be a way of life in business as well as in personal settings. A purchasing agent may want a shipment of material at a certain price and on a certain day. The supplier may be able to get the material there on the requested day but cannot do it at the price the purchasing agent wants. The compromise may be that the material will be there a day later than the purchasing agent wanted and a day before the supplier wanted at a price lower than the supplier offered and higher than the purchasing agent wanted. The result is that neither the supplier nor the purchasing agent got all of what he or she wanted, but they did reach a deal and both got some of what they wanted.

■ **Collaborating Strategy.** Under the collaborating strategy, parties are pushed to find a way that both sides can win. Collaborating involves both a high degree of assertiveness and a high degree of cooperation. This makes both parties work hard and possibly think hard to come up with the best solution. In our example, if you and your friend agreed to put all the money in high-tech stocks at the beginning and invest all the proceeds in conservative stocks, this collaborating strategy would allow both of you to have what you want over time. This is probably the ideal way to handle conflict, but it is often not used because of the amount of time, assertiveness, and cooperation it requires. Within companies this is the preferred way to handle conflict. Marketing and production may have conflicts about getting out customers' orders. By working out the best possible schedules, the two departments may be able to meet customer demands within a schedule that meets production capacity.

Based on the self-assessment test at the beginning of this chapter, what is your preferred method of handling conflict? Where is this style most effective? In what situations could this style cause you problems? You should carefully consider which conflict management strategy is most appropriate for the situation rather than simply relying on your preferred style.

What to Do When the Conflict Cannot Be Resolved

What can you do when a conflict cannot be resolved by the parties involved?

Many times the parties involved in a conflict cannot resolve it. This usually happens when the parties choose a competing strategy and are high in assertiveness. One way to help people resolve their differences is by using a third party. The third party will help get the two sides together.

■ **Conciliation.** Conciliation is aimed at trying to keep the parties talking about resolving the conflict or to get them to start talking about resolving the conflict. The conciliator cannot offer solutions or make a final decision, but he or she can keep the parties moving toward a solution.

- **Fact Finding.** A fact finder is used when the parties disagree over the facts of the conflict. An example of this may be when one neighbor claims a tree is on his property and the other neighbor claims the same tree is on his property. A fact finder would come out and determine the property line and inform the parties as to the exact location of the tree in respect to each person's lot. The job of the fact finder is simply to provide the parties with the facts relevant to the conflict. It is hoped that the facts will help the parties resolve their conflict.

- **Fact Finding with Recommendations.** Sometimes the parties want the fact finder to go a step further and make recommendations about how the conflict should be resolved. It should be noted that the fact finder can discover the facts and make recommendations when asked to do so, but the parties are under no obligation to accept the recommendations as a final settlement of the conflict.

- **Consultant.** A consultant is a person in a position to aid in the problem solving through communication and analysis, sharing of expertise and influence over the individual, group, or organization to make changes for resolution of the conflict. The consultant has no direct power to make changes or implement programs, but rather he or she assists the parties to move toward understanding and resolution of the conflict with a goal of a long-term solution.

- **Mediation.** When the parties want a third person to help them reach an agreement by keeping them talking and making suggestions about a solution, this is called *mediation*. A mediator can be anybody the parties want. Mediation has for many years been a part of labor/management conflict resolution. Now, it has popularity for resolving all manner of conflicts, including domestic, buyer/seller, neighborhood, school, and workplace. This method allows people to work through their conflicts with the aid of an outside person. Not only is the mediator allowing people to work through their conflict, but the mediator can also provide them with resolutions that they may not have found on their own. When effectively communicated to employees and properly managed, mediating workplace claims can yield quick, inexpensive, and just resolutions in a confidential and respectful manner.[109]

- **Arbitration.** When parties become deadlocked in a conflict, one solution is to turn to arbitration. An arbitrator will make the final decision to resolve a conflict. The arbitrator will hear from both sides and make a decision that is binding on the parties. Before an arbitrator will hear a case, the parties have to agree to abide by the decision made by the arbitrator. Arbitration is often used in union/management negotiations when both sides cannot reach an agreement on a contract or when the two sides cannot reach an agreement on how a grievance should be settled. Arbitration can also be used in other situations involving conflict when the parties cannot reach an agreement by themselves.

UNDERSTANDING CONFLICT

Conflict will arise in nearly all aspects of your life. There can be conflict on the job with a superior, a coworker, a subordinate, a customer, a supplier, or someone else in the business environment. One study that focused on sources of interpersonal conflicts in the workplace found approximately 62 percent of the primary issues that result in "conflict between subordinates and supervisors" derived from issues such as goal conflict, rejection of employee input, vague task assignments, performance evaluations, work scheduling, and workloads. The same study found that approximately 61 percent of the primary issues that generated "conflict between coworkers" concerned personalities, workload allocation, goal conflicts, and ethical concerns. Interestingly, an employee who is in conflict with a supervisor is generally inclined to disucss the conflict with the supervisor; however, an employee who is in conflict with a coworker is more likely to avoid the coworker and not address the conflict.[110] Failure to resolve conflicts on the job in a positive way can be detrimental to the business and/or the employee. Conflicts at home can lead to problems for both spouses and children, the most common of which are divorce and abuse. Conflict with others can explode into the violence we see more and more everyday with shootings in businesses, in schools, in churches, in community centers, on the streets, and at home.

Conflict needs to be resolved in nonviolent ways. Certainly, one thing people can do is to attack the problem or the source of conflict and not each other. The goal of conflict management is to resolve the conflict in a collaborative way where all the parties feel they have won. A compromise is also a desirable outcome in that the parties feel they have made some gains and have achieved at least a partial victory. The appropriate method depends on the parties involved as well as the situation, but the collaborative approach usually offers the best solutions if the parties are willing and able to invest the time and energy required.

SUMMARY

Are you a leader who can competently handle conflict? This chapter discussed the dynamics of conflict, helped you to understand your own behavioral tendency and reaction to conflict, provided constructive responses to conflict, and provided insights into conflict resolution.

Conflict is defined as a process where one party perceives that another party has negatively affected (or is about to negatively affect) something of concern to the first party.

Conflicts can be viewed in three ways:

- The traditional view is that conflicts should be avoided.
- The human relations view is that conflicts are a natural part of life, and people need to learn how to resolve them.
- The interactionist view is that conflicts are positive and lead to innovation and change.

Informational-based conflicts can be resolved by sharing information. Conflict may also be functional, when it supports the goals of the organization, and dysfunctional, when it hinders performance and does not support organizational goals.

Strategies for handling conflict include:

- Competing (wanting to win by creating a win/lose situation).
- Collaborating (wanting to work together for a win/win situation).
- Avoiding (deciding not make a decision).
- Accommodating (letting the other side win).
- Compromising (working to get some of what you want).

Not all conflict can be resolved between the two parties; sometimes a third party is required to intervene. Techniques for resolving a conflict involving a third party include:

- Conciliation (keeping both sides talking).
- Fact finding (getting the facts of the conflict).
- Fact finding with recommendations (getting the facts and offering a solution).
- Mediation (making suggestions about solutions).
- Arbitration (making the final decision for the parties involved).

CASE STUDY

Ted Brown was a typical 35-year-old business executive. He was vice president of the Seemore Advertising Agency. In college, he majored in marketing and the only experience he had in marketing was a summer internship with Seemore. Seemore liked him and offered him a job after graduation. Since joining Seemore, he learned the advertising business from the bottom up and now was the youngest vice president in the agency. He was married to Jill and had two children, Rick, age nine, and Ann, age five. A typical day for Ted consisted of getting up at six, taking a quick shower, having breakfast with the family, and heading off to work for a nine-to-five day that sometimes would go later, going home for dinner, having the evening with the family, and going to bed around eleven. Occasionally Ted would have to travel

out of town to meet with clients, but that was rare for a man in his position.

One day as Ted started his day, Rick asked him for $40 to buy a new video game that everyone else had. Ted said no and Rick continued to badger him about getting the game. Rick resorted to using the "c" word by calling Ted cheap. Ted ended the conversation with the "n" word no. Ted knew if he had given in to Rick he would be seen as a pushover and Rick would continue to badger him for more things. Ted was trying to teach Rick to manage his money so he could buy the things he wanted without having to ask for more money.

That same day, Jill approached Ted as he was leaving. She asked him if it would be all right for them to go to the Turners' house on Friday night. The Turners were very boring and Ted did not enjoy spending time with them. Ted could put up an argument, but it would probably make him late for work. Remembering how much Jill likes Jane Turner and figuring it would not hurt him to be a nice guy about going, he agreed to go with the closing comment that Jill "owed him one." Jill agreed and Ted was out of the door.

When Ted arrived at work, he found that he had a voice message from Don Patterson, who was trying to chair the Lion's Club major fundraiser. Ted and Don had gotten into a heated discussion about who should chair the fundraiser. Ted thought Don lacked experience, had a history of not following through on things, and Fred would make a better choice for chair. This was a big deal for Don who was trying to prove something by running this event. Initially Ted was determined not to let Don push him around in front of the other Lions. The more he thought about it, the less important the whole thing had become to Ted. The vote on the chair's position was coming at the next meeting and Ted could not care less. Ted chose not to return the call and leave the decision of choosing a chair for the fundraiser to a vote of the club.

Later that morning, Ted received a call from Charles, an angry customer. He stated that the junior marketing representative on his account had failed to listen to his suggestions about how to promote his new product. This customer was one of Ted's first accounts when he joined the agency. He tried to explain that he did not handle accounts anymore and Mark was his account representative. He told Charles he would check on this and call him back. After talking to Mark, it was apparent Mark had not listened to Charles. Mark was a young, aggressive, know-it-all with a huge ego. Mark felt like he knew more than the customers. Mark was somewhat resentful of the call from Ted. Ted realized he needed to take charge of this situation before Charles, and his large account, left the agency. First, Ted called Charles and apologized on behalf of the agency. He also told Charles that he personally would take care of the problem. Ted brought in Mark and informed him that he was very talented, but he needed to work better with the customers. He told Mark to lose the ego around the customers and to come to a meeting with Charles and him. Mark agreed and admitted he had a bit of a big head. Ted assured Mark he could be successful if he heard customers out. At the meeting, Ted assured Charles the agency wanted his business and that Mark and he were going to get this job done. Charles, seeing that Ted was back in the game, agreed to let

them keep the business. Mark was now listening to Charles and was playing on his ideas. The situation was resolved when Mark produced an outstanding advertising campaign for Charles. Charles and Mark both thanked Ted for his help.

Late in the afternoon, Ted got a call from George at *Be Fashionable* magazine about advertising rates at $60,000 per page and $40,000 for a half page. Ted offered to pay $40,000 per page and $20,000 per half page. Ted really needed to be in the magazine with a spring advertisement for his client. George, on the other hand, had more pages to sell than he had advertisers. George said he was sorry, but he could not go any lower. Ted, knowing George was a wheeler-dealer who always came down on his rates, said fine and hung up. George called back and wanted to know if Ted had changed his mind and Ted said no and that he was looking into other magazines. George replied to Ted by asking him to not commit to anyone else until he got back to him. Ted said he had a business to run and could not wait for George to make up his mind about the rates. George called back with an offer of $55,000 per page and $35,000 for a half page. Ted said that he would think about it and call him back. Ted called back with an offer of $45,000 per page and $25,000 for a half page. George said he would think about it. George called back an hour later wanting to meet Ted in the middle. Ted and George agreed on $50,000 per page and $30,000 for a half page. George complained that he had been taken to the cleaners, but both men knew they had gotten their best deal out of the other.

Ted returned home and had dinner with his family. At dinner, Rick once again brought up the $40 for the new video game. Ted looked at Rick with that fatherly look that said no way and repeated firmly his "no" from the morning. Rick, knowing that Dad was not going to give in on this matter, promptly dropped it. The family settled into a good night at home.

Questions

1. What strategy for handling conflict did Ted use on Rick and did it work?

2. What strategy for handling conflict did Ted use on Jill and did it work?

3. What strategy for handling conflict did Ted use on Don and did it work?

4. What strategy for handling conflict did Ted use on Charles and Mark and did it work?

5. What strategy for handing conflict did Ted use on George and did it work?

DISCUSSION QUESTIONS

1. What strategy do you usually use in handling a conflict?

2. Give an example of when it is appropriate to use each of the conflict-handling techniques.

3. Discuss the differences between the various forms of third-party intervention for conflict resolution.

4. Give an example of the interactionist approach to conflict.

CHAPTER 13

Negotiation

LEARNING OUTCOMES: NEGOTIATION

1. Define negotiation.
2. Contrast the distributive and integrative bargaining strategies.
3. Describe the negotiation process.
4. Review the use of the third-party negotiators.
5. Discuss the ethical issues in negotiations.
6. Outline the pitfalls in negotiating.

The Negotiation

The Contrast Company and its union, the United Brotherhood of Lawn and Garden Workers, were engaged in collective bargaining for a new contract for the workers. The company contended that it did not have the money to meet the union's demand of $15 per hour, 15 days vacation per year, and company paid insurance. The company has established its position at $13 per hour, 10 days vacation, and insurance paid equally by the company and the workers.

The union is now threatening a strike in which none of the union workers would report to work. The company is threatening to lock out the workers and not let them get to their jobs. The company is faced with a loss of revenue and the workers are faced with a loss of pay. Neither side really wants either a strike or a lock out.

What can be done to help the Contrast Company and its union reach an agreement that both of them will accept?

Welcome to Negotiations! ∎

> *"I like thinking big. I always have. To me it's very simple: if you're going to be thinking anyway, you might as well think big. . . . I don't do it for the money. I've got enough, much more than I'll ever need. I do it to do it. Deals are my art form."*
>
> —*Donald Trump*[111]

Donald Trump, the king of the deal, the consummate negotiator, lives to bargain. He loves to negotiate. When Trump was asked if he was a gambler, his answer was an emphatic "No!" He chooses those situations that are favorable to his overall business plan. Instead of gambling, he buys the gambling business. The odds and the returns are better, he contends.

This chapter will define negotiation and present the following topics:

- The Negotiating Environment
- Bargaining Strategies
- The Negotiation Process
- Third-Party Intervention
- Some Concluding Issues

Just what is **negotiation?** It is a process. From an operative point of view, it amounts to an exchange of goods and services for money or something else of value. Negotiation is one of the most important responses to conflict.

> **Negotiation** is a process; it amounts to an exchange of goods and services for something of value.

THE NEGOTIATING ENVIRONMENT

At the personal level parents and children negotiate wardrobes, use of the car, curfews, and the ratio of study time to recreation time. Individual consumers generally do not pay the list price for a home or a car and can also negotiate the interest rate on the loan. Lawyers and criminals negotiate through plea bargaining. Couples will negotiate the settlement for a divorce. Negotiation is always part of the process. Students even negotiate with teachers.

The professional scenario mirrors the personal barter process. The difference is what is at stake. The process may be formal as in the give and take that occurs between management and labor, or it may be informal, which is often the case with mergers and acquisitions.

Negotiation skills can be developed at an early age. Donald Trump would follow his father around and watch him as he negotiated with suppliers. Later, in college, Trump read listings of FHA mortgage foreclosures while his contemporaries read the sports page and comic books.

BARGAINING STRATEGIES

Walton and McKersie identify four types of bargaining strategies: distributive bargaining, integrative bargaining, attitudinal structuring, and intraorganizational bargaining.[112]

Distributive Bargaining

Distributive bargaining is sometimes referred to as **win-lose negotiating**. This strategy assumes someone wins while the other party loses. The concept assumes a fixed amount of resources that may be allocated or distributed to a particular person or function. Distributive bargaining is also considered a short-term solution. The most common example is employee pay. It could just as easily be time. For example, a company may negotiate with supervisors and managers to be on the job thirty minutes before work begins and remain thirty minutes afterward. These people are usually salaried and not necessarily subject to overtime pay. Management's purpose in establishing such a policy is to better prepare all supervisors and managers for the day's work and better tie matters together at work's end. Productivity is expected to increase; the company wins. The supervisors lose since they have less personal time.

The pay example is a clear illustration. Typically an organization, company, or business allocates a fixed sum to be distributed as pay increases for the employees. Management will direct that these limited resources be distributed according to a merit system that results in some employees receiving a larger portion than others. Those employees receiving the larger share are the winners; the others are the pay losers.

Another example is wage bargaining as a part of a collective bargaining agreement. Any time a contract is negotiated, pay and benefit issues are always material. Companies often spend as much on employee benefits as pay. Every dollar the company agrees to provide for increased wages or benefits means a dollar less for the bottom line. There is also a dollar less to distribute to the owners and shareholders. There appear to be clear winners and losers, which is a classic case of distributive bargaining. There is some evidence that performance-based pay programs can minimize distributive bargaining.

Integrative Bargaining

Integrative bargaining assumes there are no losers. Everyone wins. How can that be? Remember laundry day in the dorm? Two roommates agree at the beginning of the school year that Saturday morning will be set aside as laundry day. Each Saturday they make their way to the laundromat and share in the effort. On a particular Saturday one roommate has a chance to join a group for a weekend ski trip. If she accepts, the other roommate is left with the laundry. Prior to the weekend the ski-bound roommate negotiates that, in return for this Saturday's vacation, she will repay the favor by doing the laundry next Saturday. Thus we have two winners.

Distributive bargaining is win-lose negotiating.

Integrative bargaining is win-win negotiating.

It is reasonable to argue that given the right circumstances, all bargaining is integrative. A wage issue need not result in a winner and a loser. Creative managers can eliminate the agony and divisiveness associated with the process by agreeing to share part of the organization's profit with employees. The most common way is through performance-based pay programs. Suppose a company pays a fair base wage to all employees based on experience and level of responsibility. It becomes a simple matter to agree, probably through negotiation, that a portion of future profits will be distributed in some orderly fashion as bonuses. The employees work hard to make the company successful, and since the rewards are shared, everyone wins.

The perception of the negotiating parties often determines whether bargaining is seen as distributive or integrative. To illustrate, consider a retail sales business. This business could be a farm implement store, a landscaping business, or perhaps a large clothing chain.

For a retail salesperson, the bargaining is distributive. Most sales compensation plans actually accentuate the situation. These programs have two elements: a base salary and a bonus or profit sharing based on sales volume or gross profit on sales. The higher the cumulative gross profit or perhaps the larger the volume, the more the commission or bonus. The salesperson therefore views a sale in which a customer wins by successfully negotiating a price close to cost as a loser, since it adds little to gross profit.

Bargaining from the company perspective is integrative and has a long-term focus. Any time something is sold and delivered at retail, the company wins. Since a sale has occurred, the customer is also a winner. The company either owns the inventory or has it on consignment (meaning that ownership is retained by the manufacturer or the supplier until the product is sold). In both cases, the company absorbs interest charges until the product is sold. Therefore a sale will reduce interest costs, result in some amount of profit, and create a new or a repeat customer. Someone once asked, "When do I know if I got a good deal?" The answer is simple: "Were you satisfied?"

Attitudinal Structuring

Attitudinal structuring occurs when the parties try to improve the attitude of the other parties toward them. If the one party does not like, trust, or respect the other party, it can be difficult to enter into negotiations. Thus, prior to negotiation, one party may try to change the attitude of the other party, or both parties may engage in conduct and dialog aimed at improving the relationship with the other party. It should be noted that the best long-term strategy is to cultivate respect and trust over a long period of time by maintaining integrity at the bargaining table and in all other areas of the relationship.

Attitudinal structuring is changing the other party's attitude toward you.

Intraorganizational Bargaining

Intraorganizational bargaining is the process of convincing people on your own side that you are doing the best you can for them in the negotiations. Those on your own side must trust you, have respect for you, and feel that you are doing your best to help them get what they want. This is especially true with union workers who must ratify, or approve, the contract before it goes into effect as the final settlement. If the union workers feel that the negotiator has not done a good job for them, they are likely to reject the contract and the negotiations must continue. It is a good idea to keep the people on your side informed during negotiations, get their feedback, and secure their final approval of what the negotiator has done.

THE NEGOTIATION PROCESS

The negotiation process has three stages: preparation, action, and settling on the details.

Preparation

Stages of negotiation:
- Preparation
- Action
- Closure and implementation

The preparation stage is crucial to the negotiation setup. Where will the negotiation take place? A teen negotiating with his or her parents for the weekend use of the car may choose mealtime. Then again, he or she may choose a fleeting moment such as when leaving the house for school. Location for the teen is of lesser importance than mood or frame of mind. For the corporate negotiators, location can be critical. A neutral site away from telephones, pagers, or any other distraction is of major importance. Once the negotiation begins, any interruption can be a disaster. If there is to be a break in the action, then the negotiators should establish the terms without outside influence.

Business negotiators need to do their homework with regard to the people who will be involved in the negotiation. Who are they and what authority do they have? If one side of the negotiation sends less experienced employees whose task is to set the stage by fact-finding, then by all means, the other side should not engage in any serious give and take on the issues. The reason for sending support people initially is to gain information that may be analyzed and studied by the real negotiators. Inexperienced negotiators are lured into this trap frequently. When faced with the situation without warning, be pleasant and offer nothing of substance. This is not the time to flex your muscles or show your hand. The teenager's dilemma is simpler, "Who do I approach, Mom or Dad?" He or she may even try an end run by asking an older brother to use his wheels. In any case, a teen will rarely negotiate with both parents. Two against one is not fair, and besides, how do you get parents to both be in a consenting mood at the same time?

The early conversation in a serious negotiation is rarely substantive. This conversation may be about outside activities such as golf scores, the latest fate of a sports team, or the latest fashion. The skilled negotiator generally knows the opponent's hot button and, regardless of the negotiator's preferences, plays to the opponent.

Action

As the negotiation begins, it is important to establish the parameters, just what is to be included in the negotiation. If the issue is wages, then avoid any discussion about benefits or work hours unless such issues will be introduced as trade-offs to a potential loss of a crucial point. In other words be prepared to compromise. For example, a business owner may offer flextime, a flexible set of work hours, in exchange for a smaller increase in wages. Flextime generally has a substantially smaller cost to the employer than does the wage increase.

Agree with your team before the negotiation that under no circumstances will there be a confrontation. **Never draw a line in the sand or give the impression that you will not compromise.** It is virtually impossible to negotiate when one party refuses to compromise. If there is an impasse or the conversation becomes strained, adjourn and reconvene when cooler heads can prevail. At the same time, agree with your team before the negotiation that there is a willingness to walk away. To break off negotiations is not necessarily bad as long as a restart is an option. To end negotiations without resolution is fatal.

A young woman came home to her father after shopping for a used car. She told her father that she had found the perfect car and she wanted him to go with her to finalize the deal. She knew her father was a skilled, tough negotiator, and she wanted his help in negotiating a final price. He asked these questions: "Are you sure the car is what you want and did you get a price?" She answered, "Yes" on both counts. The father answered, "If I go with you, are you prepared to walk away if the price does not fit the product value? If the answer is no, then all you need is your checkbook. I am of no value." If a negotiator—in this case, the young woman—becomes personally involved, there is no room for negotiation.

As Harvey Mackay points out in his book *Pushing the Envelope All the Way to the Top*,[113] a skilled negotiator knows that if you make decisions or negotiate with your heart, you will get heartburn. When a negotiator becomes personally attached to an alternative, there is no room for negotiation. Coupled with this point of view is the rule that a negotiator never says yes too early. Sleep on it, think it over, and beware when people on the other side say this is the last, or only, chance. It is a rare negotiation where there is no alternative. Also if it sounds too good to be true, then it probably is. Remember the objective is for everyone to be a winner.

Experienced salespeople will usually never quote a firm price during a negotiation. To do so implies a lack of flexibility. Instead they will give a range. The person who hears the range normally hears only the low point. If the salesperson says the range is $4,000 to $7,000, the customer invariably hears $4,000. Crafty salespeople will therefore establish their low point at a level they can accept and any "up-sell" will sweeten their deal. The teenage daughter who wants to use the car may offer to mow the lawn, rake the leaves, or pull the weeds. The teen's mistake is that while she was suggesting one chore, the parent heard all three. Finally, a victory for the parent.

Body language also plays a major role in any negotiation. If one of the players frowns, makes a nervous move, or shuffles the papers, the answer is clear. That issue is failing.

A common negotiating mistake is to **talk too much.** If the other party has heard your offer and is still sitting down, then the best advice is to stop talking. Experience has shown that the next person who speaks will lose control to the other party. A skilled salesperson knows that when the presentation is complete to stop talking. If the customer is allowed to speak first, the salesperson will likely retain control of the situation.

Closure and Implementation

Obviously cleanup work needs to be done once negotiations are complete. This includes paperwork and implementation strategies. In the teen's case the issues are who buys the gas and when the car will be available. It is unwise to delegate the details to someone else, even though such cleanup work may seem mundane. The reason is often overlooked. The cleanup, the housekeeping, and the details become the setup for the next negotiation. The clever teenager never says "thanks" and moves on. Instead, she says, "Thanks and, by the way, I will wash the car tomorrow after I am finished."

In corporate America or in a sales situation, the details make the deal. If the customer sees care in the details and if there is periodic follow-up, he or she will buy again, guaranteed. If you want proof, try this simple exercise. Ask anyone who has bought a car at least six months ago to tell you his or her salesperson's name. For those who cannot remember the name, ask them if they intend to return to that salesperson for their next car. Ask the same question of those who can remember their salesperson's name. Successful salespeople never lose contact with their customers.

THIRD-PARTY INTERVENTION

Sometimes it becomes necessary to enlist the help of a **third party** to resolve a conflict. These skilled, experienced people may be mediators, arbitrators, conciliators, or consultants. You have seen some of these terms before when talking about handling conflict. Negotiation is one specific type of handling conflict.

Mediators

Mediators are people who are respected by all parties to the negotiations. They may have nothing to do with the issue at hand, but because of a perceived expertise, all parties will listen. In 1997, the Teamsters Union struck the United Parcel Service (UPS). The issues were hiring practices and pension control. UPS was, and is today, the dominant force in the parcel delivery business. When the Teamsters called the strike and the brown UPS trucks stopped making deliveries, there was a major impact on the way that the United States did business. As the strike became prolonged, Alexis Herman, the Secretary of Labor, was called on to help mediate the situation. She had no real authority, but as the Secretary of Labor and a government leader that reported directly to the president, she enjoyed a position of respect. Even though the Teamsters and UPS negotiated an agreement privately, all parties believed that Secretary Herman played an important role as a mediator. Through reasoning and persuasion she was able to get both parties to negotiate a settlement to the conflict.

In 1998, President Clinton invited the Israeli and Palestinian leadership to the United States in an effort to create a Middle East peace accord. As negotiations slowed, President Clinton asked the leader of Jordan, King Hussein, to attend the conference in a mediator role. King Hussein was considered by both negotiating parties to be a respected leader in their part of the world. King Hussein's presence was instrumental in the positive results of that particular meeting.

Arbitrator

As a third party, the **arbitrator** is the only one with authority. The negotiating parties agree that when an arbitrator is employed, they will both abide by the arbitrator's decision. The arbitrator's decision is final and binding on both parties. It is an accepted practice in some businesses to include in a contract language that should there ever be a disagreement, then binding arbitration will be accepted. During a recent National Basketball Association (NBA) season, Latrell Spreewell of the Golden State Warriors basketball team physically assaulted his coach. He was suspended from the team and from playing in the NBA for one year. When the season was complete, Spreewell appealed the NBA decision. His appeal was followed by negotiations with the NBA, which were unsuccessful in resolving any differences. Arbitration was ultimately employed. The arbitrator studied the facts as presented and ruled that Spreewell's suspension should be reduced to 90 days.

Arbitration can also be used to settle an impasse in collective bargaining for a new contract. Under traditional arbitration, the arbitrator will listen to both sides' final offers and then decide what the final settlement will be. The settlement is usually between the two parties' offers and can sometimes be a split-the-difference ruling that is halfway between both sides' final offers. An interesting form of arbitration is called **final offer arbitration**. Under final offer arbitration, the arbitrator will pick the final offer of one of the parties as the final settlement. This is a high-risk strategy for the parties, which stand to win big or lose big. Final offer arbitration is practiced primarily in professional sports for individual player contracts.

Conciliator

A **conciliator** is a trusted friend who is sometimes referred to as a *bridge*. In cases where the negotiating parties cannot find common ground, they may ask someone who is familiar with the parties and the issues to provide useful advice. Just like a trusted friend, the conciliator will use informal communications to assist the parties to find resolution. For example, consider three people who have been partners in a business with one another for 40 years. One of the partners decides to retire. There is difficulty reaching agreement as to the share value of the stock held by the retiring member. It may be useful to invite a trusted colleague from the same or a similar business to examine the situation and make a recommendation. This trusted friend becomes the conciliator. In the movie *The Godfather*, Robert Duvall plays the part of the lawyer for the ruling Mafia family. Throughout the movie, Duvall is called on to negotiate sensitive issues that arise between the feuding families. He is successful because all the parties, although bitter enemies, trust Duvall's character.

Conciliator is like a trusted friend who uses informal communication and becomes a bridge for resolution.

Consultant

A **consultant** is a skilled, trained, and experienced professional in the business of giving advice to the negotiating parties or acting as a fact finder. Ministers are frequently called on to provide advice in parent-child relationships. High school counselors play a similar role. Marriage counselors often play critical roles in saving and mending fragile marriages. A type of consultant that is becoming more useful today to resolve conflict is the **ombudsman.** This person is also often employed to examine and review business operations and then make recommendations for improvements.

Consultant is a trained professional, a counselor.

Ombudsman

An ombudsman is a person who investigates complaints and mediates fair settlements, especially between aggrieved parties such as consumers, employees, or students and an institution or organization. An ombudsman is often a government official who investigates citizens' complaints against the government or its functionaries. Some media outlets such as television or radio stations may have ombudsmen that will serve as the intermediaries for members of the public who have issues with institutions or organizations. These media outlets provide some leverage for the public through potential news broadcasts. A more recent use of the ombudsman is addressing problems with airline and travel service. In this case, a travel association such as AAA or Good Sam's Club will leverage their collective power to negotiate a resolution for the customer.

CONCLUDING ISSUES

Several related matters are either a part of the negotiation process or should be considered when anyone prepares to negotiate: ethical conduct, gender differences, the service business, and pitfalls in negotiating.

Ethical Conduct

Is it fair to take liberties during negotiations because of the assumed adversarial roles of the participants? The infamous used car salesperson is often viewed as unscrupulous and dishonest; some have compared the experience of buying a used car to having a root canal. It is common in our society during the barter process to stretch the facts. When dealing with one used car dealer, the customer tells the salesperson that a similar make and model down the street is $2,000 less costly than this car. The salesperson knows if that were the case, the customer would not still be shopping. Salespeople overstep their bounds as well when they tell prospective customers that what they see is the last available unit. That is unlikely because factories manufacture cars and trucks around the clock. Thankfully, this behavior occurs only in a significant minority of the buying experiences.

What happens when, during business negotiations, one party leaves critical documents in the conference area unknowingly? Is the information fair game or should it be returned unopened? More often than not, the material is returned unopened. Doing so actually has a positive effect on the other negotiators. Not everyone agrees that maintaining an ethical posture is an ingredient to a successful outcome, but ethical conduct rarely goes unnoticed. Ethical behavior is the perfect setup for the next negotiation, regardless of the outcome of current negotiations.

Gender Differences

Men and women are more alike than different in their abilities as negotiators.

Who is more successful at negotiating, men or women? The answer is neither. In fact men and women are more alike than different in their expertise and success at negotiating. This does not mean that men and women use the same negotiating styles or techniques. Men tend to be more direct and less patient, and they become annoyed by protracted discussion. Women, on the other hand, are conciliatory and less demonstrative. Women are generally more successful in building relationships and displaying empathy. Some of the most successful women negotiators are willing to be viewed as soft and manageable whereas in reality their manner and behavior is just part of the package. One of the best negotiating techniques today is a mixed team of men and women. While the men may concentrate on the issues, the women may quietly and skillfully maintain a favorable negotiating tone. A woman can easily switch roles with her male teammate if the need arises.

The Service Business

Customer satisfaction is central to the service business. If the customer displays any dissatisfaction, the corrective action is to negotiate a suitable compromise. "Will the customer take advantage of the situation? Sure! Do we care? As long as they remain customers, we probably don't care." This is a common theme in the service business as we know it today. The customer service practices of retail businesses today likely would permit a customer to reject a half-eaten meal and leave without paying. Further, a customer may return a half-used tube of toothpaste to a grocery store and be given a choice between a new product or a full refund. Is that ethical behavior on the part of the customer? Probably not, but negotiation or compromise may not be part of the customer expectation either.

One of the most successful styles of customer negotiation is the style employed by Jim Allen. Jim is an experienced service manager for a new car dealership. Frequently, when a customer is disappointed with the service, he or she is introduced to Jim. Jim appears to have a low-key temperament and exudes a quiet confidence. Underneath, Jim is a skilled and competent manager and an incredibly successful leader. Jim can quiet the most agitated customer with these words: "Loud, angry voices achieve nothing. Let's sit down and you can explain your problem to me. The two of us will find a solution." The words have a soothing effect. Normally after a brief discussion Jim asks the crucial question, "What would you recommend that we do that is fair?" Invariably the customer will suggest less than Jim is prepared to offer. Jim makes the agreement; the customer is satisfied and remains a customer. Some are so pleased they send Jim a thank you note.

How to Win

Now that you have an understanding of what negotiating is all about, how do you maximize success? It makes little difference whether the negotiation involves millions of business dollars or whether the issue at hand is a favor from a friend; a plan is necessary.

A critical element of any plan is what a negotiator is willing to give up. The skilled negotiator will always be prepared to give up one or more of his or her wants or demands when doing so means victory. Therefore, a successful plan will contain wants that can be discarded without jeopardizing the grand plan. For example, in a wage negotiation, the employee may ask for a $2.00 raise in pay, all the time prepared to accept anything over $1.25. Any gain over the $1.25 is viewed as a bonus. On the other hand, anything less than $1.25 requires a new plan.

Pitfalls in Negotiating

Some of these pitfalls have been mentioned in previous sections; however, a review is worthwhile.

- Never use offensive or off-color language to make a point, even if doing so is meant to be lighthearted and funny.
- Do not draw a line in the sand. An ultimatum like *take it or leave it* is always a negotiation terminator.
- If there are people on your team who act as antagonists and cannot negotiate, lock them in the closet!
- There is no such thing as a deal breaker. Some provisions are more important than are others, but remember: No lines in the sand.
- Lastly, it bears repeating, to be a successful negotiator, a person must be able to walk away from a negotiation without a deal.

SUMMARY

Negotiation is a process. It amounts to an exchange of goods and services for money or something else of value.

Negotiations can involve four kinds of bargaining:

- Distributive bargaining (win-lose).
- Integrative bargaining (win-win).
- Attitudinal structuring (changing the other side's view of you).
- Intraorganizational bargaining (getting agreement from your side).

Negotiation has three stages:

- Preparation (what issues, where the negotiation will be held, and who will be involved).
- Action (the actual negotiations, establishment of parameters, seeking clarification of requests, and movement toward problem solving)
- Settling on the details (closure and implementation).

When negotiations break down, third-party intervention is available through conciliators, mediators, fact finders, consultants, and arbitrators.

Proper ethical conduct plays a major role in a successful negotiation. A breach of ethics can destroy a negotiation and may block any future negotiating opportunities.

Donald Trump is probably correct; negotiation is an art form.

CASE STUDY

It was a bad year for Yardran Clothing. The firm had been producing clothing for the entire family for more than seventy-five years. People purchased Yardran Clothing because it was good clothing at a reasonable price. The company had never tried to be top-of-the-line, feeling that it better served middle-class families. It also refused to produce low-end clothes because of a desire to maintain its reputation of good quality. The market had changed over the years and now more people were looking for better prices when shopping for clothing. The upper-class shoppers continued to buy upscale clothing, but many middle-class buyers, faced with unstable employment and rising prices (especially for gas to run their cars and heat their homes), resorted to buying cheaper clothing largely manufactured overseas. Yardran Clothing, feeling the pressure, had started to move production to the Far East and Latin America. The three remaining plants in the United States were in Massachusetts (the oldest and the first plant), North Carolina, and South Carolina. The Massachusetts plant had a union and the other two plants did not.

The contract for employees of the Massachusetts plant was going to expire in ninety days and the union was talking about wanting more pay and benefits. Henry Mack, the plant manager, was scheduled to be the chief negotiator for the company. Henry was a veteran with the company and no other plants had unions so he was the logical choice to represent the company. He had a management degree from a state university and had been with Yardran for thirty years. He was aware that the price of gasoline had gone up and that heating oil and natural gas had also increased greatly in price. He was also aware of the fact that some production had been moved overseas. He had also seen the closing of the Vermont plant a year earlier. Just before negotiations were scheduled to start, Henry was approached by Tom Black, the company president. Tom told Henry that the company would not give him much to offer the union because of the current situation. Henry was told to be tight on the negotiations or there may be layoffs or a Vermont situation. Henry was used to negotiating with Frank Murphy, a man that had been with Yardran as long as he had. Frank and Henry were firm but fair, and they always seemed to be able to work out a deal that both company management and union workers could support.

As many of the older workers retired from Yardran, Frank lost the support that had kept him union president for more than twenty years. After the union election, Bob Franklin was the brash and cocky new union president who was eager to get Yardran to the table where he would get the workers their fair share. Bob was supported by the younger workers who wanted more money and better benefits. The older workers were somewhat leery of Bob and were afraid of what he might do to their jobs.

When negotiations started, Henry and his middle-aged management team found themselves looking at Bob Franklin and his 20- to 30-year-old union team. Bob Franklin started the negotiations by telling Henry and the management team that there was a new sheriff in town and these negotiations were not going to be business as usual. Henry began cautiously by suggesting that they would start with environmental issues and work toward the more complex economic issues later. Henry was hoping that this would buy him time and help to settle Bob down. Henry and Bob knew the existing contract had been a good one for environmental issues like safety, union shop (workers agree to join the union or pay union dues after being hired), probationary period for new workers, grievances, production process, production standards, breaks, overtime, holidays, vacations, and inspections. Both sides got through most of the contract in 30 days of less-than-intense work. There were some minor changes, but the new contract looked very much like the existing contract. The only real issues left on the table were wages and benefits. The union started out by asking for a $4.50 per hour raise over the next three years and a phase out of contributory benefits over the same period. This meant the union workers would get $1.50 per year raise for each of the next three years and that the contributory part of the benefits would decrease by 33% for the next three years. This would result in the employees getting a $4.50 per hour raise and paying no out-of-pocket costs for their health benefits after three years. On the management side, Henry started his part of the negotiations by stating that the wages and benefits would remain the same for the next three years and the company would try to keep everyone employed. Obviously, the negotiations began to bog down as each side had to consider what the other had offered.

Henry returned to the table with a raise of 50 cents an hour over the next three years and a one-time 10 percent cut in what employees had to pay toward benefit costs. Bob countered with a $1.35 per hour raise over the next three years and a 25 percent cut in what employees paid for benefits for each of the next three years. It became apparent to Henry that dealing with Bob was going to be very different than dealing with Frank. Over the next 60 days, the company and union had reached an impasse. Henry had moved to 65 cents per hour raise for each of the next three years and a one-time cut in employee benefit costs of 25 percent. Bob had refused to move from a $1.25 per hour pay raise and a one-time cut of 60 percent of the employee benefits cost.

Bob, encouraged by the younger workers, remained steadfast and said he would not give any more to the company. The younger workers were confident that their guy could put management in their place and give them what they wanted. The older workers were becoming worried that this hard line negotiating may backfire on the union. The younger workers wanted to strike and the older workers wanted to keep working when the existing contract expired. When the contract expired, the union voted to go on strike against the company.

Henry was talking to Tom about the situation and Tom continued to tell Henry to hold the line or the big bosses would not like it. Tom told Henry to let them strike. Tom informed top management of what was going on and they decided to move production from the Masachusetts plant to the plants overseas and in the Carolinas. As the strike continued, more and more production was moved.

In a dramatic move, Tom told Henry to take the offer of the union and end the strike. Henry replied that taking the offer of the union was not financially feasible and would certainly mean the death of the plant. Tom said that the top bosses had instructed him to take the offer. Henry went back to the bargaining table with Bob and union members and took their offer. Bob and the union members ratified (approved) the contract and the contract was signed by the union and Yardran management. Bob's big win turned sour in three weeks when the mandatory 60 day notice was given that the plant was closing. The reason given was that the plant was not competitive and it cost too much to keep it open.

Questions

1. Evaluate Bob's situation of representing the union in the negotiations.
2. Evaluate Henry's situation of representing management in the negotiations.
3. Were the older workers right about their concerns?
4. Did Bob ask for too much?
5. Did the union really win?

DISCUSSION QUESTIONS

1. It has been said that it is an advantage to overstate demands during a negotiation.
   a. What does that mean? Provide examples in a response.
   b. Is this statement true or false, and why?
2. Should one party to a negotiation say yes to the first offer? Why or why not? What are the advantages and disadvantages of doing so?
3. How important is it to conduct yourself ethically during a negotiation? Should unethical conduct by either party be a deal breaker?
4. Of the three stages for negotiation, discuss which stage, when done well, provides an advantage in the negotiation process.

PART 4

UNDERSTANDING ORGANIZATIONS

CHAPTER 14

Typical Structures

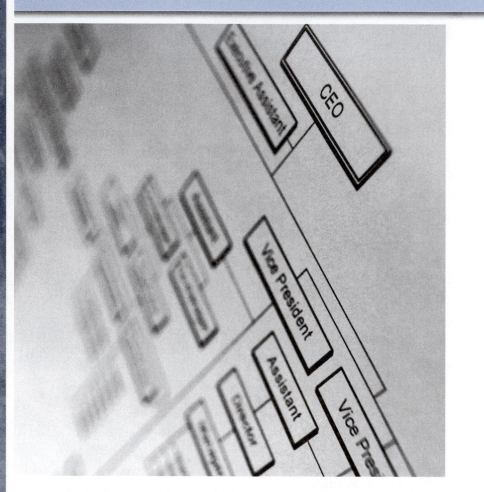

LEARNING OUTCOMES: TYPICAL STRUCTURES

1. Describe the six elements of organizational structure.

2. Discuss span of control.

3. Contrast centralized and decentralized decision making.

4. Differentiate between the simple organization, the bureaucracy, the matrix organizational design, the virtual organization, and a team-based organization.

5. Discuss the need for structure differences.

6. Through self-assessment, gain a greater understanding of one's own propensity to entrepreneurship, organization structure, and motivation to manage.

Name: _____

Section Number: _____

SELF-ASSESSMENT TESTS

Please complete the following exercises online, accessible with the Access Card Packaged with this text, before reading this chapter.

EXERCISE I.E.4: **AM I LIKELY TO BECOME AN ENTREPRENEUR?** Score _____

This instrument assesses proactive personality. That is, it identifies differences among people to the extent in which they take action to influence their environment. Proactive personalities identify opportunities and act on them. They show initiative, take action, and persevere until they bring about change. Research finds that the proactive personality is positively associated with entrepreneurial intentions. A number of factors have been found to be associated with becoming an entrepreneur. For instance, entrepreneurship tends to flourish in communities that encourage risk taking and minimize the penalties attached to failures.

EXERCISE III.A.1: **WHAT TYPE OF ORGANIZATION STRUCTURE DO I PREFER?** Score _____

This instrument measures your preference for working in a mechanistic or organic organization structure. Because the trend in recent years has been toward more organic designs, you're more likely to find a good organizational match if you score low on this instrument. However, there are few, if any, pure organic structures. Therefore, very low scores may also mean that you're likely to be frustrated by what you perceive as overly rigid structures, rules, regulations, and boss-centered leadership. In general, however, low scores indicate that you prefer small, innovative, flexible, team-oriented organizations. High scores indicate a preference for stable, rule-oriented, more bureaucratic organizations.

EXERCISE III.B.4: **HOW MOTIVATED AM I TO MANAGE?** Score _____

Not everyone is motivated to perform managerial functions. This instrument taps six components that relate to managerial success, especially in larger organizations. These are a favorable attitude toward authority, a desire to compete, a desire to exercise power, assertiveness, a desire for a distinctive position, and a willingness to engage in repetitive tasks. What meaning can you draw from your score? It provides you with an idea of how comfortable you would be doing managerial activities. Note, however, that this instrument emphasizes tasks associated with managing in larger and more bureaucratic organizations. A low or moderate score may indicate that you are more suited to managing in a small firm, an organic organization, or in an entrepreneurial situation.

EXERCISE IV.F.2: **DO I LIKE BUREAUCRACY?** Score _____

This instrument measures your preference for working in a bureaucratic organization. Bureaucratic organizations are characterized by a rigid, hierarchical structure with a high concentration of power at the top of the hierarchy. Work in bureaucratic organiztions tends to be highly formalized and routine, and there is a strong adherence to rules and policies. Bureaucratic organizations have their advantages and disadvantages. Advantages include the ability to perform tasks efficiently and with less reliance on individuals at lower levels of the organization. Disadvantages include a sometimes obsessive reliance on rules and policies, which greatly limit flexibility.

You should also record your scores on these exercises in Appendix 1.

How Many Managers?

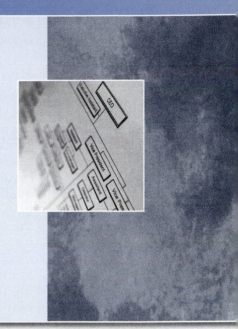

Rhonda and Chuck are very pleased about the growth of their company. The two of them are currently managing thirty-two employees. Even though the employees are well trained and productive, both Rhonda and Chuck realize that they need more managers to free up some of their time.

Rhonda says, "We need to spend more time running this business and doing strategic planning. I just don't have the time to watch sixteen people and do the other things I need to do."

"You are right. I can't do it either," Chuck replies.

"Let's hire eight new managers to supervise the employees," Rhonda suggests.

"Let's hire four new managers to supervise the crew," Chuck counters. "Eight managers are just too many"

"How do you know eight managers are too many?"

"How do you know four managers are too few?"

How many managers should they hire?

Welcome to Typical Structures!

■

"It's not always what's up front that counts. It's what's inside."

—Harvey Mackay[114]

The organization has many faces. It may be a small privately held business, a large well-established corporation, a unit associated with government, or an educational institution. Whatever the environment, the organizational structure will influence the behavior of its members.

This chapter will discuss the following five aspects of organizational structure:

- Elements of Organizational Structure
- Structure Shapes and Designs
- Organizational Models
- Why Are Structures Different?
- The Future

ELEMENTS OF ORGANIZATIONAL STRUCTURE

The organizational structure provides guidance for people toward the completion of the work to be accomplished. The structure may range from simple hierarchies along traditional lines to complex networks dependent on computer systems and telecommunications. Organizational structures can be classified into a number of types, including simple, bureaucracy, matrix, teams, and virtual. The following six elements are the guideposts for the creation of an organizational structure. Together they provide discipline to the organization. Discipline, in this context, is not meant to be punitive in nature. It is the mechanism that provides control and order.

- Division of Labor
- Characterization of Jobs

- Authority
- Control
- Decision Making
- Creativity

Division of Labor

What do the organization members do? What are their functions, and how are they grouped, subdivided, or placed into separate jobs? The accounting department has cost accountants, tax advisors, auditors, and inventory control specialists. The people in a typical production operation may be assigned tasks as assemblers, painters, inspectors, and shippers. In a large organization, a particular activity may have several levels of expertise. The quality assurance department, for example, may have several functions: first, inspect incoming raw materials; second, evaluate tolerances along the assembly line; and finally, conduct a final inspection prior to release for shipping.

The organization may be small, with a handful of people doing more than one task. For example, a manager at Wendy's is responsible for training new hires and supervising the activity of all employees. The manager may also become a line worker or cashier during peak periods.

Characterization of Jobs

Jobs and work activity are typically grouped by function, product, geography, or type of customer. These groupings may be found in a single organization.

- **Function.** What is the expertise of members? Are they engineers, accountants, or human relations specialists? A typical Circuit City or Best Buy retail store organizes by function. There is a sales staff, an office group, and unseen employees who handle warehousing, shipping, and receiving. A large corporation will likely have a marketing department, a research and development group, manufacturing, and production operations, to name a few.

- **Product.** Structuring by product is popular since it allows everyone in the organization to focus on the product being produced. Eli Lilly and Company, for example, has a well-known pharmaceutical business and a successful agricultural group.

- **Geography.** Worldwide organizations generally structure their business to focus on a particular region. Ford Motor Company includes unique operations in North America, Europe, and Asia, to name a few. Geographic specialization may be as simple as dividing the United States by regions east and west of the Mississippi.

- **Type of Customer.** The organization may have more than one distinct business. Large consumer product companies brand and produce their products for their own retail market. Michelin Tire produces tires for the retail market. In fact, many believe Michelin means quality and safety. Michelin has also contracted with Sears to provide a Sears-branded tire labeled The Roadhandler. The tire maker responds to both retail and a wholesale market.

Authority

This is the chain of command, a single path of authority that shows any employee how the guidance and direction flows. It also identifies where to go to solve a problem. The concept of **unity of command** establishes that a single source has the final word. President Harry S. Truman is an example. On his desk was a plaque that read, "The Buck Stops Here."

Unity of command establishes that a single source is the authority.

The unity of command also states that everyone should have just one superior and that one superior should have the authority, responsibility, and accountability for that employee. Under the principle of unity of command, it is fine for one superior to have several employees reporting to him or her, but it is unacceptable for the employees to have more than one superior. Having more than one superior can lead to problems for the employees in trying to figure out who to follow and what work needs to be done.

Control

The number of people one person supervises is that person's **span of control.** Figure 14–1 compares two organizations with the same number of employees but with markedly different spans of control. What is the optimum number of subordinates that should report to a single boss? What is the ideal span of control? It depends. A creative business such as an advertising company likely has a small span of control, say three to five creative people. The amount of leader-follower interaction in a creative business is substantially higher than a business where people do repetitive tasks. A supervisor's span of control is a direct reflection of the need for supervisor input, approval, and control. The superintendent of a golf course may have a crew of ten to fifteen people, some part-time and some full-time. The tasks they perform, for the most part, are routine and easy to control. Some mow, some trim, some hustle trash while others maintain equipment. One supervisor on one golf course can control the operation nicely. However, a research chemist in a laboratory working on a complex synthesis may have only two or three people in his charge: one in the fume hood, one recording data from a chromatograph, and maybe one cleaning up and maintaining supplies.

The views on span of control are changing. Michael Hammer, a leadership coach in Cambridge, Massachusetts, notes, "You need to change what it means to be a manager."[115] Hammer favors giving the workers more responsibility with the supervisors becoming more like coaches or mentors, thereby increasing the span of control. As an example, one high-tech manufacturing company increased the span of control from 24.4 employees in 1997 to an average of 30 in 2009. As a note of interest, managers with wide spans of control tend to get paid more and are viewed more favorably when being considered for promotion.

As illustrated in the above example, a major organizational survival consideration is cost or the expense of doing business. People, the number one asset, are usually the number one cost. A traditionally organized business

Span of control defines the number of people that one person will supervise.

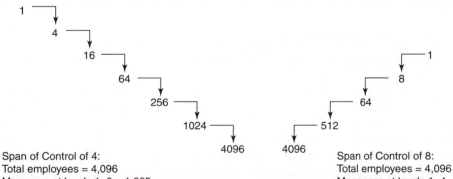

Span of Control of 4:
Total employees = 4,096
Managers at levels 1–6 = 1,365

Span of Control of 8:
Total employees = 4,096
Managers at levels 1–4 = 585

Difference in managers equal 780.

Figure 14–1 Span of control members at each level.

with narrow spans of control, typically two or three people, may find that enlarging spans of control to four to six people can significantly reduce costs by eliminating expensive supervision. The downside of such a decision is a loss of this experienced leadership. That alternative may be too expensive in terms of lost expertise and institutional memory.

Decision Making

Some organizations are structured in such a way that the decision-making authority is vested at the highest level, or a centralized approach. There may very well be a solid reason to do business that way. For example, the weapons specialist on a submarine has little opportunity to freelance since his boss, the weapons officer, retains the launch authority. Conversely, members of a university faculty have significant latitude in the development of coursework, given their decentralized approach. The decentralized decision-making approach means the decision is made at the lowest level possible. Action toward problem solving often occurs more quickly, there is more input into the decision by others, and those participating will feel more involved and in control of decisions that may affect their work lives. The effort to reduce costs, improve quality, and promote innovation and worker participation has led many organizations toward greater decentralized decision making.

Creativity

How structured are the tasks? There may be a need to be very specific, and creativity may be seen as a hindrance to business. Holiday Inn Express, an outgrowth of the successful Holiday Inn franchise, was created to tone down the frills and offer simple perks to attract the frugal customer. A standardized continental breakfast and complimentary newspaper are normal fare. It makes no difference if you stay in Morgan Hill, California, Lincoln, Nebraska, or Pascagoula, Mississippi, the experience does not vary. Holiday Inn Express offers consistent service. On the other hand, a greeting card company like Hallmark continually searches for a fresh way to say, "Happy Birthday."

STRUCTURE SHAPES AND DESIGN

The shape and design of an organization describes its philosophy and style. Is the organization flexible or rigid? Will the organization be creative, and is it customer friendly? The design may be one of three traditional designs: simple, a bureaucracy, or a matrix. We will also discuss two contemporary designs, the virtual organization and team organization.

The Simple Organization Design

Simple designs are found in smaller organizations where the need for functional differentiation is not necessary. A small privately owned business is an example (see Figure 14–2). The owner likely performs the duties of the store manager, the accountant, the buyer, and everything else. The span of control is probably wide, with virtually all employees reporting to the owner. A local fast-food business is another example. The cashiers, fry cooks, and shift supervisors may all report to the store manager. A simple structure results in a personal environment. These organizations may be stable with little or no turnover, or they may be very volatile, experiencing significant employee turnover.

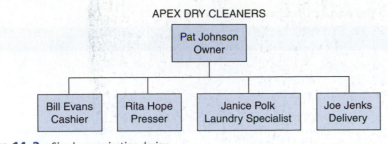

Figure 14–2   Simple organization design.

The Bureaucracy

This concept is usually thought to be reserved for companies with the need for several layers of management structure (see Figure 14–3). Some may be small with less than 100 employees, while others may employ more than 100,000. Typically these organizations are designed with small spans of control, perhaps three to six people assigned to a manager or leader. Likely there will be multiple departments organized functionally such as human resources, sales, marketing, finance, production, and engineering. These organizations by their very nature are somewhat rigid with volumes of rules, policies, and procedures. While creativity may abound in a simple structure, a large bureaucracy can be stifling. A government is a good example of a bureaucracy.

The Matrix Design

A large organization may counter the pitfalls of a bureaucracy by organizing in a matrix fashion. This is especially successful for creative businesses. Table 14–1 depicts a **matrix organization.** Traditional organizational functions are shown on the horizontal axis. Business functions are shown vertically. In this example the CEO directs the traditional functions of finance, marketing, R&D, and purchasing to allocate packages of people to a particular functional area. The aircraft team that is responsible for designing, building, and marketing airplanes is constituted with people from the traditional organization functions. The vice president for marketing is responsible for the corporate marketing strategy and also responsible for providing people to staff each team. Depending on emphasis and need, people may be reassigned as necessary.

The **matrix organization** combines the functional and product structures.

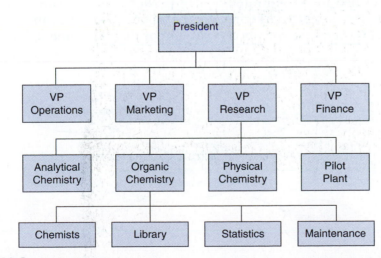

Figure 14–3   The bureaucracy.

Table 14–1   The Matrix Organization

	Finance	Marketing	Research	Purchasing
Aircraft	X	X	X	X
Automotive	X	X	X	X
Watercraft	X	X	X	X
Motorcycle	X	X	X	X
Racing	X	X	X	X
Accessories	X	X	X	X

The Virtual Organization

The **virtual organization** is a small core organization that outsources major business functions.

One of the contemporary designs is the **virtual organization.** This flexible design allows for frequent changes and adjustments based on the work environment (see Figure 14–4). A common application is the construction business. Most owners or general contractors have a small core of permanent employees that are augmented by various subcontractors during a construction project. These companies usually do not have employees such as painters, heating and cooling contractors, framers, roofers, landscape architects, and electricians on the company payroll. A construction company will, however, employ permanent job foremen, finish carpenters, and an office staff. These jobs are outsourced ensuring the company has the best skilled employee performing the job. It also keeps overhead costs lower. This type of organization can staff up or down quickly depending on work demands.

Team Organization

The concept of teams has rapidly gained in popularity in recent years. In many respects team operations look similar to a matrix structure. The concept is simple and successful. Characteristics of the team organizations include decentralized decision making and improved communications through the removal of barriers between departments. Competent people with diverse capabilities are chosen from within the organization to form a synergistic approach to business operations. Ford Motor Company did just that when **brand management teams** were created. These teams focus on specific products complete with the interface of these products with their customers. For example, the family brand team was established to concentrate on such products as minivans. This team focuses on the design, marketing, and production for minivans. Ford reasoned that by creating operations that mirror their customers, Ford could

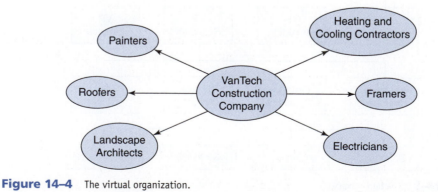

Figure 14–4   The virtual organization.

be more responsive to matching customer needs and new vehicles in two dimensions:

- **Increased efficiency** among the marketing, production, and engineering functions
- **Activity in concert** with customer preferences

These various shapes and designs have been discussed individually for purposes of clarity. However, any organization may internally configure itself to take advantage of a particular opportunity. Large bureaucratic organizations, for example, frequently constitute teams, some on a short-term basis and some on a long-term basis, to seek competitive advantage. An emerging company may begin with a simple organization but gradually begin to adopt bureaucratic tendencies as growth occurs.

ORGANIZATIONAL MODELS

Structurally, organizations fit into one of three models.

Bureaucratic

The bureaucratic model may also be called a **mechanistic model.** This type of organization operates under precise rules, policies, and regulations. If an employee has a question, he or she generally can find an answer somewhere in the policy manuals. The lack of flexibility and creativity in this model often prevents the adoption of a pure bureaucracy structure for many organizations.

*The **mechanistic model** is characterized by substantial structure and high levels of control.*

Entrepreneurial

The entrepreneurial model is called an **organic model,** the reverse of a pure bureaucracy. This model is often found in newly formed organizations and in privately held businesses. The key advantage to this model is flexibility, the ability to change, and the constant desire to create. While there may be rules, the work environment is dictated by the leader. If working specific hours is not important, then some employees may choose to work from eight to five, while others may work at night. Still others may choose to work continually for 36 hours on a particular project that has no convenient stopping point. These employees then may be absent for three days. No one seems to mind provided the work gets done.

*The **organic model** is characterized by high creativity and low structure.*

Based on the self-assessment test at the beginning of this chapter, are you more comfortable with the mechanistic model or the organic model? Are you likely to be an entrepreneur? If so, what type of business would you like to start?

The Blend

The blend is a compromise of the bureaucratic and the entrepreneurial models. Creativity may be central to success; however, specific rules and policies must be observed. In the leadership chapter (Chapter 9), we described the R&D director who departed from the normal bureaucratic routine at least once each week to allow his chemists the opportunity to work on individually creative projects. Most of corporate America may be viewed as a blend.

Which model is best? Where is your organization's best chance of success? It depends on the organization's philosophy and emphasis. Consider the following illustrations. The military represents a bureaucracy, a private enterprise represents the entrepreneurial model, and corporate America is a blend of the two.

MILITARY

There is little debate and wide acceptance that a military organization is bureaucratic and compartmentalized. In fact, it is the organization and the structure that provides the motivation for greater responsibility, rank, and pay. Everyone has a slot, place, or billet. There will always be a specific chain of command. The spans of control are narrow, typically four to five people to one supervisor. The chain of command is fixed and respected. To "go over your commander's head" and speak with his or her boss, other than socially, without prior coordination would surely result in severe criticism.

PRIVATE ENTERPRISE

Nonpublicly traded companies often are characterized by simple structures. In large measure, this is driven by business size. A sole owner, partnership, or family business defines itself. The owner is frequently visible, well known, and a hands-on operator. While some of the larger private organizations may be traditionally organized, individual or limited ownership will still make the important decisions. Therefore, control is highly centralized. Although there may be the appearance of employee involvement (empowerment), when the chips are down, the owner makes the decision.

CORPORATE AMERICA

Generally business maturity dictates and defines corporate organization and structure. Burgeoning, young companies may be somewhat "free-form" or come-as-you-are. These new companies are characterized by wide spans of control and simple structures. Younger, growing organizations adopt an organic form. As the organization matures, size, success, customers, competitors, and geography cause organizations to begin to alter the structure to be more mechanistic. Policies, procedures, rules, and regulations become the norm. Spans of control tighten, a chain of command is identified, and there is more emphasis on the publication of policy memos and procedures manuals. Some mature and maturing organizations do seek to protect employee creativity, however. They do so by stepping out of the organization on a regular basis to allow employees to work on any project of their choosing. Some may go further by removing all shields to organizational chains of command. The upfront cost can be expensive, but the benefits of achieving a competitive advantage outweigh the investment.

WHY ARE STRUCTURES DIFFERENT?

The following three factors play a major role in determining the type of structure that an organization will choose: size, technology and external influences, and focus and strategy.

Size

A newly created twenty-person business likely does not need and could not support a formal bureaucratic structure. The fourth floor dorm committee that organizes dormitory social activities is likely composed of a chair and several committee members. Some of the members serve as the liaison with other dorms and arrange publicity, while others are in charge of food and drink. A simple informal structure works just fine. Conversely, the U.S. Postal Service would not serve its customers well if each branch were allowed to determine its own pricing models based on volume or location. It is also unlikely that a branch postmaster would make a decision to run the routes twice a day during peak periods, nor would we expect the Postmaster General to adjust postage prices to generate more business. The system does not allow for that behavior.

Technology and External Influences

A Coca-Cola bottling plant will have a different routine and work environment than will the engineering school of a major university. The technology is different, but more importantly, the customer demands are not the same. The bottling plant has a production goal that must be met to maintain market share. The academic institution may be concerned with volume; however, volume takes a back seat to credible graduates. The atmosphere is different even though everyone in the Coca-Cola plant and the university faculty are fully committed to their profession. Competitors, customers, and suppliers influence structure as well. Cost plays a major role in organizational design. If a business is growing and customer demand is increasing, then business output must escalate to keep pace. The most expensive part of operating any business is people. One way to minimize increasing people costs in growing organizations is to increase the spans of control. If a supervisor today has four employees in his or her charge, it does not take that much extra effort to increase the load by one or two people, particularly if the function is routine and repetitive.

Focus and Strategy

Organization strategy has a major influence on structure. For example, is the organization's focus:

- to create and develop new products or ideas?
- to do what we do better than the competition?
- to copy the leader?

Some companies are on the cutting edge of technology. They are the **creators.** Companies like Amazon.com, eBay, and Delia's are all plowing new ground. Will a strict bureaucratic style work? Of course not. The structure will likely be one that encourages the creativity that launched the business.

A mature organization will often seek to **do what it does better than the competition.** General Motors, Chrysler, Toyota, and Ford seek to dominate the automobile market through their pricing structures. The goal may be to produce a low-priced family vehicle with the most family-oriented features such as superior crash safety and adding to or improving long-term reliability. These features can be expensive, which drives the need for efficiency and cost minimization. So how are they doing? One needs only to look at the number one selling car in the United States. It is the Toyota Camry. Efficiency and cost minimization alternatives include increasing spans of control, force reductions, replacing employees through the use of outsourcing or subcontractors, implementation of lean manufacturing principles, and team work. Pepsi recently marketed oversize cases, 30 cans instead of 24. By lowering packaging costs, Pepsi can offer products at a lower unit cost, potentially earning market share from Coca-Cola. And remember, packaging costs include more than just cardboard. Reduced packaging requires lower effort, which translates into lower demand for manpower. From an environmental viewpoint, it also reduces the waste going to landfills. These are all good business decisions.

Some adopt the strategy of **copying the leader.** The clothing industry and the sports equipment industry offer illustrations. Jeans, a universal garment, may cost $30 at Eddie Bauer; however, Members Mark jeans at Sam's Club sell for $12.99. The imitator, in this case Members Mark, will likely structure to enter and leave markets quickly while Eddie Bauer focuses on constant quality at a fair price. It is possible for a golfer to pay nearly $400 for a Callaway driver or, alternatively, she may find a small-time operation that will make a "knock-off" club for $98. The knock-off club looks, feels, and works as effectively as the expensive club for most players. Copycat businesses are usually private enterprises with minimal structure, negligible overhead, and unmatched flexibility for manufacturing.

THE FUTURE

Organizations today operate in a global environment. For example, the recent crisis in the financial markets with record numbers of foreclosures on home owners, the dramatically falling U.S. dollar, and the price of oil going to over $120 per barrel have had significant impacts on individual and organizational behaviors. Mergers and acquisitions with foreign companies have dramatically changed. Isn't it interesting that Japanese, German, and Chinese automakers can build new factories in the United States, employ American workers, and make profits while U.S. automakers struggle to break even? China and India are becoming the new economic superpowers and that will change the way we do business.

The global market must focus on customer satisfaction, and it is driven in large measure by the Japanese. Large, inefficient bureaucratic organizations and industries are being replaced with teams. New creative companies like Dell Computer Corporation, Tata Motors, Toyota, and Amazon.com are flourishing. Large bureaucratic organizations like Kodak, Ford, GM, and Chrysler have announced major downsizing and reductions in their workforces. Structure and style now take on the appearance of fast-moving, streamlined units.

Quietly the reengineering process continues. Safeway replaced the corner grocery. Wal-Mart, the most successful discount retailer in 2005, is replacing Safeway. Today customers can one-stop shop. The dry cleaners, the grocery, the clothing store, the repair shop for the family vehicle, the bank, and the McDonald's restaurant are all under one roof, or at least they are in the same retail complex. McDonald's is going head-to-head with Starbucks and serving fresh roasted coffee in their stores. E-commerce, once considered a novelty, is the world's fastest growing business system and offers an entirely new structure for businesses of the future.

Turning Inward

Large, medium, and small organizations are adjusting their structures to adapt to the growing demand for employee satisfaction. The large structure may still exist; however, creativity demands have given rise to teams. Recently an employee of a medium-size manufacturing plant was asked in what department she worked. The reply was, "I work on the paint **team.**" Structural changes now offer the employee a stake in the business, not an eight-to-five job. In the manufacturing arena, organizations are moving to a more lean process flow, or a pull system, as opposed to the traditional economics of scale type of production, or a push system. The health-care industry is reducing costs and improving patient services and patient flows by implementing the manufacturing lean philosophy, moving organizations to a team-based structure. Many organizations now have programs to grow their own leaders through innovative leadership development programs.

Turning Outward

The environment is a major issue. Organizations are moving toward recycling and away from simply throwing away trash. Organizations used to be staffed and operated with a focus on internal convenience and cost minimization. The mood is changing toward customer orientation. A local auto dealership has replaced the traditional workday of 8 A.M. to 6 P.M. with a fresh team approach that is oriented to the customer. The service department hours are now 7 A.M. to midnight daily and 24 hours on Saturday. This change necessitated a second work team of qualified technicians, which is an expensive proposition. The result is more business, not only in the service department, but also for the body shop and the sales department. Organizations are adapting to their customers, a reversal of the attitudes that prevailed from 1950 to 1980. Banks have quietly and successfully been changing the way their customers manage their deposits. Replacing tellers with ATMs was the beginning, and now there are paperless checking accounts, online account access, and debit cards. Internally banks have restructured. Where before they were open from 9 A.M. to 3 P.M., now hours include evenings and Saturdays. That emphasis on customer service requires structural changes.

APPLICATION

As you reflect on the structural principles presented in this chapter, review your responses to the self-assessments at the beginning of the chapter: your entrepreneurial appetite, your preference toward organic or mechanistic organizations, and your motivation to manage.

Let's say, for example, that you have a strong entrepreneurial inclination, that you prefer organic organizations, and that you have a high degree of motivation to manage. It is reasonable that a highly structured bureaucratic organization is not an optimum fit for you. The assessment results also suggest your preference toward creative structures, likely with wide spans of control and delegation of authority. Those with reverse assessments may have an inclination for a staff role in a bureaucratic or mechanistic organization. Many managerial failures may be traced to an incorrect match of preferences and job assignments.

The analysis, therefore, demonstrates that there is an opportunity for anyone who wants an opportunity. The point to take away from this chapter is that there is a place for someone who demonstrates your behavior; recognize your preferences and make the most of them.

SUMMARY

There are six elements of organizational structure:

- Division of labor is how workers are grouped, subdivided, or placed into jobs.
- Characteristics of jobs are defined by function, product, geography, and type of customer.
- Authority is the chain of command.
- Control is the number of people a person supervises.
- Decision making depends on the level at which decisions are made.
- Creativity depends on how structured tasks are.

There are five types of organizational shapes or designs:

- Simple organization design is used most in small businesses.
- The bureaucracy is used in larger companies and features a small span of control.
- The matrix design is used to mix function with product.
- The virtual organization is flexible.
- The team organization emphasizes groups committed to a product.

Sue Davis was a very bright and personable product engineer for Harvey Tech Corporation. One evening, she and her husband Tom, were having dinner at Mario's Restaurant with Chuck and Helen Parker. The four had gone to college together and met regularly for a night out. After talking about movies, the kids, and the weather, Chuck was not quite his usual talkative self. Sue could tell that something was on Chuck's mind.

Sue asked Chuck, "Hey, Chuck you are awfully quiet tonight. Is anything wrong?"

Chuck responded with, "I hate to be a drag on our evening, but the boss has me trying to find a part for our new product and I am stumped on where to go."

Sue shot back, "Let me look at what you want."

Chuck, using a cocktail napkin, roughed out a drawing of the part and told Sue what the specs were. Sue looked at the part and thought Harvey Tech can make this. Sue then told Chuck that the two of them should get together and work this out. Chuck agreed and they set a time for Monday afternoon for Chuck to come see Sue at Harvey Tech.

On Monday, Chuck went to see Sue and was impressed with the operations at Harvey Tech. Sue got the detailed information on the part Chuck needed made and went to work on it. Ed, Sue's boss, met Chuck and saw what Sue was doing. Ed encouraged Sue to take the ball and run with it. After four days of working on the design of the part, Sue had created a scale drawing of the part and wanted to take it to the design department for a prototype. Sue shared the drawing with Chuck who said it is exactly what he wanted. Chuck wanted to see the prototype and take it back to his company. Ed intervened to get the prototype done and back to Sue. Sue then took the prototype to Chuck. Chuck and his boss liked the work. The prototype worked in the product when tested by Chuck's company. They were ready to place an order for 1,000 on the first run, with more orders to follow if the delivery time and price were right.

Sue knew that Chuck needed to have the parts in two months and for less than $200 a part. Sue also knew that the cost of producing and delivering the part was $100. Sue was convinced she had solved the problem, helped a

friend, and generated new business for the company. She felt very good calling Chuck and telling him she thought she could take care of it in the time frame and for the price Chuck wanted.

Sue started to get the ball rolling toward closing the deal and getting the part to Chuck's company. When she put in the order for the parts, she was told that she could not place an order for production because only the sales department could do that. Larry, a pushy and cocky salesperson, was assigned to the account. Larry went ahead and called Chuck about the part without talking to Sue. Chuck was surprised by the call and by Larry's attitude toward him. Chuck called Sue and asked her what was happening with his part and why she was talking to Larry. Sue explained that Larry was the salesperson who was assigned to handle the order. Chuck was not impressed with Larry. Larry let Sue know that Chuck was a jerk and that marketing was adding 30 percent to the final price for the marketing work. Chuck asked what marketing work because he had sold the client. Larry let him know that it was company policy to charge 30 percent add-on to cover his commission and costs.

Larry sent the prototype part to design. Frank from the design department called Sue and said that they had reworked the part. Sue explained to Frank that the prototype was fine the way it was. Frank said he could live with that, but 30 percent had to be added to the cost for design work. Sue asked what design work and Frank responded "that it is company policy on all orders coming in here."

Sue was told that she still needed to run the product by manufacturing before it could go to company management for final approval. Sue took the prototype to manufacturing to talk with Al. Al looked at the product for a couple minutes and declared that it was doable for the $100 cost plus the 40 percent add-on for manufacturing. Sue left with the approval she needed and proceeded to take the prototype and proposal for production to Ed. Ed said that he would get the ball rolling by giving it to his boss, Henry.

Chuck was becoming concerned about not hearing from Larry and called Sue. Chuck explained that his boss was after him to get the product contract done. Sue explained that she had to go through the chain of command. Chuck explained the situation to his boss and was told to start talking to other manufacturers. Chuck asked Sue to give him the prototype and Sue let him have it. Chuck explained that his boss had asked him to look elsewhere for a manufacturer to do the job. Sue was still convinced that Harvey Tech would get the job.

After waiting for two weeks, Sue asked Ed how the proposal was doing. Ed said he would call Henry and find out. Henry had been on vacation for a week and his desk was piled up with papers. When Ed called Henry, he was told by Henry he had not seen any proposal, but he would try to find it. After another week, Henry processed the proposal and sent it to Julie in contract approvals. She was backed up and held it for another week. She finally approved it and sent it to the management council for the final approval. Management council met every two weeks to review and approve proposals. It sat there for a week until the next meeting. It was approved and sent back to Julie with the note to add 50 percent to the cost of the product for overhead. After two more days, Julie sent it to Henry and after three more days, Henry sent it to Ed. Ed then called in Sue and told her that the deal was approved at $250 per part. Sue wondered why the $100 part now cost $250. She was told that marketing, design, manufacturing, and overhead costs had to be added.

Sue called Chuck with the news and found out that Chuck's company had gone to a smaller manufacturer. Chuck apologized to Sue about the situation, but explained that they needed to move on the project and that Larry had refused to call him back. When Larry finally did call him back with the $250 per part price, Chuck's company had already signed with Advanced Tech. Advanced Tech had responded in days with a $185 per part cost. Chuck said that Harvey Tech had ended up taking too much time and costing too much.

Questions

1. What were the issues with Harvey Tech that prevented them from getting the part order from Chuck?
2. What could have been done to fix the situation at Harvey Tech?
3. What could Sue have done differently?
4. Did Chuck do the right thing for his company?

1. We speak of span of control and the differences between tall and short spans or, in other words, narrow and wide spans on control. What are the advantages and disadvantages of each? Discuss cost, coordination of activities, team communication, creativity, and employee job satisfaction in your response.

2. In your opinion, which organizational design:

   a. creates the best advantage for recognition and advancement, and why?

   b. is likely to result in the poorest advantage for advancement, and why?

CHAPTER 15

What Do People in Different Jobs Do?

LEARNING OUTCOMES: WHAT DO PEOPLE IN DIFFERENT JOBS DO?

1. Contrast line and staff positions.

2. Discuss the necessary interpersonal skills required for success in each of the line and staff positions.

Problems in the Line

Joe was recently hired by Norton Company as a salesperson. His job is to sell a variety of paneling, flooring, shingles, doors, windows, and other building materials to contractors. Joe is eager to sell as much as he can to impress his bosses.

Joe is talking to a contractor who needs custom-built doors and windows for a job by next week. Joe is confident that the company can deliver on this sale and sells the contractor twenty-four custom windows and four custom exterior doors. The total bill comes to $16,000. Feeling really good about the sale, Joe brags to his boss about it.

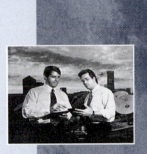

Joe's boss says he's really impressed with the sale and Joe's positive can-do attitude. He ends the conversation with a caution: "I hope you checked that order out with production before you promised the customer anything."

Joe remembers that he has not checked with production on the order. When he calls the production people, he finds that his order will take three weeks to process because none of the windows are in stock.

What mistake did Joe make and what should he do now?

Welcome to Understanding Organizations! ■

This chapter gives a general description of what kind of jobs are available in different companies. Since organizations and jobs are so varied, it is risky writing this chapter (which is probably why most people don't try!). Be warned that these descriptions may not exactly fit your experience.

We've talked a lot about organizations and people, but you might have one final question: What do people in different jobs do? What skills are required to be successful in today's organizations? I knew when I graduated from college that I had no idea what different jobs were available and what people did in those different jobs. This chapter will review some of the typical jobs available in organizations, with a particular emphasis on entry-level positions. We will also look at the needed skills to be successful in the different jobs.

One good division of various jobs in an organization is to separate by line positions and staff positions. **Line positions** are jobs that are directly related to the day-to-day business of the organization. Figure 15–1 presents a generic organizational chart for a company. Line positions include jobs in production, sales, marketing, and customer service. **Staff positions** are jobs that support the operations of the organization. Examples of staff positions are human resources, research and development (R&D), accounting and finance, management information systems (MIS), and legal services.

To help understand the difference between a line position and a staff position, think about who is the main "customer" for the job. If you work for General Motors (GM) in a sales position, your main customer is the car buyer, a consumer. **Line jobs serve an external customer.** A production person in GM is ultimately building a car that will go to the consumer, so production is a line position. If you work for GM in a legal position, your main customer is another GM employee, perhaps a

Line positions are involved in the day-to-day business of the company.

Staff positions play a supporting role.

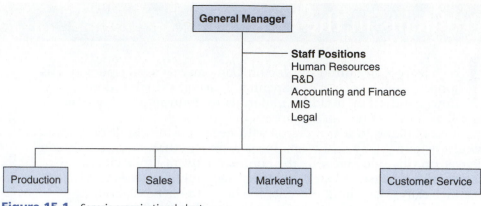

Figure 15-1 Generic organizational chart.

general manager or a marketing manager. A person in accounting for GM generates accounting statements that are used by other GM employees. **Staff jobs serve an internal customer.**

The distinction between line and staff jobs may be slightly different in various organizations. For example, in many organizations marketing is a line position because this department works with the external customer in mind on day-to-day decisions. Other organizations use marketing as a staff position that supports the sales organization. To go back to the definition, a line position is involved in day-to-day operations, whereas a staff position supports the operations.

Let's go through each of the blocks in the organizational chart in Figure 15–1 and discuss what people in these jobs do, with particular emphasis on entry-level jobs.

LINE POSITIONS

Sales

A salesperson is ultimately responsible for generating sales of the company's products. The product may be an actual physical product (like a car), a service (like a health club membership), or a financial instrument (like an insurance policy). Salespeople are some of the most critical people in an organization because if they don't generate results, nothing else matters. Sales positions are especially good entry-level positions because a job in sales forces a person to learn about the company's product, develop better interpersonal skills, and foster a strong customer perspective. A successful sales career is often a ticket to upper management.

A salesperson's typical day includes some pre-call planning: reviewing background for the day's customers, reviewing which products to discuss with each customer, and establishing a sales strategy. The salesperson then meets with the customer to discuss a product or business deal or simply to find out about any new developments with the customer. If appropriate, the salesperson may ask the customer to place an order for the product. Needless to say, sales jobs vary quite widely, but this is the general idea.

In most cases, a salesperson is a people person. Since most of the salesperson's job is focused on other people, he or she needs to be the type of person who enjoys interacting with other people. That does not mean a salesperson must be a Type A, super-extrovert. Many sales jobs, such as positions in technical sales, focus more on technical content than on negotiation and persuasion, but being a people-oriented person remains critical to any sales job.

Another important objective in a sales position is to gather information. The salesperson is the eyes and ears of the organization. If consumer tastes are changing, the salesperson needs to recognize the change and communicate this information to the organization. A salesperson can be influential in setting policies for the organization because of his or her position on the "front line."

A person working in sales needs to have or develop self-confidence. In many sales jobs, the batting average in closing deals can be quite low. It is important to be able to deal with rejection. Sometimes potential customers are not happy to hear from salespeople, and they may consider them to be pests (ever get a call from a telemarketing person at dinner?). On the other hand, the upside potential in sales can be extremely good. Salespeople may be paid on salary, commission (getting a certain amount of money per sale), or a combination of both. If any of your compensation is based on commission, you can make a lot of money if you are able to sell effectively. A salesperson can often make more money than his or her manager makes.

Sales is also a good entry-level position to consider because a person may be able to get valuable experience before having extensive family responsibilities. Sales jobs often require a lot of traveling, and it is easier to do this if a person does not yet have a family and children.

Sales is a very good entry-level job.

Marketing

Marketing and sales are similar positions in many organizations. Usually a marketing position is focused on groups of customers, whereas sales concentrate on individual customers. For example, a person in marketing may be concerned with truck buyers as a group, while a salesperson is concerned with each individual truck buyer. A marketing person may put together a rebate program for all truck buyers, while the salesperson makes the individual sale, pointing out the benefits of the marketing program on rebates.

A **marketing** person must understand customer needs.

Many people enter marketing from a sales background because both positions value the customer perspective. To put together a good marketing program, a marketing person must have a good sense of the customers and what attracts them to his or her product. If you are the marketing manager for trucks, is it better to offer an incentive of a free gun rack or a lifetime supply of air fresheners? If you are in touch with your customers, you can make the tough calls like this one.

A marketing position is split between dealing with customers and dealing with corporate managers. A marketing person will spend a lot of time with customers and salespeople to understand the direction of the market. When the marketing person formulates a program or strategy, he or she will generally need to sell this idea internally to corporate managers.

One good type of entry-level job in marketing is data analysis. A marketing department keeps track of product sales, prices, competitive activities, cost trends, advertising spending, and so forth. In these entry-level jobs employees make sense of all these numbers and use this information to formulate marketing programs and strategies.

A good quality in a marketing person is perception. A marketing person needs to develop the ability to see a product as a customer sees it. If you can do this, you have a future in marketing.

Production

An understanding of human behavior is critical in production.

Once the sales and marketing groups generate sales from customers, it is the job of production to fill these orders. In this section, we will focus on companies that make a physical product.

Within a production facility, the frontline staff are the workers who manufacture the product. Companies will have supervisor positions to manage the production workers. Other tasks like quality control, safety, and engineering are also essential for the production process.

Being a supervisor in a production facility requires great knowledge of organizational behavior. This job probably uses more of the topics discussed in this book than any other job. A production manager needs to understand the personalities and abilities of people. He or she needs to know how to motivate people. A production manager needs to facilitate good group interaction. He or she needs to deal with many human resource policies. In total, supervision is a challenging job. As production workers will tell you, a good supervisor can make all the difference, not only in the workers' job satisfaction, but also in the efficiency of plant operations.

Much of a supervisor's job is taking care of the production workers' needs. If you are a person supervising ten or twenty production workers, even handling a single issue from each worker every day can consume half of your working time. You need to develop trust and respect with your workers. Sometimes you cannot always solve a problem to a worker's satisfaction, but the worker needs to know you are doing your best to act in his or her best interests. Good people skills are essential. There are also special challenges in a union plant because there will probably be rules about what can and cannot be done, and it is important to maintain good relationships with the union.

Other jobs in production require specific job knowledge. A quality control (QC) person monitors the product to make sure it meets all specifications. If there are problems, the quality control person will work with the plant engineers and production workers to solve the problem. A typical day of a quality control person involves monitoring production records to identify possible problems and then spending time to solve or prevent problems.

Safety experts in the plant make sure that working conditions are as safe as possible. Most companies take safety seriously, not only as good corporate citizens, but also because the cost of accidents is high. Safety experts monitor working conditions, work with insurance companies to prevent accidents, and investigate any incidents. Sometimes these safety experts work with plant engineers to make changes to the plant to improve safety.

Finally, most companies have an engineering staff to maintain, improve, or expand the facility. As mentioned earlier, the engineering staff will also work with quality and safety experts.

An important attitude in production is to get the job done. In most production plants, there are always problems that need to be resolved. These problems usually have to be fixed right away with whatever resources are available. In some ways, the production department is not always appreciated as much as it should be. When things run well, nobody says anything. Quality production in the right quantity is the expectation. When things go wrong, there are lots of people who can complain to you, from salespeople to customers to corporate managers. You need to derive satisfaction for getting the product out the door, while overcoming the daily challenges associated with running a production plant and tolerating people yelling at you when things don't go well.

Entry-level jobs in production are great for getting experience. You usually have a lot of responsibility and your decisions can make a big difference. Suppose you are working third shift and a piece of equipment goes down. Do you call the plant manager? Do you alter the production schedule? Do you call in an engineer? Do you try to fix the equipment yourself? You need to make these decisions fast because every minute the equipment is offline costs money. You have to be able to handle pressure and make the call.

Customer Service

Customer service, like sales, is a direct connection with the customer. The impression that a company has of your organization is largely formed by the perception gained from the customer service representative. As a result, a customer service person needs to treat customers with respect, to solve their problems, and to handle day-to-day business like orders and simple requests.

Customer service jobs vary among organizations. Some are more clerical, some are more sales oriented, and some are more technically oriented. You need many of the same skills as a salesperson, but in customer service you are mainly dealing with established customers and spending less time on potential customers. Like a production person, a customer service representative needs to find solutions to a continuing stream of challenges. If a customer service representative has 1,000 customers, taking care of their problems and questions can be very time-consuming.

In customer service, a person needs to have a helpful attitude and represent the company well. He or she needs to derive satisfaction from solving customer problems. Like production, sometimes customer service can be a thankless job. When things run well, no one hears about it. Everybody hears about the customer service problems. Customer service representatives are valued especially when they solve an important customer's problem and retain a critical piece of business.

Depending on the organization, customer service can be a good entry-level job to help develop the interpersonal and product knowledge skills a sales position offers with the day-to-day, "get the problem solved" attitude of a production position. Before taking a customer service position, however, you should make sure the position is one of real responsibility that will help you develop.

Customer service professionals need:

- Great communication skills
- The ability to handle stressful situations
- A positive attitude

STAFF POSITIONS

Human Resources

Human resources can be considered customer service for internal customers. The human resource department deals with issues that are critical to employees: salary, benefits, new career opportunities, development, and training. There are some close analogies to a supervisor position. In human resources, a person needs to solve the problems of the employees. He or she needs to earn the trust and respect of the employees because people won't always like the decisions.

Human resources is a good job for a person who wants to make a difference in the happiness of others. A person in a human resource job can make a huge difference in an individual's life by making hiring decisions, setting up benefits plans that provide for the employee's security, and resolving employee disputes. Interpersonal and perception skills are essential.

Many people who start in human resources make it their career. There are many specialties in human resources such as compensation, benefits,

Human Resource (HR) professionals must be respected and trusted, and have great communication and problem-solving skills.

equal employment opportunity, and recruiting. Entry-level positions could involve setting up new programs, data analysis, or employee problem solving. You may even be asked to do some recruiting at your alma mater.

Research and Development

Research and development jobs come in many varieties. Some technical service jobs in a research and development group are similar to sales jobs. In this job, a person would visit a customer site to solve a technical problem the customer might be having with the product. Some detective work is usually involved, and technical representatives need to understand the customer's process as well as their own product. Sometimes the problem does not come from the product being purchased by the customer and persuasion skills are needed to convince the customer that the problem is coming from somewhere else.

Some research and development jobs interface with production. Sometimes a company will research ways to improve its existing facility or to introduce a new product into its plants. The research and development person works closely with the production department on such projects.

Finally, in some pure research and development jobs a person might work in a corporate research center to discover new technologies and products. The ideas for these new technologies and products may come from information gathered by the sales and marketing people on new customer needs.

Accounting and Finance/MIS (Management Information Systems)/Legal

Until a person gets to upper-level positions, accounting and finance jobs are pretty much what you would expect. The same would be largely true of an MIS job or a legal job. The work is pretty close to what a person does in a college course. Specific knowledge in the field is essential. These jobs require a surprisingly large amount of interaction with internal customers. Even in these jobs, interpersonal skills remain important.

SUMMARY

Organizations are divided into line jobs and staff jobs. In all the above jobs, companies must invest in training to make sure the employees have, and stay current with, the skills and knowledge required to do the job. Companies investing in training have seen improved customer satisfaction, improved quality, improved attitudes, less turnover in the management and leadership ranks, and greater teamwork, creating a more synergistic and effective organization.

Line jobs are those jobs related to the day-to-day operations of the business and are directly related to the products or services being provided by the company to the external customer.

- Sales involve selling the products or services.
- Marketing includes the promotion of the products or services.
- Production is the making of the products or delivery of the services.
- Customer service is taking care of the customer.

Staff jobs support the line jobs and serve internal customers.

- Human resources staff takes care of issues concerning employees.
- Research and development staff works to solve problems and develop new products.
- Accounting and finance workers handle the company's money.
- Management information systems keep the computer system functioning.

It is important that people in both line and staff jobs develop good interpersonal skills. Those in line jobs must foster good relations with people both within and outside of the organization. Those in staff jobs primarily need to have good relations with those people within the organization, but may also have to interact with customers and others outside the organization.

This chapter offers general descriptions of the types of jobs that are available in organizations. As a wise person once said, "Choose a job you love and you will never have to work another day in your life."

CASE STUDY

Smith Manufacturing Company was a maker of household products. Business was going well and had expanded to two divisions—production and marketing. Mr. Paul Smith continued to do the office work with his secretary, Brenda. Paul was considered a jack-of-all trades and vowed not to hire anyone who was not a line employee. Paul wanted everyone that worked for the company to contribute to the bottom line. His attitude was that if you do not make the products or sell the products, you do not work here unless you are Paul himself or Brenda.

Every morning, Paul would check the ten computers to make sure that all of them were running properly. There were five computers in the production department, three computers in the sales department, and two computers in the main office for him and Brenda. Paul

maintained the computers and updated all the software. Brenda could help when computers locked up or programs failed to operate correctly.

Paul and Brenda were also trained in first aid and helped any worker that was injured or not feeling well. If the injury or illness were serious enough, Paul or Brenda would take the employee to the company doctor or the emergency room. They also kept all the employee records, hired, and fired employees. Any trouble in the company was handled by Paul personally. He was legendary for dealing with everything from fist fights to being drunk on the job. Paul had four simple rules in the company—no drinking, no fighting, no stealing, and no firearms. The rule regarding firearms was added after an employee showed up at work with a gun and threatened his coworkers. Paul took the gun from the man, emptied out the bullets, gave the gun back to the man, and then fired him.

Paul also made all the decisions regarding any money spent by the company. Much of his day was spent dealing with purchases, ordering material from vendors, and tracking down late shipments. It was not uncommon for Paul to deal with six to seven vendors on orders to find the best prices.

At the end of the day, Paul and Brenda did the books for the company. Paul would record all purchases and payments made by the company. Brenda would account for all the money coming in from customers. Brenda also picked up the employee time cards every Wednesday for the week and processed the payroll for payday each Friday.

As the company began to grow, Paul found himself coming to work earlier in the day and leaving later at night. Brenda maintained her schedule of 8 A.M. to 5 P.M. with an hour off for lunch. Finally, Paul was coming in at 6 A.M. and leaving at 9 P.M. Even though the plant was closed on Saturdays and Sundays, Paul often found himself at the office doing paperwork. Paul's wife, Mary, began to complain that he had no time for her and their two children. Paul's response was always the same: that someone had to pay the bills around the house since Mary did not work outside the home. Mary appreciated the fact that she could stay at home with their two preschoolers, but she thought Paul was gone entirely too much.

One day, Brenda called in sick and Paul had to do all the office work himself. To start off, one of the computers in production had failed to boot up properly. He spent an hour on it before he found that the Internet connection was damaged by heat coming from one of the machines. He had to go to the computer store to pick up a new connector. He had now spent two hours on fixing the computer.

Rob, one of the production managers, reminded him that they were running low on material and needed a shipment from the supplier by next week. Paul knew that the lead time on the orders was five days and he had better place the order today to make sure it got to the company in time to keep production going.

As Paul was going back to the office, a fight broke out in the shipping area. Paul went there quickly and separated the two combatants. Determined to get this issue resolved he brought each man individually into his office to

hear what happened. After talking to both men, both were sent home for the day and told to report to his office at 8 A.M. the next morning.

It was now approaching noon and Paul was interrupted by news that an tourniquet had been injured by a machine. By the time Paul got there, the employee was bleeding from a cut on the arm. Paul applied a tourniquet to stop the bleeding, but realized that the man needed stitches to close up the wound. Paul drove the employee to the emergency room where the doctor took care of the employee's cut.

Paul returned to the office and started working on the books. After getting his books done, Paul looked at the clock and it was already 6:30 P.M. He had not even started on Brenda's books and decided to leave them for her the next day. Realizing that he was late for dinner with the family and the school play, Paul shot out of the company and headed home. He felt like he had forgotten something important and then it dawned on him that he had failed to order the material needed by Rob in production.

The next day Paul decided to go in at 6 A.M. to try to get caught up on the office work. At 7 A.M. Brenda called in sick again. At 8 A.M. the two combatants from the day before showed up at his office determined to continue from where they were the previous day. Paul quickly fired them both. Both men wanted their money now and Paul told them to come back later. At 8:30 A.M. Rob called the office to make sure his parts had been ordered. As Paul was talking to him, several people came into the office to report that the entire computer system had crashed. After working on the system nearly all day, it finally came back up after the service provider fixed their system problem. Later that day, Brenda called in to report that her doctor told her that she was under too much stress and that the stress may be job related. The doctor told her that she may have to consider taking a new job or she will have more health-related problems. Paul was quickly beginning to wonder what he should do now.

Questions

1. What are the problems Paul is having?
2. Are the problems line related or staff related?
3. Is Paul's system of using a two-person office working?
4. Is this situation likely to get better or worse on its own?
5. What needs to be done to fix the problems?

DISCUSSION QUESTIONS

1. What is the difference between line positions and staff positions?

2. Are staff positions not important because they do not serve the external customer?

3. Explain the differences in tasks between marketing and sales.

4. Describe the interpersonal skill(s) needed for success in each position.

Human Resources I: The Hiring Process

LEARNING OUTCOMES: THE HIRING PROCESS

1. Outline the human resources process.

2. Contrast job description, job analysis, and job specification.

3. Outline the recruiting and selection process.

4. Discuss the guidelines for conducting an effective interview.

5. Explain the advantages and disadvantages of the interview, written tests, assessment centers, and work sampling.

The Interview

Helen was interviewing for a factory job at the Sadapple Company. She was recently laid off from a production job she had for eight years with another company that had gone out of business. She was a hard worker and had excellent references. She had had her previous job since graduating from high school.

After meeting with the human resources people, she was told that she would be called back to interview with the supervisor. The human resources people thought she would be a good candidate for the job and sent all of Helen's information to Greg, the supervisor.

Greg was a new supervisor and had not done any interviewing. Wanting to know more about Helen, as part of the interview he asked her the following questions:

What religion are you?

Are you married?

Are you pregnant?

Have you ever been arrested?

How much do you weigh?

After this last question Helen told Greg that his questions were too personal and she left.

Was Helen right in leaving, or was Greg right in asking her personal questions?

Welcome to Human Resources I: The Hiring Process! ■

The study of organizational behavior encompasses many of the practices, policies, procedures, and functions of the human resources (HR) department within an organization. In this chapter, we want to look at the HR functions in a comprehensive manner with a focus on the behaviors of people at work.

Technology and work design continue to affect the behavior of people at work. We see and feel the accelerated pace of life increasing at all levels. Technology is available to more people. The demands for quality, customer service, and flexibility continue to challenge us and we have to address all of these issues without increasing the price of the service or product. The organization certainly has its job cut out for itself. We have to get it right in the human resources area if we hope to be in business tomorrow.

We will follow the HR function as a process. This process begins with recruiting a candidate for employment, moves to the selection of the best person, and finally ends with the programs to retain the employee. This sounds simple, but in reality everything that must happen between these events makes the process quite involved. The HR function requires a lot of forethought and planning. Let's try to view this with a flowchart to get a view of the entire process (Figure 16–1). We will then work our way down the flowchart and look at each section in detail. This chapter will cover the hiring process: "determining the job to be filled" and "recruiting and selection." Chapter 17, "Human Resources II: Company Policies," will cover company policies after the hiring decision has been made: basic concept of job design, training and development, performance evaluation, and programs to retain employees.

Determining the Job to Be Filled

Recruiting and Selection

Basic Concept of Job Design

Training and Development

Performance Evaluation

Programs to Retain Employees

Figure 16–1 The human resources process.

DETERMINING THE JOB TO BE FILLED

To begin the recruiting process, the HR department needs to have a **job description** and **job specification** that spell out the skills and experience needed to carry out specific job duties. These need to be in place before the interviewing process so the interviewer is better able to evaluate a job applicant's characteristics. Even if the opening is for an existing job, this provides an opportunity to reevaluate the job description for completeness and the job specification to determine if it offers the right combination of attributes for maximum motivation and performance.

Job Analysis

Job analysis is the investigation and determination of the skills, knowledge, and abilities required to perform a job.

For new jobs the first step is to conduct a **job analysis** prior to writing the job description and job specifications. A new job may result from combining two or more tasks into one, changing product or technology, or changing quality standards. The job analysis normally requires an investigation into the various tasks and requirements of the job.[116] In this investigation, any special and general knowledge, skill, and abilities would be determined and documented. The job analysis provides the basis for the job title, the job description, and the job specifications. The following lists several ways to acquire this information.

- **Observation Method.** In this method, the operator is observed normally by a person conducting a time and motion study through several cycles of the task. For example, when I had a new job molding five different plastic computer housings for Hewlett-Packard in San Diego, an industrial engineer actually performed a series of time and motion studies to evaluate the most efficient method to process the parts once the tools were in place. The engineer observed the equipment's operation, the various operators' movements, the workflow, and the quality checks. This information is also valuable in determining the cost for making the product and in determining whether the company can produce it at the necessary quality, safety, and profit levels.

- **Individual/Group Interview Method.** This job analysis method requires the job incumbents, supervisors, and others familiar with the job to be interviewed and the results documented. This results in a picture of the process and the operations necessary for successful completion of the tasks. In the group interview method, all of those involved with the tasks are interviewed simultaneously.

- **Structure Questionnaire Method.** In this job analysis, workers evaluate a long list of items and check off the items performed in the job.
- **Technical Conference Method.** Information is gathered from the "experts" who typically are supervisors and/or engineers with extensive knowledge of the tasks. Another source to obtain this information could possibly be with a trade association that has a catalog of similar job descriptions and job specifications.
- **Diary Method.** When the task is not highly repetitive, the job incumbent(s) could maintain a diary of their daily activities. In a plastic molding operation, the mechanical and electrical maintenance activities were combined into one job description. To develop an accurate picture of what should be included in the job description, I had each individual on each shift keep a diary for seven days. With this information, I could begin to get a description of the various types of equipment and tools the technicians used in their work and, in turn, I was able to develop an accurate job description.

Job Title

The **job title** is the name of the work position. Many people will be able to get an idea about what the job is by its title. We all know what a cook is and what a professor does. The job title helps in classifying the job for recruiting purposes as well as for establishing training, evaluation, and compensation.

The **job title** is the name associated with the job.

Job Description

The first step for recruiting is the development of a **job description**. A job description is a written statement of the necessary components an employee performs. This would include all the activities necessary to perform the job in an effective and efficient manner. As noted in the definition, the job description explains in detail what the employee is supposed to do. The employee's performance appraisal, which we will cover later, would be based on these requirements.

A **job description** is a written statement of the necessary components to do a job in an effective and efficient manner.

Job Specification

A **job specification** is a statement of the qualifications or personal characteristics needed to successfully perform a particular task or a series of tasks. The job specification identifies the knowledge, education, skills, experience, and abilities necessary to perform the job effectively.

A **job specification** is a statement of the qualifications needed to perform a job.

The job description identifies characteristics of the job while the job specifications identify characteristics of the operator. Both the job description and the job specification need to be based on a careful and informed job analysis.

RECRUITING AND SELECTION

There are several ways to go about selecting a candidate for a job. The critical part for the human resources professional is selecting the right candidate for the right job and being able to accomplish this in a timely and cost-effective manner. Let's look at several ways to accomplish this beginning with what is probably the most widely used selection techniques, the resumé (application blank) and the interview.

Recruiting

The first and easiest way to recruit people for jobs is to recruit from current employees. One method of doing this is called **post and bid.** Under this method, job openings are posted in the company and employees who are qualified bid on the jobs they want. This gives current employees the first chance at the jobs and helps maintain good employee morale.

If there are no internal candidates or the internal candidates are not right for the position, the job may be offered to the public in a variety of ways. One way to find new employees is through employee referral. If you are happy with your current employees, you will probably be happy with the candidates they bring to the company. Many companies pay their employees a bonus for finding new employees. Other ways to get applicants for jobs is to use newspaper and radio ads, job fairs, billboards, Internet job postings, employment agencies, state employment services, universities, colleges, high schools, and trade schools. These techniques are good when the company is seeking a local person for the position. With an appropriate job title and job specifications, the number of applicants can be reduced to those who have an interest and are qualified. If the job requires a national or international search, professional organizations, trade and professional publications, universities, and executive search firms may be used to find the right person.

The Resumé and Application Blank

The first contact the company has with the candidate is the resumé and/or the application blank. The resumé is a document provided by the candidate listing his or her education, experience, achievements, and interests. The content is completely controlled by the candidate. An application blank is a form given by the company to the candidate. The company controls which questions are asked and can get the information it needs to make a decision. Most application blanks will state that false information will leave the candidate subject to dismissal if hired for the job. After examining the resumé or application blank, the decision is made whether or not to proceed to the next step, which is the interview.

The Interview

An interview is a way in which the employer can try to decide if an applicant is suitable for the job. But it actually serves a dual purpose. It is also a time for the applicant to decide if he or she even wants to work for the company. To the applicant, interviews can be unnerving and frightening, but they can also be challenging, a good learning experience, and even fun. Whether interviewing or being interviewed, always remember the four 12s of the interview. What are the four 12s? They are the top 12 inches (the face), the bottom 12 inches (the feet), the first 12 steps, and the first 12 seconds. The first impression is critical for a good interview and remembering to focus on the four 12s will certainly help get you started in the interview. The topics covered in a job interview may include education, work experience, special skills and abilities, hobbies, and other interests. The job application and/or resumé would normally provide a source of topics for the interviewer.

Research has shown if the interview is unstructured on the part of the interviewer, the interview tends to be ineffective as a selection device.[117]

For example, when the interviewer asks you to, "Tell me about yourself," the question does not provide you with the proper direction and guidance to demonstrate qualifications for a particular job. The information collected from such an interview process is typically biased and may not be related to the job requirements. The interviewer needs to provide more of a structured environment, such as a standard set of questions and a standardized rating of the applicant's qualifications. Evidence suggests that interviews are most valuable for assessing an applicant's intelligence, level of motivation, and interpersonal skills. When these are related to job performance, the validity of the interview is increased.

The following guidelines provide an overview for conducting a job interview.

- Prepare in advance. The interviewer needs to prepare a standard set of questions (in advance of the interview) that will be asked of all applicants. These structured questions should be relevant to the job, organization, and candidate.
- Find a quiet place free from interruptions.
- Take notes during the interview.
- Use a brief "getting to know you" period.
- Ask open-ended questions.
- Follow an interview format.
- Ask the structured questions, expanding on them as content merits.
- Give the job candidate encouragement.
- Dig for additional details without straying into inappropriate or illegal topics. For example, ask questions relating to work ethics, additional experiences, goals, and desire for self-development.
- Stay away from issues about which it is illegal to ask. Discussing the following topics in job interviews could be a violation of antidiscrimination laws:

Race	Religion
Gender	Pregnancy
Marital status	Number of children
Age	Ages of children
Handicap	Child-care plans
Height or weight	Arrest record
Union affiliation	Workers' compensation claims

- Make limited use of a stress interview because it could upset the interviewee. A stress interview is one when the interviewer deliberately tries to put pressure on the interviewee to see how well the person handles stress.
- Spend most of the interview time listening.

The interview is also an opportunity for the interviewer to evaluate the applicant's fit within the organizational culture. Organizational culture will be discussed in more detail in Chapter 18; however, the applicant needs to be successful in and operate through the current organization's culture. The interviewee may also ask the interviewer to describe the culture of the business. Is it team focused, technologically current, conservative, liberal, customer oriented, and so forth? The interview is an attempt to find an applicant who is the right fit for the job.

For the interviewee there are also some points that may enhance your changes of selection. For example:

- Dress appropriately for the job and corporate culture for which you are interviewing. Jeans and t-shirts probably are not the right clothing selection to make a good first impression. Khakis and a sports coat with a shirt and tie or a business skirt would be better choices.

- Having a current resumé that is grammatically correct, along with a cover letter that specifically addresses the job being applied for, is always a positive sign. It shows one is prepared.
- Distinguish yourself from the rest of the applicants by offering something the other applicants don't. For example, in your interview demonstrate your preparation by correctly pronouncing a name and demonstrating knowledge of the organization's product or service.
- Say "thank you" at the conclusion of the interview. Give a short recap of what you can do for the company and say why you are the best candidate. Ask if it is okay for you to follow-up in a week with a phone call to see if there might be any additional information needed, and conclude with a firm handshake.

Written Tests

Written tests are tests of intelligence, aptitude, ability, interest, and integrity. Written tests have been used extensively in the past, but with tighter control and greater awareness of the laws on discrimination, the use of written tests has declined. Written tests have been found to discriminate against racial or culturally diverse groups of people. Written tests need to be validated, and this has proven to be expensive and time-consuming. Some tests simply cannot be validated. More employers are now using other assessment means such as assessment centers that test for greater job-related qualities.

Assessment Centers

Assessment centers provide interviewees with a series of exercises that simulate real problems they would encounter in the workplace. The performance simulation assessment may take place over several days. The exercises are based on a list of descriptive dimensions that an actual employee with the job has to meet. Activities might include interviews, in-basket problem-solving exercises, group discussions, team exercises, and business decision activities. The assessment centers, while fairly expensive, have proven to be a fairly consistent predictor of later job performance in leadership and managerial positions. As technology has changed, the performance simulation assessment has seen a renewed resurgence in the past few years. The perceived validity of the assessment over the written test has led to the increase in usage. The Subaru automotive plant has used an assessment center for the past two decades as a means to evaluate potential employees in working with the actual assembly parts and tools. The predictability of the employee's performance in the assessment to the actual operation has had a significant positive correlation.

Source: Dilbert, August 21, 1997. *Dilbert* © Scott Adams/Distributed by United Feature Syndicate Inc. Reprinted by permission.

Work Sampling

Work sampling is an effort to create a miniature replica of the actual operations or tasks to be accomplished. The candidate is given an opportunity to demonstrate his or her skills, abilities, and capabilities toward the successful completion of the required task. When I was working as a warehouse manager in the construction materials business, I was asked to use work sampling to select a material handler. The candidate had to successfully pick up and move a bag of cement (94 pounds), a bundle of roofing shingles (80 pounds), and a solid core door (100 pounds) a distance of 50 feet. Failure to do so meant the candidate would not be offered the job. This form of testing has been found to have a positive correlation between the the candidate's performance and successful accomplishment of job tasks.

Physical Exams and Drug Testing

Many companies are now requiring candidates to take a physical exam to assure their fitness for a job. This is especially true of professional athletes and those engaged in heavy physical activity. Drug testing is also required by many companies to assure that candidates are not under the influence of illegal substances. This is especially important to those operating machinery, using equipment, and driving vehicles where drug use may be hazardous to themselves and others.

Use of Recruiters for Selection of Candidates

Many organizations and potential candidates have turned to the use of workplace recruiters. Every state has its own office of workforce development and job placement for citizens seeking employment. Many employers will turn to placement companies such as Adecco, Manpower, or Express Personnel for professional, skilled, or semi-skilled workers.

SUMMARY

The job analysis is a systematic examination of a job that provides the basis for the job title (name of the job), the job description (tasks that make up the components of the job), and the job specifications (qualifications successful applicants must have to fill the job).

Recruiting is the process of getting applicants for jobs in the organization. This can be done internally and externally. Internal recruiting is done by the post and bid method. The job is posted by the company and current employees can apply for it. External recruiting is done by publicizing the job to those outside of the company through company Web sites, employee referrals, newspapers, radio, trade publications, universities, schools, and other sources.

Selection is the process of picking the right candidate for the job. To determine the best candidate, several procedures are used.

- The resumé and application provide the company with information on the applicant.
- The interview gives the company the opportunity to talk to the applicant.

- Validated written tests can be used to test for intelligence, ability, interest, aptitude, integrity, and other characteristics of the applicant.
- Assessment centers are used to put the applicant in situations to deal with problems that simulate problems or operations in the workplace.
- Work sampling can be used to see how well the applicant can do the actual job.
- Physical exams can be used to test for medical problems that affect job performance.
- Drug testing can also be done to ensure the applicant is not on drugs.

The interview is the most frequently used selection process. The unstructured interview is the least predictive. When conducting an interview, be certain to develop a list of questions in advance for all candidates that focus on job skills and responsibilities and that do not violate antidiscrimination laws.

Simpson Company was a growing retail sporting goods store. People in the area around the store had come to rely on the store for all kinds of sporting equipment. Local high school teams bought all of their equipment and uniforms from Simpson. The store featured a wide variety of equipment, targeting everyone from the amateur athlete to the professional. The growth had triggered a need for more employees. Simpson did not have a human resources department and relied on managers in the various departments to do all the hiring. There was no employee union at the company.

John Youbeck was the manger of the golf and tennis department. This department carried golf supplies from low-end irons, putters, and drivers to the ones the professionals use on the tour. They also carried a wide variety of balls, bags, clothes, and accessories. The tennis line was also varied from inexpensive racquets to the ones the professional use. They also had tennis outfits, balls, and accessories. The salespeople frequently gave advice to the customers on equipment and offered tips to improve their play. John had been highly successful in running the department and now the company was going to let him hire an additional salesperson. John was excited about hiring another person to boost his staff, which was overworked.

John identified the job as a golf and tennis equipment salesperson. The description of the job was to sell golf and tennis equipment. The job specification listed by John was to sell equipment to the customers. John thought that about summed it up and he advertised the job in the paper as follows:

Simpson Company is looking for someone to sell equipment. Interested persons should call John Youbeck at (555) 555–0909 or stop by the store to apply for the position.

The week after the advertisement ran, John was overwhelmed by calls and people coming by the store. The applicants included people with complete resumés to others with just pieces of paper with their names on them. Even though the company had an application form, John had forgotten to use it. Adding to the confusion, John had to call everyone back and get them to fill out the application form.

People were told to fill out the form and leave it for John and he would get back to them. When John starting reading the more than 200 forms, he realized he had a problem in that these people ranged from those with virtually no education to a master's degree and ranged from those with no experience to having 25 years of experience. It was going to take a great deal of time to sort this mess out. After spending more than 20 hours of his time, he had narrowed the field down to ten applicants. Wanting to screen applicants out in an interview, John developed the following questions:

1. Do you have any retail selling experience?
2. Do you play tennis and/or golf?
3. Are you married?
4. Do you get along well with people?
5. Do you get along well with children?
6. Do you have any children?
7. Do you plan on having any or more children?
8. Have you ever been arrested?
9. If so, what charge was leveled against you?
10. Do you have a handicap?
11. If so, what is it?
12. When can you start if you are hired?
13. What days and times would be the best for you to work?
14. What is your religious preference?
15. Do you attend church regularly?
16. Have you ever belonged to a union?
17. Can you run a cash register?
18. Can you process credit card sales?

John's goal was to weed out people with problems and try to hire the best people. He invited the top ten candidates to come in for an interview. After talking to two of them, he found out that they were arrested and charged with crimes, but were not convicted because they were innocent and the real criminals were found later. Three of the candidates had been union members, but were not currently with their unions. One man was a Muslim with family living in Iraq. One woman was married and indicated that she was pregnant when asked if she was planning on having more children. One man was in a wheelchair and indicated that he had a permanent handicap. After eliminating these eight, John was down to the final two applicants.

He arranged to have the two finalists go for a drug test. The results of the drug test made John's choice obvious. Cory Clark had passed his drug test and the other applicant tested positive for cocaine. John hired Clark and trained him on what to do in the department. Clark was a quick learner and the customers liked him. Clark had an associate's degree from the local community college and had played tennis in high school and college. He also played golf with the family. He was knowledgeable about golf and tennis equipment and could help people improve their game. Clark quickly became a customer favorite and one of the best salespeople in the store.

Mr. Simpson brought John into his office and complimented him on the great job he had done in hiring Clark. John replied there was nothing to it when you know how to do it and then you do it well. Mr. Simpson commented to his secretary that if they ever got big enough to have a human resources department that John would be the right man to lead it.

Questions

1. Did John really know how to recruit and select people?

2. Did John really pick Cory Clark or was he just lucky?

3. What should John have done about the job description, job specifications, and advertisement?

4. Were all the questions he asked appropriate to ask the candidates?

5. Did John discriminate against anyone in the interview screening?

1. What are the values of job specifications?
2. Discuss the advantages of assessment centers over the interview.
3. Why would work sampling be an important way to screen applicants?
4. Generate a list of questions you feel would be appropriate to assess the knowledge, skills, abilities, and traits of an interviewee.

Human Resources II: Company Policies

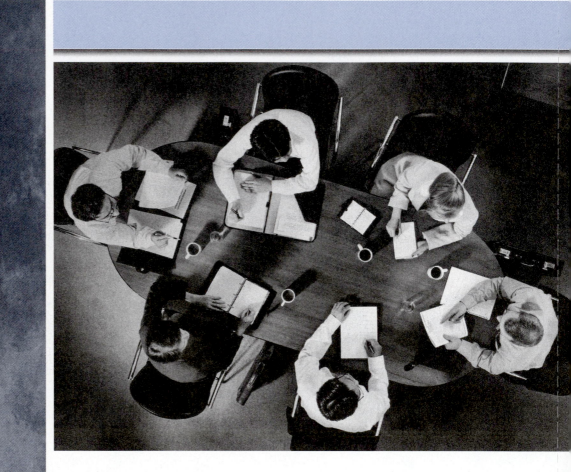

LEARNING OUTCOMES: COMPANY POLICIES

1. Explain the job characteristics model.

2. Discuss the MPS model.

3. Describe TQM.

4. Outline the PDCA model for continuous improvement.

5. Contrast TQM and reengineering.

6. Explain the implementation of the various work redesign considerations.

7. Discuss the component for employee training and development.

8. Explain the purpose of performance evaluation.

9. Discuss programs to retain employees.

10. Through self-assessment, identify your MPS in the job characteristics model.

Name: _____

Section Number: _____

SELF-ASSESSMENT TEST

Please complete the following exercise online, accessible with the Access Card packaged with this text, before reading this chapter.

WHAT'S MY JOB'S MOTIVATING POTENTIAL?

SKILL VARIETY	_____
TASK IDENTITY	_____
TASK SIGNIFICANCE	_____
AUTONOMY	_____
FEEDBACK	_____
MPS (TOTAL)	_____

This questionnaire allows you to calculate your Motivating Potential Score (MPS) from the Job Characteristics Model. The MPS represents a summary score indicating how motivating the job is that you have described.

You should also record your score on this exercise in Appendix 1.

NOTES

The New Hire

Fred has been hired by the company to operate the stamping machine during the night shift. The night shift, which runs from 11 P.M. to 7 A.M., is where new hires typically start. The day shift and the evening shift jobs are usually filled by employees with seniority.

On Fred's first shift he is greeted by the only human resources person on night shift, Allen. Allen has only been with the company for three weeks, and he is still trying to figure out the system. Allen gives Fred a pile of books, pamphlets, and brochures and tells Fred to read them and if he has any questions, to let him know. Allen then introduces Fred to Bill, the night supervisor.

Bill takes Fred to the stamping machine and shows him how to work it. Then, Bill says he needs to check out the other operations and leaves. Fred, thinking he knows what to do, begins using the machine to make parts. Fred continues until the end of the shift on the machine. The day operator comes in at 7 A.M. and yells at Bill and Steve, the day manager, to come over. All the parts produced are wrong and unusable and the machine is damaged.

Bill yells at Fred, "You idiot, you're fired!"

Fred leaves, totally upset by the whole situation.

What happened here?

Welcome to Human Resources II: Company Policies!

In the previous chapter we followed human resources practices through the identification of a job and selecting and hiring a candidate. In this chapter, we will cover company policies that affect employees after they have been hired.

The previous chapter presented the flow diagram shown in Figure 17–1 of the human resources process.

In this chapter, we will pick up with step 3 in the flow diagram, Basic Concept of Job Design.

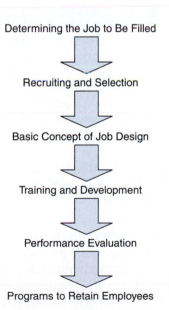

Figure 17-1 The human resources process.

BASIC CONCEPTS OF JOB DESIGN

Understanding how tasks are subdivided begins with job design.

Job Characteristic Model

John Hackman and Richard Oldham created the job characteristic model identifying five dimensions to evaluate a task for employee motivation, satisfaction, and performance. This model provides a method to focus on the task, interpersonal dimensions of a job, and job enrichment. The characteristics are

- **Skill variety.** This is the degree to which there are a variety of skills to perform. The worker can use a number of different skills and talents. This relates to job enlargement and job enrichment, which will be covered later in this chapter. Skill variety provides an opportunity to take boredom out of the job. For example, I worked for a company that molded the hood scoop for the 1999 Ford Mustang. When we began the operation, four people were involved in the process, from operating the press to packing the part. Through an employee involvement effort, the job was redesigned to have the operator running the press also remove the excess material from the molding and then load the part into a polishing cabinet. After the part was done, the operator would check the part for quality requirements and pack the product. The job was enlarged and enriched through the use of skill variety.

- **Task identity.** The degree to which one worker can do a whole job, from beginning to end, with a tangible and visible outcome is task identity. In the hood scoop example, the operators initially thought they were making door handle components for the side of a car. Once everyone understood what they were making and how important it was to the overall appearance of the car, the workers took ownership and a greater interest in what they were producing.

- **Task significance.** This is the degree to which work has a significant impact on others in the immediate organization or those around them. This impact may be in the work or lives of other people. The ultimate example of this would probably be the nurses working in the emergency room or the intensive care unit of a hospital. In this example, their care and decisions have life-or-death implications. A less dramatic example would go back to the Ford Mustang hood scoop. The skill variety and task identity issues were addressed; however, we still were not satisfied with the workers' commitment to the project. To help the workers understand the significance of this part, we first brought in a Mustang hood to show how the part fits and why appearance is important. However, we still didn't get the impact desired. Only after we brought in a new Ford Mustang and parked it next to the molding operation did the operators understand the significance of their work to the entire car.

- **Autonomy.** The degree to which a job offers freedom, independence, and discretion in scheduling work and in determining procedures involved in carrying out the various tasks is autonomy.

- **Feedback.** The degree to which a job provides direct information about the effectiveness of the employee's performance is feedback.

The strength of an employee need provides guidelines for managers. Combining the five characteristics of the job characteristic model into a single index, we can reflect the overall potential of a job to trigger high internal work motivation. This index is called the Motivating Potential Score (MPS) and is computed in Figure 17–2.

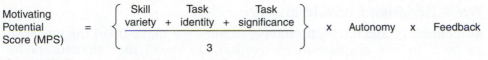

Figure 17–2 Computing a motivating potential score.

Source: Computing a Motivating Potential Score, reprinted from *Organizational Behavior and Human Performance,* J. R. Hackman and G. R. Oldham, in "Motivation through the Design of Work: Test of Theory," pp. 250–79, copyright © 1976, with permission from Elsevier.

> **Based on the self-assessment test at the beginning of this chapter, how motivating is the job you described? What characteristics of the job would need to change to raise the MPS? Where could you find such a job?**

Evaluating Work Designs

In today's competitive environment, we have to look continuously for ways to find improvement. The past decade of intensified competition and this pressure will continue through the new millennium. Continuous improvement needs to become a way of life for any business or organization to keep introducing improvements and change. This continuous improvement process is referred to as **Total Quality Management** (TQM). The philosophy of the TQM concept is one of a structured system for meeting and exceeding customer needs and expectations by creating organization-wide participation in the planning and implementation of breakthroughs and continuous improvement of the processes.[118] Under TQM, when is good, good enough? And the answer, of course: it never is. As an example, if IRS employees throughout the country are giving just 99.9 percent of themselves on the job, then the IRS will lose two million documents this year. Furthermore, 811,000 rolls of faulty 35-mm film will be loaded this year, 880,000 credit cards in circulation will turn out to have incorrect cardholder information on their magnetic strips, 114,500 mismatched pairs of shoes will be shipped this year, and on it goes. There will always be ways to improve on the product and/or customer service. The **Plan, Do, Check, Act Model** (Figure 17–3) is the continuous improvement model. It treats all organizations as if they are in a state of change.[119] Employees at all levels of the organization will plan for improvement and change, make the change, check on how the change for improvement has worked, and then act to revise or continue to implement the improvement. The process then recycles.

In some organizations we experience reengineering. What does reengineering mean? Reengineering allows us to reexamine the total organization and then, if necessary, do a wholesale change. **Reengineering** means rethinking and redesigning those processes that will add value to the product or service. Michael Hammer coined the term *reengineering,* contending that a changing global environment and organizational structure have gotten top heavy and a dramatic change is required.[120] We often read or hear of downsizing or changing a product orientation as reengineering takes place. Reengineering can dramatically change the work specifications and job descriptions discussed at the beginning of this chapter.

Total Quality Management is a process seeking continuous improvement throughout the organization, involving all employees and driven by customer satisfaction.

Reengineering means rethinking and redesigning processes to add value to the organization.

Figure 17–3 Model for continuous improvement.

Work Redesign Considerations

As technology and products change, so must the make-up of the job. If we go back to our chapter on motivation, we recall the opportunity for growth, sense of achievement, responsibility, and recognition are all motivators. When looking at **work redesign,** we certainly want to consider how our redesign will affect employee motivation. The first redesign concept we want to discuss is **job rotation**. This is often referred to as *cross training*. Job rotation means having the operator move from one job to another. There are several reasons for this. One reason is for health and safety considerations. In a repetitive operation where one runs the risk of carpal tunnel syndrome or a cumulative trauma disorder, job rotation is necessary. The repetitive motion of the job may cause physical discomfort if job rotation is not available. A second example would be for an employee who is working in a job where the environment is hot. On a regular basis, the employee would be rotated out to do other jobs. A third example would be to provide job rotation to eliminate boredom. In one department, the operator may begin by working on a drill press and then be rotated to a lathe, and then to another operation or piece of equipment within the department, just to reduce the boredom of the job and the possible accidents caused by inattention.

Another possibility in work redesign is that of **job enlargement.** In job enlargement, the number of jobs the operator completes is expanded. This is a horizontal expansion. If we go back to the example of the hood scoop from the discussion on skill variety, we could see an example of job enlargement. The employee at the press simply completed more tasks. His or her decision-making responsibilities were not increased. The number of tasks was simply enlarged.

The final work redesign concept to consider is **job enrichment.** Job enrichment means we enrich the operators by giving them decision-making responsibility over part or all of their task.[121] If operators are allowed to decide in what order they want to accomplish various tasks to complete a job, take corrective action to control quality, or take action based on problem solving while also working, the operators are enriched. Some suggestions for enriching a job would include combining tasks to form a new operation and providing open feedback on the task completion and on the operator's performance. Of the alternatives cited in this section, job enrichment may deserve the most attention. If a job can be enriched, the operator is more likely to be motivated to accomplish the tasks and feel good about the results.

Another area for consideration when evaluating the work design or redesign is the **work schedule.** As technology has been introduced into the workplace at an accelerating pace, we want to also evaluate the work schedules that allow us to be responsive to our customers, meet the demands of the workplace, and yet be receptive to the time needs of our people. First, let's look at **flextime.** Some organizations are able to permit some degree of flexibility in their work schedule. Flextime means there is a core time period that the employee must be at the work station, let's say 10 A.M. until 2 P.M.; however, the employee has flexibility to come in early or stay late to get his or her work completed and work the required amount of time. For example, on one day the employee may decide to begin work at 6 A.M. and work until 2 P.M., and the next day elect to come in at 10 A.M. and work until 6 P.M. In principle, this eliminates all tardiness, and it certainly does allow flexibility in one's schedule.[122]

Another possibility for a work schedule is to have a **shorter work week.** A shorter work week may be accomplished by working ten hours per day for

Job rotation is cross training by moving from one job to another.

Job enlargement is a horizontal expansion of the job.

Job enrichment is a vertical expansion of the job.

a four-day period, thus giving the employee three consecutive days off to use at his or her discretion. This may not be feasible in all situations; but when it is, it is often a popular choice.

Another alternative schedule is called **job sharing.** With job sharing, two or more employees do the same job but they are scheduled to share the work. As an example, a plastic molding company in the Midwest has customers on the East Coast as well as the West Coast. To provide a touch of personal service, the company decides to have one receptionist begin work at 6 A.M. to be available for calls coming from the customers on the East Coast where there is a one-hour time difference. The first receptionist would work until 12:30 P.M. and another receptionist would begin work at noon and work until 6:30 P.M., thus providing receptionist coverage for the West Coast. This job sharing idea also provides a trained backup in the event one receptionist is not able to work for some reason.

The final alternative schedule is called **telecommuting.** Telecommuting is possible where employees can do their work at home on a computer connected to their office.[123] Advances in technology have made this possible, and it is becoming more prevalent. For example, the employee can complete accounting reports, schedules, customer contacts, and a whole host of other activities through a home-based computer.

TRAINING AND DEVELOPMENT

One of the key components for getting new employees started right is to do a good job of **orientation training**. Too many times an individual is hired for a job, and the organization does not provide adequate time to orient the employee about the history of the organization, organizational culture, various departments, policies, procedures, quality and customer concerns, safety, compensation, performance evaluations, and other points necessary to ensure success.

On-the-job training (OJT) is another effective employee training strategy. Most people seem to learn better when they have a chance to practice what they will be doing. On-the-job training provides this opportunity. In fact, most training is accomplished through this means. In many cases another employee or supervisor will serve as a mentor to the worker.

Off-the-job training provides training to the new or seasoned employee. Off-the-job training means training will be done away from the job. This may be necessary due to safety issues or to learn new technology. Personnel from within the organization may do the off-the-job training. It may also require outside consultants for specific technical training. Many businesses work with local colleges and universities to develop a program where instructors from the college will go to the business to

Source: *Dilbert*, March 12, 1997. *Dilbert* © Scott Adams/Distributed by United Feature Syndicate, Inc. Reprinted by permission.

conduct training. Off-the-job training may be done in any number of ways. It is best when a combination of learning devices is used since workers have different learning styles. Some of the most popular training aids are videotapes, lectures, role-playing, games, audiotapes, case studies, and computer-based training.

PERFORMANCE EVALUATION

Every employee hired wants and needs to have feedback on his or her job performance. Performance evaluations are often viewed as an opportunity for conflict to arise but really need to be seen as an opportunity for growth. Too often the evaluator will spend a minimum amount of time working on a performance evaluation of an employee and yet that same evaluation will be used for pay increases, promotion, professional development, retention, areas for improved performance, human resources planning, and a whole host of other possibilities.

What Is Evaluation?

When doing the performance evaluation, we need to ask what must be evaluated to gain an accurate picture of the individual. Three critical areas should be considered: task measurements, behaviors, and traits.

Let's look at the **task measurements** first. How productive has the worker been and what are we using as measurements? For example, we might want to include a quality measurement, an efficiency measurement, total sales, number of customers served, a customer satisfaction measurement, and/or number of units sold. We are looking at objective measurements that reflect performance.

The second area is **behaviors.** Often it may be difficult to identify specific task performance that reflects all those things an employee does. We can also look at behaviors such as attendance, tardiness, timely submission of reports, or timeliness of follow-up on customer complaints or service.

The third area is that of **traits.** This area is often the most difficult and it is certainly the most subjective. Traits such as attitude, dependability, leadership, and honesty are often used.

Who Should Do the Evaluations?

The performance evaluation is an excellent opportunity for the supervisor to provide feedback. Too often supervisors have not been trained in how to evaluate and conduct performance reviews and are left to doing the exact same thing their supervisors did. There is a feeling one has to find people doing things wrong and evaluate that behavior; however, why not find people doing things right? But we need to ask the question, "Who should be doing the performance evaluation?" Traditionally the immediate supervisor completes the performance evaluation. Research tells us that the employee's immediate supervisor completes about 95 percent of all performance evaluations at the lower and middle management levels. The immediate supervisor should know the employee's performance the best; however, as the workforce changes, the responsibility for performance evaluations will change. Other possibilities include the employee's peers, immediate subordinates, and a self-evaluation. Let's look at each of these in a little greater detail.

Peer evaluations have been found to be one of the most reliable sources of task measurements. The employee interacts with his or her peers almost on a daily basis and this interaction provides a fairly comprehensive and accurate perception of the employee's performance.

Another possibility is to have employees evaluate **their own performance.** This approach is especially beneficial when used in conjunction with the evaluation of the immediate supervisor. This evaluation method will point out the difference in perception and will yield a positive and interactive discussion when conducting the performance evaluation. Employee self-evaluation is also consistent with employee empowerment and self-management concepts.

Yet another possibility is to have **immediate subordinates** conduct performance evaluations on their supervisor. Again this provides an opportunity to evaluate any misperceptions between the supervisor and employees. The obvious concern with this form of evaluation is the fear of reprisal from the "bosses" given unfavorable evaluations. For this reason, if this form of evaluation is used, anonymity is crucial if the evaluations are to be accurate.

The last area of evaluation is called the **360-degree evaluation.** This has been around for some time; however, it has gained considerable acceptance over the last few years. The 360-degree evaluation provides for performance feedback from everyone the worker interacts with on a regular basis. Those providing performance evaluation feedback could include the manager, suppliers, clients, peers, subordinates, and anyone else having interaction with the worker. This method of evaluation is also consistent with those organizations using self-directed work teams, employee involvement, or TQM programs.

Remember, as a rule, feedback on performance evaluations, positive or negative, normally leads to higher performance. Workers really want to know how they are perceived by their superiors, and performance evaluations provide us with a tool to do this.

How Are Evaluations Done?

Most companies use the graphic rating method of employee evaluation. Under this method, the evaluator marks the box on a scale that best describes the employee's performance on a variety of job-related activities. The scale can be based on quality of performance (very poor to poor to average to good to excellent), frequency of performance (never to rarely to sometimes to often to always), or agreement with good performance (strongly disagree to disagree to undecided to agree to strongly agree). All evaluations are done independently of the other employees and their performance. Other methods of evaluation compare one employee to other employees. These methods include ranking (best to worst employee), paired comparison (comparing all employees to each other), and forced distribution (assigning employees to groups based on performance). Management by objectives (MBO) involves seeing how well the employee has met the goals for the year established at the beginning of the year by the employee and the supervisor. Other methods include the critical incident method (based on either a good or bad incident), narrative forms (written comments usually not alone but in conjunction with the graphic rating method), and methods based on type and frequency of behavior.

How Can Evaluations Be Done Right?

The person doing the evaluation needs to evaluate the employee fairly and base the evaluation on actual job performance. Errors in evaluations occur when evaluators are too hard, too easy, or biased and when they consider characteristics of the employee other than job-related factors, fail to evaluate for the whole period, let one incident greatly influence the evaluation, or try to rate everyone as just average. The evaluators need to clearly make an effort to be aware of these problems and avoid them.

PROGRAMS TO RETAIN EMPLOYEES

A relatively recent strategy to retain employees is creating a family-friendly workplace. The workplace is in a constant state of change. The U.S. workforce is now approaching a 50/50 distribution of male and female workers. The single-parent family seems to be becoming the norm rather than the exception. Individuals are living longer. Many, if not most, households have both husband and wife working on careers. Due to the aging population, many families find themselves with the responsibility of caring for their elderly parents. In 1993, Congress passed the Family and Medical Leave Act, which provides up to twelve weeks of unpaid leave for employees who have a need to stay at home to care for a child or other family member who requires attention. This act requires employers to continue health benefits during this leave and guarantees employees the same or a comparable job upon return to the workplace.

As the workplace changes, employers must continue to change to meet the needs of their employees. Many companies are considering on-site child care and elderly care. For example, Subaru of Indiana Automotive, Inc., in Lafayette, Indiana, has a child development center for associates' children from six weeks to six years of age.[124] Many other companies are offering flexible hours, compressed work weeks, job sharing, and telecommuting. Creating a family-friendly workplace needs to be a goal for those organizations that want to remain competitive in the future. Organizations that have created family-friendly workplaces have found it easier to recruit and retain their workers, one of the key goals of human resources.

Job design embraces the three major areas of job characteristics, continuous improvement, and work redesign. The job characteristics model includes skill variety, task identity, task significance, autonomy, and feedback. It is important to incorporate all five components into the design of a new job.

Continuous improvement can best be described as plan, do, check, and act, also known as the TQM model. Under the TQM model, improvement is never ending. Reengineering allows us to reexamine the total organization and then, if necessary, do a wholesale change. Reengineering means rethinking and redesigning those processes that can add value to the product or service. Work redesign includes job rotation, job enlargement, job enrichment, work schedule, flextime, shorter work week, job sharing, and telecommuting.

One can use the motivating potential score model to measure the level of motivation in a given job. Once this is known, the task(s) may be modified using the tools discussed in this chapter to improve the MPS score.

Training, the process of preparing people for jobs, consists of orientation training, on-the-job training, and off-the-job training.

Performance evaluation is done to provide feedback to employees as to how well they are doing their job for purposes of pay increases, promotion, professional development, retention, and human resource planning. The employee is evaluated on task measurements, behaviors, and traits. This evaluation can be done by the immediate superior, peers, the employee, subordinates, or everyone having interaction with the employee (the 360-degree evaluation).

Employee retention is focusing more and more on creating a family-friendly workplace. Consideration for older workers and workers with children has given rise to better work schedules and leave policies.

This chapter concludes our two-chapter description of human resources, starting from determining the job to be filled and ending with programs to retain employees. HR needs to be viewed as a process to help bring about improvement in the employee and the workplace.

CASE STUDY

The Belton Company was ready to do the yearly evaluations for all the employees. The evaluations were done every December. The evaluations were completed by the immediate supervisor for all employees and were used for pay increases, year-end bonuses, additional training, and promotions. Everyone wanted to look good this time of year because the bonuses could run from $200 to $2,000 for production workers, not mentioning the pay raises. Promotions were usually not that important to production workers because a promotion meant being made supervisor and going on salary. Many production workers made more than supervisors because they could get overtime pay and supervisors did not get overtime pay even though they may work the extra hours. All the supervisors used the graphic rating method of evaluation, with the categories being excellent, good, fair, poor, and very poor.

Harry Krug was the supervisor for the drill press operators. Harry had problems among his employees with attendance, waste, and scrap for most of the year except for the months of November and December. During November and December, everyone was at work on time and worked the full shift. The number of mistakes also dropped during this time period. When Harry did his evaluations, he always looked at what was going on at the time of the evaluation. His workers were always rated fair to good. Management could not figure out why his department, with one of the worst records for attendance and production over the course of the year, was staffed with average-to-good workers. The workers in this department typically got an average bonus of $1,250 and a 4 percent raise.

Dan Goins was the supervisor for the metal cutters. Dan was tough on the workers. He was very demanding and expected the best out of the employees. Even though they were one of the best departments in the company, his workers were rated from very poor to fair. A fair rating was as good as it got for Dan's workers. Management could not figure out why a department with an outstanding performance rating had no good or excellent workers. Workers in this department typically got a $500 bonus and a 2 percent raise.

Fred Few was a likable welding supervisor and got along extremely well with his workers. The workers liked Fred and made an effort to do well on the job. They were considered by management as just average in productivity and attendance. Fred was not demanding on them, but he did manage to get the job done. When evaluation time came around, Fred would give everyone an excellent or good rating. Management again was surprised that an average department had top-rated employees. Workers in this department typically got an average bonus of $1,750 and a 6 percent raise.

Randy Tarr was a material handling supervisor who had a reputation for being distant from the workers in his department. He was away from the job as much as possible pursuing his interest in NASCAR racing. He would typically be gone on Fridays and Mondays during the racing season. The workers knew that if they did an average job that they would all be rated fair. Every year Randy rated everyone fair and they all got the same bonuses and pay increases. People knew that they could count on a $1,000 bonus and a 3 percent raise.

Sammy Ray was the supervisor for the shipping department and tried to give his employees a fair evaluation of their work. He would keep notes all year long on how the workers were doing. He quickly tried to correct mistakes as soon as they happened. He would meet with the workers individually to discuss how they were doing. Sammy had a reputation of being firm but fair. His ratings were ranged widely from poor to excellent. Sammy would usually fire anyone that was very poor. The average bonus is this department was $1,250 and average raise was 3.5 percent. Management rated the department as being good and the bonuses and raises were close to being right.

Mike Harris was supervisor of the grinders. His department was considered by management to be the best in the company. They had the lowest absenteeism and the highest productivity. They consistently surpassed standards. Mike had a veteran group of workers with a strong work ethic. Mike was quick to fix mistakes and take action when it was needed. Mike gave all of his men an excellent rating because he felt like they deserved it. The department received an average bonus of $2,000 and a 7 percent pay raise. Management went along with Mike on the bonuses and raises because he had the numbers to back up his ratings of the employees.

As usual management accepted the evaluations of the supervisors and gave out the bonuses and raises accordingly. Bob Parker, a known goof-off and slacker from Fred's department, was talking to some of the workers from Dan's department at the Sundown Bar and Grill after work. Bob reported he had just gotten a $1,550 bonus and a 5.3 percent raise. After Bob left, Joe Jenkins, one of hardest working men in Dan's department, commented that something is very wrong with the company when that can happen. He had only gotten $1,000 and a 3 percent raise. As more and more of the workers talked to one another, some felt that they had done really well and others felt they had been cheated.

As management was reflecting on the bonuses and pay raises based on the employee evaluations sent to them by the various managers, several workers approached them about the lack of fairness in the evaluation system. Management began to check into the complaints about evaluations and found that most of the complaints were coming form the departments headed by Dan and Randy. There were some complaints from Harry's department, but none from the departments headed by Mike, Sammy, and Fred. As management looked at the overall situation, it became apparent that the correlation between departmental performance and employee evaluations did not make much sense. This problem, which was thought to be only in one or two departments, may be more widespread.

Questions

1. Discuss which supervisors seem to be doing a good job of evaluating employee performance.

2. Discuss what is wrong with the supervisors who are not doing a good job of evaluating employee performance.

3. Why were no complaints lodged against Fred's evaluations even though he was not doing them correctly?

4. What needs to be done to correct the problem in this company?

DISCUSSION QUESTIONS

1. Why is orientation training important?
2. Explain task significance in the job characteristic model and the implications.
3. Why is feedback important to the employee?
4. Using the motivation potential score model, evaluate a task for possible improvement.
5. Demonstrate your understanding of TQM through the PDCA model by describing a project when TQM has been used.

CHAPTER 18

Organizational Culture

LEARNING OUTCOMES: ORGANIZATIONAL CULTURE

1. Define organizational culture.

2. Describe how organizational culture dictates issues.

3. Identify ways organizational culture is nurtured and sustained.

4. Contrast the dominate culture and the subculture.

5. Through self-assessment, gain a greater insight to the right culture for you.

Name: _____

Section Number: _____

SELF-ASSESSMENT TEST

Please complete the following exercise online, accessible with the Access Card packaged with this text, before reading this chapter.

EXERCISE III.A.1: **WHAT TYPE OF ORGANIZATION STRUCTURE DO I PREFER?**

Score _____

This instrument measures your preference for working in a mechanistic or organic organization structure. Mechanistic structures are characterized by extensive departmentalization, high formulation, a limited information network, and centralization. In contrast, organic structures are flat, use cross-hierarchical and cross-functional teams, have low formalization, possess a comprehensive information network, and rely on participative decision making.

You should also record your score on this exercise in Appendix 1.

NOTES

Culture Shock

Phil is looking forward to his first day on the job. He has been hired by a well-established company that has been around for more than 100 years. He is eager to show his new company that he is an aggressive, take-charge person who can lead the company into the future.

On Phil's first day, he is led into a room with all the other new employees for an orientation. The company has handbooks and procedure manuals for everything. There are also forms for everything. After a series of meetings that last all day, Phil has what seems like a ton of material to read, analyze, comprehend, and obey.

The next day, Phil meets with Linda, his boss, and is told how things are done. When Phil asks Linda why certain things are done the way they are, she responds, "That is the way we have always done it." When Phil asks what he will have to do to get promoted, she responds, "Obey the rules and don't rock the boat."

After eight months of obeying the rules and putting all requests in triplicate, Phil has had enough. No one listens to his ideas. In fact, no one even cares about his ideas. He is viewed by the company as pushy and overly aggressive. He views the company as stuck in the mud. Phil resigns his job and leaves for a more dynamic company. Both Phil and the company are pleased with his departure.

What happened here between Phil and the company?

Welcome to Organizational Culture! ■

What are the unwritten rules in a company? Most of the real rules for behavior are determined by an organization's culture. If you want to understand a company, learn its culture.

If you want to understand organizational culture, watch the movie *Gung Ho*. In this movie, a Japanese company takes over an American car factory. The Japanese managers come in to instill their culture in the factory because they believe organizational culture is one of the key factors for their company's success. They hire the character played by Michael Keaton as the liaison between the Japanese managers and the American workers.

One of the first changes the Japanese company makes is to start the working day with morning exercises. This is a common practice in a Japanese factory but a little unusual in America. The Japanese workers have no problem with the exercises, but the American workers make a half-hearted effort, trying to make sure they don't look silly. Later in the movie, the Japanese and the Americans play a "friendly" softball game. The Japanese come in coordinated uniforms and do team-oriented warm-ups. The Americans come wearing t-shirts and jeans and just throw the ball around a little to get ready. During the game, the Japanese hit a bunch of singles to try to score the most runs. The Americans try to hit home runs.

Organizational culture varies widely. In the movie *Gung Ho*, the Japanese company and its American workers exhibit widely different cultures. This creates a series of organizational problems. For example, an aspect of the Japanese culture is to sacrifice individual goals to help the company. When the American workers in the movie are unwilling to do this, they are punished.

Let's compare two companies in my career history, Air Products and Chemicals and PPG Industries. Air Products was founded around World War II on the idea of cryogenically liquefying air to separate it into oxygen, nitrogen, and trace gases. (If you want to know what "cryogenically" means, think of Mr. Freeze in *Batman*.) The company has been successful through aggressive growth and hard selling. The other company I worked for, PPG Industries, was founded in the 1800s. Their original business was making plate glass (not glass for plates, but big, flat pieces of glass used for windows and such). There was much less emphasis on growth at PPG. Instead, the organization focused more on efficiency and costs.

As you might imagine, Air Products and PPG developed totally different organizational cultures. Air Products was dynamic and encouraged creativity and aggressive ideas, especially ideas that generated new opportunities and growth. PPG, on the other hand, was a formal company. Its managers did not really like new ideas, but if you had a suggestion to lower costs, it might be considered.

You could really tell the difference between the two company cultures at the annual sales meetings. At Air Products, we would usually have our annual meeting in Florida in February. A lot of the meeting would be social events, especially sports contests. Given the competitiveness of the employees, we would usually have more "lost time accidents" at the annual softball game than accidents in our regular jobs for the whole year. The meeting would be more about motivation than anything else. One year, we made army videos for the sales meeting by dressing up in combat fatigues to talk about how we were going to beat the competition.

At PPG, we also had the annual sales meeting in February, but we had it in Chicago at a golf resort that offered good rates during the winter. This was good cost control, even if it was not much fun. There was little social time during the meeting and certainly no sports contests. Instead, we reviewed financial results, financial goals, and technical specifications for new products.

This is not to say that one culture was better than another; they were just different. If PPG people went to an Air Products sales meeting, they would ask why so much money was being wasted on extraneous activities. If Air Products people went to a PPG sales meeting, they would ask how the employees could be motivated to work hard after such a boring meeting. Each company's meeting was designed for its specific culture.

BEHIND COMPANY CULTURE

First, we must recognize the corporate organizational culture is a dramatic force behind every employer. The corporate culture is unique to that particuliar organization. A lot of organizational culture comes from the founder. Air Products was founded by a creative man who decided to pursue a high-technology idea. Most people said his idea would never work. He aggressively sold his idea to potential customers, actually convincing the customers to sign long-term contracts before plants were even built. He then used these long-term contracts as collateral for getting bank loans to build the plants. His strong personality became part of the company culture. He hired people with a similar drive as his, and new people in the company were taught that aggressiveness and creativity were rewarded. For decades, Air Products grew around these core values established by the founder. **Organizational culture** is defined as individuals in an organization having a common perception and sharing core values. In essence, it is a set of basic rules or guidelines to give the group members a common basis for understanding and interacting with one another.[125] People who

Organizational culture is individuals in an organization having a common perception and sharing core values.

work for Air Products know the story of how the company was founded and the common perception and shared values continue even today.

PPG, on the other hand, was founded with the idea of being more cost-effective than the competition. PPG expanded from glass into other businesses like paint and commodity chemicals with a strategy of finding a way to make their products at a lower cost than the competition through tight cost controls. New hires were selected based on their ability to work with tight cost controls, and once hired, they were taught to sharpen their pencils and look for ways to save a tenth of a cent per pound. People that work for PPG also have a common perception and shared values. In this case, the culture is based on a philosophy of efficiency and tight cost controls.

These examples show that organizational culture is nurtured and sustained through **hiring practices** and the **socialization** of new hires (telling new employees what is expected of them and how the reward system is structured). In their book *Primal Leadership*,[126] Goleman and McKee stress the importance of culture when they refer to building "emotionally intelligent organizations." This points out that in the best organizations, people share a vision of who they are collectively, and they share a special chemistry. They have the feeling of a good fit, of understanding and being understood, and a sense of well-being in the presence of others. Some companies send all new employees to an orientation training program. Teaching these people the company culture and how to be successful within the established culture is an important objective in this training.

Amy Miller, founder of Amy's Ice Creams, has built a series of premium ice cream shops in Austin and Houston, Texas, using the corporate culture to give her a competitive advantage.[127] Miller has created a culture of fun and entertainment in her business. As a customer, you may see the servers performing in a manner you won't forget. For example, on a Friday or Saturday evening you may see the servers juggle with their serving spades, toss scoops of ice cream to one another behind the counter, or break-dance on the freezer top. They may invite the customers to sing or dance or recite a poem or mimic a barnyard animal to win fee samples of ice cream. They may be wearing pajamas (because it is sleepover night) or you may be served by candles (romance night) or by strobe lights (disco night). They wear costumes. They bring props. They create fun. Miller has created a corporate culture of fun that sells entertainment along with ice cream and it has given her a competitive advantage.

Organizational culture is a critical determinate of whether a person will be satisfied working for a company. Organizational culture largely dictates issues like:

- Attitude toward innovation and creativity
- Attitude toward risk taking and aggressiveness
- Formalization of rules and procedures
- People orientation
- Team orientation
- Attitude toward women and minorities
- Work hours and dedication to the company
- Dress code
- Décor of the offices
- Language on the job
- Tolerance of fun
- Discipline
- Ethical standards

Forces that sustain a culture:
- Top management
- Selection process
- Socialization

The transformation begins with an effective orientation program.

Source: Dilbert, October 7, 1996. *Dilbert* © Scott Adams/Distributed by United Feature Syndicate, Inc. Reprinted by permission.

Most companies do not have written rules covering these issues, but a company's culture will take a clear stance on them.

ORGANIZATIONAL CULTURE AND CAREER PLANNING

Organizational culture should be a main factor that you consider before accepting a job. Some people want to work for a Silicon Valley company because they can wear shorts or jeans to work, the hours are flexible, and there are not many formal rules or regulations. Books are written on what companies are the most "friendly" for women. Some companies are more tolerant of the fact that some employees have children, and they might offer flexible working hours or a day-care center at the company. All of these factors are part of organizational culture.

This is not to say that all companies have a uniform culture. Large companies today are made up of many different divisions, and each division or work group might have their own **subculture.** Trying to blend all these subcultures into the **dominant culture** of the company can be a challenge, especially in cases where one company acquires another and tries to unify the culture (such as the *Gung Ho* example, in which a Japanese company acquires an American factory).

> Organizations may have subcultures that are different from the dominant culture.

When I worked for PPG, I was comfortable with the subculture in my division. This division was originally a small, privately owned company (with a culture similar to Air Products) that was acquired by PPG. At first PPG decided to leave this division alone, but that turned out to be contrary to the PPG culture of tight control. The company then tried to mold this division into the dominant culture of PPG. This failed, and the division was ultimately sold to another company. It was the division's subculture as much as business performance that led to the divestiture.

If you decide to work for a company because you like a division's subculture, you should also consider whether you are compatible with the company's dominant culture. Many policies come down from corporate management. Even if you feel safe in a division's subculture, some decisions and policies still trickle down. Dominant culture also plays a big role in promotion possibilities. If you do not fit in with the company's dominant culture, your upward mobility could be limited.

Based on the self-assessment test at the beginning of this chapter, what type of organizational culture is best for you? Where are you likely to find such a culture?

THINKING GLOBALLY

Just like an organization, each country has a different set of cultural values apart from the company culture. As we see more mergers and acquisitions between domestic and international companies, the corporate culture may become fragmented. As organizations are transformed by the greater global marketplace, the understanding of cultural differences and practices is critical. Making global differences a part of corporate culture can be a valuable endeavor. The diversity offered by the different cultures will lead to greater understanding and provide a competitive edge in the marketplace. Education, training, and awareness make all the difference to being successful.

Toyota Motor Company has been successful in building new automotive assembly plants in the United States. The Toyota way incorporates the Toyota and Japanese culture and philosophy toward a new manufacturing philosophy called "lean manufacturing." The training of the American worker and the incorporation of some of the Japanese culture through education, use of terms, teams, dress, and work ethic has provided the Japanese auto manufacturer with a competitive advantage in its United States venture. The book title *The Toyota Way* describes this competitive advantage and the power of culture.

Geert Hofstede conducted research in the 1970s analyzing the differences in culture.[128] His research involved more than 116,000 IBM employees in 40 countries and looked at five cultural dimensions. The five dimensions are

- **Power distance.** Power distance is the degree to which people in a country perceive that the power in organizations and institutions is distributed unequally. Those high in power distance have limited interactions between low-status and high-status individuals where as those low in power distance are at ease interacting with people from different backgrounds and power positions. Malaysia is a good example of a country high in power distance.

- **Uncertainty avoidance.** Uncertainty avoidance is the degree to which a country prefers structured over unstructured situations. Those with high uncertainty avoidance try to avoid the unpredictable and unstructured situations. South American countries tend to be higher than other countries in uncertainty avoidance. Those with low uncertainly avoidance have greater ease in working in unstructured and unpredictable situations. Cultures low in uncertainty avoidance are more accepting of ambiguity. They are less rule-oriented and more accepting of change.

- **Individualism versus collectivism.** Individualism reflects a national culture in which the primary concern is for self and family. The United States would be a country high in individualism. Collectivism reflects primary concern for the interest and well being of the larger group. Cultures high in collectivism expect others in the groups in which they belong to help and protect them. Japan would be a great example of a country high in collectivism.

- **Masculinity versus femininity.** Masculinity is the striving for achievement, power, and control. Cultures high in masculinity are assertive, task oriented, and more materialistic. The United States would score fairly high on masculinity. Femininity places the emphasis on good working conditions, security, feelings, and intuition. Cultures high in femininity see little difference in the capability of male and female roles and treat women as equals in all aspects. Denmark, Finland, Norway, and Sweden would be good examples of countries high in femininity.

- **Short-term versus long-term orientation.** Cultures with short-term focus appear to focus more on quantity of life as opposed to the long-term orientation and quality of life. Long-term focus is looking to the future and valuing the environment. Asian countries tend to have greater long-term orientation.

Hofstede has been influential and is one of the most cited social scientists. As nations and cultures evolve, his work will continue to be examined and evaluated.

ORGANIZATIONAL CULTURE IS A TWO-EDGED SWORD

A company's culture can be both an asset and a liability. Culture can be a great help in explaining the rules to employees and fostering camaraderie. Culture can be a disadvantage, however, if the company needs to make changes. An organization's culture may prove a barrier to diversity, acquisitons and mergers, communication, and the approach to leadership. PPG has a difficult time fostering creativity. It goes against their culture. Air Products has a difficult time getting employees to follow strict rules. Their culture encourages breaking rules. Organizational culture can be a two-edged sword.

A major factor in determining how well a person will be satisfied with the company is organizational culture. Organizational culture is defined as individuals in an organization having a common perception and sharing core values. As a result, organizational culture is a critical determinant in the establishment of organizational policies and actions toward a wide range of issues. Organizational culture is a determinant in such things as the dress code and the language used on the job, the establishment of a team environment, and ethical standards.

Organizational culture is nurtured and sustained through hiring practices and the socialization of new hires. In reality, the interview process one goes through to obtain a job is also an assessment to see if one will be able to "fit" into the organization's culture

An organization's culture can be both an asset and a liability. As an asset it provides boundaries within which to work. As a liability, it may limit acceptance of needed change. It is indeed a two-edged sword.

CASE STUDY

Charles Brown was a gifted and talented mechanical engineer. He had earned his bachelor's degree from a prestigious university and passed his engineering exam (PE) on the first try. Rather than going to work right away, he received a scholarship from another prestigious engineering school and got his master's degree.

When he started his career, he went to work for one of the best engineering firms in the country. He was well liked and well respected by his colleagues. He impressed management in the way that he took charge of projects and solved problems. He was progressing well in the company and was named senior engineer in four years. It usually took people five to seven years to get promoted to senior engineer. The money was good and the raises were predictable.

The environment of the engineering firm was friendly and open. The managers were always available to talk to Charles about projects or anything that was on his mind. His peers were friendly and the environment was collegial and not competitive. The comment was often made that everyone around the company are team players. The company definitely had a family-type atmosphere. The company paid for all the employee benefits and let people take up to ten days off per year for personal reasons in addition to giving employees ten paid holiday days and ten paid vacation days. The company discouraged employees from working evening and weekends if at all possible. The company president often said the family should come first and employees needed to be home in the evenings and on weekends. No one ever worked on Sunday as the company was built on the principle that Sundays were God's days. Although the company did not advocate that people go to church on Sunday, the officers generally did attend the churches of their choice. Everyone seemed to appreciate the fact they had Sundays off and on most weekends they had Saturdays off.

Charles also had a good home life and was in excellent physical condition. He had married his high-school sweetheart, Mary, after finishing his college work. They had a nice home in the suburbs. They had one child, a two-year old girl, and another child on the way. Mary often commented on how much she loved Charles and the way he treated her. Charles also was admired by his in-laws as being a real stand-up man and a good husband to Mary. Charles had helped out members of the family both financially and with solid business advice.

Charles had an excellent reputation in the community. He was a deacon in his church. The pastor often commented on how fortunate the church was to have a deacon like Charles.

He was also the youngest ever president of the local Lion's Club. Charles had built a reputation of getting things done at the club. Before being president, he had led several community activities and fundraisers. Charles' neighbors were also positive about him. They often commented that Charles and his family were assets to the neighborhood.

Everything was definitely going Charles' way when he was approached by a rival engineering firm to come work for them. Charles generally ignored the offer because he was very happy where he was. One day while having lunch, Charles was approached by the recruiter from the rival firm again. As Charles was about to dismiss the man in as tactful a way as possible, the man asked Charles to just hear him out and then he could decide what he wanted to do. The man offered Charles $10,000 more per year than he was making. Charles said that he was not interested. The man left and promised to see him again. Later that week, the man called Charles at his home and offered him $20,000 more than he was making. Charles then agreed to meet with the man. The man came to the meeting prepared with a contract and told Charles to take it home and think about it.

Charles went home and began talking to Mary about the deal. Mary indicated that she was happy with things just the way they were, but if he wanted to make the move she would stand behind him. Charles thought about it for a while and decided that $20,000 is a lot of money and he would not have to leave town to take this job. Charles turned in his two week's notice at his company. People there tried to persuade him to stay, but they could not match his new offer. The company gave him a going away party and wished him well with his new job.

When Charles arrived at his new company, he was surprised to see a very different kind of organization. People generally kept to themselves. People were also very competitive and viewed Charles as a threat to their jobs. When introduced to one engineer, he was told that if he wanted to get ahead in this organization he was going to have to beat the other engineer out and that was not going to be easy. The management there insisted that projects get finished on a tight timetable, which meant working evening and weekends. The stress was high in this organization as people jockeyed for position and attempted to save their jobs. There was always the threat of being fired if an employee messed up. When the first month's paycheck was given to Charles, he was shocked to receive less money than he thought he was going to get. When he asked about it, he was told that the employees paid all the costs of benefits here. When he asked about days off, he was told that he got ten holidays and five vacation days.

The longer he was in the organization, the worse the situation got for Charles. He was under the constant threat of being fired and now had to work most weekends to save his job. He had become a no-show at church and at Lion's Club. He was eventually removed from office in the Lion's Club and no longer served as deacon at the church. The neighbors began to complain about the condition of his lawn. Mary and the two children barely saw him at all. When they did see him, he was always short-tempered. Even his family noticed that he had changed for the worse. Charles realized that he had made a terrible mistake and the extra $20,000 per year could not fix the problem. The extra $20,000 a year was only $6,000 after he paid for his benefits. Even his doctor noticed changes in Charles as his weight and blood pressure had both increased since changing jobs.

Questions

1. What was the company culture like for his first company?
2. What impact did this company's culture have on Charles?
3. What was the company culture like for his second company?
4. What impact did the second company's culture have on Charles?
5. What do you feel should be the appropriate action for Charles to make with his current situation?

DISCUSSION QUESTIONS

1. What kind of organizational culture would suit you the best?

2. Are there some organizational culture issues that would prevent you from taking a job or staying with the company?

3. Describe the dominant culture of an organization with which you are familiar.

4. Discuss ways organizational culture may be a liability.

5. Give examples of ways organizational culture may be an asset.

CHAPTER 19

Motivation in Organizations

LEARNING OUTCOMES: MOTIVATION IN ORGANIZATIONS

1. Relate motivational programs for organizations to the relevant motivational theory.

2. Describe MBO.

3. Explain the significance of recognition programs.

4. Cite the merits of quality circles.

5. Discuss the various variable pay programs.

6. Differentiate between profit sharing and gain sharing.

Management by Objectives

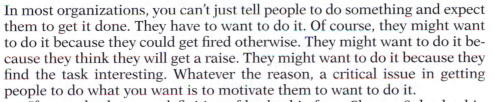

Sue is getting ready for a performance evaluation by Candy, her boss. The company uses a management by objectives (MBO) system that was implemented for the first time last year. This is Sue's first MBO evaluation. She had agreed with Candy to do better this year in tardiness, absenteeism, productivity, and errors. Last year Sue was tardy 12 times, absent 15 times, produced at a rate of 84 (100 being the standard), and committed 123 errors.

In their meeting last year, Candy and Sue agreed that Sue should do better. This year Sue was tardy 11 times, absent 14 times, produced at a rate of 85, and committed 122 errors. When Candy reveals the numbers to Sue, she is quite pleased that she has been so successful.

Sue says, "I guess I really came through because I improved in every single area!"

Candy replies, "What do you mean 'came through'? These numbers are about the same as last year! Where's the improvement?"

Sue says, "You and I agreed I needed to better and I did better!"

What is wrong here between what Candy and Sue believe? Didn't they agree to the same thing?

Welcome to Motivation in Organizations! ■

In most organizations, you can't just tell people to do something and expect them to get it done. They have to want to do it. Of course, they might want to do it because they could get fired otherwise. They might want to do it because they think they will get a raise. They might want to do it because they find the task interesting. Whatever the reason, a critical issue in getting people to do what you want is to motivate them to want to do it.

If we go back to our definition of leadership from Chapter 9, leadership is the art and science of getting the job done through the willing efforts of others. The operative word here is "willing." We want them to become willing workers. The bottom line in motivating people is giving them a chance to satisfy a need. If their needs are to keep their jobs, you can motivate them by giving them tasks that help them to keep their jobs. If their need is money, you can give them tasks that help them make more money. If job challenge is their need, you can give them tasks that satisfy their need for interesting work. **If you want to motivate people, first think about their needs.**

Traditional motivational programs might involve bringing in an inspiring speaker to create a surge of energy and motivation that quickly dissipates. Instead of doing this and getting short-term results, several long-term proven programs have been developed to motivate people in organizations. These programs are based on successful motivation theories discussed in the section on the individual. The following programs are discussed in this chapter:

MOTIVATIONAL PROGRAM FOR ORGANIZATIONS	THEORY
Management by objectives	Goal-setting theory
Recognition programs	Positive reinforcement
Quality circles	Participative management
Variable pay programs	Expectancy theory

MANAGEMENT BY OBJECTIVES

Management by objectives (MBO) is a motivational program based on goal setting.

A proven way to motivate employees is through a **management by objectives (MBO)** program.[129] The idea behind an MBO program is the goal-setting theory. If a person has a specific difficult goal, he or she is more likely to be motivated to achieve this goal. If you are a track coach, you do not say, "Run as far as you can and then hit the showers." You will motivate the team more if you say, "Run ten laps and hit the showers." That gives the runners a specific, difficult goal.

This is the way MBO works in an organization. Let's say you are a sales manager for a company, and eight salespeople report to you. You get a call from your boss who tells you she wants to meet with you to discuss next year's goals. You have the meeting and jointly decide that the goal for your sales group next year is to increase sales by 6 percent compared to this year. You both understand that this is a stretch, but it is definitely doable. You also jointly decide that all of your salespeople should go to a sales training class in the next two years and half of them should go next year. You want to space out the training evenly so you don't disrupt business. Finally, you jointly decide that your group's travel costs will be no more than $80,000 next year. The travel costs for this year are projected to be $85,000, so the group will have to get a little smarter about spending money next year. After the meeting, you go back to your office and write the following memo:

MY OBJECTIVES FOR NEXT YEAR:

1. Increase sales by 6 percent.
2. Send one person to sales training each quarter.
3. Keep travel budget below $80,000.

What are the characteristics of these objectives? First, they are **mutually agreed** to by the supervisor and the subordinate. Second, they are **difficult but achievable** goals. Third, the goals are **specific.** Finally, the goals have a well-defined **time frame.** The supervisor will be able to measure if these objectives were met at the end of the year and give **feedback** to the subordinate.

Next, you schedule meetings with your eight salespeople. You know what the group has to achieve, so now you break up these objectives between your salespeople. Your first meeting is with Andy. He is in a fast growing territory, and you mutually agree that he can increase sales by 12 percent next year. He is busy with this growing territory, so you mutually decide not to send him to sales training next year. He needs to fly to visit many of his customers, so his travel costs are pretty high. You both agree on a limit of $15,000 for travel expenses next year. By the end of the meeting, you and Andy agree on the following objectives for next year:

ANDY'S OBJECTIVES FOR NEXT YEAR:

1. Increase sales by 12 percent.
2. Keep travel expenses below $15,000.

Next you meet with Jane. She has a mature territory with few opportunities for growth. She looks forward to the chance to go to sales training as soon as possible. Her travel costs are about average for the group. You and Jane come to the following agreement for next year's goals:

JANE'S OBJECTIVES FOR NEXT YEAR:

1. Increase sales by 2 percent.
2. Attend sales training in the first quarter.
3. Keep travel expenses below $10,000.

You continue meeting with all of your salespeople. When all of the salespeople's objectives are done, you work it out so the sum of their objectives equals the total of your objectives. This process continues down the management chain until everyone has objectives that are consistent with the goals of the organization as a whole.

Why does this process work? It comes down to goal-setting theory. People are more motivated if they have a specific difficult goal. By going through this process, the supervisor and subordinate mutually agree on objectives that are specific and difficult. They are clearly spelled out so the supervisor can give feedback on performance, another aspect of goal-setting theory that increases motivation. With an MBO program, people know exactly what they need to achieve to succeed.

Consider what happens without an MBO program. What if you had a boss who told you to increase sales a lot next year? What is "a lot"? What if you increase sales by 6 percent, but at the end of the year your boss tells you that wasn't good enough? How motivated are you going to be the following year?

With a management by objectives program, good goals are SMART goals:

Specific

Measurable

Attainable

Results-oriented

Time-related

RECOGNITION PROGRAMS

One of the most powerful ways to motivate people is through **recognition**.[130] Everyone likes to look good. If you do something right, recognition can be powerful, positive reinforcement. You want to keep doing things right to get more recognition.

> **Recognition** is the most powerful workplace motivator.

There are many examples of recognition programs: award ceremonies, employee-of-the-month programs, or a letter from your boss commending you for a job well done. One of the best things about recognition programs is they don't have to cost a lot of money. Let's say a mechanic did an especially good job for you, and you send a letter to the manager of the repair shop. The manager in turn sends a memo to the mechanic with his congratulations. This process did not cost anyone much money, but the recognition can be a powerful motivator to the mechanic. You should actively look for opportunities to recognize someone for good performance. The best employee recognition programs use multiple sources of recognition and recognize individual accomplishments and group accomplishments. The programs help encourage employees to repeat the good performance.

QUALITY CIRCLES

Quality circles are a form of participative management, based on the theory that people will be more motivated if you get them involved in participating in decisions for the organization.

Let's say your company is having a problem with late deliveries. You are not sure if this is caused by orders being placed wrong, the production department missing deadlines, or problems in the shipping department. One way to resolve this problem would be to meet with the manager of each department, decide where you think the problem lies, and then take corrective action. This process may miss an innovative solution to the problem and it certainly does not create any buy-in by the different departments. In fact, each department may try to shift the blame to a different department.

Another way to solve the problem would be to form a **quality circle.** A quality circle is a team that includes people from different departments who come together to solve a problem. In the aforementioned case, you would form a quality circle from people in the order department, the production department, and the shipping department. You tell them to solve the problem with late deliveries. The quality circle would set up meetings and discuss how to solve the problem. The team would come up with a recommended solution and present it to management for approval. The quality circle approach gets people involved in the company's management. It motivates people to recognize that they can play an important role in the management and success of the organization.

Let me share a real situation that illustrates how effective this quality circle effort can be. The last company I worked for made fiberglass reinforced products for the electrical, automotive, business machine, and power tool markets. When machining a part, fiberglass dust was released into the air around the operators. There was a vacuum system available; however, the fixture for the operation did not contain all of the dust. I put together a "dust collection problem-solving team" of volunteers to help focus attention on this problem. After conducting team development training, the team starting meeting and the results were impressive. Shortly after that, Hewlett Packard came to the plant and wanted to put a team together to focus on reducing the cost and improving the quality of a series of business machine parts we were making for them. HP brought in blue baseball caps to identify the members "HP quality improvement team" and work began. Within four months, the team was able to reduce the labor cost by taking the operation from 16 operators to 9 operators and virtually eliminated all scrap by introducing new process control tools. The excitement was high. The employees asked, since we have an HP team and it has been successful, can we have an Allen-Bradley team? How about a Westinghouse, GE, GM, Ford, and Chrysler team? Why not? When I left that operation we had over 21 quality improvement teams working with amazing results. The key point is the motivation was self motivation rather than an external reward like money. It worked!

Variable Pay Programs

Another basic program to motivate people in organizations is through a variable pay program. The basic idea is to link their pay with their results. One notable advantage of a variable pay program is that it turns a fixed

Quality circles are a good way to get people involved.

cost into a variable cost. The more one contributes, the more one gets rewarded. In a **piece work plan,** for example, employees would get five cents for every letter they fold and put into an envelope. In a **commission** plan, salespeople would get $500 for every car they sell. A variable pay plan is based on expectancy theory, where people are motivated to work based on what they expect to receive.

Some companies offer **gainsharing** and **profit sharing** plans. Under gainsharing, employees' bonuses are based on group productivity improvements and lowering costs. Under profit sharing plans, part of the company's profit is distributed to the employees. Therefore, in both cases, employee compensation is tied partly to company performance.

Practical Application

What is your goal? What are your goals for yourself and your organization? What do you want to achieve? What could make your life better? What could you do to make this a better world to live in?

Setting goals is part of a vibrant life. Without goals, whether individually or as an organization, we move aimlessly from day to day. Many people think that goal setting is easy and perhaps outdated in our fast-paced information age, but such is not the case. However, two prolific researchers, Edwin A. Locke and Gary P. Latham, have arrived at the following conclusions:[131]

1. Rational, goal-directed action is essential for happiness and survival.
2. Difficult but realistic goals, if committed to, lead to greater effort, persistence, and achievement.
3. People can successfully pursue more than one goal at a time.
4. Confidence in achieving any specific goal is essential.
5. Specific and challenging goals direct a person's or organization's knowledge and skills more than vague and general goals.
6. Feedback is essential.

Goal setting, while important to a satisfying life, is not an easy process. Goal for it!

SUMMARY

One of the greatest challenges today for those in leadership roles is to keep workers motivated and organizations energized. A recent survey of workers found that as many as 50 percent of workers admitted that they only put enough effort into their work to hold onto their jobs.[132] Eighty-four percent said that they could work better if they wanted to do so. True organizational motivation requires leadership and good communication.

Motivation in organizations can be accomplished in various ways, including management by objectives (MBO), recognition programs, quality circles, and variable pay plans. Under MBO, the employee and the supervisor set goals for the employee and the employee is held accountable for achieving these goals. For best performance the goals are mutually agreed to, difficult but achievable, and specific. They have a well-defined time frame and provide a means for feedback to the subordinate.

Under recognition programs, outstanding employees are recognized for their efforts. Recognition programs are powerful motivators and often do not cost a great deal. Quality circles were early ways to introduce employees to participative management. Under quality circles, workers can get involved in decision making.

Variable pay programs change fixed cost into variable cost. Under variable pay programs, workers are paid for their performance with a piece-work plan for production workers, a commission plan for salespeople, gainsharing for cost savings, and profit sharing for increased profits. Variable pay programs are closely linked to the expectancy theory for motivation.

CASE STUDY

Harry Jones was about to start his second year with Yex Company. Yex was a mail-order shipping company. Customers would call, e-mail, or mail their orders to Yex. Yex would process the orders using the customer's credit card, debit card, cash, or personal check. Most customers used their credit card or debit card to make purchases that could be shipped after credit card or debit card approval. Some customers would mail in a check with the order. These orders would be sent to the customers when their checks cleared. People with cash could use the collect on delivery (COD) system where they paid the delivery person. The additional cost of using the COD system led Yex to ask people to send a certified check or money order for the price of their orders. This would allow people without credit cards or checking accounts to buy Yex products. It also allowed Yex to send products immediately after receiving the payment because certified checks and money orders are the same as receiving cash.

Harry was a processor in the area of orders paid by certified check or money order. It was his job to process the orders by sending the paperwork to warehousing. Warehousing would find the products in the order and send the order to the checker. The checker would make sure that payment had been made, the products were the right ones, and the products were in good condition. The checker then sent the products to shipping and handling. Shipping and handling would box up the products, put the customer's name and address on the shipping box, affix the proper postage to the box, and take it to the post office or a parcel service. Harry also had to make deposit slips out on sales and send them to accounting. The volume in Harry's part of the business was considerably less than the other two areas of credit card/debit card sales and mail-in orders with personal checks, but he had more errors and more lost time than the other processors.

The management of the company brought the errors and lost time problems to George Turner, Harry's boss, for resolution. It was time for Harry's year-end evaluation and goal setting for next year. George had been to the mandatory 30-minute seminar on the new management by objectives (MBO) system that the company was now implementing. George informed Harry that 203 errors had been made by the checker's count on orders. He also told

Harry that he had missed 11 days and been late for work 20 times in the past year. Harry looked surprised at the numbers and when confronted with the reports and timecards agreed that there was a problem. George informed him that they would be trying MBO to fix the problems. He asked Harry to think about what he was going to do to fix the problems and come up with some goals to achieve. George would also work on the matter and they would get back together next Friday at 3:30 P.M.

At 3:30, Harry came into George's office for the MBO meeting. George had gotten busy that week and really did not have anything for Harry. George did not want to look bad or give Harry the impression he did not care, so he decided to go along with whatever Harry said he would do in the way of goals. George started the meeting by asking Harry what he had done. Harry, not knowing much about MBO, said that he would do better this year than last on both errors and lost time. George told Harry that his plan sounded fine and that they would go with it. George and Harry were both glad to have the big MBO meeting behind them.

When Bill Harrison from management contacted George about the MBO meeting with Harry, he reported that things had gone fine. He and Harry had come up with a plan to take care of the problems of errors and lost time. He reassured Bill that they were on it. George now felt relieved about getting management off his back.

Another year went by and it was time again for the annual MBO meeting between George and Harry. Neither George nor Harry had watched the numbers closely this year. Harry felt he had done a better job in eliminating errors and lost time. George remembers hearing some complaints from the checkers, but did not think it was serious. Prior to the meeting, George asked the checkers for the error numbers on Harry and asked payroll for Harry's attendance record.

When the reports that were filed by the checkers and by payroll came to George, the news was not as good as George thought it should be. The errors had dropped to 199, the absences dropped to 9, and the days tardy dropped to 19. Bill called George to discuss the situation. Bill informed George that management was not happy about Harry's performance for the year. George tried to explain to Bill that the numbers were better than last year. Bill explained to George that was not the kind of improvement that they were looking to achieve. Bill invited George to his office next Tuesday to explain what had happened or, in this case, had not happened. George was shocked and immediately set up an MBO meeting with Harry. George had his secretary send the error numbers, attendance, and tardiness information to Harry.

On Monday, George and Harry met in George's office. George asked Harry how he felt about the numbers. Harry perked up and said that the numbers were great. He went on to say that they had proved that MBO was working because he said he would do better in all three areas and he had done it. George started in by saying that the numbers were not good enough. Harry reminded George that he had agreed with him that things needed to improve and that they had improved. Harry reiterated the fact that he had achieved the agreed on goal of doing better. Not having any reply to what Harry had said, George ended the meeting without discussing future goals.

On Tuesday, Bill explained to George that Harry needed to do much better in error reduction, attendance, and coming to work on time. Bill wanted to know what kind of goals George and Harry had set for last year. George explained to Bill that they had agreed that Harry needed to do better and that he had. Bill then asked what kind of goals they had set for this year. George explained that they had not gotten around to setting goals for this year. Bill asked George if he was using MBO at all and George responded that he and Harry had mutually set goals and Harry had achieved them. Bill, starting to lose both his temper and his patience, asked George to leave.

The MBO system had certainly caused a variety of reactions. Bill was mad at George and Harry for failing to significantly improve performance in the department. George was wondering what in the world was going on with Bill and the MBO system. Harry was pleased that he had been able to achieve success and improve in all three problem areas.

Questions

1. What was wrong according to Bill in his view of the MBO system?

2. What was George's problem with the MBO system?

3. What was Harry's problem with the MBO system?

4. What needs to be done to correct the problems with the MBO system at Vex?

DISCUSSION QUESTIONS

1. What are some of the positive features of management by objectives (MBO)?

2. Demonstrate setting an objective using the S.M.A.R.T. model.

3. Provide examples of recognition programs. Describe one form of recognition and explain why it works.

4. Would you like to be involved in a quality circle? Explain your answer.

5. Explain how variable pay programs change fixed cost into variable cost.

Organizational Change

LEARNING OUTCOMES: ORGANIZATIONAL CHANGE

1. Describe the driving forces for change.

2. Define the role of change agents.

3. Identify why people resist change.

4. Discuss the ways organizations may overcome the resistance to change.

A Change for the Better

When I was a graduate student in the late 1970s, I was on a team to make changes in an accounting office. My task was relatively simple, or so I thought. All I had to do was to collect all the old hand crank adding machines and replace them with desk calculators. Things were going well for me until I met the 33-year veteran, June. June informed me that I was not going to get her machine.

June said, "This is my machine and you can't have it."

When I reported this to my boss, he said I should just leave her alone and she would come around. So, all ten workers in the office had a new calculator except for June, who kept her hand crank adding machine.

After two weeks, June reported that her adding machine was broken and needed to be fixed. We informed her that she would have to take a new calculator while her machine was being repaired.

I picked up her old machine and gave her a new calculator. When I asked my boss about fixing the old machine, he replied that it would not be necessary. He was right. June never asked about her old machine and continued to use the new calculator.

Why was June not interested in the new calculator at first?

Why did she not want her old machine back after using the new calculator?

Welcome to Organizational Change! ■

"Change is about traveling from the old to the new, leaving yesterday for a new tomorrow."

—*P. Dejager*[133]

In the movie *Stripes*, Bill Murray plays John Winger, an unusual man who decides to join the Army with his friend Russell (played by Harold Ramis). John Winger is not your typical soldier, and the drill sergeant is not too impressed with his level of work ethic and discipline. Near the end of basic training, the drill sergeant gets hurt, and John Winger completes the unit's training.

John's training methods are somewhat unconventional, but at the closing ceremony, his unit receives the highest rating. John is complimented on introducing modern training methods to the Army. The drill sergeant, who wants to keep things the same, is not too happy. He does everything he can to get John into trouble through the rest of the movie (which does not turn out to be too difficult).

If there is one thing that is constant in organizations, it is change. Organizations need to adapt to changing times. Some people are not comfortable with change, like the drill sergeant in *Stripes*. Other people, like Bill Murray's character, drive change and are called **change agents.**

In all my years of hiring new personnel, I never hired anyone to keep things the same. Every leader is hired to bring about positive change. I was hiring change agents to become leaders. In this chapter, we will talk about the factors that drive organizational change. Then, we will discuss the reasons why people do not always like change. Next we will talk about why organizations do not always like change. Finally, since change is inevitable, we will talk about ways to get people to be more comfortable with change.

People who drive change are called **change agents.**

LEWIN'S CHANGE MODEL

Kurt Lewin developed a three-stage model that illustrates a simplistic approach for planned change (Figure 20–1). Lewin's model explains how to initiate change by "unfreezing" the situation, how to manage change by making a "transition," and how to stabilize the change by "refreezing" the new behavior or attitude.[134]

Unfreezing

The driving force in this first stage is to encourage a change in behavior or attitude as a means to move the organization or individual in a positive direction. People will often resist the change for any number of reasons; however, the most powerful reasons are the lost feeling of security, the fear of the unknown, economic factors, habits, and perceptions. A manager can begin the unfreezing process by creating a sense of urgency and dire need for the change.

Movement and Transition

To get people and organizations to move to the desired level of change, the leader may aid the transition by reducing the resistance for change. This could be done through education, employee participation in the change and decision making, economic incentives, individual and team support, greater communication, and negotiation. The leader may need to force the change out of necessity. Issues involving new safety procedures or following government regulations would be examples where the change is a must.

Refreezing

To complete the change process so that the new behaviors and attitudes become the new standard, refreezing must take place. The refreezing stage allows a period of time for the success of the change to become the "new way to do things." Once the change has been implemented, the leader offers encouragement, recognition, and other forms of positive reinforcement to strengthen the stability of the change.

DRIVING FORCES FOR CHANGE

There are five main driving forces for change:

- Technology
- Nature of the workforce
- International effects
- Mergers
- Economic shocks

We will discuss each of these driving forces for change in this chapter.

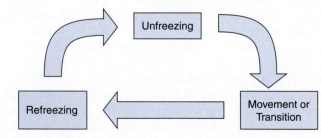

Figure 20–1 Change model.

Technology

My father was a typesetter. These are the people who once laid out the text letter by letter to make all the margins straight in a book. When he first learned to be a typesetter in the 1940s, he worked with metal type, actually putting the letters and spaces into something called a *composing bar* (think of a Scrabble® game). In the 1950s, he learned something called Monotype, a typewriter that generated tape, and in turn put the metal tape in the right place (think of a player piano and the roll of tape that plays the notes). In the 1960s, typesetting moved to photo typesetting, which generated something that looked like a photograph negative. Finally, in the 1970s and 1980s, typesetting moved into the computer age and was done on sophisticated word processors.

Each of these advances in technology forced organizational change. People needed to be trained on the new technology, departments were rearranged, and the physical layout of the company was changed to accommodate the new equipment. Some people, like my father, adapted to the change. They were retrained and resumed their jobs, although their jobs changed in responsibility and scope. Other people could not adapt and ended up changing careers.

You do not have to look very hard to see how technology is changing organizations. Technology marches on at an accelerating rate: typewriters to computers, memos to e-mail, and mimeographs to photocopies (I may have lost people with the mimeograph, but check a museum sometime). Employees must either change with the technology or get left behind. Every business is an ongoing source of change due to the nature of technology, customer demands, competition, and the changing marketplace.

Nature of the Workforce

Another driving force for organizational change is the nature of the workforce. Many men still say, "I could never work for a woman." Well, they'd better learn how, because women make up a growing percentage of managers. In the old days, people worked their way up the ladder. Now many new college graduates come into a company as management trainees, skipping several rungs of the ladder. Some people do not adapt well to these changes in the nature of the workforce, but the workforce is changing and will continue to do so. Every professional discipline is in a process of change. It is said that the life of an engineer is about eight years and is continuously getting shorter. Due to new materials, methods, processes, technology, and discoveries, engineers must commit to lifelong learning and keep reinventing themselves to stay competitive in the marketplace. Get used to the new nature of the workforce or get left behind.

International Effects

World political and economic conditions change constantly, resulting in another source of organizational change. One day, the United States has a favorable trading partnership with Venezuela. Then, there is a change in political leadership and the United States no longer has a favorable relationship with Venezuela. In the future it will change as political leadership changes in both countries.

One day the Japanese make low-quality knock-offs. Then Japan becomes a quality leader. Then, the United States is considered the quality leader again. Political alignments and international economics constantly change. China, India, and Brazil are emerging as the new world powers. The threat of global warming is now recognized and is changing the way we do business locally and internationally. The search for new energy and alternative fuel sources will force change. Political alignments and international economics constantly change. Get used to the changing international world or get left behind.

Mergers

I know a person in the publishing industry who had the same office for three years but worked for four different companies. Companies are constantly acquiring, merging, and divesting. It can be difficult to keep track of these company changes without a scorecard. This constant corporate reshuffling is unnerving to people working for the companies affected by the changes. Mergers often mean downsizing and layoffs. Get used to the changing corporate alliances or get left behind.

Economic Shocks

The economy tends to run in cycles. We may get economic growth for a few years and then fall into recession. Unemployment goes up and down. The U.S. economy has been relatively stable for the past decade, but even during this period, there has been great volatility in the stock market and major changes in exchange rates. We have seen the U.S. budget go from a positive balance to a deficit. I am reminded of the joke that a recession is when your neighbor loses his job, and a depression is when you lose your job. Get used to economic shocks (and be prepared for them) or get left behind.

A key point in this section is that change is inevitable. You don't have the option of avoiding change. Unfortunately, most people don't like change.

WHY (MOST) PEOPLE DON'T LIKE CHANGE

Many people do not like change because it disrupts their **habits.** Drill sergeants in the military know how to run basic training. They have done it many times. New recruits arrive, are then put through the regular training process, and graduate at the end. And then, the same thing is done over and over again. Many college students do not understand why people want to stick with the same routine. The people reading this book are probably more likely to enjoy new challenges. Most of the rest of the world sees things differently. Try taking away a person's Apple computer and replacing it with a PC if you want to see what I mean.

Many people do not like change because it threatens their **security.** What if the drill sergeant cannot lead the new type of training? What if a typesetter cannot learn to use the new computer-based system? A person who cannot adapt to change can lose his or her job or lose influence.

WHY MANY ORGANIZATIONS FIND IT DIFFICULT TO CHANGE

Once an organization starts going in a certain direction, it is difficult to get it to change, due to **group inertia.**

Just as individuals have habits, organizations have **group inertia**. Once an organization gets moving in a certain direction, it is difficult to get the organization to change course. The U.S. auto industry was good at producing big fuel-guzzling cars. Even with a major economic shock, the OPEC oil embargo, the U.S. auto industry kept producing big cars, assuming that was what American consumers wanted. It was not until Japanese compact cars started taking away market share that the U.S. auto companies (slowly) moved to smaller more fuel-efficient cars. Since people do not like change, most organizations include a number of individuals who want to preserve the status quo as long as possible, making organizations slow to change. As the pace of change increases, it seems that people are adapting better, and so organizations do seem to be responding faster. However, group inertia remains a limiting factor.

Change threatens not only an individual's security, but also an organization's security. What if the Army changes the way it does basic training and it does not work? What if a company changes to a new computer system and it crashes? Many times an organization thinks the safest decision is to do nothing. It may be safer in the short run, but it is usually suicide in the long run. Change is inevitable. Either change with the times or get left behind.

HOW TO GET PEOPLE AND ORGANIZATIONS TO CHANGE

Few principles in the management of change are as well documented or understood as the idea that involvement breeds commitment, yet organizations continue to ignore this principle.[135] As a rule, managers do not involve their workers in decisions that affect them because it takes too long, but we need to stop and ask ourselves, "What is the cost of failed implementation?" The first step in getting people to cope with change is to make them understand that change is imminent. Keeping things the same is never an option. People need to change with the times, or they will get left behind.

Once they understand that change is inevitable, some specific techniques can be used to help people and organizations change: education, participation, support, and economic incentives along with increased communication, negotiation, and even coercion are the driving forces of implementing change.

- **Education.** My father adapted to change in his typesetting job because he was given training on each new technology. If people are trained well and comfortable with the new job, they will be less resistant to change.

- **Participation.** People react better to change if they are part of the decision to make the change. If a company is thinking about changing from PCs to Apple computers, people will be more comfortable with the change if they are part of the decision. Setting up review panels, selecting people to try the new system, and having people research how the new equipment works in other companies are all ways to get people to buy into the change.

- **Support.** Sometimes people have emotional difficulties dealing with change. This can lead to stress, as discussed earlier in this book. Sometimes people need counseling and support to deal with a new situation.

- **Economic Incentives.** I once worked for a company that decided to move its entire research group to another state. This was not well received because people had built ties to the community. Once the company offered substantial economic incentives to make the move, people saw things much differently. As we discussed in the section on motivation, monetary rewards do not always work, but they usually do not hurt!

- **Increase Communications.** People may resist change simply because they don't understand the need. Increased communication to the point of over-communication may help create the sense of urgency and the need to change. The old adage, "if you tell it to them enough times, they will start to believe it" applies.

- **Negotiation.** Another possible stimulus to help bring about change is to negotiate the needed change. It may be possible to negotiate the time, level of involvement, and degrees of change just to get the process started. We read, for example, of local and state government agencies negotiating with the affected members of a community to bring the needed change for highway improvement or area planning.

- **Coercion (if necessary).** If change is necessary and for whatever reason it is not being accepted, a leader may have to resort to coercion to bring about change. Coercion is the use of force to make changes and is not the most desirable outcome; however, it may be necessary. For example, a new government regulation requires the use of specialized safety equipment to protect workers in the performance of their work. It is a change and some employees are resisting the change because the equipment takes a lot of time to put on and is cumbersome. To get the employees to comply with the change, the leadership may have to force compliance until it becomes accepted. The mandatory seat-belt law would be a good example. Some have resisted, and some still do, in which case they may be stopped by law enforcement and issued a ticket for noncompliance.

SUMMARY

Change is everywhere, the pace of change is getting faster, and everyone is affected by change. Still, we fight change. Today's organizations need to do things differently to remain competitive. This process is known as *organizational change*. The people who drive this change are called *change agents*.

The driving forces of change are technology, nature of the workforce, international effects, mergers, and economic shocks. Most people do not like change because of disruption of their habits, fear of the unknown, economic factors, and threats to their sense of security. Most organizations find it difficult to change because of group inertia (difficulty in changing direction when moving in a certain direction over time) and because of the threat change makes to organizational security. Organizations will also resist due to the threat to power, resources, and expertise.

The change process introduced by Lewin consists of three steps: unfreeze, movement or transition, and refreezing to the new standard.

Although change can be implemented by manipulation and coercion, the preferred approach is to use education, participation, support, and economic incentives. People have to understand that change is coming whether they like it or not.

And one last thought that I almost forgot: Change with the times or get left behind!

CASE STUDY

Wellcare Company made a wide variety of home health-care products. The product line consisted of hospital-type beds, ramps, shower and tub railings, toilet seat extensions, walkers, canes, and wheelchairs. The production workers were all local residents and many were second- and third-generation Wellcare workers. Most of the workers had been with the company for more than ten years. The company was non-union as most workers were very happy with their jobs and their pay. Many workers felt a sense of security in working for Wellcare because there had never been a layoff and the plant had been in town for 75 years.

The stability of the company could also be seen in the non-production areas, as most of the workers in the office had been with the company for more than 20 years. It was viewed by the community as a good place to work. The office staff carried on the business of the company by doing the human resource functions, paying bills, collecting and processing payments from customers, and managing the day-to-day operations.

The sales and marketing department was composed of 15 full-time salespeople, three supervisors, and three secretaries, as well as the vice president of sales and marketing. The sales people all had territories they serviced. It was common practice for the salespeople to have a list of customers and they called those customers every two weeks for orders. The customers could also call their sales representative at anytime and place an order. The customers were very pleased at the prospect of calling the same person for all their health-care equipment needs. The company purchasing people were more like old friends to the sales staff than customers. The sales staff averaged more than 17 years on the job. Sam Black had been a Wellcare salesperson the longest, with more than 35 years on the job.

George Anderson, the company president, was looking at the sales figures, which had been fairly constant over the last two years. He was wondering what he should do to try to increase sales. He decided to ask Tom Brown, the vice president of sales and marketing, what he thought the company could do to increase sales. Tom explained that most of the health stores and pharmacies that handled their products were small and that their customer base had not grown despite many baby boomers getting older and needing health-care products. George asked Tom where these baby boomers were going to get health-care products. Tom replied that many were going to large discount stores where lesser quality items were sold. Tom and George both agreed that they could not compete with manufacturing companies using equipment made in foreign countries and serving the large discount store chains because of cost considerations. Wellcare products were considered the best in the health-care field and neither man wanted to lower quality to increase business. Tom told George there was another way to increase sales by selling on the Internet.

Tom convinced George to use the company Web site to sell direct to customers. The Web site previously had been used to tell the company's story and showcase products. A Web site marketing firm was hired to convert their Web site into a marketing tool. The Web site was created to allow purchasers to review products, to select products to be put into a shopping cart, and to pay for their purchases with a credit card or debit card. All transactions were secure for both the customer and the company. The Web site marketing company also agreed to train all the salespeople in how to use the system. Each salesperson was made responsible for all online customer orders in his or her territory. The system would automatically route the order to the appropriate salesperson. The salesperson would then send the order to production and the customer's bill and credit/debit card information to the secretary for processing.

Just before the new system was to start up, the employees were told about the online sales. Several salespeople were taken aback by the announcement. Several people were concerned that management had not even told them what was happening until it was over. Several salespeople started to worry about their jobs. Many salespeople started to wonder about working with a new system that they did not know. The salespeople got together to discuss the situation. After a brief meeting, the salespeople and the secretaries approached the supervisors. They told the supervisors they had been successful using the old selling techniques and they would not change the way they did business. The mottoes of the salespeople and secretaries became, "if it isn't broken, don't fix it" and "we've always done it this way."

The supervisors went to Tom and told him the workers were opposed to change and did not see the need for it. The supervisors further told Tom the employees felt like that they had been completely left out of the loop on the decision to start selling online. Tom agreed with that, but added that change needed to happen now. Tom agreed to have a meeting with the salespeople and secretaries to discuss their concerns.

The supervisors returned to the department reporting that Tom was going to meet with them all the next day at 4 P.M. The workers were happy that Tom had agreed to meet with them, but they were also apprehensive about what he was going to say about their jobs. Many of the salespeople and secretaries had worked for the company their whole careers. Many were concerned that they would be laid off and replaced by a bunch of computer nerds.

Tom met with them the next day and told them that all their jobs would be safe and that the online sales would increase their commissions. He also told them that they would be fully trained by the Web site company on how to use the system. He encouraged them to give the new system a try. They all agreed to give it a try, but they were still apprehensive. The Web site people did an excellent job of explaining the system and showing them how easy it was to use.

After giving the system a six-month try, the salespeople and secretaries were happy with it. The salespeople and the company were actually making more money. After some modifications to the system, some of the old customers starting using the system to place orders and charge the equipment to their accounts with the company. The salespeople admitted that the new system worked fine, but they missed talking to some of their old customers on the phone.

Questions

1. What caused the need for change?
2. What was the reaction to the change by the salespeople and secretaries?
3. What could the company have done to help better bring about this change?
4. Describe the processes of unfreezing, movement and transition, and refreezing?

DISCUSSION QUESTIONS

1. Discuss the characteristics of a change agent.

2. Explain why people do not like change.

3. Discuss ways to overcome the restraining forces to change.

4. Explain how you would propose to start the change process in an organization that is resisting (a) new technology, (b) new leadership, and (c) new competition.

Power and Politics

LEARNING OUTCOMES: POWER AND POLITICS

1. Define power.

2. Discuss the importance of understanding the power and dependency relationship.

3. Identify the five bases for power.

4. Explain why sexual harassment is actually an issue of power.

5. Explain political behavior in organizations.

6. Identify the seven impression management techniques.

7. Through a self-assessment, learn of your preferred type of power.

8. Through a self-assessment, gain insight into how politically oriented and astute you might be.

Name: _____

Section Number: _____

SELF-ASSESSMENT TESTS

Please complete the following exercises online, accessible with the Access Card packaged with this text, before reading this chapter.

EXERCISE II.C.1:   **HOW POWER-ORIENTED AM I?**   **Score** _____

This instrument was designed to compute your Machiavellianism (Mach) score. Machiavelli wrote in the sixteenth century on how to gain and manipulate power. An individual with a high Mach score is pragmatic, maintains emotional distance, and believes that the ends justify the means. High Machs are likely to manipulate more and win more and are persuaded less and persuade others more than do low Machs. High Machs are also more likely to shade the truth or act unethically in ambiguous situations where the outcome is important to them.

EXERCISE I.C.2:   **WHAT'S MY PREFERRED TYPE OF POWER?**

Score   Reward   _____   Expert   _____

           Coercive   _____   Referent _____

           Legitimate _____

Managerial positions come with legitimate, reward, and coercive powers. However, you do not have to be a manager to have power. If you are not in a position of formal authority, you can still be a powerful person in your organization if you focus on developing your expert and referent power bases.

EXERCISE II.C.3:   **HOW GOOD AM I AT**
                    PLAYING POLITICS?   **Score** _____

Politics are a natural part of organizational life. This instrument was designed to give you some insights into how politically oriented you are. Those who fail to acknowledge political behavior ignore the reality that organizations are political systems. Researchers have identified certain personality traits, needs, and other factors that are likely to be related to political behavior. In terms of traits, we find that individuals who are high self-monitors possess an internal locus of control, have a high need for power, and are more likely to engage in political behavior.

You should also record your scores on these exercises in Appendix 1.

NOTES

The Lunch

Five old friends decided to meet for lunch. After the usual discussions about their families, the conversation turned to work and more specifically to the kind of boss each one of them has.

Bob said, "My boss is a jerk. He is always threatening to fire us. Most of us put up with him out of fear of losing our jobs."

Tom replied, "My boss isn't much better. All we hear is, 'If you want a raise or a bonus, you had better do what I tell you.' His cronies always get all the good money."

Frank said, "My boss is always reminding us that he is in charge, the company put him there, and we had better do it his way because he is the man."

Andy replied, "My boss sounds better than all of your bosses. At least he is very knowledgeable in the materials area, and all of the people respect him for that."

Dick added, "I really like my boss. He is hard working and honest. I like the way he tells it like it is. I respect him and can count on him to look after me and other employees."

Which of these bosses would you like to have?

Which of these bosses would be the most effective in the long run?

Welcome to Power and Politics! ■

"Power. Libraries have been written about its use and abuse. It has motivated the great (and the greedy) throughout history. It has been called the ultimate aphrodisiac. But what is it? A dirty word that connotes backroom politics, conniving end-runs, and secret deals? Or a normal part of everyday life? Both, no doubt. But I'm mightily predisposed to the latter definition."

—*Tom Peters* [136]

Power is the engine that drives the train. Bill Walton, the former All-American basketball player from UCLA, said this of his former coach John Wooden,[137] "A boss has to boss. In a group, someone has to make the final decisions. At UCLA that was (John) Wooden. When we'd (the players) disagree, he would say, 'Bill, we've enjoyed having you here. We're sure going to miss you.' End of conversation." Wooden had the influence and the team depended on him. Power is the capacity a person, or even a group, has to influence another to respond in a certain manner.

> **Power** is the ability to influence another to respond.

This chapter will cover the following topics:

- Power and Dependency
- Sources of Power
- Sexual Harassment
- Political Behavior
- Impression Management

POWER AND DEPENDENCY

Power may be latent; it may not be apparent or exercised even though the capacity is there. In 1999 American Airlines was virtually grounded due to an apparent sick-out by a large number of the pilots. In the course of a normal day's business, the pilots as individuals do not demonstrate much power. However, the banding together to form an informal coalition severely constrained the ability of the airline to conduct business. The potential for the exercise of power exists, but without action, there is no demonstration of power.

Dependency gives power its influence.

The perception of **dependency** gives power its influence. The greater the dependency an individual or a group has on another person or an organization, the greater the intensity of power. The Microsoft antitrust action brought by the government in 1998 is just such an issue. Does Microsoft gain an unfair market advantage by the way it conducts business? The basis for the antitrust laws in our country is to ensure that no one entity can create an unfair business advantage over another. We establish laws to control power relationships.

The most expensive media advertising is television during the annual Super Bowl. The advertisers are at the mercy of the network. The network has the power and it makes sure it is well paid for the advantage. If dependency is to exist then the following three parameters must be established. First is **scarcity;** there is only one Super Bowl opportunity each year. Second, is **importance;** millions of potential customers will see the television ads. Third, there can be **no substitutes;** no other advertising can reach so many so efficiently.

Are power and leadership equal since both have a basis in influence? The definitions may have a resemblance; however, leadership and power are not the same. Leadership focuses on a downward influence that seeks goal satisfaction. Power seeks to create a dependency and may be directed downward—the influence of parents on their children, for example. Power may also be lateral like the influence within peer groups. In the form of employee coalitions such as labor unions, the influence is upward. The American Airlines pilot sick-out is an illustration of upward influence.

SOURCES OF POWER

There are two kinds of power: formal power, which consists of the organization chart, meetings, rules, regulations, and policies; and personal power, which consists of relationships, personal knowledge or expertise, and the grapevine.[138] Where is power derived, or more directly, what are the **sources of power?** French and Raven created a useful model[139] identifying five sources of power: coercive, reward, legitimate, expert, and referent.

- **Coercive Power.** This is formal power of a sort and is based on **fear,** not necessarily physical fear but perhaps the silent stare of a teacher when you are talking at the wrong time. A supervisor who practices leadership in an authoritarian manner is seen as using coercive power. The threat of job loss, a withheld promotion, or perhaps harassing treatment are examples of the use of coercive power.

- **Reward Power.** This source of formal power is based on **the ability to control and distribute** rewards that are seen as valuable. Creation of pay programs that include bonuses or special payments beyond normal pay is an example. A professor may offer an added voluntary course-related assignment and include ten bonus points for successful completion. Providing a day off for exemplary performance and special recognition for a job well done are further examples of reward power. Reward power is the flipside of coercive power.

- **Legitimate Power.** This power comes with **position.** Legitimate power is formal power defined by the organizational chart and is often referred to as position power. The chairperson of a local committee, the

CEO of Wal-Mart, and the teaching assistant for a chemistry lab all possess legitimate power by virtue of their office. The power dimension most often found in the military is legitimate, the power associated with the chain of command.

■ **Expert Power.** The one who holds an advantage over another because he or she **possesses a special expertise** is demonstrating expert power. This personal power is intrinisic to the individual. Doctors, lawyers, and professors are all considered experts. When the lawn mower fails to start, the mechanic at the small engine shop becomes an instant expert. Many intelligent, well-informed, and well-traveled consumers never make a major purchase without consulting *Consumer Reports* magazine for expert advice.

■ **Referent Power.** The power that is derived from **personal traits, attributes,** or **charisma** is **referent power.** This is another personal source of power and is intrinsic to the individual. Before her death, Princess Diana became a spokesperson for the elimination of land mines and buried explosives. She may have never had an hour's worth of training disarming explosives, but she was revered because of the respect for her as a person. Does it make any difference that race car driver Jeff Gordon's picture is on a Pepsi can? It must, because millions of dollars are spent annually using celebrities to promote or endorse products. That is referent power in action. Referent power is derived by others giving the leader the right to have power over them. In reality, people actually give the leader the right to have power over them and if the leader doesn't do a good job, the followers will take the power away. Based on this assessment, referent power probably has the greatest impact toward positive leadership and the follower's commitment to the leader and the organization.

These sources of power are not mutually exclusive. Michael Jordan has demonstrated each. He endorses Gatorade, Hanes, and Nike, which are examples of his referent power. He had no peer on the basketball court, giving him expert power. He is the president of his own company, which gives him legitimate power. Jordan delivered in the clutch, earning six world championships and millions of dollars for his sponsors, the team owners, and his teammates. They were all recipients of his reward power. And finally, he could strike fear into the heart of a teammate, an opponent, and maybe even an official with a stare, showing Jordan's masterful use of **coercive power.**

Based on the self-assessment test at the beginning of this chapter, what is your preferred type of power? Are you a high Mach? What situations are best for the way you use power? In what situations could you be at a disadvantage?

Nahavandi and Malekzadeh describe the "Dark side of power: Corruption."[140] They remind us of the old adage, "power corrupts and absolute power corrupts absolutely." The abuse of power occurs when the abuser feels he or she is not required to respect established standards or norms. For example, in 2006 the politically ambitious Durham, North Carolina, District Attorney Mike Nifong filed rape charges against three Duke University lacrosse players. District Attorney Nifong was spotlighted on major stories in the *New York Times*, *Newsweek*, The *New Yorker*, *Rolling Stone* magazine, *Sports Illustrated*, and thousands of other media outlets. The case also was featured on five segments of *60 Minutes* and several tabloid television shows. In 2007, after a thorough investigation, North Carolina Attorney General Roy Cooper announced the three lacrosse players were innocent of the charges. District Attorney Nifong, because of his effort to convict the three, was charged by the state bar association for ethics violations for withholding exculpatory evidence and making inflammatory statements about the case. In June 2007 a North Carolina state bar disciplinary panel concluded after a trial that Nifong had made inflammatory and prejudicial comments about the case, intentionally withheld DNA evidence, and lied to court officials. The panel called for his disbarment and Nifong resigned his office.[141]

Some may make the case that Wal-Mart abuses its power to offer big discounts when it establishes a new store in a community. Wal-Mart advertises that it will not be undersold, and it practices what it advertises, often to the detriment of the small, locally owned shops that line Main Street.

SEXUAL HARASSMENT

Abuse of power is most acute in cases of harassment. Whether it is the prison guard force in the movie *Shawshank Redemption*, the abusive coach who mentally demeans his players in public, or the supervisor who suggests sex in return for a promotion, harassment is a serious matter.

The issue of **sexual harassment** is likely one of the more sensitive subjects in today's organizational environment. Just what is sexual harassment? The law stipulates sexual harassment as: Unwelcome sexual advances, requests for sexual favors, and other verbal or physical conduct of a sexual nature (will) constitute sexual harassment when:

- submission to such conduct is made either explicitly or implicitly a term or condition of any individual's employment,
- submission to or rejection of such conduct by any individual is used as the basis for employment decisions affecting such individuals, or
- such conduct has the purpose or effect of unreasonably interfering with an individual's work performance or creating an intimidating, hostile, or offensive working environment.[142]

The range of illicit actions cuts a wide path and may include pornography displayed on a toolbox or taped to the outside of a locker. It may take the overt form of unwanted touching, obscene gestures, or requesting sexual favors. There is no reference to gender. Sexual harassment can be male to female, the form most often reported, or female to male, as in the case of Demi Moore's character's actions with Michael Douglas's character in the movie *Disclosure*. The harassment can also be same sex, male to male, or female to female. Same-sex harassment reached media proportions with the report of an offshore oil rig worker who claimed that he was sexually harassed by male supervisors. He filed suit and won a judgment. It may seem innocent enough to pass someone in the aisle or other close quarters and make what is meant to be a harmless touch; however, in short order, this act can become the focus of a sexual harassment allegation.

It is unlikely that the incidence of sexual harassment will go away soon, although education in the workplace is making headway. At a minimum, there must be a stated policy denouncing such activity and a further stipulation of severe consequences for offenders. There should be an effort to occasionally remind all employees of the policy as well. If alleged sexual harassment is reported to a supervisor, manager, or leader, the first step is to conduct an investigation. It can be a fatal mistake to ignore the situation or delegate responsibility for action. The question the courts ask the boss is specific, "What initial action, if any, did you take?" If the suspected offense is serious or inflammatory, it may be necessary to send the involved parties home, with pay, until the investigation is complete and the situation is resolved. Options available as corrective action may include reprimand, suspension without pay, or, in severe cases, termination for offenders.

Immediate action is crucial. The legal system places a high value on whether the situation was investigated properly and an appropriate action was taken. Proper action may save a conviction; however, the damage to a business and its reputation by an unnecessary lawsuit can be terminal.

POLITICAL BEHAVIOR

Power is the essence of **political behavior** in the workplace. It is the degree to which and the method people use to flex their power muscles within the organization. There is no politics-free environment. Whether it is the local university or the local factory, the teacher in the classroom, or the church on the corner, every organization has "office politics" and exercises political behavior.

Political behavior is the method that organization members use to demonstrate power.

Who has the power? On Friday night, it is the person who has a car with gas and on Sunday, it is the student who stayed in over the weekend and has the assignment completed. Someone once made the observation that not all corporate vice presidents seem to enjoy equal status. They all share equal billing on the organization chart, but a particular function seems to be favored, perhaps with funding or with rewards. The answer may be simple. What was the career path of the corporate president? If he or she is an engineer, then we may see favor to the engineering vice president. If the corporate president earned his or her stripes in the financial community, then the chief financial officer or the vice president of finance may be the favorite. Harvey Mackay, the owner of a successful envelope business, will tell you without hesitation that the salesperson is the king at his company. He reasons that no one works unless the salesperson sells something. The fact that Harvey Mackay was initially a successful salesperson probably has something to do with his opinion.

Political behavior is not bad; in fact, it is quite necessary for a healthy organization. Politics helps the flow of communication. There is, however, acceptable and unacceptable political behavior.

Here are some examples of acceptable political behavior:

- People may band together to petition the leadership for a change in routine. For example, the dorm cafeteria breakfast hours are established as 7 A.M. to 9 A.M., Monday through Friday. Starting at 7 A.M. causes those with 7:30 A.M. classes to rush or miss breakfast altogether. The residents band together and generate majority support for adjusting the hours to 6:30 A.M. to 8:30 A.M. and present the alternative to the dorm leadership for a decision.

- In the movie *Hoosiers,* the final scene depicts Hickory High School, an enormous underdog, in a team huddle with seconds to play and the state basketball championship on the line. The coach calls a play, which the players do not acknowledge. The coach asks, "What is the matter?" in a panicked voice, and the players respond with a play of their own. The rest is history: The play works and Hickory wins the championship.

- A new professor in the leadership department of a major university wanted a new printer for his office. The one he had been given was old, took "forever" to print, and the quality was not very good. He had a friend, Scott, who worked in the budget office of the university and that office seemed to have all the latest and greatest in new computer equipment, including printers. While out to lunch the new professor saw Scott and asked in a somewhat joking manner, "Hey, do you have any printers you want to get rid of? I really need one for my new office." Scott replied that they did have a used one that needed some minor repair but overall was a good HP Series IV printer. Scott indicated he could have it sent over to the office, "If you'd buy my lunch!" The printer arrived the next day; the minor repairs were made. A professor in the same department who had been with the university over 15 years saw the printer and noted, "It's just not fair. I have been here 15 years and you have been in four months and you got a new printer. How do you do it?" The answer is to know how to use political behavior. As a side note, the new professor was able to get a second printer from Scott for the older professor.

In understanding and using political power in an organization, one's people skills are critical. To be successful, getting along with people is mandatory, not optional. For whatever reason, it appears those in the sciences and technology finds this concept difficult to learn. During their studies, everything is task focused and not as much people focused. Perhaps, this limits the student's understanding of office politics or the political behavioral necessary in an organization for success. Individuals found to be successful in office politics are high self-monitors and sensitive to the issues of the organization. They normally have high internal loci of control, control their own environments, and will have high expectations for success. As such, they will be able to relate to others in the organization with vast amounts of experience and have power themselves.

There are always questions about organizational or individual political action being ethical. There is a series of questions people could ask themselves to help provide guidance in deciding if the behavior is ethical. They are

- Does the political action respect the rights of the individuals affected? If the answer is "NO" then it is unethical.
- Is the political activity fair and equitable? Again, if the answer is "NO" it is probably unethical.
- Is the political action motivated by self-serving interests detrimental to the organization's goals? If the answer is "YES" then it is probably unethical.

Here are some examples of unacceptable political behavior:

- Disgruntled employees sabotaging machines or company equipment
- Employee violence
- The sick-out by American Airlines pilots
- An unauthorized employee strike

IMPRESSION MANAGEMENT

Impression management is a form of political behavior that influences how others see a person.

Political behavior is also used to influence the way others see a person, the concept of **impression management.** The following short statements demonstrate each of seven impression management techniques.

1. **Conformity.** I am a team player. I'm not going to rock the boat.
2. **Excuse.** I am truly sorry that I missed your class on Monday, but I was scheduled for an employment interview—I think I got the job!
3. **Apology.** I apologize, but I will be ten minutes late for our appointment. Please forgive me. I know your time is valuable.
4. **Acclaiming.** There is no question about it, if they select me, I will be an immediate impact player.
5. **Flattery.** Your course may be the best I have taken. You have inspired me to consider a change of major.
6. **Association.** I drive a BMW.
7. **Favor.** A potential customer is offered tickets to see Sammy Sosa and Barry Bonds play in the same major league baseball game.

   Source: "Impression Management: A Literature Review and Two-Component Model," by Mark R. Leany and Robin M. Kowalski, *Psychological Bulletin*, January 1990, Vol. 107, No. 1, pp. 34–47. Copyright 1990 by the American Psychological Association, Inc.

Each example of impression management is an effort to influence another to favor the speaker. The first example, conformity, suggests that we avoid being obnoxious and go with the flow. Regarding the missed class for the job interview, it was hoped that an excuse would turn a negative situation into a positive. The telephone apology is preferred to showing up ten minutes late and saying, "Hey, I'm sorry."

"I am good. Aren't you glad I am here?" is an example of acclaiming. The course compliment demonstrates flattery. A job applicant employs this technique when she is complimentary of a prospective employer's business success. "I drive a BMW," "I sat next to Tiger Woods on a flight to Cleveland," or "Britney Spears invited me backstage after the concert" are all examples of association.

It may appear to the reader that impression management is marginal behavior. If politicking is to be successful, then a favorable impression is central. If the impression is not favorable, then it should be at least neutral. The final example of the baseball tickets warrants wider consideration. It is the concept of **favors,** not to be confused with bribes. A bribe is an illegal act; a favor is a legal act. Business is frequently conducted away from the office. When a potential customer has a significant amount of potential business, a salesperson must make every effort to earn the opportunity to have a share of the business. Tickets to *Lion King* or *Ragtime*, a golf outing, or tickets to the Indianapolis 500 are favors that are door openers. The objective of these favors is to create an opportunity to call on potential clients to demonstrate a product or service. It would be rare for a customer to award business based on a favor. It is also rare for a potential customer not to give a supplier an opportunity to make a presentation in response to a favor.

EXERCISES

A Sexual Harassment Issue

You are employed by a freight company loading and sorting packages on the night shift. Your team consists of four people: three men and one woman. Your team leader is a man. Jokes and stories are commonplace to make the time pass, many of which are off color, and all team members joke about a woman's anatomy. The female worker is offended and objects, but her coworkers only laugh at her. The leader is not present at the time.

1. What action, if any, do you recommend the woman take, and why?
2. Does this situation fit the definition of sexual harassment?
3. What would you do if you were the leader and the woman reported the incident to you?

A Political Behavior Issue

You have graduated from college and have been hired by a large company. You are required to participate in a four-week education and orientation program. Each week you and your new fellow employees are arranged in a different five-person work group for study, research, and presentation purposes.

1. Since you want to impress your peers and the instructor group, what is your best course of political behavior?
2. What actions would you take to emerge as the leader among your peers?
3. For each of the five sources of power, prepare a real-life example of your experience with each. Be original.
4. Barbara Pachter, career coach and author once said, "Tactful self-promotion is a business skill. You don't want to be obnoxious, but learning when and how to speak well of yourself is a key to getting and staying ahead. If you don't who will?" How would you engage in tactful self-promotion?
5. What can you do and what should you do to promote yourself in the workplace?

SUMMARY

Power is the ability to influence another to respond. It is through the perception of dependency that power generates influence; the greater the dependency relationship, the greater the power. The three parameters to establish dependency are

- Scarcity
- Importance
- Lack of a substitute

Power and politics are present in all organizations. A person's power base may come from one or more of five sources:

- Coercive power
- Reward power
- Legitimate power
- Expert power
- Referent power

Sexual harassment is more about power than it is about sex. Sexual harassment occurs primarily due to an unequal power relationship between two or more people.

Political behavior is the method that organization members use to demonstrate power. Understanding the organizational culture will go a long way in helping you to understand how to be successful in the organizational political climate. One must recognize the difference between acceptable and unacceptable political behavior.

Finally, individuals use several forms of impression management as a way to influence their acceptance by others. Successful salespeople and business negotiators understand the usefulness of the favor.

CASE STUDY

Stratford Corporation was having its yearly retreat for managers. Managers were put into discussion groups and asked to discuss how things were going at the company. This exercise was seen as an ice breaker to get people talking to one another. The managers were picked to get different points of view. The groups were composed of new managers just starting their jobs, managers with less than five years of experience, mangers with five to ten years of experience, managers with ten to twenty years of experience, and managers with more than twenty years of experience. It was hoped by upper-level management that the young managers would learn how to manage from the veterans. Several managers were discussing their operations when the subject of handling employees arose.

Frank, who was the oldest at 63 years old, had the most experience with 26 years and was probably the meanest manager in the company; he was the first to speak on the subject. "My style is simple. It is my way or the highway. If you do not want to work for me, I will help you right out the door. This new age 'touchy feely

stuff' is for the birds. We have company rules and standards of performance and I enforce them. Things get done right in my department and that is final." Frank also said employees who failed to follow rules or meet standards were punished immediately. Frank was viewed by upper management as being old school, loyal to the company, and a hard worker. Employee turnover was high in Frank's department, but that was viewed by Frank as separating the wheat from the chaff.

Bill was hired into management from the ranks of the hourly workers. He had been a line worker for seven years before moving into management. He was given his title and new status by the company ten years ago. Bill was a manager and that meant that he supervised the hourly workers in his department. When confronted by employees and their problems, Bill would remind them that he was the boss. Bill told the others that employees did what they were told because he was the manager designated by the company to run the department. Older workers in Bill's department saw him as the company's choice because of the time he spent in the ranks with them. Younger workers were aware of his position and service with the company. Bill was not a great leader, but he did manage to get things done.

Diane was a popular boss. She had been hired into the company right out of college and had been a manager for eight years. She had worked at the company during summers to pay for her education. She was a hometown girl who had been a cheerleader, president of her senior class, prom queen, and salutatorian of her high school class. Her employees liked her, wanted to be around her, and enjoyed working for her. She was one of them, but she had a certain charisma about her. Diane always spoke about her employees as her loyal following. She loved and respected the people that worked for her. She was very attractive, dressed well, had a winning personality, and always had a smile on her face. No matter how bad the problem was, she was always able to settle people down and get the problem solved. Nobody had anything bad to say about her. The men in the department were very protective of her and treated her like she was their sister. The women idolized and respected her for making it into management. Things seemed to run smoothly in her department and turnover of employees was low. Diane said that she treated people like she would like to be treated by her boss. You treat people right and they will work hard for you.

Ralph had been with the company for five years as a manager. He had been hired from another company in town that had gone through some downsizing. He was very protective of his job and certainly did not want to upset anyone. He remembered how hard it was to find this job after he had been laid off by the other company. At fifty-six, he was not getting any younger and job prospects were scarce. Ralph related that he gave pay increases, bonuses, and some promotions to people who worked well for him. Ralph was seen as a boss that took care of his employees. Frank viewed Ralph as a lazy slacker who would not stand up to his employees. Ralph viewed Frank as a bully and tyrant.

Mike was a veteran manager with more than twenty years of experience. Mike had a bachelor's degree and a master's degree in engineering. He always read any information he could get on products or machines in his area. His department was the most technically advanced group in the company. His workers knew that Mike was the man when it came to knowing what to do. He was regarded by upper management as the one employee who must be retained at all costs because of his knowledge of the field. People followed Mike because he knew what he was doing. People liked working for Mike, and his department had high productivity and low employee turnover. Mike told the group to never stop learning about the technology of the business. Everybody in the room respected Mike and valued his opinion. Even Frank had to admit that Mike knew more about technology than anybody in the company or in any other company in this business.

Helen, Allen, and Beth, the three rookie managers, heard the tales these five managers had told. The president of the company came in to address the group and looked right at the three of them and said, "I hope that you have learned how to be good managers from our veteran management team." He went on to say that "these are some of our best and brightest managers."

After the group had broken up, the three new managers began to talk.

Helen said, "I am really confused. I thought I was going to learn how to handle people and these managers cannot seem to agree on anything."

Beth said, "I got the feeling that Frank and Ralph do not agree at all on how to manage people."

Allen remarked, "I don't feel that I have the personality to be Diane no matter how hard I try." Beth agreed and said that she did not feel that she could be forceful like Frank. Helen said she did not have the experience in the ranks like Ralph has to lead people. All of them were left wondering how to take what was said by the managers and use it in their departments.

Questions

1. What was Frank's source of power to manage his workers?
2. What was Bill's source of power to manage his workers?
3. What was Diane's source of power to manage her workers?
4. What was Ralph's source of power to manage his workers?
5. What was Mike's source of power to manage his workers?
6. What types of power are preferred and why?

1. Explain the relationship between dependency and power.

2. Discuss the three parameters necessary for dependency.

3. Choose one of the five sources of power and explain the power source and its limitations (if any).

4. Explain the difference between leadership and power.

5. Discuss how sexual harassment is really an issue of power.

6. When is political behavior in an organization appropriate?

7. When might political behavior in an organization not be appropriate?

PART

5

PUTTING IT ALL TOGETHER

CHAPTER 22

Effort and Ethics

LEARNING OUTCOMES: EFFORT AND ETHICS

1. Define effort.

2. Discuss how ethics and ethical behavior govern individuals or groups.

3. Identify five areas in which ethical behavior is necessary for success.

4. Through self-assessment, compare your aptitude toward ethical behavior to the national norms.

Name: _____

Section Number: _____

Self-Assessment Test

Please complete the following exercise online, accessible with the Access Card packaged with this text, before reading this chapter.

Exercise I.D.2: How Do My Ethics Rate?

Record your scores against the norms provided with the instrument.

	Norm Score	Your Score		Norm Score	Your Score		Norm Score	Your Score
1.	3.09	_____	6.	2.88	_____	11.	1.58	_____
2.	1.88	_____	7.	3.62	_____	12.	2.31	_____
3.	2.54	_____	8.	2.79	_____	13.	3.36	_____
4.	3.41	_____	9.	3.44	_____	14.	3.79	_____
5.	3.88	_____	10.	1.33	_____	15.	3.38	_____

You should also record your score on this exercise in Appendix 1.

NOTES

The Garage

Luke and Rob are working on a car in for an oil change and filter at the Main Street Garage. The car is in good repair and there is nothing wrong with it. Then Luke takes Rob aside and tells him how to make real money around here.

Luke says, "This car needs a brake job in the worst way."

Rob replies, "I didn't see anything wrong with those brakes."

Luke reaches into his pocket and pulls out a small container of brake fluid. He sprays some on the axle of the car and then goes to get the owner of the car.

Luke says to the owner, "See that brake fluid on your axle?"

The owner replies, "What about it?"

Luke says, "This car is unsafe to drive because those brakes are going to fail. You could kill someone driving a car in that condition!"

The owner replies, "Well, I guess I had better get them fixed. How much is that going to cost me?"

Luke says, "A full brake job will run you around $700."

The owner replies, "You had better go ahead and do it."

After the car owner leaves the work area, Rob asks Luke why he did that.

Luke says, "We get paid on commissions, and I just got $105. Besides, I won't have to do anything."

Rob, after seeing this happen, walks over to the boss and quits.

Was Luke right in what he did?

Was Rob right in quitting?

Welcome to Effort and Ethics! ■

> *"I believe that a life of integrity is the most fundamental source of personal worth. I do not agree with the popular success literature that says that self-esteem is primarily a matter of mindset, of attitude—that you can psych yourself into peace of mind."*
>
> —Stephen Covey[143]

Effort and ethics "go together like peas and carrots," to use the words of Forrest Gump. Ethical conduct, or the lack thereof, shape the effort and color the outcome. The questionable ethical conduct of the fictitious politician in the movie *Primary Colors,* in place of legitimate political effort, demonstrates how the resulting circumstances can reach the lowest of lows. John Travolta plays the part of an aspiring Southern governor who wants to be the president of the United States. The governor, in an effort to discredit his opponent, encourages his aides to dig up dirt. The aides find proof that the opponent had a one-time drug dependency, long since history. The aides suggest the findings be ignored since the conduct is no worse than the governor's past behavior has been. The governor, supported by his wife, disagrees. The aide who discovered the drug dependency then commits suicide to avoid participating in the publication of the information. This prompts the governor to turn the incriminating findings over to the opponent as a sign of good faith. There is no question that the opponent will withdraw rather than risk embarrassment, thus clearing the way to a tainted victory. The governor may have achieved his goal, but he failed to consider that "what goes around comes around."

This chapter begins with a discussion of the principles of effort. The concept of effort is reinforced through the use of various examples. The second part of the chapter focuses on ethics. This is followed with a description of the five dimensions of ethical conduct. Each dimension is supported by a case study example.

EFFORT

Peter Sacks, the author of *Generation X Goes to College*,[144] wrote in 1996 that the movie *Forrest Gump*, "idealizes naïve stupidity as something to strive for in life." Some would challenge that point of view and offer instead that the movie's title character exemplifies honest effort untainted by petty jealousy or personal agenda. Either way, Forrest does display an undying effort. We respect effort. How else can we explain our admiration for the Special Olympics, the Spinners' basketball wheelchair competition, or any gallant effort by an underdog?

It is a common convention that success is rewarded while anything less than success is ignored. Since real success is relative, we need another measure, and that measure is effort. Let me illustrate with an academic example. If I were to choose one student from my classes this past semester to hire, that student would be an individual who earned a B. I would pass over all the A students for the B student. Why? Because this particular student demonstrated an effort that signaled extraordinary potential. He or she does not realize that you have to open the door to pass through. Sometimes, there is no time to waste in opening doors. In this book *Pushing the Envelope All the Way to the Top*,[145] Harvey Mackay writes about a large company that will not hire students with A averages because of the fear that there might be too much conformity to rote knowledge with a potential loss of creativity. Maybe this is true or maybe not.

Did the company president or college dean realize his or her trash can was empty this morning? Did these very successful people notice the cleanliness of the executive restrooms? What would be the impact if the dean took the time to find out who cleaned his office and then sent that employee a note of thanks for the effort? How many times does a customer tip the server before the meal at a restaurant? What happens when we send a thank you note or even an occasional gift certificate to the greens keeper of our favorite golf course? The point is this: **Routine effort is expected and seldom rewarded.** Sometimes effort needs a hug, and sometimes effort needs a nudge.

As employees are recruited and hired, experience has shown that the successful leader seeks subordinates or support staff who have skills and expertise the leader lacks. The organization that depends on the CEO or the vice presidents for all ideas, creations, and innovations will be mediocre at best. The leaders set the tone, establish the parameters, and fund the organization.

Three children in one family demonstrate effort at an early age. The oldest boy plays second string junior varsity football as a high school sophomore and is told at the end of the season not to return the next season because of a lack of size and lack of speed. He was the point guard on the basketball team in junior high school; however, he is cut from the high school basketball team that winter because he lacks size and speed. These are tough sets of circumstances to face back to back when you are sixteen years old. Disappointment leads to a determined effort to improve.

The following football season, he ignores the earlier advice and reports for early camp. He makes the junior varsity team as a starter and is selected for the varsity traveling squad. In the second game of the varsity season, an injury to the starting right offensive guard gives this young man his first varsity opportunity. He starts every subsequent game. When he is a senior, he is named an offensive captain, earns mental attitude honors, and is named to the first team all-state. His younger sister and brother earn three more mental attitude awards as they pass through the same high school.

If that is not enough of a challenge, these three siblings all score less than nine hundred on their precollege SAT. However, all three complete their college work, earning GPAs in excess of 3.0 out of 4. The oldest completes graduate work in civil engineering and now is one of a handful of experts in the aggregate recycling business in the United States.

Here are four illustrations that emphasize the impact of effort over apparent talent:

- Tom Hanks portrays a Federal Express employee in the movie *Castaway*. He becomes the sole survivor of an airplane crash somewhere in the Pacific Ocean. He has no tools, no food, and virtually nothing for survival when he is washed onto the shore of a deserted South Pacific island. He learns to make fire, he teaches himself to fish, and he survives for years. Finally, at exactly the right seasonal moment, he sets out on a homemade raft intent on riding the trade winds to the sea shipping lanes. This extraordinary effort results in his rescue and return home.

- Russell Crowe is cast as the Roman general Maximus in the movie *Gladiator*. After winning a decisive victory for the Roman Empire, it appears that Maximus will ascend to become the next Caesar when the current emperor, who is in failing health, dies. The nefarious son of the ailing Caesar successfully plots the destruction of Maximus's family. He also believes that his bandits have killed Maximus, thus leaving the son the throne. No one realizes that Maximus, although badly wounded, survives. He is captured by a slave trader and turned into a slave gladiator who performs to amuse the crowds of bloodthirsty Romans in the arena games.

  Maximus wears a mask when he returns to fight in the Roman arena, thus not revealing his identity to the young Caesar who is in attendance. In scene after scene, Maximus defeats all comers at the grand gladiator contest. In the presence of the wicked son, Maximus reveals his true identity. He subsequently slays the Caesar in battle while losing his own life.

- Fred Franks, a recently retired Army four-star general, lost a leg in combat in the 1960s. Despite rules to the contrary, Franks proved he could function as well as anyone despite his prosthetic leg. His effort and determination were keys to his success. Few realized that Fred Franks, the ground force commander in Desert Storm, only had one human leg.

- And how about that young Indiana high school basketball player who moved to a new community? He tried out for and made the high school varsity team and then shocked the community as he waved his artificial leg from the window of a school bus. That demonstration was the first time anyone realized the young man's apparent disability.

If all that is difficult to remember, then consider these quotes from Pat Riley's book, *The Winner Within*:[146]

> *"If at first you don't succeed, you are running about average."*
> —*M. H. Alderson*

> *"The only place where success comes before work is in the dictionary."*
> —*Vidal Sassoon*

ETHICS

Meriam Webster's Collegiate Dictionary defines **ethics** as "the discipline dealing with what is good or bad and with moral duty and obligation . . . the principles of conduct governing an individual or group."

The operative words are

- **Discipline.** Discipline is not used here in a punitive sense, but as a term that guides, directs, and gives order to one's actions.
- **Good or Bad.** The issue of choice (see *obligation*).
- **Obligation.** The implication of choice. Ultimately, everything can be seen as a choice between alternatives. You may sleep or go to class, you may go to class or study for an exam, or you may call in sick and play golf. There are only a few things that "have" to be done; everything else is a choice.
- **Principles.** Rules, norms, and standards. When a standard of performance is established, it becomes the rule or the norm. Any relaxation will result in a new standard. It is easy to run with the wind at your back. Running into the wind is a different story.
- **Governing.** This is not politics. Instead, we are talking about conscience, which is always our counsel.

If these operative words are the **what**, then how about the **where?** We will discuss five areas where ethical conduct is important in an organization:

- Customers
- Employees
- Peers
- Suppliers
- Competitors

Customers

Customers come in all shapes, sizes, and disciplines. They may be the students at a college or university, subscribers to MSN services, a department store retail consumer, or the soccer mom who pumps her own gas at the BP station. Customers are the reason the business or organization exists.

CASE STUDY ON CUSTOMER ETHICS

Melanie has just landed her dream job as part of a sales and product development team for a major maker of state-of-the-art computer electronics. Melanie is slated to replace Jeff in sales and marketing; Jeff is a gifted salesperson and has been promoted. As part of Melanie's education, she is reviewing the last six months' business with the three major accounts. One of these accounts is Burton Labs. Burton has been a long-term major customer and most orders are electronically passed between the companies. Melanie discovers a three-month-old order where Burton was shorted in shipment. Burton ordered 1,000 units and received only 900. The invoice value is $1 million. Burton paid the invoice, and apparently no one discovered the error. Melanie immediately brings the short shipment to Jeff's attention. Jeff is paid based on invoice value, as is Jeff's immediate boss. Jeff asks Melanie if Burton Labs is aware of the error. She tells him no. The invoice was paid and several other shipments, in the correct quantity, have been made, and those invoices also were paid. Jeff tells Melanie to forget it; Burton Labs' loss is our good fortune.

Discussion:

1. Is there an ethical dilemma?
2. What are Melanie's alternatives?
3. What are the consequences of each alternative?

Employees

A pencil here, a pad of paper there, maybe a few paperclips, making personal vacation arrangements while at work, and calling in sick on Friday to enjoy a three-day weekend—any one or more of these and other similar seemingly harmless acts occur in numbers too large to count or chart. To some, doing so is accepted practice. Often, these are the practices of management or supervisors in plain view of all employees. Will the company or organization seek bankruptcy protection or otherwise cease existence because of a loss of ten paperclips or 10,000 paperclips? Probably not. Lost paperclips are not the problem. They are the symptom, a symptom of loose control and a lack of discipline. Such lack of control can be disastrous.

Consider the cashier for a service business with loose controls. He has been a loyal and honest employee for more than ten years, and he has little supervision. As he was reconciling the cash drawer on a particular night, the cash was over by $25. The accepted practice is to include the $25 in the night deposit and make a report the next day. In this case, the employee is short of personal cash and needs to stop by the grocery store on the way home. Why not "borrow" the $25 and repay it after going to the bank tomorrow? No one will ever know. Is the behavior ethical?

Peers

We may shape our future ethical conduct at an early age. A mother asks her son who is responsible for the mess in the basement. It is Friday and this is no time to face discipline over the weekend; therefore, the mess has to belong to his sister. That is just the way it is. A white lie? Harmless, probably, but does the action result in some learning? We are probably not going to get many to argue that any brother-sister disagreement will create a serious

---

CASE STUDY ON EMPLOYEE ETHICAL CONDUCT

Andy, a middle-level supervisor, has been with Lake Landscaping for eight years. He began as a laborer and worked his way to be supervisor of lawn services. Andy is a hard worker and generally works at least twelve hours per day during the heavy work season. On one particular day, Andy does not return to the yard until 10 P.M., well after everyone else has departed. During the day Andy has the use of a company-owned truck, but he is not permitted to take it home. Each evening after work, Andy is required to complete and file his daily reports and service the truck including fueling it up at a secure pump on the company grounds. This night after Andy completes his chores, he remembers he forgot to get gas for his personal pickup truck on the way to work. Most gas stations are now closed. The nearest opportunity is 30 miles away and making it there will be a gamble. Andy now considers his options:

- "Borrow" five gallons of fuel and charge the fuel to his company truck.
- Call his wife and have her bring him some fuel in a gas can.
- Try to make it on what fuel remains.

Discussion:

1. How do you think Andy will handle the situation?
2. If Andy asked you for advice, what would you say?
3. Are there other options available to Andy?

ethical crisis. It does not take much imagination to extrapolate to the high school classroom, the high school marching band, and the volleyball team.

Suppliers

This is the reverse situation from the customer circumstance. Some would agree that suppliers are, by their nature, greedy and untrustworthy. Any time we can be a step ahead of a supplier, we should improve the profitability of our own organization. We are all suppliers—it just depends on where we are in the food chain. Suppliers are too often seen as the enemy. In reality, the supplier is as much a part of your organization as the customer. Successful suppliers are competent and they ensure constant quality. Some suppliers have cheaper prices, but you get what you pay for.

Competitors

There is usually little business or organizational love between competitors. It makes no difference if you are a Republican challenging a Democrat, two athletic teams squaring off, two emerging businesses, or two college graduates who are finalists for one job opportunity. There is going to be a winner and there will be a loser in absolute terms. If a political candidate discovers that his or her opponent is going to make a major announcement the next day about an issue of pivotal proportions, it is likely the candidate who makes the discovery will make arrangements to be on the evening news, thus

CASE STUDY ON ETHICS WITH PEERS

Sara is stepping down as the volunteer head of the regional arts museum and preservation society. Her appointed replacement is Phil, who recently retired from an executive position at the bank. Sara invites Phil to accompany her to a conference so that Phil can make the necessary contacts that are vital to funding the society. Sara has taken the society further than any of her predecessors have been able to do. She is also well respected in the community and among her peers. The travel, sponsored by the society, is reimbursable for out-of-pocket business expenses.

Sara explains the procedure to Phil and tells him that she will handle all the reimbursable expenses and file for repayment after the trip. During the trip Phil happens to notice that in several cases, Sara modestly adjusts some of the out-of-pocket expenses in her favor as she is completing the expense report. Generally she does this for expenses that are under $20 that do not require receipts for justification. Phil cannot help himself, and he asks Sara why she is claiming more reimbursement than the actual costs. Sara is not offended and answers that there are always costs involved that may not be apparent during travel away from home that are not reimbursable. In Sara's opinion, taking some liberty with the expenses is therefore justified. Phil is puzzled and asks what Sara means. Sara's justification includes interruption of her normal routine and the difficulties of travel.

Discussion:
1. Is there an ethical dilemma?
2. What are Phil's options?
3. Is Sara justified?
4. Place yourself in Phil's position. What do you do?

upstaging the opponent. Is that ethical conduct, or is that the way the game of politics is played? It is common practice for companies to recruit and hire the best performers from their competitors. Volkswagen did just that to General Motors. Many companies require new hires to sign confidentiality agreements if they will be working in business-sensitive positions. These agreements usually require nondisclosure of company proprietary information for some defined time period should an employee resign and go to work for the competition. While these agreements are legally binding, they rely more on ethical conduct than any court of law.

Most unethical or unprincipled behavior found in organizations happens for one of five reasons. Individual managers need to be ever vigilant to make sure they are not committing one or more of these five deadly sins:

1. Favoring the organization's interest to the detriment of its stakeholders: customers, employees, and the community.

2. Rewarding behavior that violates ethical standards (e.g., rewarding managers who are "under budget," even though it meant they pushed employees too hard to cut corners when they should not have).

3. Creating a corporate environment that encourages separate standards of behavior for work and home (e.g., punishing people for being honest about mistakes and thereby encouraging secrecy and deceit, or rewarding individuals who grandstand while ignoring solid, but quiet, team players).

4. Allowing individuals to abuse power to further their own interests (e.g., executives who promote "friends" over more qualified employees in order to surround themselves with friendly faces).

5. Creating managerial values that undermine integrity. This "Madison Avenue mentality" holds that anything is right if the public can be convinced it is right.

CASE STUDY ON ETHICS AND COMPETITORS

Jennifer and Samantha both graduated recently with similar degrees but from different universities. Jennifer and Samantha are the finalists for a position with Watergate Cosmetics. The interview and selection process has been particularly arduous and lengthy. Neither Jennifer nor Samantha has another serious offer pending. The position is at the corporate headquarters and the initial salary is $55,000 plus a 25 percent add-on for living expenses. They both think the job is perfect. Over the past few months, Jennifer and Samantha have become good friends, and they actually thought the company might hire both of them.

This week Watergate Cosmetics asked both candidates to visit the corporate headquarters for final interviews. As it turns out, Watergate can only make one offer. The night before the final interviews, Jennifer and Samantha meet for dinner. They both feel nervous and apprehensive. Each wishes the other good luck and they retire.

Shortly thereafter, Samantha receives a phone call from Frank, the sponsor at Watergate.

He goes over the final details for the next day. He did the same for Jennifer earlier, but Frank inadvertently lets it slip to Samantha that the CEO is on the interview schedule tomorrow. Frank also mentions that the CEO believes business is largely influenced by current events nationally and internationally and will likely raise the issue. Samantha hangs up the phone and makes a dash for the newsstand where she buys *Time, Business Week,* and the *New York Times* to study. On the way back to her room Samantha meets Jennifer.

Discussion:

1. Is there an ethical dilemma here?
2. What should Samantha say to Jennifer?
3. What are Samantha's options?
4. Should Samantha raise the issue of Frank's added information when she meets the CEO?

A FINAL THOUGHT

As you conclude this study of effort and ethics, consider the following ideas:

- "Always show positive attitudes toward your job (task) so that your subordinates will 'pick up' right thinking."
- As you approach your job each day, ask yourself, "Am I worthy in every respect of being imitated? Are all my habits such that I would be glad to see them in my subordinates?"[148]

It is impossible to anticipate all the different ethical dilemmas that a person might face. Instead, let us leave you with twelve good questions to ask to understand the ethics of a situation and help you find the proper solution.[149] It is not necessary to ask all twelve questions in every situation, but you may want to pick two or three of these questions to ask yourself in difficult situations.

1. Is it legal?
2. How do I feel about this? Am I feeling unusually anxious? Am I fearful?

3. Will any rules, policies, or regulations be violated?

4. Is the proposed action consistent with past practice?

5. Does my conscience bother me?

6. How would I feel if the details of this situation appeared on the front page of the local newspaper?

7. Does this situation require that I lie about the process or the results?

8. Do I consider this to be an extraordinary situation that demands an unusual response?

9. Am I acting fairly? Would I want to be treated this way?

10. Would I be able to discuss the proposed situation or action with my immediate supervisor? My family? My company's clients? The president of the company?

11. If a close friend of mine took this action, how would I feel?

12. Will I have to hide or keep my actions secret? Has someone warned me not to disclose my actions to anyone?

SUMMARY

Effort and ethics go together in that ethics shape the effort. Effort is a serious attempt to accomplish a task. Effort is important to one's success in business and in life. Take the time to recognize individual effort as a means to give recognition and show appreciation.

Ethics is centered on discipline (guide to one's action), good or bad (choice), obligation, principles (rules, norms, and standards), and the conscience that governs us. Ethical conduct is important to customers, employees, peers, suppliers, and competitors. We have seen a great deal of unethical behavior in business over the past few years. There are five basic managerial mistakes organizations often participate in that will lead to a lack of trust and respect. These are

- Favoring organizations' interest over the interest of the stakeholders
- Rewarding behavior that violates ethical standards
- Creating a corporate environment that encourages separate standards of behavior for work and home
- Allowing individuals to abuse power to further their own interests
- Creating managerial values that undermine integrity

1. Discuss what you think must be done to improve the ethical standards in business and government today.

2. Should routine effort be rewarded? Explain your answer.

3. When faced with an ethical business decision, explain the process you would undertake to seek direction for the decision.

CHAPTER 23

Succeeding in an Organization

LEARNING OUTCOMES: SUCCEEDING IN AN ORGANIZATION

1. Outline the five points on which success is largely determined.

2. Discuss *The West Point Way of Leadership*.

3. Identify the two types of human failure.

4. Recite the seven principles serving as guideposts for successful leaders.

Name: _____

Section Number: _____

SELF-ASSESSMENT TESTS

EXERCISE IV.A.3   HOW CONFIDENT AM I IN
                MY ABILITIES TO SUCCEED?   Score _____

    Confidence has an influence on many things we do. People who are confident have high self-efficacy that generalizes across a variety of situations. They believe that they have the capability to mobilize the motivation and resources required to perform successfully on different tasks they encounter. Ultimately, this confidence translates into better performance. Why? One reason is that efficacious individuals set more goals for themselves, are more committed to their goals, and even persist in achieving their goals in the face of failure. In fact, when individuals who are confident about themselves are given negative feedback (say, by a supervisor), they respond by *increasing* their effort and motivation. Perhaps not surprisingly, individuals with such positive self-concepts are more satisfied with their jobs and obtain higher levels of career success.

You should also record your scores on this exercise in Appendix 1.

NOTES

The Clerk

Betty has just been hired as a clerk at Wallace's Pharmacy. She is excited about the prospect of making money even though the job only pays $6 per hour to start. Mr. Wallace trains her on how to operate the cash register and how to wait on customers. He tells her about the products and gives her pamphlets and books on the products carried in the pharmacy. The bulk of the nonprescription business is in over-the-counter drugs and cosmetics.

Betty enjoys talking on the pharmacy's phone with her friends. She also enjoys sampling the cosmetics. Her friends hang out at the store and talk to her while she is on the job. Customers start to complain to Mr. Wallace about her lack of product knowledge and poor service. Once, she continued to talk on the phone with one of her friends until a customer left the store because no one would take her money at the cash register.

Mr. Wallace has asked you about what to do about Betty.
What is Betty's problem?
What do you tell him?
Welcome to Succeeding in an Organization! ■

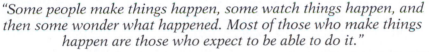

"Some people make things happen, some watch things happen, and then some wonder what happened. Most of those who make things happen are those who expect to be able to do it."

—*Charles Garfield*[150]

In large measure, **those who expect to be successful are successful.** It is not luck and it is not because someone else gave that person a break. Successful people make their own luck and they make their own breaks. Or perhaps successful people just recognize when they create luck and when they create a break. In Chapter 4, we shared one of the magical points for success. We noted that successful people must think, act, talk, and conduct themselves as successful people would. That means those wanting to be successful must believe in themselves, learn the behaviors needed to act successful, and learn to talk successfully. If becoming successful is a goal of yours, and I hope it is, this means you will take the extra time, go to the extra training session, learn the additional skills, and so on, to prepare yourself for success. Those who wait for success are usually run over by the success train. *Success* is a relative term and everyone has his or her own definition. The band director for the high school may see success as a state championship. A research scientist sees success in the creation of a new compound, and a business bases success on market share and profitability. As the old adage says, "those who say it can't be done need to get out of the way of those who are doing it!"

When you start a job, the first thing managers look for is whether you can manage yourself. They will want to see if you can meet deadlines and whether you can finish a project without giving a lot of excuses about why you can't get it done. There are always many reasons, often good reasons, why a project will not get done. Managers are looking at new people to see if they can get the project done with "whatever it takes" (within legal and ethical bounds, of course).

If you demonstrate that you can manage yourself, the next step is to show that you can manage a project. This is often challenging because you need to influence people without having them actually report to you. You need to find ways to motivate these people to get the project done.

If you successfully demonstrate that you can manage a project, the next step is to give you responsibility to manage people. Many nonmanagers have the romantic idea that managing people means you tell them what to do. Unfortunately, it usually doesn't work that way. The most successful way that a person manages people is to use reason. A common complaint from first-line managers is that the people who work for them do not do what they are told to do. Welcome to the exciting world of management.

Frankly, the first-line manager often exerts more effort than seems worthwhile. At times, it feels like a person is doing more babysitting than managing. In some respects, your first management experience is like being a parent. You need to be fair with all your people, but they are all different and you need to manage each one differently. You will quickly build your skills in understanding what motivates different types of people. As you advance in management, the task becomes easier. You will be managing people who are already managing other people, so they are usually more understanding.

Success often has a direct relationship with confidence. No matter where their life goals take them, people who are confident about their abilities are more likely to succeed. This list of recommended readings demonstrates the connection between confidence and success:

1. *The Go-Getter*, by Peter B. Kyne.[151] This is an older book; it is a quick read and its message is timeless.
2. *The Magic of Thinking Big*, by David Schwartz.[152] This short paperback is powerful.
3. *The Millionaire Mind*, by Thomas J. Stanley.[153] This work conveys a super message.

Success is largely the combination and interaction of the following:

- Preparation
- Selection and adaptation
- Motivation and stimulation
- Leadership
- Reference Points

PREPARATION

A case may be made that everything we have experienced and all of our informal and formal education are mere precursors to entry into the world of work. Some people may hold part-time jobs or work on the family farm or in the family business, and some may pursue intense athletic activity. The skills and discipline learned and practiced early in life usually make a difference.

Formal education plays a major role. More people are seeking higher education today than ever before. Advanced formal education at the university level is not always the right direction for everyone. There are some excellent trade schools and occupational schools that focus on learning specific work skills.

An interesting article in *Time* magazine reported on the amount of time young people spend today in preparation for school.[154] The average weekly homework investment increased from 85 minutes in 1981 to 134 minutes in 1997 for six- to nine-year-olds. For nine- to eleven-year-olds, the trend was from just over two and a half hours to more than three and a half hours weekly. Is that enough or is that too much? The time investment is not necessarily the issue. Instead, the emphasis is on the importance of preparation at an early age.

Real world experience through an internship will yield significant dividends in the future. When the labor market is uncertain, those people who have prepared themselves with job experience will certainly have a greater chance for success. Employers want workers with practical experience, and internships and cooperative training programs provide that experience. After the Organizational Leadership program at Purdue University made internships a requirement for graduation, the average starting salary for graduates increased over $4000.[155]

Interviewing seems to be the culmination of the preparation stage. Everyone interviews for something sometime. How to present yourself in a résumé, how to dress, how to sit, and how to answer interview questions seem to get the greatest attention when preparing for an interview. The prospective employer considers all those matters to be relevant, but he or she is normally using a "selection out" process. In other words, of all the applicants, whom should we consider for the next step? Successful businessman and author Harvey Mackay, in his book *Sharkproof*,[156] offers a list of various questions that goes well beyond questions about what classes prospective employees took and what summer jobs they held. Do not overlook this excellent resource as you prepare for an interview.

The concept of teaming is so well accepted today that invariably the subject is discussed during most interviews. That horrific lab experience, the group project in a communications class, and the other academic-level teaming exercises now take on extraordinary proportions. Get involved, solve problems, and seek solutions in team projects. Don't be a social loafer.

The bottom line never changes. The one hosting an interview is looking for someone who can be an impact player. Not too long ago an individual interviewing for a position was being questioned by an especially difficult interviewer. The interviewer controlled the hiring selection even though several other managers were on the agenda. The interviewer became demanding, asking on more than one occasion what made the prospective candidate feel he should be selected. After several more tough questions the candidate said these words, "I am my own best critic. I will know well before you or anyone else for that matter, whether I can or cannot handle the tasks assigned. If I am unable to compete, I will tell you so. I will find the door; you will not have to show me." Powerful words, interview over, send everyone else home; we have found our newest team member. Sometimes you just have to be unique.

SELECTION AND ADAPTATION

Everyone has a choice, and one of the best opportunities to exercise that choice occurs when searching for the right professional fit. Throughout this book you have been encouraged to survey and evaluate yourself. Values, personality, conflict, negotiation, power and politics, and leadership all play a role in selection and adaptation. Now would be a good time to reflect on your assessment survey responses again. Look for a trend. If one is not apparent, ask for help. Your attitude toward others and your strengths and weaknesses are your guideposts. For example, will you prefer a bureaucratic or an entrepreneurial environment?

If you tend to enjoy creativity and freedom, then pass up a job with the U.S. Post Office. On the other hand, if structure and order fit your preferences, a more bureaucratic environment may be a better fit. You may find creative and entrepreneurial people in what might be considered bureaucratic organizations. The subculture within the larger organizational culture may seem to be different and that can well be the case. The marketing department may be dominated by free spirits who appear to operate with little direction or boundaries. The engineering department of the same organization may be just the opposite, demanding strict adherence to practices and norms. A word of caution: If the head of the organization came from an engineering background, there may be little tolerance for sales and marketing types. Matching an organization's structure and culture with one's own preferences may be the most critical issue in the selection and adaptation process.

How can you know if a mistake or a bad match has occurred? It may not be an immediate revelation; sometimes, it takes years. On other occasions the fit is correct, but then the people change. Author Marilyn Kennedy wrote the following advice in *U.S. News and World Report:* "I think there are two times when it's wise to change jobs: when you stop growing and when you realize that nothing you do is going to make management value you because their values are different from yours (ethics and moral conduct are included)."[157]

What about that job offer? The following tips, adapted from Stephen Robbins, provide a good roadmap for choosing a job.[158]

- **Observe the physical surroundings of the organization.** Does it fit your style? If you talk to a mechanic about car repairs, does it make a difference if his or her work area is disorganized and dirty? Do you apply the same test to a prospective job opportunity? What are the current employees you observe doing?

- **Who did you meet?** Did the HR people handle everything, or did you have an opportunity to talk with a prospective boss and peers? It sends a powerful message to a prospective candidate when he or she is permitted to go one-on-one with a future peer.

- **How would you characterize the style of the people you meet?** Was there a smile and a kind word or perhaps just a nod? It is interesting that we always feel good when someone takes the opportunity to smile and speak. Employees of Wal-Mart and Blockbuster Video, for example, try never to miss the opportunity to greet every customer.

- **What about formal rules and regulations?** This comes back to which organization structure you prefer.

- **Ask questions.**

- **How are new employees integrated into the organization?** Are the new people assigned mentors? What makes up the training program, if one exists?

- **Can you identify the fast trackers? What do you see?** This is usually a good barometer as to what the organization views as important.

- **How does the organization react in a crisis?** This may be difficult to determine for smaller organizations; however, there is usually an answer for larger companies such as Enron, World.Com, and Martha Stewart Living Omnimedia, Inc. Competitors are sometimes a source of this information.

The work world does not stand still. The impact of women in organizations has been one of the single most important dimensions to affect all organizations in the past quarter-century. Geraldine Layborne, a successful cable industry leader, is a CEO with offices overlooking Central Park in New York City. Not too shabby. She gives us her perspective in a interview,[159] "Right now 80 percent of all new businesses are being run by women."

Tenure is fading as a benchmark for assessing success. In the past, conventional thinking held that anyone with five or six different jobs in ten years is probably a risky hire. That attitude is changing, particularly in the technology business. New, rapidly growing ventures seek those who have been successful in like businesses and then recruit them away. A better measure for those who have changed jobs frequently may be growth track, not the number of jobs held. If each move is to a position of greater responsibility and, in each case, there is achievement and success, then it makes sense to place less emphasis on tenure.

Change is certain, and each generation brings new ideas and new challenges. *Business Week* reported on the generation of people from ages fifteen through thirty. The article labeled these young people *Generation Y*.[160] The article reported that Generation Y is trading L. L. Bean for Delias, Coke for Mountain Dew (more bang), and Nikes for Vans.

MOTIVATION AND STIMULATION

There is a good deal of wasted effort today trying to motivate groups and teams. Teams and groups are not motivated as such; instead, they are made up of large numbers of motivated individuals. Football coach Lou Holtz, an outstanding motivational speaker, reports that he will never try to motivate a group, even though those who hire him do so for that reason. Instead he focuses on what individuals can do, the culmination of which makes the team successful.

Select from memory any successful group, team, organization, or business. The success of that unit is likely a direct reflection of the leader's personal involvement. The auditorium speeches and pep sessions are replaced with a leader who is visible throughout the organization, providing encouragement and reinforcement. Herb Kelleher built Southwest Airlines into a market leader with just such a philosophy. Ken Blanchard echoed this idea in his book, *The One Minute Manager*.[161] He writes, "Help people reach their full potential, catch them doing something right."

Be visible. A director of operations manager for a 400 person company had his secretary put everybody's anniversary date with the company on his calendar. This was a 24-hour manufacturing operation. Whenever an employee's anniversary date came up, he made a special effort to go to the production floor or office and congratulate the employee. It didn't matter if it was the employee's first year with the company or the 42nd year, or if it was the president of the company or the janitor, he made himself visible to every employee and spent some quality time with each of them. There were times when he would go into work at 11:00 P.M. or 5:00 A.M. to meet with an employee, and he made a special effort to talk to every employee and learn more about him or her.

Be unique. Be different, but not to a fault. Remember our earlier example of the research manager who stopped scheduling work every week for a half-day. The chemists and technicians in his charge were encouraged to experiment with new ideas and concepts. They were encouraged to discover something new or search for a way to do something better. The leader spent his half-day moving from lab to lab, chemist to chemist, encouraging and reinforcing their efforts.

Here's another example, this time of a successful salesperson among a group of average performers. The boss often wondered how the one salesperson could do so well. To better understand, he invited himself to travel with the successful subordinate for one week. Where it was conventional practice to schedule appointments between the hours of 9 A.M. and 3 P.M., this particular salesperson rarely did so. He asked secretaries and other support people at his client companies when the purchasing agents and buyers were least busy. The answer was from 7 A.M. to 9 A.M. and from 3 P.M. to 5 P.M. He would show up at the buyer's desk or office at 7:15 A.M. with coffee and donuts, or perhaps he would visit at 4:30 P.M. with cold drinks and cheese wedges. In the beginning he ate a lot of donuts and cheese alone; but over time, his program worked. It did not necessarily work because he had a better product or service. He was just different.

LEADERSHIP

In an organization anything that happens or fails to happen is generally related to leadership. Any discussion of leadership and success suggests the following question: What should we expect from a successful leader? It is likely that no one answers the question in the same way. Here is an example from the book *The West Point Way of Leadership.*[162]

- **Care** more than others think is wise.
- **Risk** more than others think is safe.
- **Dream** more than others think is practical.
- **Expect** more than others think is possible.

Care: Take care of your people and your organization. **Risk:** Do not be reluctant to explore new opportunities; do not get mired in old paradigms. **Dream:** What else can be done? **Expect:** Be disciplined and ordered, and maintain high standards.

Why do employees fail to do what they are supposed to do? Author Ferdinand Fournies gives us five reasons to consider:[163]

- They don't know what they're supposed to do.
- They don't know how to do it.
- There are no positive consequences for them to do it.
- They're punished for doing what they're supposed to do.
- They have personal problems that distract them from work.

A leader or manager must be clear and complete with all instructions. Any time there is ambiguity or uncertainty, the job either does not get done or there is a failure in some part of the execution.

Any function that is new requires some sort of education and practice if it is to be done satisfactorily. It does not make sense to consider that we can ask a teenager to watch videos and read books that describe how to drive a car and then be able to drive with proficiency. There is nothing wrong with the videos and books, but driving skills must be practiced to be learned with any proficiency. The same concept holds true for a follower. Do not expect excellence and accuracy without practice and experience. In most cases, it is wise to make sure that practice takes place away from customers.

Knowing what to do and how to do it raises another issue. What is correct performance? With the possible exception of precision machine and instrument work, a follower will typically not duplicate a leader's or manager's routine to get the job done. Housepainters paint differently, but they all paint houses. Salespeople sell differently, but they all sell. Leaders and managers must be able to allow employees and followers to use their own devices, provided they do not endanger people or property or do not create unacceptable damage or waste.

There also needs to be some sort of positive recognition for the job or task accomplishment. The recognition may be in the form of encouragement or an approving smile or perhaps it is more tangible in nature. In any case, it is important that management value employees and their performance.

Incorrect criticism is a disease that infects many leaders and managers. For example, employee A is one of six employees who does much the same task on generally the same schedule. If employee A arrives for work early and stays late, the others will jeer and criticize. This may cause the employee to change his or her behavior to fit in. The supervisor may view employee A's change in behavior as laziness and lacking in commitment. Managers must not permit their people to become average.

Roughly one-third of the typical day is spent in the charge of a work leader. If an employee has an illness or financial crisis outside work, then efficiency will likely be impaired. Left unattended, personal problems often deepen, which will impact more people than just the individual employee. Involved leadership can often prevent a serious problem.

Unfortunately, some followers are not able to be followers. Every attempt must be made to properly train, educate, and motivate followers, but in some cases, it just does not work. Some people may not have the mental or physical ability to do a job. If reassignment within the company is not possible then the ultimate reassignment is necessary—termination. It is never a sign of weakness or failure on the part of a manager to discharge an unacceptable worker. Sometimes it is necessary for the health and growth of the organization.

Self-discipline is also crucial to successful leadership. Consider these words from an old Chinese proverb, "Being patient in one moment of anger will allow one to escape 100 days of sorrow." The best medicine for anger or frustration often is to sleep on it. Somehow things always look different the next morning.

REFERENCE POINTS

Reference points are tips or ideas that have been found to be useful in the practice of success in an organization. These include the following:

- Failure
- The Magnificent Seven
- The New Discipline
- Remember Me

Failure

We all know what **failure** is, but do we know what kind of failure it is? Picture a new employee with less than two months' experience. The employee has been trained and trained well. Despite the education, the employee makes a mistake and does something wrong that results in a failure. Perhaps it is damaged goods, a lost customer, or an incorrect billing that cannot be corrected. What happens? All too frequently the leader or manager is frustrated with the situation and acts before thinking. The leader may publicly reprimand the employee or maybe the criticism is handled in private. In any case, there is often an immediate action without thinking or checking.

Failure occurs when someone does not accomplish an assigned task.

There is failure in this example, but what kind of failure is it? The question may seem strange, but there are only two types of human failure:

- **Ability.** The person did not know how to complete a task.
- **Motivation.** The person did not want to complete the task.

Take a moment to find out what kind of failure exists. It will make all the difference in the selection of the corrective action. An incorrect application of the corrective action will never solve the problem.

An **ability failure** is related to education and training.

A **motivational failure** is related to a choice not to accomplish a task.

- An **ability failure** should result in more education or training.
- A **motivation failure** may generate the necessity of disciplinary action and may even be punitive in nature. Consider this formula: lead, coach, inspire, or, as a last resort, fire.

If discipline is used to respond to an ability failure, the frustration level will increase. If training or education is used to handle a motivation failure, little will be accomplished. A person habitually late to work benefits little from videos on how to start up a production line.

The Magnificent Seven

These seven principles can serve as guideposts for successful leaders and managers:

1. **Take care of your people.** An organization should always ask the question, "Do I treat my customers better than I treat my people?" This is a tough question and the answer is often disappointing. We may be talking about recognition programs, compensation, stress minimization, evaluation programs, flexible benefits, and so on. We are not necessarily seeking happiness; the objective is job satisfaction.

2. **Take care of your customers.** If you don't, someone else will. We all know that. How many businesses waste precious resources trying to capture new customers while their current customers are ignored? Why does that happen? What can be done to reverse the situation? Do we ignore our current customers (or friends)?

3. **Hire people who are smarter than you.** No one has the corner on ideas. In a successful environment, the boss spends a lot of time evaluating new ideas. The CEO of Highsmith, Inc., a $55 million mail-order business, spends two hours each week with his librarian. The librarian is his principal idea person. Pat Carrigan, a GM plant manager, admits that she would never make or measure a part; smarter people do that. It is interesting to evaluate why companies that once were at the top of their game falter. If we look closely, we may have a situation where the senior leader was the idea bank and intimidated the chain of command. Then, suddenly the leader is out of the loop due to health, resignation, or retirement. The company flounders and can fail if the vacuum is not filled quickly.

4. **Be able to speak convincingly.** After all the e-mail and all the memos, face-to-face interaction gets the order. The order may be 1,000 units of raw material, or it may well be the final negotiation for a merger or an acquisition. Effective speaking is required in all of the following situations:
   - Any sales/service/product presentations.
   - In negotiations. On a one-to-one basis or team-to-team approach, a speaker must be able to convince and earn respect. An incompetent speaker never wins.
   - To motivate. An athletic coach may not always choose the correct words, but the principal way he or she motivates is to speak convincingly.

5. **Write with clarity and conviction.** If people cannot read it or understand it, it will find its way to the trash can.

6. **Always put fear behind you.** It will frequently get in the way. Never permit fear to alter your course. How does an unranked team defeat the number one team in the nation? The team has no fear, only confidence. The lack of fear must be felt throughout the organization. The attitude may be read this way, "Don't worry about the closed door. I will go through it without opening, if necessary." A salesperson, for example, must be absolutely confident he or she can get the order. That does not imply that there is always success. A short-term setback usually generates an increased intensity to succeed. Do not fear the assignment where others have never been successful. You may find a way to succeed where others have failed.

7. **Avoid divisive engagement.** Divisive engagement occurs when an individual or an organization has lost its ability to influence the action. If a boss and an employee confront one another in a threatening manner, there may be no choice. The employee must go. That employee very well could be the organization's best resource for ideas. People with ideas who have no fear often are extremely difficult to lead and manage. It takes a unique leadership skill to keep a group of free spirits functioning as a team.

The New Discipline

In the book *The Discipline of Market Leaders*[164] Michael Treacy and Fred Wiersema describe three distinct value disciplines that identify organizational focus: operational excellence, product leadership, and customer intimacy.

The thrust of their argument is that the success of an organization is built on the concentration of one of the disciplines. It does not mean the others are of no importance, only that the primary discipline is the focus. Attempting to balance all three will result in marginal success at best. The authors believe that as historians critique the 1990s, they will conclude that success is directly related to an organization adopting a primary discipline and then sticking with it.

- **Operational excellence.** The target is "low price and hassle free service." It is very difficult to travel the interstate highway system in the Midwest and know where to find the least expensive gas. That has changed. The lowest price for gas from Ohio to Nebraska is now the *Flying J*. For those who have never heard of the *Flying J*, the company made its mark as a high-quality truck stop. Truck stops do not advertise on national television; they advertise on CB radios. Today, the *Flying J* continues to be a quality truck stop, but now it also offers a low-price gas service. Some may briefly match the price but no one beats it. Wal-Mart operates on the same principle. The stores are not fancy and the merchandise is not designed by Tommy Hilfiger, but the prices are often the lowest.

  Operational excellence targets the best price and convenient service.

- **Product leadership.** The goal is to "offer the best product, period." General Motors appears to have adapted this strategy. The company has reorganized to develop a closer relationship with the customer and the product. GM has not been reluctant to trim model offerings in the process. Gone is the entire line of Oldsmobiles. At the same time GM has fielded a series of heavy-duty pickups and SUVs, including the Avalanche, the Envoy, and the Hummer H2, billed as the ultimate driving experience. The focus is the product, the right product in the right configuration, to satisfy the customers' wants.

  Product leadership results in providing the best product possible.

- **Customer intimacy.** Sometimes it is not the lowest price but a blinding orientation on the customer that counts. Applebee's Neighborhood Grill and Bar is full of customers from open to close. At peak times there is

  Customer intimacy focuses on customer service and satisfaction.

always a wait, and there are always people willing to wait. Perhaps it is because of the personalized service that never changes from location to location. Applebee's bills itself as the hometown place to eat. An entry into the home shopping or catalog business is Delia's. In *Business Week*, Newborne and Kerwin write,[165] "The morning after the Delia's catalog arrives, the halls of Paxton High School in Jacksonville, Florida, are buzzing." The catalog creator has figured out how to become intimate with a consumer group between the ages of five and twenty.

Remember Me?

- *I am the person who sits in the restaurant patiently while the waitress does everything but take my order.*
- *I am the woman who stands quietly while the department store clerks finish their chitchat.*
- *I am the man who drives into the service garage for an oil change and I don't blow my horn, but I wait patiently while the attendant finishes his book.*

Yes, you might say that I am a nice person. But guess who else I am? I am the customer that never comes back. It amuses me that you spend thousands of dollars to get me back into your store when I was there in the first place. All you had to do was to give me a little service and show me a little respect. The author is unknown, but he or she really makes the point!

Last but Not Least

We hope you have enjoyed the material presented in this book. We wrote it to help the reader realize the importance of understanding human and organizational behavior for effective leadership. There is a quote by Winston Churchill we believe sums up the material and the knowledge gained as we move through this text. Churchill noted:

> *To every man (person) there comes in his lifetime that special moment when he is figuratively tapped on the shoulder and offered the chance to do a very special thing, unique to him and fitted to his talent. What a tragedy if that moment finds him unprepared or unqualified for the work which would be his finest hour!"*[166]

Hopefully the material covered and knowledge gained in this study have helped you become prepared for that moment when opportunity knocks.

SUMMARY

Success is largely the combination and interaction of preparation, selection and adaptation, motivation and simulation, leadership, and reference points. Preparation means obtaining the education, skills, and discipline to succeed. Selection and adaptation means choosing a good fit and being able to adjust. Motivation and stimulation means helping people in the organization achieve their potential. Leadership can be summed up as care (take care of your people and your organization), risk (explore new opportunities), dream (what else can be done?), and expect (be disciplined, ordered, and maintain high standards). Reference points refer to tips and ideas that can help you and your organization achieve new levels of success.

The West Point Way of Leadership states:

- Care more than others think is wise.
- Risk more than others think is safe.
- Dream more than others think is practical.
- Expect more than others think is possible.

There are two types of human failure:

- Ability failure—the person did not know how to complete a task
- Motivation failure—the person did not want to complete the task

The seven principles serving as guideposts for successful leaders are

- Take care of your people.
- Take care of your customers.
- Hire people who are smarter than you.
- Be able to speak convincingly.
- Be able to write with clarity and conviction.
- Always put fear behind you.
- Avoid divisive engagement.

DISCUSSION QUESTIONS

1. How do you feel about *The West Point Way of Leadership?*
2. Have you ever been treated poorly by an employee of a store, restaurant, or other business? What did they do and how did you react?

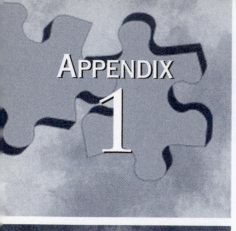

APPENDIX 1

PERSONAL PROFILE

This appendix is provided for each student to record his or her scores from various self-assessment exercises. In several of the text chapters you will be instructed to complete various personal assessments. For the most part, these assessments were on-line and accessed via the access card packaged with the text.

Individually, these assessments have marginal value. Collectively, however, they will provide a valuable profile. The profile becomes an information source that identifies preferences, strengths, and weaknesses. You will be well served to maximize your strengths while minimizing your weaknesses.

Chapter 2
PERSONALITY, ABILITY, AND LEARNING

EXERCISE I.A.2:   WHAT'S MY JUNGIAN 16
PERSONALITY TYPE?   Result _____

The Jungian 16 Type Indicator (J-16) is a popular personality framework. It classifies people as extroverted or introverted (E or I), sensing or intuitive (S or N), thinking or feeling (T or F), and perceiving or judging (P or J). These classifications can then be combined into sixteen personality types. What value can the J-16 have for you? It can help you understand your personality—your strengths and your weaknesses. It can help you in making successful career decisions when you try to find jobs that align well with your strengths and avoid those jobs that are a poor fit.

EXERCISE I.A.3:   AM I A TYPE A?   Score _____

This instrument measures the degree to which you're competitive and rushed for time. The Type A personality describes someone who is aggressively involved in a chronic, incessant struggle to achieve more and more in less and less time. More specifically, Type As are always moving, walking, and eating rapidly. They feel impatient with the pace of most events. They strive to do two or more things at once, they do not cope well with leisure time, and they are obsessed with numbers. They measure their success in terms of how many or how much of everything they acquire. Type Bs are the exact opposites of Type As.

Exercise I.A.4: How Well Do I Handle Ambiguity?   Score _____

One who has intolerance for ambiguity tends to perceive situations as threatening rather than promising, and prefers more structured situations. In contrast, people who score high on tolerance for ambiguity respond better to change and tend to be more creative. A high tolerance for ambiguity makes you more likely to be able to function in a work world where there is less certainty about expectations, performance standards, and career progress.

Exercise I.A.5: How Creative Am I?   Score _____

Creativity is the ability to combine ideas in a unique way or to make unusual associations between ideas. Creative people develop novel approaches to doing their work or unique solutions to problems. For managers, creativity is useful in decision making. It helps them to see options that others might not. All jobs, of course, don't require high creativity.

Pathways to Learning (from textbook)

Scoring

Bodily-Kinesthetic	(total for questions 1–6)	_____
Visual-Spatial	(total for questions 7–12)	_____
Verbal-Linguistic	(total for questions 13–18)	_____
Logical-Mathematical	(total for questions 19–24)	_____

What is the best style for you to learn? What study techniques can you use?

_____

_____

_____

Chapter 3
Perception

Exercise II.C.4: How Well Do I Manage Impressions?

Score _____, _____, _____, _____, _____.

This instrument assesses one's management of image. As the analysis notes, most of us are concerned with the image that others have of us, their perception. Impression management is a process by which people attempt to control the impressions others form of them. The instrument itself assesses five impression management strategies from self-promotion to ingratiation to exemplification to intimidation to supplication. It is important for people to know their style and how it might fit into an organizational culture.

Chapter 4
Values and Attitudes

Exercise I.B.1: What Do I Value?

Record your top four terminal values:

1. _____
2. _____
3. _____
4. _____

Record your top four instrumental values:

1. _____
2. _____
3. _____
4. _____

Values are basic convictions of what is right, good, or desirable. Your values reflect what you think is important. There are, of course, no right or wrong values. This self-assessment merely gives you some directive insights into your value structure.

Chapter 5
MOTIVATION

EXERCISE I.C.1:   WHAT MOTIVATES ME?

    Growth Needs Score   _____
    Relatedness Needs Score _____
    Existence Needs Score   _____

This instrument taps the three needs of growth, relatedness, and existence. It is based on the ERG theory. If you consider all four items within a need category to be extremely important, you would obtain the maximum total of 20 points. College students typically rate growth needs highest. However, you may currently have little income and consider existence needs as most important. Note that a low score may imply that a need is unimportant to you or that it is substantially satisfied. The implication is that everyone has these needs, so a low score is usually taken to mean that this need is substantially satisfied.

EXERCISE I.C.4:   WHAT'S MY VIEW ON THE
                          NATURE OF PEOPLE?   Score _____

This instrument was designed to tap your view of human nature. It is based on Douglas McGregor's Theory X and Theory Y. McGregor proposed that individuals tend to view others in either negative or positive terms. The negative stereotype, which he called *Theory X*, sees human beings as primarily lazy and disinterested in working. In contrast, *Theory Y* views them as responsible and hard working under the right conditions. Your score can give you insights into your inherent view of people. However, you are not locked into a particular management or leadership style based on your view of human nature. Your views reflect a tendency, not a mandate.

    Other questions:

1. What are your needs?

2. What is your most important objective in life?

3. What event has motivated you to do your best or work the hardest?

Chapter 6
STRESS

EXERCISE III.C.3: AM I BURNED OUT? Score _____

Burnout is exhibiting chronic and long-term stress. This instrument is designed to provide insights into whether you're suffering from burnout.

EXERCISE III.C.2: HOW STRESSFUL IS MY LIFE? Score _____

Stress and change go hand in hand. Stress is part of our daily lives and it will probably always be. It is up to us to try and learn how to manage stress. This instrument measures the impact of life changes on people and how stress is created. Several of the questions relating to retirement may not appear applicable; however, the rest of the questions offer insights and can easily apply.

Chapter 7
TURNING PEOPLE INTO TEAM PLAYERS

EXERCISE II.B.6: HOW GOOD AM I AT BUILDING AND LEADING TEAMS? Score _____

The authors of this instrument propose that it assesses team development behaviors in five areas: diagnosing team development, managing the forming stage, managing the conforming stage, managing the storming stage, and managing the performing stage. Based on a norm group of 500 business students, your score will help you determine in which quartile you fit.

Chapter 9
LEADERSHIP

EXERCISE II.B.1: WHAT'S MY LEADERSHIP STYLE? PEOPLE SCORE _____
Task Score _____

This leadership instrument taps the degree to which you are task or people oriented. Task orientation is concerned with getting the job done, while people orientation focuses on group interactions and the needs of individual members. The best leaders balance their task orientation and people orientation to various situations. A high score on both would indicate this balance. If you are too task oriented, you tend to be autocratic. You get the job done, but at a high emotional cost. If you are too people oriented, your leadership may be overly laissez-faire.

EXERCISE II.B.4: DO OTHERS SEE ME AS TRUSTWORTHY? Score _____

Effective leaders have bult a trusting relationship between themselves and those they see to lead. This instrument provides you with insights into how trustworthy others are likely to perceive you. The higher the score, the more you are perceived as a person who can be trusted. If you want to build tgrust with others, look at the behaviors this instruemtn taps then think about what you can do to improve your score on each.

Chapter 11
COMMUNICATION

WHAT'S MY FACE-TO-FACE COMMUNICATION STYLE?   Score _____

Dominant	_____	Dramatic	_____
Contentious	_____	Animated	_____
Impressive	_____	Relaxed	_____
Attentive	_____	Open	_____
Friendly	_____		

The higher your score for any dimension, the more that dimension characterizes your communication style. When you review your results, consider to what degree your scores aid or hinder your communication effectiveness. High scores for being attentive and open would almost always be positive qualities. A high score for contentious, on the other hand, could be a negative in many situations.

EXERCISE II.A.2: **HOW GOOD ARE MY LISTENING SKILLS?**   Score _____

Effective communicators have developed good listening skills. This instrument is designed to provide you with some insights into your listening skills.

Chapter 12
CONFLICT

EXERCISE II.C.5: **WHAT'S MY PREFERRED CONFLICT HANDLING STYLE?**

Score:
Competing	_____
Collaborating	_____
Avoiding	_____
Accommodating	_____
Compromising	_____

Research has identified five conflict-handling styles:

- **Competing.** A desire to satisfy one's interests, regardless of the impact on the other party to the conflict.

- **Collaborating.** The parties to a conflict each desire to satisfy fully the concerns of all parties.

- **Avoiding.** The desire to withdraw from or suppress the conflict.

- **Accommodating.** Willingness of one party in a conflict to place the opponent's interest above his or her own.

- **Compromising.** Each party to a conflict is willing to give up something.

Ideally, we should adjust our conflict-handling style to the situation. For instance, avoidance works well when a conflict is trivial, when emotions are running high and time is needed to cool them down, or when the potential disruption from a more assertive action outweighs the benefits of a resolution. In contrast, competing works well when you need a quick resolution of important issues, where unpopular actions must be taken, or when commitment by others to your solution is not critical. However, the evidence indicates that we all have a preferred style for handling conflicts. In tough situations, this is the style on which we tend to rely. Your score on this instrument provides you with insight into this preferred style. Use this information to work against your natural tendencies when the situation requires a different style.

Chapter 14
TYPICAL STRUCTURES

EXERCISE I.E.4: **AM I LIKELY TO BECOME AN ENTREPRENEUR?**

This instrument assesses proactive personality. That is, it identifies differences among people to the extent in which they take action to influence their environment. Proactive personalities identify opportunities and act on them. They show initiative, take action, and persevere until they bring about change. Research finds that the proactive personality is positively associated with entrepreneurial intentions.

A number of factors have been found to be associated with becoming an entrepreneur. For instance, entrepreneurship tends to flourish in communities that encourage risk taking and minimize the penalties attached to failures.

EXERCISE III.A.1: **WHAT TYPE OF ORGANIZATION STRUCTURE DO I PREFER?**

This instrument measures your preference for working in a mechanistic or organic organization structure. Because the trend in recent years has been toward more organic designs, you're more likely to find a good organizational match if you score low on this instrument. However, there are few, if any, pure organic structures. Therefore, very low scores may also mean that you're likely to be frustrated by what you perceive as overly rigid structures, rules, regulations, and boss-centered leadership. In general, however, low scores indicate that you prefer small, innovative, flexible, team-oriented organizations. High scores indicate a preference for stable, rule-oriented, more bureaucratic organizations.

EXERCISE IV.F.2: **DO I LIKE BUREAUCRACY?**

This instrument measures your preference for working in a bureaucratic organization. Bureaucratic organizations are characterized by a rigid, hierarchical structure with a high concentration of power at the top of the hierarchy. Work in bureaucratic organiztions tends to be highly formalized and routine, and there is a strong adherence to rules and policies. Bureaucratic organizations have therir advantages and disadvantages. Advantages include the abilty to perfrom tasks efficiently ans with less reliance on individuals at lower levels of the organization. Disadvantages include a sometimes obsessive reliance on rules and policies, which greatly limits flexibility.

Chapter 17
HUMAN RESOURCES

EXERCISE I.C.8: **WHAT'S MY JOB'S MOTIVATING POTENTIAL?**

Skill Variety   _____

Task Identity   _____

Task Significance	_____
Autonomy	_____
Feedback	_____
MPS	_____

This questionnaire allows you to calculate your Motivating Potential Score (MPS) from the Job Characteristics Model. The MPS represents a summary score indicating how motivating the job is that you have described.

Chapter 18
ORGANIZATIONAL CULTURE

EXERCISE III.B.1: WHAT'S THE RIGHT ORGANIZATIONAL CULTURE FOR ME?   Score _____

This instrument taps the seven primary dimensions of an organization's culture. They are innovation and risk taking, attention to detail, outcome orientation, people orientation, team orientation, aggressiveness, and stability. Organizational cultures differ and so do individuals. The better you can match your personal preferences to an organization's culture, the more likely you will be able to find satisfaction in your work. You will be less likely to leave, and there is a greater probability that you will receive good performance evaluations.

Chapter 21
POWER AND POLITICS

EXERCISE II.C.1: HOW POWER ORIENTED AM I?   Score _____

This instrument is designed to compute your Machiavellianism (Mach) score. In the sixteenth century, Machiavelli wrote on how to gain and manipulate power. An individual with a high Mach score is pragmatic, maintains emotional distance, and believes that ends justify means. High Machs are more likely to manipulate more, win more, and be persuaded less and persuade others more than are low Machs. High Machs are also more likely to shade the truth or act unethically in ambiguous situations where the outcome is important to them.

EXERCISE II.C.2: WHAT'S MY PREFERRED TYPE OF POWER?   Score _____

Reward	_____
Coercive	_____
Legitimate	_____
Expert	_____
Referent	_____

Managerial positions come with legitimate, reward, and coercive powers. However, you do not have to be a manager to have power. If you are not in a position of formal authority, you can still be a powerful person in your organization if you focus on developing your expert and referent power bases.

Politics are a natural part of organizational life. This instrument was designed to give you some insights into how politically oriented you are. Those who fail to acknowledge political behavior ignore the reality that organizations are political systems. Researchers have identified certain personality traits, needs, and other factors that are likely to be related to political behavior. In terms of traits, we find that individuals who are high self-monitors, possess an internal locus of control, and have a high need for power, are more likely to engage in political behavior.

Chapter 22
EFFORT AND ETHICS

EXERCISE I.D.2:   HOW DO MY ETHICS RATE?

Record your scores against the norms provided with the instrument.

	NORM SCORE	YOUR SCORE		NORM SCORE	YOUR SCORE		NORM SCORE	YOUR SCORE
1.	3.09	____	6.	2.88	____	11.	1.58	____
2.	1.88	____	7.	3.62	____	12.	2.31	____
3.	2.54	____	8.	2.79	____	13.	3.36	____
4.	3.41	____	9.	3.44	____	14.	3.79	____
5.	3.88	____	10.	1.33	____	15.	3.38	____

Do you tend to be more or less ethical than the student norms presented? Where do you differ? Large discrepancies might be a warning that others do not hold the same ethical values you do hold. Comment on any large discrepancies below:

_____

_____

_____

_____

_____

_____

_____

Chapter 23
Succeeding in an Organization

Personal Profile Assignment

In this class you have learned a great deal about yourself and how you work with others. Drawing upon the self-assessment tests in the textbook and your own life experience, address the questions below in a minimum five-page paper (double-spaced, one-inch margins, twelve-point type).

1. **How do you see yourself?** Chapter 1-6 explored discovery of yourself as an individual and leader. Describe your personality, abilities, learning style, handling of stress and workplace preferences. Use concrete examples wherever possible.

2. **How do other people see you?** Discuss this with someone in your group or a friend. Think of how you might characterize a person that you know (e.g., very smart but a little obnoxious). In the same way, how do people characterize you? Do you give people the right impression or the wrong impression? How can you improve the impression that people have of you?

3. **How do you work with others?** What is your team role? What are your strengths and weaknesses in group situations? Are you better working in a team or by yourself? Do you have good communication skills? What communication mistakes are you prone to make? What conflict-handling techniques do you use? Give concrete examples wherever possible.

4. **What are your goals in life?** Where do you want to be in ten years? What motivates you? What do you value? If you didn't have to worry about money, what would you do?

5. **What is one area for improvement?** Based on the personal profile that you have constructed, what is one area that you could improve on in the next twelve months? How would improving in this area help you meet your goals?

Please attach the results from your self-assessment tests (Appendix 1) to your paper.

WORKBOOK

C.A.P.S. STUDY: A SUMMARY OF PERSONAL STYLES

CAPS Study—A Summary of Personal Styles, adapted from Personal Styles and Effective Performance by David W. Merrill, Ph.D., and Roger H. Reid, M.A. (Radnor, PA: Chilton Book Company, 1981). Reproduced with permission in the format Textbook via the Copyright Clearance Center.

C.A.P.S. Personal Style Inventory

The following instrument is designed to assess your tendency to behave in a manner consistent with one of the four quadrants in the C.A.P.S. Model. As in any model, such as the C.A.P.S. Model, there may be a tendency to regard them as indicating there is one "better" way to behave. This tendency must be avoided if the model is to be useful. It is designed to simply illuminate different styles of behavior, not to imply that one is superior to others. Please keep this thought in mind as you assess yourself by the results of this instrument.

The following items are arranged in pairs (a and b), and each member of the pair represents a preference you may or may not hold. Rate your preference for each item by giving it a score of 0 to 5 (0 meaning that you really feel negative about it or feel strongly about the other member of the pair, 5 meaning that you strongly prefer it and do not prefer the other member of the pair). The scores for a and b MUST ADD UP TO 5 (0 and 5, 1 and 4, 2 and 3, etc.). Do not use fractions such as 2 1/2.

I Prefer:

1a. _____ making decisions after finding out what others think.

1b. _____ making decisions without consulting others.

2a. _____ being called imaginative or intuitive.

2b. _____ being called factual or accurate.

3a. _____ making decisions about people in organizations based on available data and systematic analysis of situations.

3b. _____ making decisions about people in organizations based on empathy, feelings, and understanding of their needs and values.

4a. _____ allowing commitments to occur if others want to make them.

4b. _____ pushing for definite commitments and ensuring that they are made.

5a. _____ quiet, thoughtful time alone.

5b. _____ active, energetic time with people.

6a. _____ using methods I know well that are effective to get the job done.

6b. _____ trying to think of new methods of doing difficult tasks.

7a. _____ drawing conclusions based on unemotional logic and careful step-by-step analysis.

7b. _____ drawing conclusions based on what I feel and believe about people and life from past experiences.

8a. _____ avoiding making deadlines.

8b. _____ setting a schedule and sticking to it.

9a. _____ alking a while and then thinking to myself about the subject.

9b. _____ talking freely for an extended period and thinking to myself at a later time.

10a. _____ thinking about possibilities.

10b. _____ dealing with actualities.

11a. _____ being thought of as an exciting person.

11b. _____ being thought of as a feeling person.

12a. _____ considering every possible angle for a long time before making a decision.

12b. _____ getting the information I need, considering it for a while, and then making a fairly quick, firm decision.

13a. _____ inner thoughts and feelings others cannot see.

13b. _____ activities and occurrences in which others join.

14a. _____ the abstract or theoretical.

14b. _____ the concrete or real.

15a. _____ helping others explore their feelings.

15b. _____ helping others make logical decisions.

16a. _____ change and keeping options open.

16b. _____ predictability and knowing in advance.

17a. _____ communicating little of my inner thinking and feelings.

17b. _____ communicating freely my inner thoughts and feelings.

18a. _____ possible views of the whole situation.

18b. _____ factual data about each part of a situation.

19a. _____ using common sense and conviction to make decisions.

19b. _____ using data, analysis, and reason to make decisions.

20a. _____ planning ahead based on projections.

20b. _____ planning as necessities arise, just before carrying out plans.

21a. _____ meeting new people.

21b. _____ being alone or with one person I know well.

22a. _____ ideas.

22b. _____ facts.

23a. _____ convictions and beliefs.

23b. _____ verifiable conclusions.

24a. _____ keeping appointments and notes about commitments in note books or in appointment books as much as possible.

24b. _____ using notebooks and appointment books as minimally as possible.

25a. _____ discussing a new, unconsidered issue at length in a group.

25b. _____ puzzling out issues in my mind, then sharing the results with another person when I am sure of my answer.

26a. _____ carrying out plans quickly and immediately.

26b. _____ designing plans and structures without necessarily carrying them out.

27a. _____ lively people.

27b. _____ feeling people.

28a. _____ being free to do things on the spur of the moment.

28b. _____ knowing well in advance what I am going to do or what I am expected to do.

29a. _____ being the center of attention.

29b. _____ being reserved and in the background.

30a. _____ imagining the nonexistent.

30b. _____ examining details of the actual.

31a. _____ experiencing emotional situations, discussions, movies, music, and so on.

31b. _____ participating in lively events.

32a. _____ starting meetings punctually at a prearranged time.

32b. _____ starting meetings when all are comfortable or ready.

33a. _____ speaking loudly so that everyone is certain to hear me.

33b. _____ speaking in a low voice so that I don't stand out.

34a. _____ taking over the leadership of a group when it is poorly organized.

34b. _____ waiting for someone else to lead the group.

35a. _____ being patient when solving people problems or conflicts.

35b. _____ quick solutions to problems or conflicts between people.

36a. _____ that my decisions be carried out without being questioned.

36b. _____ that people question my decisions before acting.

37a. _____ to stay distant from people when I first meet them.

37b. _____ to quickly get to know people very well.

38a. _____ letting people work out the details of plans and goals I give them.

38b. _____ to work with people until plans are very carefully laid out.

39a. _____ that I do most of the talking when working with people on problems.

39b. _____ to let people talk when we are working together.

40a. _____ to use my authority to achieve goals.

40b. _____ to rarely use my authority to get things done with people.

Name: _____

C.A.P.S. PERSONAL STYLE INVENTORY SCORING SHEET

Instructions: Transfer your scores for each item of the pair to the appropriate blanks. Be careful to check the a and b letters to be sure you are recording the scores in the right blank spaces. Then total the scores for each dimension in the spaces at the bottom of each column.

C	A	P	S
4b. _____	2b. _____	1b. _____	1a. _____
6a. _____	3a. _____	2a. _____	3b. _____
12b. _____	5a. _____	5b. _____	4a. _____
16b. _____	7a. _____	6b. _____	7b. _____
18a. _____	8b. _____	8a. _____	9b. _____
19a. _____	9a. _____	10a. _____	11b. _____
21b. _____	10b. _____	11a. _____	15a. _____
23a. _____	12a. _____	13b. _____	21a. _____
24b. _____	13a. _____	14a. _____	27b. _____
26a. _____	14b. _____	16a. _____	29b. _____
28b. _____	15b. _____	17b. _____	31a. _____
32a. _____	17a. _____	20b. _____	32b. _____
33a. _____	18b. _____	22a. _____	33b. _____
34a. _____	19b. _____	25a. _____	34b. _____
35b. _____	20a. _____	26b. _____	35a. _____
36a. _____	22b. _____	27a. _____	36b. _____
37a. _____	23b. _____	28a. _____	37b. _____
38a. _____	24a. _____	29a. _____	38b. _____
39a. _____	25b. _____	30a. _____	39b. _____
40a. _____	30b. _____	31b. _____	40b. _____
TOTAL _____	TOTAL _____	TOTAL _____	TOTAL _____

Note: As a check of your math, the sum of the four TOTAL numbers above should be 200.

THE C.A.P.S. MODEL

The thrust of this exercise is to expand on the process described earlier. The exercise provides a way of holding the "why" behind what people do. To a productive manager or supervisor, however, the why of people's action is not as important as the "what." It is far easier to work with people at the level of action than it is at the level of interpersonal motivations. In other words, what we are concerned about as managers is changing what people do, how they behave on the job—not why they do it. To do this we must interact with people more effectively, and to do that, we must have greater insight into where they are "coming from."

The C.A.P.S. (or CAPS) model is designed to help give some insight into this element of human behavior. Many models seek to simplify and categorize human behavior in a meaningful way. Entire "catalogs" have been created with this goal in mind. An entirely new jargon has been created in an effort to describe the various "styles" people exhibit. Unfortunately, many of these models have served to merely confuse that which they sought to clarify.

For a model to be useful, it must be specific enough to be meaningful yet broad enough to be widely applicable. It should also address the issue of behavior styles in a language that everyone can easily understand. The C.A.P.S. model meets these requirements.

The Quadrants of the C.A.P.S. Model

The C.A.P.S. model divides observable behavior into four basic and easily recognizable categories. These categories, or a combination of any two, include nearly everyone and can be readily observed in normal, day-to-day social interplay. The quadrants describe typical "modes of operation" that we all will exhibit on the job and at home.

While quite obviously people can exhibit an infinite range of behaviors, much of the time they will fall into one of the C.A.P.S. modes. This will be referred to as their high or primary behavior. Another way of looking at it is that while people may, in any given instance, act in any manner, they will still find it easier to act in certain predictable ways. These might be referred to as *comfort zones*. That is, while they are capable of doing things differently than they normally do, it is much easier and "safer" for them to do things in a cheerful way. This is particularly true in those situations that people may feel are threatening, unusual, unique, or stressful. And, of course, these are precisely the situations that a manager must handle carefully and wisely, and the ones that usually aren't handled that way. Thus, we see even greater importance being attached to this model.

The four modes of operation, the C.A.P.S. quadrants, are

Controllers   Analyzers   Promoters   Supporters

Let's examine each of these modes, with its distinguishing characteristics.

Controllers

Controllers are often seen as "take-charge" people. They are often quite demanding and insistent that things be done "their way." They are usually outgoing socially and typically are not afraid to speak out or give their opinion on an issue, often unsolicited. They demand fast action from people who work for and with them, often without being willing or able to give real guidance about how they expect those people to accomplish what is demanded of them. They are not afraid to use authority to get the job done. They will sometimes make quick, shortsighted decisions and statements, and they do not apologize easily. They will occasionally overlook the "human elements" in management in pursuit of what they consider important. RESULTS: They are real doers and highly value getting the job done. Their traits magnify under pressure, and they can get intense at times. They greatly fear having their control usurped by those around them and can be territorial. They don't take criticism gracefully and absolutely detest being pinned down to providing detailed plans of action.

Analyzers

The analyzers are the real "thinkers" of the organization. They are logical, rational, linear-sequential types of people. They carefully weigh and consider numerous options before making a decision. While this may sometimes be a strength, it can, if carried too far, also be seen as their greatest weakness. Analyzers are usually socially reserved and tend to be "observers" at social events and group meetings rather than participants. They rarely voice their opinion on an issue unless they are absolutely certain of their position. They tend to be organized, accurate, and careful of details. They make great planners and forecasters, but many times fail at the task of execution. They highly value concrete plans, goals, objectives, benchmarks, milestones, deadlines, schedules, and so on, and they demand that proposals be well thought out and specific. They fear quick decisions and proceeding with what they consider to be insufficient information. As a result, they are often slow to act and miss many opportunities because of it. Analyzers can be difficult to be with because they will often appear to be scrutinizing and assessing you rather than listening to what you have to say.

Promoters

Promoters are usually the "cheerleaders" of organizations. They are enthusiastic, high-energy people who approach tasks with spirit. They tend to look at the "big picture" and as a result can be sloppy with details and follow-up. They are oriented toward the future, with what comes next, and because of this, often leave tasks unfinished. They are usually quite creative (sometimes to a fault), and tend to make elaborate, often unworkable, plans. They will often have several projects going on at the same time, some quite successful and others disastrous. They are impatient and will occasionally make great intuitive leaps forward. They can be overly vocal and are, as a rule, outgoing and personable. They are movers who highly value continuous action. They have a terrible fear of boredom and detest back-tracking.

Supporters

Supporters are the "people-people" of organizations. They are seen as the "really nice" people whom everyone likes and of whom everyone speaks well. They are empathetic and considerate of other people's feelings. They can be quite emotional, even excitable, and feel things deeply. It is easy to wound these people with a thoughtless comment though they would never let you know. Supporters are warm and easy to be with and are usually good listeners. They are communicators who can receive and send messages with good effect. Supporters will sometimes be overly honest and open and, as a result, can sometimes be embarrassed easily. Many times supporters will be the real leaders of groups, though at first it may not be obvious. They highly value personal relationships and close contact with other people. They fear being alone and are particularly subject to peer pressure. They are also afraid of being taken advantage of, many times with good reason.

The Limitations of C.A.P.S.

While the C.A.P.S. model can be a useful paradigm in creating more understanding, and as a result creating more effective interaction, the following considerations must be kept in mind:

1. People will exhibit behaviors that fall into any one of the four quadrants of the C.A.P.S. model at any time. No one will act a given way all of the time.

2. People will exhibit behaviors that are consistent with one or two of the quadrants a majority of the time. This is particularly true in times of stress, perceived threat, unusual pressure, or unique situations.

3. There is no "right" or "best" style to be an effective manager. A manager can be effective operating predominantly from any quadrant.

4. Effectiveness is more a product of flexibility and appropriateness. That is, for a manager to be optimally effective, he or she must be able to operate comfortably from any style regardless of what is personally most comfortable. The manager must be able to alter personal behavior depending on the circumstances.

5. In order to fully use the model, a manager must:

   - recognize and be aware of his or her own personal predominant style,
   - be able to quickly recognize what style the person with whom he or she is interacting is most comfortable with or is operating from at the time,
   - be willing and able to adjust his or her own style to one that will make the other person the most comfortable and produce the best results, and
   - be prepared to shift types at any given moment.

In terms of more effective interaction, a person will generally respond to someone who is using an approach that corresponds to the style of behavior with which the person is comfortable.

Ultimately, what is necessary is that a person must be able to "speak" controller, analyzer, promoter, and supporter. That is, an effective communicator will be able to transmit thoughts, ideas, requests, corrections, and questions in a manner that takes into account what the other person feels is important.

For example, to approach a strong analyzer with an idea or a plan that needs to be implemented, it is essential that it be well thought out, detailed, and specific. Approaching a promoter with the same plan might entail less details but might demand that it be presented with a great deal of enthusiasm and energy. Focusing on the results that the plan will produce (with less emphasis on exactly how it's going to work) might be more effective with a controller. In approaching a supporter, it would be a good idea if a lot of thought and attention were given to the impact the plan might have on the people involved in it.

In terms of style, it might be possible to "sell" a plan to a promoter or a controller, but any hint of "hype" should be avoided with an analyzer or a supporter.

In other words, it is more effective to adjust one's own style to suit the person with whom one is interacting, rather than either ignoring what suits the person or trying to force the person to operate in a style unsuited to him or her. While this might demand a great deal more attention, insight, and versatility, it also produces more communication and more effective inter-action, not to mention a more satisfying experience.

The C.A.P.S. Instrument

This training exercise is designed to place each participant of the training in the C.A.P.S. quadrant quantitatively. It is a forced-choice instrument that makes a person choose between a range of preferred behaviors. The instrument has been proven to be reliable and useful and can provide each participant with a great deal of insight into oneself and the other people in the training and/or workplace.

You may be divided into teams for a course project based on scores from this exercise. The results can be used to help you throughout the semester in understanding the interaction among team members and assist you in achieving better performance. The profile is designed to make each participant of the training aware of other team members' profiles and can also serve as an indicator of the balance of the team as a whole.

Obviously, it is a good idea if all members of the team are able to operate with equal ease in any of the four quadrants. Failing that, the team should be well balanced among the different styles. A well-balanced team will be able to approach a problem or a situation with a wide variety of perspectives and will be able to communicate with a great many different people. One goal of this training is to create just such a situation—a manager and a team that can operate from a variety of contexts and thus have available to them a greater number of options in dealing with people and achieving the results required.

TIPS FOR BETTER PRESENTATIONS

Be Prepared

1. **Know Your Audience.** By knowing your audience, one can better focus the material being presented to be interesting and applicable to the audience.

2. **Do Your Research.** The first step in giving a presentation is developing a talk that is well researched and one is able to support all the points and positions with illustrations and examples.

3. **Seek to be Understood.** Design your presentation to be understood by your audience.

4. **Dress for Success.** Make sure the dress is appropriate for the audience and the type of presentation being given.

5. **Rehearse! Practice the Presentation.** Give your presentation to a friend or family member and ask them to critique the material and presentation.

Prior to the Presentation

6. **Have an Opening, Body, and Conclusion.** Your presentation needs to have a beginning, a middle, and an ending.

7. **Open with a Bang.** A startling question, illustration, story, or challenging statement will grab the audience's attention.

8. **Use Visual Aids.** Visual aids can be used to dramatize your point(s) and help the audience to remember the message. When using a chalkboard or flipchart, be sure to face the audience when talking and not the visual aid.

9. **Check Your Equipment.** Make sure that the microphone, overhead, computer, and projectors are working properly.

10. **Attitude Is Important.** It is your attitude toward the audience that will determine their attitude toward you. While you may know the material, this is your audience's first time. You only have one opportunity to make that first impression. Attitude is everything.

11. **Rehearse.** This is so important it bears repeating. An alternative to rehearsing your presentation to a friend or family member as noted above, one could also video tape themselves and watch the results with a critical eye.

During the Presentation

12. **Show Passion, Commitment, Conviction, and Enthusiasm.** The greater the level of preparedness, the greater the ability one has to capture the audience's attention.

13. **Make Eye Contact.** While making your presentation, make direct eye contact with individuals throughout the entire audience. Don't stare but rather look directly at one person and then move to another moving from side to side and front to back.

14. **Be Eloquent and Speak with Authority.** The greater the level of preparation the greater the ability to speak with authority in making your point of view known.

15. **Involve Your Audience in Your Presentation.** Ask questions. Ask for a show of hands on a particular point. Create some role-playing situations. Involving the audience will create greater interest and learning opportunities

16. **Use Humor.** Audiences want, actually need, the opportunity to relax and reflect a bit in a presentation. Humor will work.

17. **Use Facial Expression.** People watch a speaker's face throughout the presentation and will believe what they see more than what they hear. Make certain the facial expression match the message you want to deliver.

18. **Use Body Language.** Body language that looks unnatural can ruin the presentation. It is difficult to use body language and make it look natural and spontaneous. Match your gestures with your words.

19. **Use Your Voice.** Speak clearly articulating your words with enough volume to be heard and with the right inflections to reflect your intent.

20. **Use Short Words.** Effective presentations must be immediately understandable to the ear. The most effective and memorable words to listeners are short words that are familiar with the audience.

21. **Use Short Sentences.** Long, complex sentences are difficult to follow and almost impossible to remember. It is best to use a mixture of short and medium length sentences to add some variety and still allow the audience to follow the presentation.

22. **Use Notes Very Sparingly.** Too much time spent reading notes reflects on the lack of preparedness, conviction, and excitement for the topic being presented.

23. **Watch the Time.** Don't go too fast to try and get more in. Don't go so slow that the audience will be bored. Know when to stop talking.

24. **Ask for Questions.** At the end of the presentation, seek feedback through a brief question-and-answer session.

25. **Say Thank You.** Your audience has given you a very precious gift, the gift of time. Thank your audience for giving you this gift and for listening.

FINAL NOTE

The Rule to Tell 'em seems to work and it does make good sense. It goes:
First Tell 'em what you are going to tell 'em,
Tell it to them, and then
Tell 'em what you told them.

GUIDELINES ON GROUP MEETINGS

- Distribute the agenda and background material in advance.
- Clarify the objective.
- Compose the group appropriately.
- Encourage the expression of minority viewpoints.
- Separate idea generation from evaluation.
- Make assumptions explicit.
- Legitimize questioning attitudes.
- Control irrelevant discussions.
- Test the level of support for a decision.
- Evaluate the groups' effectiveness.
- End on a positive note and assign responsibilities.
- Summarize main decisions or accomplishments of the meeting.
- Set next meeting date and restate agenda or goal for next meeting.
- Follow up with written summary, if appropriate, along with next meeting information.

TEAM ROSTER

Assigned Team Number _____

Team Leader _____ Phone _____

Team Member Names	Phone #	E-mail
_____	_____	_____
_____	_____	_____
_____	_____	_____
_____	_____	_____
_____	_____	_____
_____	_____	_____

Group Project/Presentation Title: _____

Group Project/Presentation Date: _____

Provide your instructor with one completed copy.

GROUP PROJECT

Objectives

1. To convey information to the class on a specific aspect of organizational behavior in the world of work that is not directly addressed in depth in the regular class presentation.
2. To participate in a group working toward a common goal, observe the workings of individuals in the group, and experience the group dynamics involved.
3. To learn about one's own reactions, responses, and feelings (interpersonal) resulting from the group interaction.

General Flow of Events and Timetable

1. [_____] Explain project; groups will consider general subject of preparation and areas of interest and be prepared (at a later date) to select, and rank in order, three topics from the attached list.
2. [_____] Groups submit proposed presentation topic choices. Selection should be narrowed to three topics. Favorable rationale will determine the selection. No two groups can have presentations on the same topic. (Enclosure 1)
3. [_____] Group leader will submit the objectives and basic plan for presentation (based on group's planning). (Enclosure 2)
4. An outline with details of presentation and with specific team participants' names is to be handed in no later than **one session** prior to group's presentation. (Enclosure 3)
5. Presentation Schedule—[Dates assigned]:

    [_____] Team Number 1
    [_____] Team Number 2
    [_____] Team Number 3
    [_____] Team Number 4
    [_____] Team Number 5
    [_____] Team Number 6
    [_____] Team Number 7
    [_____] Team Number 8
    [_____] Team Number 9
    [_____] Team Number 10

6. [_____] Project Wrap-up. During the course and the exercise, the material for this report is being developed. Complete Forms A and B with your team following your presentation and then *write a three- to five-page paper reflecting on your group experience*. Attach Form C, evaluation of individual effort, to Forms A and B upon submission.
7. [_____] Submit individual project report within one week following your team's presentation.

Participation

All members of the group are expected to contribute and participate in the presentation. At the first meeting, the members should discuss and mutually agree (make a contract with one another) on "What are the expectations of the other members of my group in respect to meeting outside class, doing library research, planning, and executing my part of the final presentation?" This is also a time to consider the role of the leader. The grades assigned for the presentation will be the same for *all* members *except* in those cases of nonparticipation that have been brought to the attention of the instructor by the group. The group leader, as part of his or her report, will provide a schedule of the meetings held and the attendance record of each group member.

Group Project Proposal

The group project proposal will be submitted on the form (Enclosure 1) included in this packet.

Presentation

Your presentation may not be less than _____ minutes or more than _____ minutes and should allow for questions either during or after the presentation. The format of your presentation is up to you, except as noted under evaluation. Timing is generally five to six minutes per team member (i.e., twenty-five to thirty minutes for a five-person team).

Evaluation of the Presentation

Your presentation will be evaluated using the following questions:

1. Did your group present information of interest and usability to the class?
2. Was the presentation the result of the closely coordinated work of the group? Did all members of the group participate?
3. Did the remainder of the class become involved in the presentation through questions, comments, and participation?
4. Did the presentation inform the class on a specific aspect of human relations in the work world that is *not* directly addressed in depth or duplicated in the regular class lectures/presentation/textbook?
5. Did the presentation stay within the time allotted?

An evaluation form for the presentation can be found on pages 357, 359, and 361.

Peer Evaluation

Each of the other groups will be asked to evaluate each presentation (see presentation analysis sheet), with the group leader being responsible for coordinating a single group evaluation per presentation. The five items listed previously should be a major focus of that evaluation. A major rationale for this type of evaluation is the fact that as a supervisor, you will be asked to evaluate your employees' performance on an "objective-performance" scale, and this is training toward that goal.

You will also be asked to evaluate the individual members of your team and your team as a whole following the presentation. Forms will be provided on that day for those evaluations.

Individual Reports

Individual reports will be the subject of a separate handout during the session following the presentations (mentioned in the previous paragraph). This report on your group experience is required within one week following your team's presentation.

Notes:

GROUP PROJECT

Possible Topics for Presentations

(Not limited to this list, however!)

Working with People/Motivation
Do we expect too much of our employees?
Do we expect too little of our employees?
Is the work ethic dead?
What can be done to stimulate motivation?
Employee recognition
Money as a motivator, pay for comparable worth

Leadership/Discipline/Supervision
Positive discipline
Decentralization of authority
Power and politics
Improving the role/image of the supervisor
Is there still a need for Theory-X-type supervisors?
Are "nice guys" successful/needed/appreciated?
Supervising women
Supervising workers who are older/younger than yourself

Communications

Should the supervisor have an increased voice in management?
Body language
The need for improved communication
Effective listening and feedback techniques
Interviewing
Rumor and its effects
Polygraphs at work: A case for and against
Communications and interpersonal skills

Participation

Quality circles
How much participation is too much?

Unions

Featherbedding/marginal labor productivity
Have unions ruined the work ethic?
Have unions ruined our industrial productivity?
Is striking cost-effective for labor? Management?
Have unions surpassed their usefulness?
Labor's changing role

Management

What is the price for worker happiness? (Job satisfaction vs. productivity)
Teamwork in management
Union participation in the management decision-making process
De-unionization procedures

Is a potential strike preferable to arbitration?
How to successfully manage/lead people

Women

Women in executive positions
Are women getting preferential treatment?
Are there still barriers to women achieving executive positions?
How do women cope with executive stress/demands?
The changing role of women in the workplace

Affirmative Action

EEO and reverse discrimination
Blue/white-collar discrimination
Sexual harassment
The growing impact of workers from different cultures
ADA and its effect on business, good or bad?

General

The workplace of tomorrow—some predictions
Burnout
Conformity vs. change
Demotions and dismissals
Office politics
Should robots replace workers?
Flexible schedules
Compulsory retirement at age 65? 70?
Theft in the workplace
Why is time management important?
Groupthink
Paradigms

Performance Appraisals Systems

Firing employees tactfully
How is the "baby boom" generation affecting the labor market?
Outplacement techniques (firing, retiring, etc.)

Drug Abuse/Alcoholism

Recognition of the problem
What management should and can do about it
Drug testing in the workplace (issues and answers)

Training

On-the-job training
Training minorities
Training less educated employees
New employee orientation
Time management
Team building

Productivity

Advantages and applicability of Theory Z
Time management techniques
Fitness centers: Costs and their effects on employees and managers
Profiles of effective management

Motivation

Bring out the best in your people
Self-development—Is it important?

Enclosure 1

GROUP PROJECT PROPOSAL (ONE PROPOSAL PER GROUP)

Group Number _____   Group Leader _____

Section Number _____

List three proposed topics in priority order with rationale for the selection of each topic. Based on your rationale, the professor will grant approval to the project he or she deems most worthy and productive.

PROPOSAL #1

Topic: _____

Rationale for Selection:

PROPOSAL #2

Topic: _____

Rationale for Selection:

PROPOSAL #3

Topic: _____

Rationale for Selection:

TO BE COMPLETED BY YOUR INSTRUCTOR:

Approval for Proposal # _____

Topic Title_____ Signed _____

Enclosure 2

(Only one plan per team)

GROUP PROJECT OBJECTIVES AND BASIC PLAN FOR PRESENTATION

Group Leader _____   Group Number _____

Section Number _____

Approved Topic _____

Objectives of Presentation: What specific learning should result from your group's presentation? (This should be developed by your group.)

Proposed Method of Presentation: How will your group present this material? Provide some detail in your explanation. (Video clip description, class involvement details, etc.)

Enclosure 3

Outline of Completed Presentation (due one session prior to date of presentation)

Team Leader _____ Team Number _____

Section Number _____

Approved Topic _____

Outline: (Complete with names of each participant and points to cover.)

Presentation Analysis and Scoresheet

Team Number _____   Title of Presentation _____

Presenting members present   _____   _____
for presentation:

                 _____   _____

                 _____   _____

EVALUATION	POINTS POSSIBLE	POINTS AWARDED	COMMENTS
Introduction/Interesting Approach	10	_____	

- Stated primary subject
- Background and history
- Team members introduced

Knowledge of Subject Matter	10	_____	

- Assumptions versus facts
- Principles and opinions

Organization	30	_____	

- Creativity in presentation
- Real-world examples
- Use of visual aids
- Class involvement

Professionalism	10	_____	

- Presentation skills
- Appropriate dress

Communication Skills	20	_____	

- Presented or did they read
- Presenter presented material

Did it appear that there was equal contribution and participation by all members?	10	_____	
Summary:	10	_____	

- Conclusions, solutions
- Was this a team effort?

TOTAL SCORE	100	_____	

When completed, turn this form into your instructor.

Presentation Analysis and Scoresheet

Team Number _____ Title of Presentation _____

Team members present   _____   _____
for presentation:
                              _____   _____

                              _____   _____

EVALUATION	POINTS POSSIBLE	POINTS AWARDED	COMMENTS
Introduction/Interesting Approach	10	_____	
■ Stated primary subject ■ Background and history ■ Team members introduced			
Knowledge of Subject Matter	10	_____	
■ Assumptions versus facts ■ Principles and opinions			
Organization	30	_____	
■ Creativity in presentation ■ Real-world examples ■ Use of visual aids ■ Class involvement			
Professionalism	10	_____	
■ Presentation skills ■ Appropriate dress			
Communication Skills	20	_____	
■ Presented or did they read ■ Presenter presented material			
Did it appear that there was equal contribution and participation by all members?	10	_____	
Summary:	10	_____	
■ Conclusions, solutions ■ Was this a team effort?			
TOTAL SCORE	100	_____	

When completed, turn this form into your instructor.

Presentation Analysis and Scoresheet

Team Number _____   Title of Presentation _____

Team members present   _____   _____
for presentation:

_____   _____

_____   _____

EVALUATION	POINTS POSSIBLE	POINTS AWARDED	COMMENTS
Introduction/Interesting Approach	10	_____	
■ Stated primary subject			
■ Background and history			
■ Team members introduced			
Knowledge of Subject Matter	10	_____	
■ Assumptions versus facts			
■ Principles and opinions			
Organization	30	_____	
■ Creativity in presentation			
■ Real-world examples			
■ Use of visual aids			
■ Class involvement			
Professionalism	10	_____	
■ Presentation skills			
■ Appropriate dress			
Communication Skills	20	_____	
■ Presented or did they read			
■ Presenter presented material			
Did it appear that there was equal contribution and participation by all members?	10	_____	
Summary:	10	_____	
■ Conclusions, solutions			
■ Was this a team effort?			
TOTAL SCORE	100	_____	

When completed, turn this form into your instructor.

Individual Reaction Report

1. In a narrative form, prepare a typewritten report of at least three pages, addressing the "sense" of the group's interactions. At a minimum, your report will consist of:

   - An assessment of answers/conclusions arrived at during discussions and your comments or qualifying statements relative to each point **(Form A).**

   - The rating arrived at for your group and explanations as to the ratings arrived at, noting the differences between your ratings and the group average **(Form B).**

   - Using **Form C**, rate each group member's contribution toward the ten listed elements. **This does not need to be shared with your group.** The extent to which you reveal your ratings in detail is your business and WILL NOT affect your grade. This form is to be attached with the others, to the report.

   - An objective discussion of what you learned during this group exercise/experience and a report of how your team acted during the course of the project—and WHY you feel team members responded the way they did.

   - An in-depth evaluation of your own feelings and reactions to the others in your group: How did you handle criticism, rejection of your ideas or proposals, frustrations of inability to research exact material or communicate your ideas to others, leadership selection, or praise from others? What did you learn about yourself that will improve your effectiveness in future group situations? What did you learn about yourself that you would like to change? What are you going to do about it specifically?

2. Your report will be evaluated essentially on the scope, depth, and objectivity of your analysis and comments (especially the final two bullets above) in addition to the answers to the survey questions, on forms A, B, and C. Any comments about another group member's performance will not affect the other person's grade. **(ATTACH FORMS A, B, AND C TO THE BACK OF YOUR REPORT.)**

3. The cover sheet for the report must contain the following information:

   Section Number_____
   Team Number_____
   Individual Reaction Report
   Student's Name _____

4. Proofread the report for content, spelling, and grammatical errors before submitting. Do not put the report in any kind of folder—simply staple the cover sheet to the report in the upper-left corner. Take your time to do a good job on this report. It is one of the few written reports for this course and should reflect your true writing ability.

Form A Group Project

The group wrap-up is on _____. **Prior to the group wrap-up, complete the sections identified as** *individual* **evaluations.** The items identified as either *group* or *consensus* evaluations will be completed by the entire group on the date of the wrap-up.

Discussion:

I. Individual Evaluation

   A. In solving problems and carrying out assignments in the group planning and presentation, what three qualities in this group contributed to its success?

     1. _____

     2. _____

     3. _____

   B. What major obstacles did the group have to overcome?

     1. _____

     2. _____

     3. _____

II. Consensus Evaluation

   A. What were this group's three strongest and three weakest points?

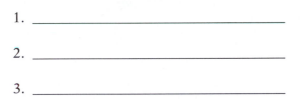

    Strong   *Weak*

    1. _____   1. _____

    2. _____   2. _____

    3. _____   3. _____

   B. What two things could be changed to make this group more effective in future assignments?

     1. _____

     2. _____

Name _____

Group Number _____   Date _____

Form B Group Project

Rate each point from 1 to 10 with 10 being the highest and 1 the lowest.

DESCRIPTION	YOUR RATING	CONSENSUS* GROUP RATING
1. Group members trust one another and are confident of one another's abilities.	_____	_____
2. Group members are ready to discuss openly their true feelings about the group.	_____	_____
3. Everybody participated equally (as opposed to one or two individuals dominating or carrying this group).	_____	_____
4. Group members valued and respected each other (as opposed to "taking advantage of," "using," or "playing games" with one another).	_____	_____
5. Sufficient time was spent on important decisions.	_____	_____
6. All members accepted and understood the goals the team set out.	_____	_____
7. The group worked constructively and hard.	_____	_____
8. All members shared the load equally.	_____	_____
9. The group's resources were fully used.	_____	_____
10. This group is organized and ready for new challenges.	_____	_____

Can be numerical average of the entire group's individual ratings or a "negotiated" value determined by the group if no consesus is achieveable.

Form C Group Project: Peer Rating Form

Name _____   Group Number _____

Rate each member of your group (including yourself) on each of the items listed below. Use a scale of 1 to 5 where 5 is the highest and 1 is the lowest. The peer rating and personal reaction paper will be confidential. Take the necessary time and be honest in all your responses to the questions.

Member's initials*   ___ ___ ___ ___ ___ ___

	A	B	C	D	E	F
Willingness to work in group environment	___	___	___	___	___	___
Reliability in completing assignments	___	___	___	___	___	___
Amount of effort put forth	___	___	___	___	___	___
Willingness to follow as well as lead	___	___	___	___	___	___
Commitment to group, no hidden agenda	___	___	___	___	___	___
Leadership provided to the group	___	___	___	___	___	___
Consideration for other group members	___	___	___	___	___	___
Ability to listen and discuss others' views	___	___	___	___	___	___
Ability to consider minority viewpoints	___	___	___	___	___	___
Good group member, would want to work with this person again	___	___	___	___	___	___
EACH MEMBER'S TOTAL SCORE	___	___	___	___	___	___

*Member's Names:

A. _____

B. _____

C. _____

D. _____

E. _____

F. _____

How Well Is Your Team Doing?

Directions: At **mid-semester,** rate the extent to which your work unit is experiencing problems in the following areas:

	No Problems	Some Problems	Lots of Problems
1. Unclear goals	1	2	3
2. Lack of commitment to goals	1	2	3
3. Confusion about assignments	1	2	3
4. Low performance (productivity)	1	2	3
5. Complaints/grievances within the team	1	2	3
6. Conflicts among team members	1	2	3
7. Hostility among team members	1	2	3
8. Apathy or lack of interest (involvement)	1	2	3
9. Lack of taking initiative	1	2	3
10. Lack of trust between leader and members	1	2	3
11. Mistrust among team members	1	2	3
12. Poor listening	1	2	3
13. Fear of dealing openly with conflicts	1	2	3
14. Members not talking together	1	2	3
15. Team dominated by one person	1	2	3
16. Decisions made without team agreement	1	2	3
17. Individuals feel their work is not recognized	1	2	3
18. People in team resist changes	1	2	3
19. Members not committed to meeting	1	2	3
20. Workload not being evenly balanced	1	2	3

Instructor/Course Evaluation
(Mid-Semester Evaluation)

Evaluation is a serious topic to professors. We are always interested in trying to improve the course and the course of instruction. This enables us to improve ourselves and our courses. Please consider your answers; your input will affect future students.

Professor:

1. How well do you like the **textbook?** What topics are not covered that you feel should be?

2. Did you find the **videos** used in the presentation of the course applicable?

3. Things I like about the **class** and/or **instructor:**

4. Things I would like to see changed:

5. How much of your time/effort is spent preparing for class?

6. You are nearly halfway toward the completion of this course. What effect has the course, or the instructor, had on you? What will you remember from the course?

ENDNOTES

[1] M. Friedman and R. H. Rosenman, *Type A Behavior and Your Heart* (New York: Alfred A. Knopf, 1974).

[2] *See* R. R. McCrae and P. T. Costa, Jr., "Reinterpreting the Myers-Briggs Type Indicator from the Perspective of the Five Factor Model of Personality," *Journal of Personality,* March 1989, 17–40; and C. Fitzgerald and L. K. Kirby (eds.), *Developing Leaders: Research and Applications in Psychological Type and Leadership Development* (Palo Alto, CA: Davies-Black Publishing, 1997).

[3] D. Shuit, "At 60, Myers-Briggs is Still Sorting Out and Identifying People's Types," *Workforce,* 2003, http://www.workforce.com/section/06/feature/23/57/09/index.html, p. 2.

[4] "Personality Assessment Soars at Southwest," *Training,* Vol. 45, Issue 1, January 2008, 14.

[5] Ibid.

[6] E. Krell, "Personality Counts: Personality Assessments are Being used in New Ways Throughout the Employee Life Cycle," *HR Magazine,* November 2005.

[7] R. E. Riggio, S. E. Murphy, and F. J. Pirozzolo, *Multiple Intelligences and Leadership* (Mahwah, NJ: Lawrence Erlbaum, 2002).

[8] D. Goleman, *Working with Emotional Intelligence* (New York: Bantam Book, 1998, 317–318).

[9] I. P. Pavlov, *The Work of the Digestive Glands,* trans. by W. H. Thompson (London: Charles Griffin, 1902).

[10] B. F. Skinner, *Contingencies of Reinforcement* (East Norwalk, CT: Appleton-Century-Crofts, 1971).

[11] A. Bandura, *Social Learning Theory* (Englewood Cliffs, NJ: Prentice Hall, 1977).

[12] C. Carter, J. Bishop, J. Kravits, and J. Block, *Keys to Success in College, Career and Life* Englewood Cliffs, NJ: Prentice Hall, 2002).

[13] H. H. Kelly, "Attribution in Social Interaction," in E. Jones et al. (eds.), *Attribution: Perceiving the Causes of Behavior* (Morristown, NJ: General Learning Press, 1972).

[14] L. M. Keller, T. J. Bouchard, R. D. Arvey, N. L. Segal, and R. V. Dawis, "Work Values: Genetic and Environmental Influences," *Journal of Applied Psychology,* February 1992, 79–88.

[15] For example, D. J. Cherrington, S. J. Condie, and J. L. England, "Age and Work Values," *Academy of Management Journal,* September 1979, 617–623.

[16] D. Gaylor, "Generational Differences," April 2002, http://www.reachtheu.com.

[17] D. Knight, "Employee Exodus," *The Indianapolis Star,* September 3, 2007, Section C1.

[18]R. T. Mowday, R. M. Steers, and L. W. Porter, "The Measure of Organizational Commitment," *Journal of Vocational Behavior*, 14, 1979, 224–247.

[19]R. Kanungo, *Work Alienation* (New York: Prager Publishers, 1982).

[20]Charles Swindoll, www.readandsucceed.biz/swindoll.html.

[21]Lou Holtz, www.cyber-nation.com/victory/quotations/authors/quotes_holtz_lou.html.

[22]William James, www.brainyquote.com/quotes/authors/w/william_james.html.

[23]Adapted from Abraham H. Maslow, "A Theory of Human Motivation," *Psychological Reviews*, July 1943, 370–396; Maslow, *Motivation and Personality* (New York: Harper & Row, 1954, Rev. Ed. 1970) Chapter 5.

[24]Clayton P. Alderfer, "An Empirical Test of a New Theory of Human Needs," *Organizational Behavior and Human Performance*, May 1969, 142–175.

[25]Frederick Herzberg, Bernard Mausner, and Barbara Snyderman, *The Motivation to Work*, 2nd ed. (New York: John Wiley & Sons, 1959).

[26]Frederick Herzberg, "One More Time: How Do You Motivate Employees?" *Harvard Business Review*, 46, January–February 1968, 53–62.

[27]Adapted from McGregor, *The Human Side of Enterprise* (New York: McGraw-Hill, 1960) p. 23; Craig C. Pinder, *Work Motivation in Organization Behavior* (Upper Saddle River, NJ: Prentice Hall, 1998) p. 52.

[28]N. Harter, "The Shop Floor Schopenhauer: Hope for a Theory-X Supervisor," *Journal of Management Education*, 21 1997, 87–96.

[29]D. C. McClelland, *The Achieving Society* (New York: Van Nostrand Reinhold, 1961); D. C. McClelland, *Power: The Inner Experience* (New York: Irvington Publishers, 1975) pp. 3–29.

[30]Adapted from David C. McClelland, "Business Drive and National Achievement," *Harvard Business Review*, July–August 1962, 99–112; David C. McClelland, *The Achieving Society* (New York: Van Nostrand, 1961).

[31]David C. McClelland and David H. Burnham, "Power Is the Great Motivator," *Harvard Business Review*, 54, March–April 1976, 100–110; R. E. Boyatzis, "The Need for Close Relationships and the Manager's Job," *Organizational Psychology: Readings on Human Behavior in Organizations*, 4th ed. (Upper Saddle River, NJ: Prentice Hall, 1984) pp. 81–86.

[32]J. B. Miner, *Studies in Management Education* (New York: Springer, 1965).

[33]Edwin A. Locke and Gary P. Latham, *A Theory of Goal Setting and Task Performance* (Englewood Cliffs, NJ: Prentice Hall, 1990).

[34]Adapted from E. Walster, G. W. Walster, and W. G. Scott, *Equity: Theory and Research* (Boston: Allyn & Bacon, 1978).

[35]Developed in part from Hamner, "Using Reinforcement Theory in Organizational Settings," in Henry L. Tosi and W. Clay Hamner, (eds.), *Organizational Behavior and Management: A Contingency Approach* (Chicago: St. Clair Press, 1977) pp. 388–395.

[36]V. H. Vroom, *Work and Motivation* (New York: John Wiley, 1964).

[37]A. Sanow, "The Real Reason Employees Work: 36 Proven Ways To Motivate," Expert Magazine, July 19, 2002.

[38]Kerri Strug quote.

[39]K. C. Brewer, *Managing Stress*, (West Des Moines, IA: American Media Publishing, March 1995), p. 10.

[40]Adapted from R. S. Schuler, "Definition and Conceptionalization of Stress in Organizations," *Organizational Behavior and Human Performance*, Vol. 25, Issue 2, April 1980, 189.

[41]Adapted from "Stress Levels Aren't Rising in America Like They Are Overseas," *Workforce Management* (Crain Communications, Inc., 2005).

[42]Ibid., p. 14.

[43]Ibid., p. 13.

[44]J. L. Xie and G. Johns, "Job Scope and Stress: Can Job Scope Be Too High?" *Academy of Management Journal*, October 1995, 1288–1309.

[45]Adapted from L. R. Murphy, "A Review of Organizational Stress Management Research," *Journal of Organizational Behavior Management*, Fall–Winter 1986, 215–227.

[46]S. J. Motowidlo, J. S. Packard, and M. R. Manning, "Occupational Stress: Its Causes and Consequences for Job Performance," *Journal of Applied Psychology*, November 1987, 619–620.

[47]Ibid.

[48]Adapted from J. J. House, *Work Stress and Social Support* (Reading, MA: Addison Wesley, 1981); S. Jayaratne, D. Himle, and W. A. Chess, "Dealing with Work Stress and Strain: Is the Perception of Support More Important Than Its Use?" *The Journal of Applied Behavioral Science*, Vol. 24, No. 2, 1988, 191–202.

[49]M. Friedman and R. H. Rosenman, *Type A Behavior and Your Heart* (New York: Alfred A. Knopf, 1974).

[50]This model is based on D. F. Parker and T. A. DeCotiis, "Organizational Determinants of Job Stress," *Organizational Behavior and Human Performance*, October 1983, p. 166; S. Parasuraman and J. A. Alutto, "Sources and Outcomes of Stress in Organizational Settings: Toward the Development of a Structural Model," *Academy of Management Journal*, June 1984, 333; R. L. Kahn and P. Byosiere, "Stress in Organizations," in M. D. Dunnette and L. M. Hough (eds.), *Handbook of Industrial and Organizational Psychology*, 2nd ed., Vol. 3, 571–650 (Palo Alto, CA: Consulting Psychologists Press, p. 592). Adapted from K. C. Brewer, *Managing Stress* (West Des Moines, IA: American Media Publishing, 1995), p. 13.

[51]Adapted from K. C. Brewer, *Managing Stress*, p. 17.

[52]Ibid., p. 63.

[53]U.S. Department of Health and Services, National Institutes of Health.

[54]*Risk Management*, Vol. 53, No. 11, Nov. 2006, 8–9.

[55]P. Riley, *The Winner Within* (New York: Berkeley Books, 1993).

[56]See the review of the literature in S. E. Jackson, V. K. Stone, and E. B. Alvareq, "Socialization Amidst Diversity: The Impact of Demographics on Work Teams of Old-timers and Newcomers," in L. L. Cummings and B. M. Staw (eds.), *Research in Organizational Behavior*, Vol. 15 (Greenwich, CT: JAI Press, 1993), p. 64.

[57]T. Walton, *Leadership, Creativity, Teamwork, Design Management Review*, ProQuest Information and Learning Company, Summer 2006.

[58]V. Sadowski, "Trends," *Training Magazine*, October 1995, 69–74.

[59]T. D. Wall, N. J. Kemp, P. R. Jackson, and C. W. Clegg, "Outcomes of Autonomous Workgroups: A Long-Term Field Experiment," *Academy of Management Journal*, June 1986, 280–304; and J. L. Cordery, W. S. Muller, and L. M. Smith, "Attitudinal and Behavioral Effects of Autonomous Group Working: A Longitudinal Field Study," *Academy of Management Journal*, June 1991, 464–476.

[60]L. R. Sayles, "Work Group Behavior and the Larger Organization," in C. Arensburn et al. (eds.), *Research in Industrial Relations* (New York: Harper & Row, 1957), pp. 131–145.

[61]B. W. Tuckman, "Developmental Sequences in Small Groups," *Psychological Bulletin*, June 1965, 384–399; B. W. Tuckman and M. C. Jensen, "Stages of Small Group Development Revisited," *Group and Organizational Studies*, December 1977,

419–427; and M. F. Maples, "Group Development: Extending Tuckman's Theory," *Journal for Specialists in Group Work*, Fall 1988, 17–23.

[62]Lencioni, P. *The Five Dysfunctions of a Team* (San Francisco: Jossey Bass, 2002), pp. 187–190.

[63]Ibid.

[64]C.C. Manz and H.P. Sims, Jr., *Business Without Bosses: How Self-Managing Teams Are Building High Performance Companies* (New York: Wiley, 1993).

[65]T. D. Wall, N. J. Kemp, P. R. Jackson, and C. W. Clegg, "Outcomes of Autonomous Workgroups: A Long-Term Field Experiment," *Academy of Management Journal*, June 1986, 280–304; and J. L. Cordery, W. S. Muller, and L. M. Smith, "Attitudinal and Behavioral Effects of Autonomous Group Working: A Longitudinal Field Study," *Academy of Management Journal*, June 1991, 464–476.

[66]E. J. Thomas and C. F. Fink, "Effects of Group Size," *Psychological Bulletin*, July 1963, 371-384; A. P. Hare, *Handbook of Small Group Research* (New York: Free Press, 1976); M. E. Shaw, *Group Dynamics: The Psychology of Small Group Behavior*, 3rd ed. (New York: McGraw-Hill, 1981).

[67]D. R. Comer, "A Model of Social Loafing in Real Work Groups," *Human Relations*, June 1995, 647–667.

[68]For a more detailed breakdown on team skills, see J. J. Stevens and M. A. Campion, "The Knowledge, Skill, and Ability Requirements for Teamwork: Implications for Human Resource Management," *Journal of Management*, Summer 1994, 503–530.

[69]J. R. Katzenbach and D. K. Smith, *The Wisdom of Teams* (Boston: Harvard Business School Press, 1993).

[70]P. L. Schindler and C. C. Thomas, "The Structure of Interpersonal Trust in the Workplace," *Psychological Reports*, October 1993, 563–573.

[71]B. Norton and C. Smith, *Understanding the Virtual Organization* (Hauppauge, NY 1997).

[72]P. W. Paese, M. Bieser, and M. E. Tubbs, "Framing Effects and Choice Shifts in Group Decision Making," *Organizational Behavior and Human Decision Processes*, October 1993, 49–65.

[73]B. M. Staw, "The Escalation of Commitment to a Course of Action," *Academy of Management Review*, October 1981, 577–587.

[74]D. Shula and K. Blanchard, *Everyone's a Coach* (New York: Harper Business, 1995).

[75]Fritz, W., What CEO's Say About Leadership: Center for Creative Leadership and Chief Executive Survey Uncovers CEO Attitudes on Leadership, *Chief Executive*, 2005, *http://www.centerforcreativeleadership.com/leadership/news/2002/chiefexecutive.aspx?pageId=677.*

[76]D. Hoppe, "Leadership/Management," *The Business Journal of CNY*, http://www.dhoppe.com/published_articles/cynarticle6.html.

[77]R. Giuliani, *Leadership* (New York: Little, Brown, 2002).

[78]R. M. Stogdill and A. E. Coons (eds.), "Leadership Behavior: Its Description and Measurement," Research Monograph No. 88 (Columbus: The Ohio State University, Bureau of Business Research, 1951).

[79]R. Kahn and D. Katz, "Leadership Practices in Relation to Productivity and Morale," in D. Cartwright and A. Zander (eds.), *Group Dynamics: Research and Theory*, 2nd ed. (Elmsford, NY: Row, Patterson, 1960).

[80]http://forums.bucknuts.com/showthread.php?t = 19272.

[81]Wikipedia Exxon Mobil and Rex Tillerson.

[82]J. N. Fuller and J. C. Green, "Leadership is Critical to Forming and Implementing Strategy and Without it, Good Strategy Does Not Happen," *Graziadio Business Report*, Vol. 08, No. 2, 2005.

[83]B. M. Bass, *Leadership and Performance Beyond Expectation* (New York: Harper and Row, 1978); B. M. Bass, "From Transactional to Transformational Leadership: Learning to Share the Vision," *Organizational Dynamics,* Winter 1990.

[84]Daniel Goleman, "Leadership That Gets Results," *Harvard Business Review,* March–April 2000.

[85]Daniel Goleman, *Primal Leadership* (Boston: Harvard Business School Publishing, 2002).

[86]M. Mallinger and J. Banks, "Use Emotional Intelligence to Cope in Tough Times," *Graziadio Business Report,* Vol. 6, No. 1, Pepperdine University, 2003.

[87]Ibid.

[88]Ibid.

[89]D. C. McClelland, "Identifying Competencies with Behavior-Event Interviews," *Psychological Science,* 1988, 331–339.

[90]M. Ashby and S. Miles, *Leaders Talk Leadership* (Oxford University Press, 2002), p. 6.

[91]M. Weinstein, Leadership Leader, *Training,* Vol. 45, No. 2, February 2008, 42.

[92]H. Mackay, *Pushing the Envelope All the Way to the Top* (New York: Ballantine Books, 1999).

[93]U.S. Securities and Exchange Commission. www.sec.gov. Retrieved on 4 June 2003.

[94]http://en.wikipedia.org/wiki/Martha_Stewart.

[95]Brousseau, K.R., "The Seasoned Executive's Decision Making Style," *Harvard Business Review,* February 2006, 111.

[96]H. A. Simon, *Administrative Behavior,* 3rd ed. (New York: Free Press, 1976); J. Forester, "Bounded Rationality and the Politics of Muddling Through," *Public Administration Review,* January–February 1984, 23–31.

[97]P. O. Soelberg, "Unprogrammed Decision Making," *Industrial Management Review,* Spring 1967, 19–29; and D. J. Power and R. J. Aldag "Soelberg's Job Search and Choice Model: A Clarification, Review and Critique," *Academy of Management Review,* January 1985, 48–58.

[98]Kepner and Tregoe, *The Rational Manager* (New York: McGraw-Hill, 1965); Kepner and Tregoe, *Problem Analysis and Decision Making* (Princeton, NY: Princeton Research Press, 1973).

[99]Osburn, A. F., *Applied Imagination: Principles and Procedures of Creative Thinking.* (New York: Scribner's, 1941).

[100]R. Tannenbaum, and W. H. Schmidt, "How to Choose a Leadership Pattern," *Harvard Business Review,* 51, 1973, 162–180.

[101]A. L. Delbecq, A. H. Van de Ven, and D. H. Gustafson, *Group Techniques for Program Planning: A Guide to Nominal and Delphi Processes* (Glenview, IL: Scott Foresman, 1975).

[102]M. S. Poole, M. Holmes, and G. DeSanctis, "Conflict Management in a Computer-Supported Meeting Environment," *Management Science,* August 1991, 926–953.

[103]"Work Week", *The Wall Street Journal,* December 19, 1998, p.1.

[104]"When Leaders go Wrong," *Training Today,* August 2006, p. 11.

[105]K. W. Thomas and W. H. Schmidt, "A Survey of Managerial Interests with Respect to Conflict," *Academy of Management Journal,* June 1976, p. 317.

[106]P. Clampitt, R. DeKoch, and T. Cashman, "A Strategy for Communicating About Uncertainty," *The Academy of Management Executive,* November 2000, 14, 41–57.

[107]K. Davis, cited in R. Rowen, "Where Did That Rumor Come From?" *Fortune,* August 3, 1979, 134.

[108]Adapted from L. Smith (ed.), *Preventing Early Pregnancy* (Rapid City, SD: West River Community Health Center, 1986), p. 12.

[109]J. Schieber, "Resolving Intra-Organization Conflicts," *Graziadio Business Report*, Vol. 8, Issue 2, 2005, Pepperdine University.

[110]Ibid.

[111]D. Trump, *Trump, The Art of the Deal* (New York: Random House, 1987).

[112]R. W. Walton and R. B. McKersie, *A Behavioral Theory of Negotiations* (New York: McGraw-Hill, 1965).

[113]H. Mackay, *Pushing the Envelope All the Way to the Top* (New York: Ballantine Books, 1999).

[114]Ibid.

[115]Anders, G. "Overseeing More Employees—With fewer Managers," *The Wall Street Journal*, 2008.

[116]J. V. Ghorpade, *Job Analysis: A Handbook for the Human Resource Director* (Englewood Cliffs, NJ: Prentice Hall, 1988).

[117]M. A. McDaniel, D. L. Whetzel, F. L. Schmidt, and S. D. Maurer, "The Validity of Employment Interviews: A Comprehensive Review and Meta-Analysis," *Journal of Applied Psychology*, August 1994, 599–616.

[118]M. Sashkin and K. J. Kiser, *Putting Total Quality Management to Work* (San Francisco: Berett-Kochler, 1993); J. R. Hackman and R. Wageman, "Total Quality Management: Empirical, Conceptual, and Practical Issues," *Administrative Science Quarterly*, June 1995, 309–342.

[119]M. Sashkin and K. J. Kiser, *Putting Total Quality Management to Work* (San Francisco: Berett-Koehler, 1993), p. 44.

[120]"The Age of Reengineering," *Across the Board*, June 1993, 26–33.

[121]J. R. Hackman and G. R. Oldham, *Work Redesign* (Reading, MA: Addison Wesley, 1980).

[122]D. R. Dalton and D. J. Mesch, "The Impact of Flexible Scheduling on Employee Attendance and Turnover," *Administrative Science Quarterly*, June 1990, 370–387; K. S. Kush and L. K. Stroh, "Flextime: Myth or Reality," *Business Horizons*, September–October 1994, 53.

[123]R. Maynard, "The Growing Appeal of Telecommuting," *Nation's Business*, August 1994, 61–62.

[124]"SIA Breaks Ground for Child Center," *Lafayette Leader*, May 1999, 1.

[125]D. Goleman and A. McKee, *Primal Leadership: Realizing the Power of Emotional Intelligence* (Boston: Harvard Business School Press, 2002).

[126]Ibid.

[127]J. Case, "Corporate Culture," *Inc.*, November 1996, 42–53.

[128]G. Hofstead, *Culture's Consequences: International Differences in Work-Related Values*, (Beverly Hills, CA: Sage, 1980).

[129]P. K. Drucker, *The Practice of Management* (New York: Harper and Row, 1954).

[130]Cited in S. Caudron, "The Top 20 Ways to Motivate Employees," *Industry Week*, April 3, 1995, 15–16.

[131]E. A. Locke and G. P. Latham, *A Theory of Goal Setting and Task Performance* (Englewood Clifts, NJ: Prentice Hall, 1990).

[132]C. G. Springer, "Organizational Motivation," *PA Times*, American Society for Public Administration, November 2006, p. 8.

[133]P. Dejager, "Resistance to Change. A New View of an Old Problem," *The Futurist*, May–June 2001, 24.

[134]K. Lewin, *Field Theory in Social Science* (New York: Harper & Row, 1951).

[135]C. G. Worley, "Leading Change Management Involves Some Simple, but Too Often Forgotten Rules," *Graziadio Business Report*, Pepperdine University, Vol. 8, Issue 2, 2005.

[136]T. Peters, *In Search of Excellence* (New York, Harper and Row, 1982).

[137]B. Walton, "Life Is in the Details," *USA Today Weekend*.

[138]M. M. Kennedy, "What Campus Employers Teach Students About Office Politics," *Journal of Student Employment*, Brockport Education, www.iris.nyit.edu/ose/article_what_campus_employers_teach_stud.htm, 1999.

[139]J. R. P. French and B. Raven, "The Bases of Social Power," in D. Cartwright (ed.), *Studies in Social Power* (Ann Arbor: University of Michigan, Institute for Social Research, 1959).

[140]A. Nahavandi and A. Malekzadeh, *Organizational Behavior* (Upper Saddle River, NJ: Prentice Hall, 1999).

[141]"Looking Back at the Duke Lacrosse Case," *Duke University Office of News and Communications*, 2007.

[142]29 CFR 1604.11.

[143]S. Covey, *Seven Habits of Highly Successful People* (New York: Simon and Schuster, 1990).

[144]P. Sacks, *Generation X Goes to College* (Chicago: Open Court, 1996).

[145]H. Mackay, *Pushing the Envelope All the Way to the Top* (New York: Ballantine Books, 1999).

[146]P. Riley, *The Winner Within* (New York: Berkeley Books, 1993).

[147]Thomas J. Stanley, *The Millionaire Mind* (Kansas City, MO: Andrews McMeel Publishing, 2000).

[148]D. Schwartz, *The Magic of Thinking Big* (New York: Simon and Schuster, 1981).

[149]K. Blanchard and Norman Vincent Peale, *The Power of Ethical Management* (New York: Ballantine Books, 1996).

[150]C. Garfield, *Peak Performers: The New Heroes of American Business* (New York: Avon Books, 1991).

[151]Peter B. Kyne, *The Go-Getter* (Burlington, NC: Eagle Books, 1983).

[152]D. Schwartz, *The Magic of Thinking Big* (New York: Simon and Schuster, 1981).

[153]Thomas J. Stanley, *The Millionaire Mind* (Kansas City: Andrews McMeel Publishing, 2000).

[154]R. Ratnesar, "The Homework Ate My Family," *Time*, January 25, 1999, 55–63.

[155]J. Albrecht (personal interview, April 10, 2008).

[156]H. Mackay, *Sharkproof* (New York: Ballantine Books, 1998).

[157]M. Kennedy, Playin,"Office Politics Now Necessary," *U.S. News and World Report*, January 12, 1981, 35–36.

[158]S. Robbins, *Organizational Behavior*, 8th ed. (New York: Prentice Hall, 1998).

[159]G. Layborne, www.timedigital.com, article by Anita Hamilton.

[160]E. Newborne and K. Kerwin, "Generation Y," *Business Week*, February 15, 1999, 81–88.

[161]K. Blanchard, *The One Minute Manager* (New York: Morrow, 1982), p. 280.

[162]L. Donnithorne, *The West Point Way of Leadership* (New York: Doubleday, 1994).

[163]F. Fournies, *Why Employees Don't Do What They're Supposed To Do and What to Do About It* (Blue Ridge Summit, PA: Liberty House, 1988).

[164]M. Treacy and F. Wiersema, *The Discipline of Market Leaders* (Boston: Addison-Wesley, 1993).

[165]E. Newborne and K. Kerwin, "Generation Y," *Business Week,* February 15, 1999, 81–88.

[166]Winston Churchill.

INDEX

Negotiation, 180–194
    action, 184–185
    case study, 190–191
    closure, 185
    ethical conduct and, 187–188
    gender differences and, 188
    implementation, 185
    organizational change and, 275–276
    pitfalls in, 189
    preparation, 184
    in service business, 188–189
    success in, 189
    third-party intervention and, 186–187
Nifong, Mike, 285
Noise, communication process, 159–160
Norming, group development, 105f, 106

O

OB. *See* Organizational behavior
Obama, Barack, 48, 131
Off-the-job training, 241
Ohio State University (OSU) study
    consideration, 123
    initiating structure, 123
    leadership, 123
OJT. *See* On-the-job training
Oldham, Richard, 238
Ombudsman, 187
On-the-job training (OJT), 241
Operant conditioning, learning and, 27
Operational excellence, 319
Organic organizational models, 203
Organization(s), 8
    attitude in, 50–51
    behavioral differences within, 13
    communication within, 160–161, 161f
    human behavior in, 7
    motivation in, 262–269
    team, 202–203
    virtual, 202, 202f
Organizational behavior (OB), 2–15
    assumptions regarding, 13
    case study, 13–14
    study of, 8–9
Organizational change, 270–279
    communications and, 275
    dislike of, 274
    driving forces of, 272–274, 272f
    economic incentives and, 275
    economic shocks and, 274
    education and, 275
    habits and, 274
    international effects and, 273–274
    negotiation and, 275–276
    participation and, 275
    principles of, 275–276
    security and, 274
    support and, 275
    technology and, 273
    workforce and, 273

Organizational commitment, 51
Organizational culture, 3, 248–259
    career planning and, 254
    global thinking and, 255–256
    SA test, 249
Organizational models, 203–204
    application, 207
    blend, 203–204
    bureaucratic, 203
    case study, 209–210
    corporate America, 204
    entrepreneurial, 203
    focus/strategy, 205–206
    future of, 206–207
    mechanistic, 203
    military, 204
    organic, 203
    private enterprise, 204
    size, 204–205
    technology influences, 205
Organizational structures, 194–211
    authority and, 198–199
    bureaucracy design of, 201, 201f
    characterization of jobs and, 198
    control and, 199–200
    creativity and, 200
    decision making and, 200
    division of labor, 198
    elements of, 197–200
    matrix design of, 201, 202t
    SA test, 195–196
    shapes/design, 200–203
    simple design, 200, 201f
OSU study. *See* Ohio State University study
Output evaluation, equity theory, 67

P

Participating/supporting, in situational leadership
    model, 128
Participation, organizational change and, 275
Pavlov, Ivan, 26
Peers, ethical conduct and, 301–302
Perceivers, 36
Perceiving type
    Jungian 16-type personality, 19
    MBTI, 23
Perception, 32–39
    case study, 41–42
    SA test for, 33
    selective, 36, 40
    stress and, 81
Performance evaluation, 242–244
    case study, 245–246
Performance-to-reward expectancy, 69–70
Performing, group development, 105f, 106
Personality type, 18–31
    case study, 30–31
    definition, 21
    extroverted, 21
    factors composing, 22